The Philosophy of
MARSILIO FICINO

~~~

NUMBER SIX OF THE
COLUMBIA STUDIES IN PHILOSOPHY
EDITED UNDER THE DEPARTMENT OF
PHILOSOPHY, COLUMBIA UNIVERSITY

The Philosophy of
MARSILIO FICINO

By PAUL OSKAR KRISTELLER
ASSOCIATE IN PHILOSOPHY AT
COLUMBIA UNIVERSITY

Translated into English by
VIRGINIA CONANT

GLOUCESTER, MASS.
PETER SMITH
1964

The publication of this volume has been aided by a grant from the American Council of Learned Societies from a fund provided by the Carnegie Corporation of New York.

To my friends

PREFACE

THE PLAN for this study of Ficino's philosophy goes back to 1931. The German manuscript was finished, after several interruptions, in 1937. An Italian version was ready for the press and accepted for publication in 1938. Now at last the work is to appear in an English translation. The book has thus shared the fortunes of its author, and personal and political circumstances as well as the necessity of having it twice translated account for the long delay in its publication. The time and effort spent on the work might seem out of proportion to its size and importance, especially in a time like this. Yet in a period of great change and uncertainty, concentration on a definite task is a source of strength. Moreover, even a limited subject often has larger implications and may thus justify and reward an accurate investigation.

Since it was first completed the manuscript has not undergone any basic changes. A few passages, many notes, and the bibliography have been brought up to date. The first chapter has been thoroughly revised. Since there is no previous study of Ficino in English, I have added in the English version some general information on his background, life, works, and influence, which now forms the earlier part of the second chapter. Some chapters have been already published as separate articles: Chapter II, Part II (*Civiltà Moderna*, V [1933], 438-45); Chapter VII (*Giornale critico della filosofia italiana*, XV [1934], 395-423); Chapter X (*ibid.*, XVIII [1937], 234-56); Chapter XIII (*ibid.*, XIX [1938], 185-214); and Chapter XV (*Journal of the History of Ideas*, I [1940], 299-319). A few chapters were also delivered as lectures at different American Universities in 1939: Chapter II at Michigan; Chapter VII at Harvard and Yale; and Chapter XIII at Michigan and Columbia.

The figure of Ficino merits our interest for various reasons. As translator and commentator of Plato he represents one of the most important epochs in the history of Platonism. As leader of the Platonic Academy in Florence, he occupies a central position in the history of Renaissance civilization. Continuing the work of the earlier humanists, he was the first who gave that work a philosophical significance. Absorbing a vast body of ideas from ancient, early Christian, and medieval sources, he was able to incorporate them into a comprehensive system of Christian Platonism which displays many original and important characteristics of its own. Both as an original thinker and as a transmitter of earlier ideas he exercised a widespread and powerful influence on subsequent generations, and traces of this influence are found in many philosophers, scientists, theologians, moralists, poets, and artists of the later Renaissance, in Italy as well as in France, England, Germany, and other European countries.

The literature on Ficino is very large if we include all the works in which he is mentioned incidentally; it is still considerable if we take into consideration only biographical and historical studies; it is rather scanty and recent so far as a study of his philosophical thought is concerned. From Schelhorn (1730) to Della Torre (1902) most authors treated only his life and influence, saying little or nothing of his philosophy. Their assumption, implied or explicit, is that he did nothing but translate and repeat the doctrines of Plato and of the Neoplatonists. The brief studies of Ferri (published in 1883–84, but based on lectures delivered in 1866) and of Galli (1897–99) are no more than summaries of a few limited passages. Stein gives a balanced judgment on Ficino (1875), but does not proceed to an elaborate interpretation.

Ficino's philosophical importance was first recognized by Cassirer (*Erkenntnisproblem,* 1897) and by Gentile (*Giordano Bruno e il pensiero del rinascimento,* 1920), who indicated his epistemology and his conception of man, respectively, as original aspects of his thought. The first philosophical monograph on Ficino was published by Saitta (1923), who gives a lively exposition of Ficino's thought, emphasizing such important aspects as his theories of religion, of the dignity of man, of knowledge, and of love. It is an exaggeration for critics to assert that Saitta, with his "idealistic" interpretation, makes of Ficino a pure pantheist; but he certainly tends to underestimate the medieval elements in Ficino and to overemphasize his modern, "immanentistic" aspects. The monograph by Dress (1929) is valuable for the author's many acute observations and for his theological analysis of Ficino's commentary on St. Paul. Yet the "mystical" aspect of Ficino's thought mentioned in the title of Dress's book does not receive adequate treatment. Dress agrees with Saitta that Ficino's thought is "anthropocentric" and "immanentistic," but what for Saitta, an idealist philosopher, had been a virtue, becomes a vice for Dress, a Protestant theologian, who assigns to Ficino a place quite inferior to that of the Reformers. The three most recent monographs are of a more limited scope. Horbert (1931) gives but an elementary paraphrase of a few chapters of the *Theologia Platonica*. Hak (1934) treats mainly Ficino's life and influence and has only a brief section on his doctrine, limiting himself almost entirely to his theories on dogmatic theology. Anichini (1937) studies Ficino's theological position with respect to orthodoxy, but does not touch on his basic philosophical doctrines.

Besides these monographs, many recent articles and sections in books on larger subjects treat of Ficino. But with the exception of Cassirer, who repeatedly deals with Ficino in his work on the philosophy of the Renaissance, these scholars either give a short summary of Ficino's thought in general (Olgiati, Semprini, Robb, Moench, Kieszkowski) or illustrate some special problems: his medical theories (Kahl), his theory of melancholy (Giehlow and Panofsky-Saxl), his attitude toward astrology (Baron and Thorndike), his conception of religion (Pusino and Corsano), his epistemology (Meier), his theory of love (Festugière, Meylan, Ivanoff, and Nygren), or his moral doctrine (Trinkaus). Most important among these special contributions are the various articles by Heitzman, although I cannot subscribe to all his historical conclusions. It is greatly to be desired that his larger study, published in Polish, should be made available in some more widely read language.

With respect to these previous studies, I have followed no polemic intention. I have tried only to give a more complete and more methodical analysis of Ficino's thought and to understand his various teachings in the light of a few basic doctrines. I have not tried to report all the details to be found in his writings, but have selected those of philosophical importance. The aspects of his thought most frequently discussed—such as his theories of universal religion and of love, his attitude toward astrology, and his epistemology—I have tried to analyze in their proper context. I have given a new interpretation to a few other theories—such as his theories of Platonic love, of the five substances, of the central position of the Soul, and of immortality. Certain doctrines not mentioned in the previous literature I have treated for the first time, for example, the theories of the *Primum in aliquo genere* and of the *Appetitus naturalis*. I have included numerous quotations from Ficino, in order to support my interpretation and also to acquaint the reader with the words of Ficino, since he has never been translated into English. The English version of these translated passages often presupposes an emendation of the Latin text of the Basel edition, which is full of misprints; but it has not always been possible to mention the corrections explicitly. In the notes I have referred to previous treatments of the same point or passage. This does not necessarily mean that I have followed the statements of previous interpreters or that I share their opinions, although I do gladly admit that in many respects I am indebted to most of them.

The scope of my study has been to reconstruct the essential elements of Ficino's philosophy. Other important questions, such as his early philosophical development, his sources, his influence, and his relations to contemporary philosophical and intellectual movements, I have mentioned but incidentally in the second chapter and wherever they seemed to have some bearing on my major topic.

An exhaustive treatment of these questions would require a separate study, but I do not think it is a prerequisite for our present purpose. Therefore I have resolved not to present in this study a few such facts which have recently come to my knowledge and which would have distracted the reader from my basic intention.

I should like to express my thanks and appreciation to the institutions and persons who have helped me to undertake and to finish the present study. The libraries of Freiburg, Berlin, Florence, and Pisa placed at my disposal the valuable volumes of the old Basel edition. From the Notgemeinschaft der deutschen Wissenschaft, Berlin, in 1932–33, from the Academic Assistance Council, London, in 1935, and from the Oberlaender Trust, Philadelphia, in 1939–41, I received research grants which enabled me to continue my work. I have learned how to interpret a text from my former teachers, Professors Ernst Hoffmann, of Heidelberg, Werner Jaeger, of Berlin, now at Harvard, and the late Eduard Norden. For valuable advice and guidance in the selection of the subject and in the initial stages of my work I am indebted to Professor Martin Heidegger, of Freiburg. Among my Italian friends who gave me help and encouragement I should like to mention Professors Gaetano Chiavacci, of Pisa, Ernesto Codignola, of Florence, Leonardo Olschki, now in Cambridge, Mass., and above all Professor Giovanni Gentile, who actually made it possible for me to finish my manuscript. My friend Dr. Alessandro Perosa, of Pisa, helped me to revise the Italian version on which the present English translation is largely based. In the United States, I am particularly indebted for help and encouragement to Professors H. M. Ayres, D. Bigongiari, H. L. Friess, A. Livingston, G. Prezzolini, J. H. Randall, Jr., and H. W. Schneider, all of Columbia University, and to Professors R. H. Bainton and E. Cassirer, of Yale, A. O. Lovejoy, of Baltimore, and R. McKeon, of Chicago, as well as to the Committee on Renaissance Studies. Miss V. Conant, my former pupil, now instructor at Smith College, was generous of her time in the first draft of this English translation, which was later revised, with respect to philosophical terminology, by Messrs. S. Daugert and W. Owen, and with respect to literary style, by Miss E. Abbott. The Department of Philosophy and the Casa Italiana, of Columbia University, contributed to the costs of these revisions. For valuable help in the editorial preparation of the final manuscript I am indebted to Miss G. Savini and Miss G. Cazzola, of the Casa Italiana. The publication of the manuscript was finally made possible by the Columbia University Press and by a subsidy granted by the American Council of Learned Societies. This list is as long as the story of my manuscript, and it is far from being complete. All others whom I have not mentioned explicitly may feel that they are included among my friends to whom I wish to dedicate this volume.

PAUL OSKAR KRISTELLER

Columbia University
September 23, 1942

CONTENTS

Part One

INTRODUCTION

I

METHODOLOGICAL QUESTIONS

MARSILIO FICINO, the Florentine, is well known as a man of the Renaissance and as the outstanding translator and commentator of Plato and Plotinus. As a philosopher in his own right he has rarely been appraised. This is due primarily to his apparent lack of originality, since in philosophy he keeps explicitly to tradition and professes merely to be restating the doctrines of Plato and of the ancient Platonists. If one chooses to accept this statement literally, one is tempted to conclude that everything that Ficino learned from Plato and Plotinus can be found set forth in a more attractive and original form in those writers themselves and that anything that may distinguish his thought from theirs must be of scant importance—a reasoning somewhat like that which, according to the legend, led the Caliph Omar to burn the library at Alexandria. Actually the mere revival of a tradition that had been extinct, or at least without direct influence, for centuries is in itself a phenomenon of no little interest. Not only do the old ideas undergo a peculiar change under the influence of the Christian and scholastic traditions and of Ficino's own manner of thinking, but even when they recur apparently unchanged, they are not just mechanically repeated, but are recreated on the basis of a fresh and original conviction and in terms supplied by a new intellectual content.

In this connection it may be appropriate to examine somewhat closely the significance of intellectual tradition as regards philosophy and its history. All human beings, primitive and civilized alike, seem to be prone spontaneously to reflect upon the nature of their own being and upon the relation of their being to reality as a whole, expressing their conclusions in the form now of myth and poetry, now of aphorism and proverb. Such prephilosophic theories are not necessarily comprehensive or even consistent in their various parts. Though always visibly related to a specific historical background, they do not seem to rest consciously upon any doctrinal tradition. Philosophy properly so-called begins only with the appearance of a conscious effort to arrive at logical coherence in such expressions and at a systematic interpretation of the whole of reality in its manifold aspects and content. Systematic perfection, mastery of the whole of reality in the full richness of its content, is unattainable in the short span of a single human life. The philosopher therefore is obliged to fall back upon theories, ideas, and concepts that have been formulated by others. Examining these with continual reference to his own experience of reality, he will necessarily discard anything that strikes him as devoid of significance and work over into his own speculative structure things that he finds richer in meaning. So in passing from one "system" to another in this process of philosophical examination and discussion, ideas, singly or in the mass, necessarily change in form and in function and therefore in internal structure and in their mutual and external relations, much as corporeal matter, in the physical alternations of birth and death, may belong successively to any number of different concrete objects. In the course of repeated discussions of this sort a philosophical tradition grows up, due to a succession of thinkers who possess a common fund of basic postulates and utilize common materials and common forms of expression. There is, for instance, the Western tradition in philosophy, which extends from Thales down to the present time. More narrowly speaking, there are Platonic and Aristotelian traditions that can be traced throughout the ages. When we say that a man belongs to a philosophical tradition, we do not mean that he merely repeats ideas that have come down to him in a mechanical sort of way— in such a case we could scarcely call him a philosopher. We mean that he accepts certain ideas of the past and restates them in terms of the significance that he ascribes to them. In interpreting his masters and predecessors he translates their doctrines into new language, reconstructing them according to his own views, altering them in more-or-less numerous details, now omitting, now adding certain essential elements. In the development of a philosophical tradition basic ideas are not merely repeated and passed along; they are continually adapted to the changing intellectual problems and needs of successive periods and thinkers.

It is in just this sense that we must try to think of Ficino as a representative of the Platonic tradition. We must not, fixing our main attention upon new and original elements in his thought, regard him as an isolated figure; nor should we, considering traditional elements exclusively, think of him as a mere repeater of conventional ideas. Our effort, rather, should be to describe and explain the peculiar and particular form of expression that he gives to the basic principles of Platonism.

Only in the light of this conception of tradition can Ficino's independence and originality as a philosopher be soundly appraised. If by independence in thought we mean an individual and unmediated approach to truth, Ficino must be considered an independent thinker—a conclusion which it remains for our study to prove. But "independence" taken in this sense must not be confused with "originality" taken in the ordinary sense, as a capacity of saying "things new and never before said." While Ficino holds his ground in any comparison with other philosophers from the standpoint of "independence," in point of "originality" he is certainly inferior to his contemporary Pico, who makes frequent boast of being "original," especially during his earlier years. But such "originality," if we consider carefully, may be the outward manifestation of a very superficial "independence." One may readily conceive of a genuine independence that does not result in any idea that is outwardly new, just as one may conceive of a very conspicuous "originality" that in the deeper sense may be lacking in substance and therefore in independence. For that matter, "originality" is one of those specious values, secondary at best, that are either mere natural endowments or else incidental by-products of the process of thinking. Any attempt to achieve one of these superficial qualities is doomed at the outset to sterility, and its products have never actually succeeded in being what they are claimed to be. No thinker has ever been great by simply trying to be "original." In view of all this we cannot hesitate with respect to our choice between the criterion of "independence" and the criterion of "originality." The expositor must no more succumb to a mania for the sensational than the philosopher to personal vanity.

Ficino's evident and explicit indebtedness to the Platonic tradition readily leads the expositor to identify and to evaluate now the conventional, now the original elements in his doctrine; but his peculiar method of thinking would seem to require a very special method of philosophical interpretation. In the first place his writings, taken in the mass, notably his principal work, the *Theologia Platonica,* contain so many different ideas that it is difficult to find one's way among them, to distinguish essential from incidental elements, and to recognize the principles that are basic to his system as a whole. Then, again, repetitions, more-or-less extensive, are not at all infrequent in the mass of his writings, though particular arguments, taken by themselves, are well constructed, have a precise wording, and cannot be reduced to shorter formulas. From the latter point of view Ficino can lay claim to a rather noteworthy succinctness of expression.[1] Finally the separate propositions and developments —in other words, the primary elements in the exposition—have, taken in themselves, a peculiar ambiguity and vagueness, not from any lack of precision in thought, but because each particular idea is always related to a comprehensive view of the universe. These traits seem to be characteristic of the Platonic tradition, but they are neither common to nor characteristic of Ficino's

---

[1] *Marsilii Ficini Opera omnia,* pp. 615, 618, 756; cf. p. 728. Henceforth all quotations from Ficino's works will refer to this edition (*Op. om.*) or, less frequently, to the *Supplementum Ficinianum,* 2 vols., Florence, 1937 (*Suppl.*).

age. The exact opposite may be said of his contemporary Pico. In Pico's works as a whole very few leading ideas stand out among the others. The separate sections are devoted invariably to a single idea that can be easily summarized in a brief formula, and the separate propositions can be exactly understood without reference to the general context or to any total conception of the *(Heptaplus ?!* world. In the two men evidently, we encounter two different methods of reasoning, the one aiming at a clear formulation of isolated ideas, the other at a detailed exposition of a complex conception of the universe. We are not called upon just here to determine the respective philosophical merits of these two methods. It is sufficient to note that one of them can be disposed of by a mere description of its formal characteristics, whereas from the very outset the other has to be understood and interpreted in the light of a system.

We may therefore conclude that a type of thought such as Ficino's cannot be adequately interpreted by merely restating the author's various positions. It requires a more thoroughgoing philosophical analysis. A listing of his positions is, to be sure, indispensable as a foundation for any sound interpretation, and that such restatements be accurate is of the utmost importance. All the same, summaries of this sort are likely to be too much influenced by the formal structure of the work under discussion, and they always run the risk of obscuring inconsistencies that otherwise are apparent enough and of presenting a philosophical system as a mere antiquarian collection of arbitrary and unrelated opinions. Actually the formal structure of a system is mere surface. Inconsistencies may be the clue to a deeper understanding of the author's thought, and the separate ideas have each their own specific relation to the whole philosophical structure in which they occupy now a more, now a less significant place. A philosophical analysis must examine the reasons that are advanced in support of each conclusion and so lay bare such doctrines as are basic in the sense that the writer does not regard their certainty as dependent upon the validity of other ideas.

These basic conceptions, these starting points, so to say, are themselves philosophical doctrines. The philosophical analysis of the author's process of thought is therefore something basically different from any psychological interpretation derived from nonintellectual elements. These starting points once found, the expositor is in a position to repeat the author's whole process of thought. From these basic doctrines he can reconstruct their various speculative derivations and even the traditional postulates with which they are combined, and so arrive in the end at the formal structure of the system as the author actually expounds it. If it does not go astray, therefore, the philosophical interpretation will reach the same conclusions which the merely descriptive method records without ever getting beyond them. It will grasp in terms of basic principles ideas that description regards as mere factual data.

This method of philosophical interpretation we intend to apply to the doctrine of Ficino. It involves two procedures, which move in opposite directions. On the one hand we move analytically from text to principles; on the other, we return, synthetically, from the principles so discovered back to text. Since at the start of our study we have the text before us, not the principles as yet, the analysis must necessarily precede the synthesis. It is the basic method on which the conclusions of our present study rest. The synthesis is mainly a sort of counterproof of our conclusions, but because of its clarity we shall make use of it in our exposition. Part Two of this study will be devoted to an exposition of Ficino's ontological concepts and his peculiar logical methods of procedure. In Part Three we shall show how the basic experience of internal ascent is subjected to speculative interpretation and contributes, along with other ideas, to the construction of the system as a whole. We shall make frequent mention of Ficino's historical premises and the influence of his sources throughout our study; a more detailed consideration of these relations would exceed the limits of the present exposition. As a historical background for our interpretation, however, we shall first state briefly a few basic facts as to Ficino's place in history, his own opinion of that place, and the particular task that he consciously assumed as his mission in life.

II

FICINO'S HISTORICAL POSITION

BEFORE beginning to analyze Ficino's philosophy we shall give a brief outline of his background and sources, of his life and works, and of his influence on the later Renaissance. Then we propose to consider in greater detail the opinions he himself held as to his own historical task and position.

Since the brilliant work of J. Burckhardt the term "Renaissance" has come to stand for a distinctive period in European history and civilization. Its temporal limits coincide, roughly speaking, with the fifteenth and sixteenth centuries, and its main characteristic in the field of literature is classical humanism—in other words, the study, imitation, and revival of Greek and Roman antiquity. Recent studies have considerably modified our conception of the Renaissance. Many new details have been discovered: in particular it has become increasingly clear that there was more continuity between the Middle Ages and the Renaissance than most humanists or their modern interpreters care to admit. However, we cannot eliminate the concept itself as some modern scholars are inclined to do. We must rather be ready to adjust our concept of the Renaissance to the complexity of the known historical facts, instead of expecting the facts to agree with our artificial notions.

Whereas Burckhardt and most of his followers among the historians paid slight attention to the philosophy of the period, other scholars, such as Fiorentino, Dilthey, and Cassirer, began to speak of a "philosophy of the Renaissance." This does not merely mean that certain thinkers happened to live during that period; it means, rather, that those thinkers gave philosophical

expression to the prevailing intellectual tendencies of the age and
that underlying all differences between various schools and traditions there were certain characteristic problems common to all
philosophers of the Renaissance. The attempt to give a concrete
and conclusive definition of the philosophy of the Renaissance
involves considerable difficulty. But the concept, as such, is fruit-
ful and indispensable—especially when we do not take it for
granted, but use it as a guiding principle for further research.[1]
In the earlier part of the fifteenth century we find that in Italy
there was a rather complex and obscure situation with respect
to philosophical studies. Most teachers of philosophy at the
various universities, such as Bologna, Pavia, and especially Padua,
were developing a particular type of Aristotelianism, which was
by no means uniform and was to reach its most mature conclusions
in the sixteenth century. The roots of this Aristotelianism lie in the
fourteenth century, its orientation is medical rather than theological, and its chief interest is in the fields of logic and natural
philosophy. On the other hand, the humanists were writing a
number of treatises and dialogues in the Ciceronian manner,
which often dealt with more-or-less philosophical subjects. The
humanists were either men in public office or, more often,
teachers of grammar, rhetoric, and the classics at the universities,
as well as in the secondary schools of various cities. They continued the traditions of medieval grammar and rhetoric, but they
received a new impulse and inspiration from Petrarch. Their
philosophical interest was limited to ethics, political theory, and
education, but of even greater, though indirect, importance was
their philological study of the ancient thinkers. The humanists
tended to be slightly amateurish in their philosophical works,
but in compensation they were inclined to give direct expression
to the modern ideas of the age. The theological writers of the

---

[1] Burckhardt, *Die Kultur der Renaissance in Italien;* Baron, "Renaissance
in Italien," *Archiv fuer Kulturgeschichte,* XVII (1927), 226–56; XXI (1931),
95 ff.; Huizinga, "Das Problem der Renaissance," in *Wege der Kulturgeschichte,* pp. 89–139; Kristeller and Randall, "The Study of the Philosophies
of the Renaissance," *Journal of the History of Ideas,* II (1941), 449–96.

time represent a third group which has not yet been sufficiently investigated. While the authors of the more popular devotional literature continued the tradition of medieval Augustinianism, the more scientific theologians followed the line of Thomas Aquinas or that of Duns Scotus. In the period with which we are concerned many of these theologians were partly influenced both by the more recent type of Aristotelianism and by classical humanism. Most of them were connected with the flourishing schools of the various religious orders. Their influence in the Italian universities was at first very slight, but it increased gradually during the fifteenth and sixteenth centuries. Since its foundation in the fourteenth century, the university of Florence, alone, had been a stronghold of the theologians and it retained that characteristic far into the fifteenth century. The foreign scholars living in Italy during that period represent a fourth group of philosophical writers. Nicholas of Cusa, probably the most vigorous thinker of the fifteenth century, spent much of his later life in Italy and counted numerous friends and pupils among the Italians. Even more important were the Byzantine scholars who came to Italy in increasing numbers after 1397. The famous polemic between Greek Platonists and Aristotelians took place, for the most part, in Italy during the fifteenth century. Though the Italians did not take a very active part in this discussion, the Byzantine scholars helped to popularize the knowledge of ancient Greek philosophy through their teaching and their writings, a knowledge based on the original text and on ancient interpretations rather than on medieval translations and commentaries.[2]

It is against this background that we must understand the Platonic Academy of Florence and the philosophy of its founder and leader, Marsilio Ficino. In so far as Ficino attempted to express the new ideas of the humanists in a strictly speculative

[2] I am at present engaged in research on the teaching of philosophy in the Italian universities during the Renaissance.

metaphysical form, he may be called the first philosopher of the Italian Renaissance.

Ficino's close connection with the humanistic movement is obvious. Born and brought up in Florence, which was one of the most important centers of humanism, Ficino moved in the same social and cultural circles as the earlier humanists. Among his friends and correspondents we find many representatives of contemporary literature and educated society. His Latin style reflects the formal education of the humanistic school and a tendency to imitate the classical writers. Furthermore, he was an assiduous letter writer, collecting his correspondence for publication after the fashion of the earlier humanists. Ficino's correspondence is rhetorical in form, but it is also a direct reflection of his personal life and sentiments. Following a particular trend of Florentine humanism in his day, he was interested in the old Tuscan poets, translated Dante's *De monarchia* and some of his own works into Italian, and even wrote certain tracts in the vernacular. Through his translations and commentaries Ficino did for Plato, Plotinus, and other ancient philosophers what the other humanists did for the ancient Greek orators, poets, and historians. His revival of Platonism may be considered the realization of an old humanistic dream. Even since the days of Petrarch many humanists had made a point of praising Plato at the expense of Aristotle, the great authority of the Middle Ages—for the most part without much direct knowledge of Plato's works. Many of Ficino's philosophical problems originated in the modern tendencies of humanistic thought and owed their wide influence to that fact. This is particularly true of his theory of love, his doctrine of the dignity of man, and above all of the emphasis he gives to the position of man, who now becames the center of the universe, in contrast to the medieval emphasis on God.

On the other hand, we find in Ficino a strong and definite element of medieval Aristotelianism, a point generally less emphasized by modern scholars. Traces of the logical tradition, which goes back to Suiseth's *Calculationes,* appear in the doctrine of the "primum in aliquo genere." The polemic against Averroism, as developed in the fifteenth book of the *Theologia Platonica,* shows his acquaintance with the teachings of his opponents. Elsewhere he quotes Aristotle and the Arabic Aristotelians with great respect, and he never launched a general attack against Aristotelianism or scholasticism, as so many humanists did.[3] Some of Ficino's earliest works are largely Aristotelian and scholastic in form and content and are written in the typical form of "Quaestiones." His principal work, the *Theologia Platonica,* preserves the form of a "Summa de immortalitate animorum" and follows throughout the scholastic method of demonstration, enumerating many successive arguments for or against a given statement. Certain important concepts, such as "essentia" and "esse," "perfectio," and "hierarchy of being," are derived directly from the Scholastics, while other important theories, such as the "primum in aliquo genere" and the "appetitus naturalis," clearly contain scholastic elements. Hence we may conclude that Ficino owed to humanism his literary form and his preference for certain problems; to medieval Aristotelianism his metaphysical terminology and his logical method of argumentation.[4]

The influences which Ficino felt from the Aristotelian philosophers of his time were apparently strengthened by, and combined with, theological influences. A reliable tradition mentions St. Antoninus, the famous Thomist, as one who exerted a personal influence on Ficino in his youth. In any case, the influence of Thomas Aquinas and of Augustine is very strong in Ficino's work, and we are inclined to attribute this to the theological environment at Florence. Many metaphysical statements and arguments show a close relationship to Thomas, especially to his *Summa contra Gentiles.* Even more profound is the influence

[3] Cf. Garin, "Recenti interpretazioni di Marsilio Ficino," *Giorn. crit.,* XXI (1940), 307.

[4] See my article "Florentine Platonism and Its Relations with Humanism and Scholasticism," *Church History,* VIII (1939), 201 ff.

of Augustine, from whose works Ficino quotes entire pages. Augustine is Ficino's guide and model in his attempt to reconcile Platonism with Christianity. Many of Ficino's shorter treatises are Augustinian in style. His emphasis on the relation between the Soul and God is also due to Augustinian inspiration.[5]

Ficino mentions Nicholas of Cusa in one letter, but the evidence of a direct philosophical relationship is not very clear. It is possible that Ficino's theory of the infinity of the human mind may have been derived from Cusa. Of much greater importance was the work of the Byzantine Platonists, especially of Pletho. Ficino tells us in the Preface to his translation of Plotinus that Pletho's lectures given at Florence in 1438 inspired Cosimo de' Medici with the idea of founding the Platonic Academy. We cannot doubt that Pletho's personal appearance left some traces in Florence. Yet his direct influence on Ficino is less tangible than the quoted statement suggests. Ficino was still a child when Pletho came to Florence. By the time he had entered into correspondence with Pletho's pupil Bessarion, Ficino had already elaborated his own philosophy. There is also a basic difference between Pletho's position and that of Ficino. Pletho was primarily a political reformer, using Platonic philosophy to combat Christian theology and to give an allegorical interpretation of ancient Greek mythology. Ficino was not interested in political problems and always sought to maintain harmony between the Platonic philosophy and the Christian dogma. However, Ficino obviously derived at least one characteristic idea from Pletho— the idea of an ancient tradition of pagan theology that led directly from Zoroaster, Hermes Trismegistus, Orpheus, and Pythagoras to Plato and his followers.[6]

[5] On Ficino and Thomas cf. Taylor, *Thought and Expression in the Sixteenth Century*, II, 273 ff. On Ficino and Augustine cf. my article "Augustine and the Renaissance," *International Science*, I (1941), 7 ff.

[6] On Zoroaster see Kieszkowski, *Studi sul Platonismo del rinascimento in Italia*, pp. 113 ff. On the Hermetics see my article "Marsilio Ficino e Lodovico Lazzarelli," *Annali della R. Scuola Normale Superiore di Pisa*, Ser. II, VII (1938), 237 ff.

A final important factor for Ficino's doctrine was, of course, his direct contact with Plato and the ancient Neoplatonists, whom he studied and translated. Many of his central concepts are derived directly from those ancient sources, for example, the theory of Ideas, the hierarchical series of forms, and the concept of Soul and of its ascent to God. It would, however, be a mistake to say that Ficino's Platonism is a mere repetition of Plotinus or of other Neoplatonists. Many factors render this impossible: among others, the great span of intervening time, the medieval and Renaissance elements in Ficino's thought, and his own quality as a thinker of wide interests and of remarkable speculative force. Ficino did not repeat Platonic theories just because he translated Plato and Plotinus. As his early tracts show clearly, he was rather led to study and to translate these thinkers because he had first become interested in their ideas. In restating their thought he could not fail to combine it with the original impulses of his own philosophy.

The basic facts of Ficino's biography may be easily summarized. He was born on October 19, 1433, in Figline, near Florence, the eldest son of a physician called Diotifeci. Of his youth and early studies we know very little. It is probable that he studied grammar in one of the public or monastic schools in Florence and later philosophy and medicine, with perhaps also some Latin and theology, at the university of Florence. There is a tradition that he studied at Bologna, but this is not supported by sufficient evidence. About the year 1456, at a time when he had already written his first philosophical treatises, he took up the study of Greek in order to become acquainted with the sources of ancient philosophy. His relations with Cosimo de' Medici, which date from 1452, took a decisive turn in 1462, when Cosimo bestowed on him a grant of a villa at Careggi, near Florence, at the same time placing several Greek manuscripts at his disposal, with the understanding that he would dedicate himself to the interpretation and teaching of Platonic philosophy. This was the origin of the Platonic Academy. Ficino spent the rest of his life teaching and writing, remaining constantly in close relation with the Medicis and their circle. In 1473 he turned priest, and he received several benefices. In 1487 he became a canon of the Cathedral of Florence. After the death of Lorenzo de' Medici (1492) and the expulsion of the Medici from Florence (1494) Ficino retired to the country. Although at first an admirer of Savonarola, he became increasingly bitter about political conditions in Florence. He died on October 1, 1499.[7]

The earliest works of Ficino must be attributed to 1454. A number of treatises written between 1454 and 1462 are preserved. They show the various influences which he underwent in that period of formation: the traditional Aristotelianism of the Schools, some eclectic knowledge of ancient philosophy derived from Cicero, traces of Epicureanism derived from Lucretius, and of Platonism based on Augustine and other Latin writers. It would be interesting to reconstruct more carefully his early philosophical development on the basis of those treatises. That task is made difficult by the fact that the major work of that early period, the *Institutiones ad Platonicam disciplinam* (1456), has been lost. In 1463 Ficino finished the translation of the important *Corpus Hermeticum*. In the same year he began his Latin version of Plato's works, the first complete translation of all the dialogues into an occidental language. At the time of Cosimo's death, in 1464, Ficino had translated ten dialogues, completing his work under Piero about the year 1468. He then wrote his commentaries on Plato's *Symposium* and *Philebus* in 1469, and between 1469 and 1474 his principal philosophical work, the *Theologia Platonica,* in eighteen books. In 1474 he wrote his theological work, *De Christiana religione.* The following years were dedicated to the writing of numerous small treatises, now inserted among his letters, and to the revision of the *Theologia*

---

[7] The standard work for Ficino's biography is Arnaldo della Torre's *Storia dell'Accademia Platonica di Firenze.* A few corrections are found in my article "Per la biografia di Marsilio Ficino," *Civiltà moderna,* X (1938), 277 ff.

and of the Plato translation, works which were printed in 1482 and 1484, respectively. From 1484 to 1492 he worked on his translation of Plotinus and wrote his commentaries on that author. In 1488 he made translations of Porphyry, Proclus, and other Neoplatonic sources, and in 1489 he wrote his medical work, *De vita*. His translation of Dionysius the Areopagite was completed in 1492. His letters were collected and printed in 1495, his commentaries on Plato in 1496. The incomplete commentary on St. Paul's Epistle to the Romans seems to be the latest of Ficino's extant works.[8]

Ficino was never connected as a teacher with the University of Florence, but he gave many public lectures in the city. The foundation of the Florentine Academy must be dated from the year 1462, when he took possession of his villa at Careggi, which he used to call his "Academia." There he held private lectures and seminars in which he dealt chiefly with the interpretation of Plato and Plotinus, not neglecting the direct discussion of metaphysical and theological problems. There, too, he received foreign visitors and held informal discussions with his friends. His famous Platonic symposia reveal a characteristic combination of social intercourse and philosophical teaching. There was no distinction between Ficino's doctrine and the doctrine of the Academy; the Academy was merely the circle of persons in which and through which Ficino's doctrine was diffused. Among his friends only Pico della Mirandola was a philosopher with an independent standpoint. Among his pupils only two produced philosophical works: Alamanno Donati and Francesco da Diacceto, the latter continuing the Platonic tradition at Florence in the sixteenth century. Lorenzo de' Medici, Cristoforo Landino, and many others also were profoundly influenced by Ficino's teaching. It is, perhaps, not too much to say that all of educated Florence in the second half of the fifteenth century came under

[8] The list and chronology of Ficino's works is given in my *Supplementum Ficinianum*, I, lxxvii–clxvii.

the intellectual influence of Ficino's Academy. Through his writings and his correspondence he was in touch with other Italian centers, such as Rome and Venice, his relations extending also to Germany, France, Belgium, Poland, and Hungary. Ficino's influence survived his death and the dissolution of his Academy. His works were reprinted and studied throughout the sixteenth century. In Florence, and later in Pisa, a local tradition of Platonic philosophy flourished over a long period of time. Other philosophers, such as Patrizi, Bruno, and Campanella, were strongly influenced by Ficino's Platonism. The treatises on immortality written by the Aristotelians of the sixteenth century made constant reference to Ficino's arguments. His concept of natural religion may well have had some bearing on the theological discussions of the period of the Reformation. The traces of his theory of love appear in many poets, from Lorenzo to Michelangelo, and in the extensive literature of the "Trattati d'amore," which includes Bembo's *Asolani,* Castiglione's *Courtier,* and the prose works of Torquato Tasso. Outside Italy the influence of Florentine Platonism was specially persistent in France, the main centers of this influence being Lefèvre d'Etaples and his group, including Symphorien Champier, the humanists and poets of Lyons, and Marguerite de Navarre and her circle. In England, John Colet shows some trace of Ficino's Platonism. But the Platonic trend, probably transmitted through French channels, becomes more tangible toward the end of the sixteenth century in poets such as Spenser. The Cambridge Platonists, whose activity extends far into the seventeenth century, carry on the philosophical tradition of the Florentines. But with the seventeenth century a new epoch in the history of science and philosophy begins, and the direct influence of Florentine Platonism as of most Renaissance philosophy tends to disappear. However, Ficino continued to exercise a subtle and anonymous influence through his translations and commentaries, which were still reprinted and widely read. Everyone who read Plato and Plotinus in Latin absorbed, along with the ideas of these ancient thinkers, many ideas that actually belonged to their Renaissance interpreter. In this form Ficino's influence continued at least up to the end of the eighteenth century. It was not until the nineteenth century that his translations were definitely replaced by other versions in modern languages. They were, however, still being reprinted as late as 1840. Since that date he has been buried in the *apparatus criticus* of modern editions of Plotinus. Further research will doubtless throw more light on many of these influences, and it is this broad historical perspective that increases our interest in a genuine understanding of Ficino's own doctrine.[9]

We have touched on the basic historical facts concerning the origin, development, and influence of Ficino's Platonism. There is, however, another problem which is in a certain sense even more important: What was Ficino's own idea of his historical position, and how did he understand the "Renaissance of Platonism?" In developing this problem we shall not only be completing our historical considerations, we shall be making a first approach to Ficino's own thought.

The term "Renaissance" as it is used to designate a certain historical period is purely of modern origin. Yet not only does it describe quite accurately an intellectual movement which took place during that period, it also expresses an idea present in the minds of the writers of the period itself. In varied phrases they mention a "renewal" of arts and learning (either hoped for or

[9] For the Academy and Ficino's friends see Della Torre, *op. cit.* For Pico see Garin, *Giovanni Pico della Mirandola;* Anagnine, *G. Pico della Mirandola;* Kibre, *The Library of Pico della Mirandola;* Dulles, *Princeps concordiae;* Cassirer, "Giovanni Pico della Mirandola," *Journal of the History of Ideas,* III (1942), 123–44; 319–46; Alamanno Donati's tract *De intellectus voluntatisque excellentia* was published by Lamberto Borghi, *La Bibliofilia,* XLII (1940), 108 ff. I am working on an edition of the unpublished works of Francesco da Diacceto. On Lorenzo de'Medici see Buck, *Der Platonismus in den Dichtungen Lorenzo de' Medicis,* and my review in *Giornale critico della filosofia italiana,* XIX (1938), 149 ff. Cristoforo Landino's poems were recently published by Alessandro Perosa (Florence, 1939). On Ficino's influence in France see Moench, *Die italienische Platonrenaissance.* See also Robb, *Neoplatonism of the Italian Renaissance.*

already accomplished).[10] Referring to his translation of Herodianus, Poliziano uses a phrase that was already common when he mentions a "revival" of historiography, and again, speaking of painting that had become extinct, he says that it was "brought to life again" by Giotto.[11] The idea of a "rebirth" of arts and human institutions as a whole means that a period, conscious of its own value, has detached itself from a preceding age of decline and has attached itself to a more distant past of recognized perfection—in other words, to classical antiquity. This is the origin of the conventional division in history between antiquity, the Middle Ages, and the modern period. Only in part, however, can the movement be called a "revival of classical antiquity" (the title of a well-known book), particularly if by that term we understand merely the rediscovery of ancient writings, monuments, and historical data. It is a desire for original creation that sends us to antiquity as a model to be imitated, and only when studied as a stimulus to imitation do ancient remains acquire a real interest. This motive was clearly expressed by Poliziano in his letter to Paolo Cortesi and also in his Preface to Statius' *Sylvae*.[12] Later Winckelmann was to hold the same view, though under entirely different circumstances.[13] It would be more accurate, therefore, and more in accord with contemporary assertions to speak of a "rebirth of the arts guided by antiquity." As Burdach's researches demonstrate, this idea of "rebirth" (as well as the idea of "reformation") is derived from certain religious notions of the Middle Ages that referred originally to a personal and individual regeneration and were later applied to the arts and to social institutions. In the light of this origin "rebirth" is

[10] For this humanistic self-interpretation see the large documentation given by Ferguson, "Humanist Views of the Renaissance," *American Historical Review*, XLV (1939), 1 ff.

[11] "historiae renatae," "per quem pictura extincta revixit" (*Opera*, Basileae, 1553, p. 621).

[12] Poliziano, *Opera*, pp. 113 f., 492 ff.

[13] See his "Gedanken über die Nachahmung der griechischen Werke in der Malerei und Bildhauerkunst," *Kleine Schriften und Briefe*, I, 59–105.

understood, not as a mere repetition of the former life, but as a resumption of that life on a higher level.[14]

As to Burdach's results, we must call attention to the fact that in Ficino also we find the religious idea of rebirth in its original and personal significance,[15] as well as in its application to social conditions.[16] Of particular interest on this point is Ficino's own statement that he "was born of his father, but reborn of Cosimo de' Medici, who consecrated him to the divine Plato." [17] However, this religious concept of rebirth is not central in his thought, and in these examples there is apparently no direct connection with the historical concept of the rebirth of the arts. Yet there are other assertions in Ficino that make it quite clear that he was acquainted with this historical concept and made use of it even in judging his own life work. For example, he characterizes his translation as a "rebirth" or "resurrection" of Plato [18] and calls his own doctrine and school a resurrection of the ancient Academy.[19] In a like sense Poliziano praises Ficino, who "more fortunate than Orpheus, brought back to life the true Eurydice, in other words, Platonic wisdom." [20] Here we are close to the concept that the rebirth of Platonic philosophy is part of the universal revival of the arts, an idea clearly expressed by Ficino himself in his letter to Paulus Middelburgensis.

Our century [he says], like a golden age, restored to light the liberal arts that were nearly extinct: grammar, poetry, rhetoric, painting, sculpture, architecture, music, the ancient performance of songs with the Orphic lyre, and all that in Florence. And accomplishing what had

---

[14] Burdach, *Reformation, Renaissance, Humanismus*, 2d ed., Part I: *Sinn und Ursprung der Worte Renaissance und Reformation.*

[15] *Op. om.*, pp. 611, 1523.   [16] *Ibid.*, pp. 559, 1031.   [17] *Op. om.*, p. 493.

[18] ". . . dum Plato quasi renasceretur" (*Op. om.*, p. 1537); ". . . resurgenti Platoni" (*ibid.*, p. 948); ". . . in suscitando Platone" (*ibid.*, p. 918).

[19] "Antiquam Academiam resurgentem" (*Op. om.*, p. 909).

[20] "Marsilio Ficino Florentino cuius longe felicior quam Thracensis Orphei cithara veram ni fallor Eurydicem hoc est amplissimi iudicii Platonicam sapientiam revocavit ab inferis" (*Opera*, p. 310). The allegorical explanation of the name Eurydice occurs also in Ficino (*Op. om.*, p. 918).

been revered among the ancients, but almost forgotten since, it united wisdom with eloquence and prudence with military arts as exemplified . . . particularly in Frederic, Duke of Urbino. . . . And in you, oh, Paul, it seems to have perfected astronomy. And in Florence it restored the Platonic doctrine from darkness to light.[21]

Ficino is evidently convinced that he is doing for Platonic philosophy what, in the opinion of his contemporaries, Giotto had already done for painting and Dante for poetry. The Platonism of the Renaissance was really conceived as a genuine renaissance of Platonism, in other words, Ficino's Platonism is not a philosophical conception that just happened to appear during the period of the Renaissance, it is, so to speak, the Renaissance become philosophical—in other words, the philosophical expression and manifestation of its leading idea.

The philosophical ideas which may be considered the real content of Ficino's Platonism will be made apparent during the course of our study. Here, however, we must pause and ask ourselves by what right and in what sense Ficino chose to attach himself to ancient Platonism in particular, among the various trends of philosophical tradition, and sought to bring about a revival of that Platonism. At first we may answer that from the beginning of Renaissance humanism some philosophical writings of the Greeks had gradually become better known, along with many other works of ancient literature. In this process the humanists emphasized, not so much the internal unity of ancient philosophy, as the differences between the four major schools that had developed in the Hellenistic age. Just as the humanists sought to imitate ancient models in every field, so in that period all those philosophical schools found new followers. Ficino's adherence to the Platonic school, therefore, appears to be merely a personal preference, a supposition confirmed by some of his earlier works in which he limits himself to reporting the positions

[21] "Florentiae quinetiam Platonicam disciplinam in lucem e tenebris revocavit" (*Op. om.,* p. 944).

of all four schools.[22] In his later development, however, Ficino
tends to give a more profound and also more independent foundation to his Platonism.

The scholastic theology of the Middle Ages sought to confirm
doctrines based on the ecclesiastical tradition, in other words, on
the "auctoritas" of the Bible and of the church fathers, by means
of "ratio," that is, of independent philosophical reflection. Ficino,
who was himself a convinced Christian and wished to avoid any
scandal in the Church, found himself confronted with a similar
task. "I believe," he says in the Preface to his Theologia Platonica,
"and this belief is not fallacious, that divine Providence has decided that the perverse minds of many persons who do not easily
yield to the authority of the divine law alone, should be satisfied
at least by Platonic arguments that are brought to the aid of religion." [23] In this way he consciously compares the "rationes
platonicae," or as he says elsewhere, the "ratio platonica" [24] with
the authority of the divine law. Ficino here replaces Aristotle,
who prevailed in the preceding period, with Plato (a choice
made possible only through the recently acquired knowledge of
ancient literature), basing his decision on the agreement between
the Platonic doctrine and the Christian religion and on the judgment of St. Augustine and of the other church fathers. "Confid-
ing in them," he writes to the Archbishop of Amalfi, "I thought
it worth while—it being necessary to philosophize—to philosophize rather in the Academy," in other words, in the Platonic
tradition.[25] It is significant that the medieval principle of "ratio"

[22] "De voluptate" (Op. om., pp. 986 ff.). "De Quatuor Sectis Philosophorum" (Suppl., II, 7 ff.). The Platonic tendency in Ficino, which appeared in the lost Institutiones ad Platonicam disciplinam (see Op. om.,
p. 929) and in some other early tracts (see my article in Church History,
VIII [1939], 201 ff.) did not prevent him from being influenced by the Epicureanism of Lucretius, as we can see from some of his early and hitherto
unknown letters (Suppl., II, 81 ff.). On Ficino's Epicureanism see also
Gabotto, "L'epicureismo di Marsilio Ficino," Rivista di filosofia scientifica,
X [1891], 428 ff.).

[23] Op. om., p. 78; Cf. ibid., p. 855.   [24] Ibid., p. 930.   [25] Ibid., p. 855.

in general appears in Ficino with the special qualification of "ratio platonica." In this way Plato's name is identified with independent philosophical consideration and the difference between "ratio" and "auctoritas" is repeated within the field of "ratio" itself. Ficino therefore says of the Neoplatonists (and not incidentally) that "they rely mainly on two principles, their own reason and Platonic authority." [26] And in a letter to Johannes Pannonius he writes that "divine Providence at present supports the Christian religion with philosophical authority and reason." [27] Plato's authority thus acquires for Ficino a value similar to that of the Bible, and in one place he uses the characteristic expression: "the Platonic doctrine is related to divine law . . . as the moon to the sun." [28]

It is obvious that Ficino's conviction of the truth of the Platonic doctrine excludes, in his opinion, any basic contrast between the authority of the doctrine and his own opinion. On the other hand, however, it is important to note his effort to give a historical explanation concerning the authority of Plato and the Platonists and his judgment of their relation to the Christian tradition in particular. To Ficino, Plato is not only an admirable philosophical thinker, he is also the exponent and perfecter of an old tradition of "theology." The writings attributed to the ancient wise men and now recognized by modern criticism as the apocryphal products of a later period are for Ficino authentic testimony of that venerable tradition.

Mercurius Trismegistus [he writes in the Preface to his translation of the *Corpus Hermeticum*] was the first philosopher to raise himself above physics and mathematics to the contemplation of the divine. . . . Therefore he was considered the original founder of theology. Orpheus followed him and held second place in ancient theology. Aglaophemus was initiated into the Orphic mysteries. Aglaophemus' successor in theology was Pythagoras, and his pupil was Philolaus, the master of

---

[26] ". . . ratione propria et authoritate platonica" (*ibid.*, p. 393).
[27] ". . . authoritate rationeque philosophica" (*ibid.*, p. 872).
[28] *Ibid.*, p. 855; cf. Dress, *Die Mystik des Marsilio Ficino*, pp. 4 f., 9 ff.

our divine Plato. So six theologians, in wonderful order, formed a unique and coherent succession in ancient theology, beginning with Mercurius and ending with the divine Plato.[29]

The same series reappears in Ficino's later writings, with the sole difference that Zoroaster is inserted at the beginning and Philolaus omitted at the end.[30] The great value of this tradition is derived from its supposed antiquity, an ancestor of Mercurius being by some authorities said to have been a contemporary of Moses. In this way the tradition is not far removed from the Biblical tradition.[31]

This theology is, moreover, an esoteric doctrine, and in this we recognize another indication of its divine origin. "The ancient theologians covered all the sacred mysteries of divine things with poetic veils, that they might not be diffused among profane people." [32] Though the series of ancient theologians ends with Plato, it is continued in the series of the Platonic schools of antiquity.

The multitude of Platonic interpreters was divided into six "academies," three in Athens and three abroad. In Athens the oldest flourished under Xenocrates, the next under Arcesilaus, and the last under Carneades. Among foreign academies the Egyptian under Ammonius, the Roman under Plotinus, the Lycian under Proclus.[33]

With Proclus' school the continuous tradition, reaching back to Plato and even further to Zoroaster and Trismegistus, was broken for the first time. However, in the succeeding centuries there were still a few scattered traces and effects of the Platonic tradition. These Ficino investigated in part and with great care. From the Byzantines he translated Psellus,[34] and he commented on Nicolaus of Methone.[35] He recommends for their Platonic

---

[29] *Op. om.*, p. 1836. For the Platonic tradition see Saitta, *La filosofia di Marsilio Ficino*, pp. 58 f.; Cassirer, *Individuum und Kosmos in der Philosophie der Renaissance*, pp. 2 f.; Dress, *op. cit.*, pp. 5 f.

[30] *Op. om.*, pp. 386, 871; cf. p. 156.

[31] *Ibid.*, p. 1836.   [32] *Ibid.*, p. 386; cf. p. 871.

[33] *Ibid.*, p. 386.   [34] *Ibid.*, pp. 1939 ff.

[35] Cf. *ibid.*, p. 1171 (not preserved).

tendency [36] Avicebron, Alfarabi, and Avicenna, among the Arabic and Hebrew philosophers of the Middle Ages, and among the Scholastics, Henry of Ghent and Duns Scotus. Among the thinkers close to his own period he mentions Pletho only incidentally,[37] and he praises more explicitly the Platonism of Bessarion and Cusanus.[38] Ficino also quotes Dante and Guido Cavalcanti as Platonists.[39] However, calling himself a renewer of Platonism, he sought to attach himself directly to the tradition of ancient Platonism. So Ficino's celebration of Plato's birthday in the circle of his "Academy" [40]—the first time since the days of Plotinus and Porphyry—after an interval of 1200 years, acquired a symbolic significance. Working to spread the Platonic philosophy among his contemporaries by his writings, by his translations, and by his personal activity, he tried to bring back an ancient and divine truth to its eternal destination.[41]

Though Platonic philosophy has its own authority and tradition, it is in no way opposed to Christian doctrine and tradition. More than any other system it is able to give Christian doctrine a philosophical confirmation. The Platonic doctrine is a religious philosophy.[42] It guarantees the accord between philosophy and religion and may therefore even be called "theology," as the title of Ficino's principal work indicates. As to the intimate affinity of Platonism with the Mosaic and the Christian doctrines, Ficino quotes Numenius and Augustine again and again,[43] even writing two small tracts to prove the agreement between the Mosaic and the Platonic doctrines and between the Socratic and the Christian conduct of life.[44] He considers "religious philosophers" such as Pythagoras, Socrates, and Plato precursors of Christianity and allows them a share in eternal salvation, along with the prophets

[36] Platonem redolent (ibid., p. 899).   [37] Ibid., pp. 327, 1049.
[38] Ibid., pp. 616 f., 899; see also Suppl., I, 35. Cf. Klibansky, The Continuity of the Platonic Tradition during the Middle Ages (London, 1939), pp. 42 ff.
[39] Suppl., II, 184 f.; Op. om., pp. 1355 f.; see also Suppl., II, 257.
[40] Op. om., pp. 1320 f.   [41] Cf. ibid., p. 883.
[42] Ibid., p. 871 ("pia philosophia"); cf. Cassirer, op. cit., p. 65.
[43] Op. om., pp. 855, 769, et passim.   [44] Ibid., pp. 866 ff.

of the Old Testament.[45] In the same sense he assigns to Platonic philosophy the task of furthering religion and of bringing men back to the Christian faith.[46] Anyone who has had a philosophical education and as a result is wont to follow reason alone, can find the way to religion and to eternal salvation only through a religious philosophy, in other words, through Platonic reason (*ratio platonica*). Along with and in accord with the Christian tradition, therefore, the Platonic tradition fulfills a mission necessary to the divine scheme of world history. As a follower and renewer of that tradition Ficino does not hesitate to consider himself an instrument of divine Providence.

We must not think [he writes to Johannes Pannonius] that the subtle and philosophical minds of men can ever be gradually enticed and led to the perfect religion by any lure other than a philosophical one. For subtle minds trust themselves only to reason, and if they receive religion from a religious philosopher, at once and of their own volition they recognize religion in general and from there pass more readily to the best species of religion included in that genus. It was, therefore, by the will of divine Providence, which leads all men unto itself admirably as befits the nature of each particular individual, that a religious philosophy arose among the Persians under Zoroaster and likewise among the Egyptians under Trismegistus, that it was then nursed by the Thracians under Orpheus and Aglaophemus, to be later developed among the Greeks and Italians under Pythagoras and finally perfected in Athens under the divine Plato. . . . The whole world is now in the hands of the Peripatetics and is divided mainly into two sects, Alexandrists and Averroists. Both deny any form of religion. If anyone think to destroy by the simple preaching of faith an impiety so diffused among men and defended by such subtle minds, he will soon be refuted by the results. Stronger measures are needed: either divine miracles manifested on all sides or at least a philosophical religion to which philosophers will listen more readily and which will some day succeed in convincing them. But in these times it pleases divine Providence to confirm religion in general by philosophical authority

[45] *Ibid.*, p. 806; *Suppl.*, I, 12 ff.
[46] *Op. om.*, p. 930; cf. Anichini, *L'umanesimo e il problema della salvezza in Marsilio Ficino*, p. 26.

and reason until, on a day already predestined, it will confirm the true religion, as in other times, by miracles wrought among all peoples.[47]

From the above passages it is obvious that Ficino strove to give an historical perspective and meaning to his life work, viewing it in a broad historical context. To this end he combined the historical ideas of the Renaissance and those of the Middle Ages. The renewal of Platonic philosophy is, on the one hand, part of the general rebirth of human arts and institutions. On the other it is intended to lead men to salvation in accordance with the Christian religion and so to serve as a necessary instrument for the eternal plan of divine Providence.

[47] *Op. om.,* pp. 871 f. See Dress, *op. cit.,* pp. 11 ff. The quoted sentences are in most part repeated literally in the Preface to the translation of Plotinus (*Op. om.,* p. 1537). Since the letter to Pannonius must be dated 1484, the division of Aristotelians into Alexandrists and Averroists must belong to that period. We can therefore hardly make Pomponazzi, who was born in 1462, responsible for this division, as does Ueberweg (III [12th ed., 1924], 22).

Part Two

BEING AND THE UNIVERSE

IN HIS PRINCIPAL WORK, the *Theologia Platonica,* Ficino sets forth the philosophical doctrine of Platonism as a whole. The subject matter is not divided systematically, as might be expected, but proceeds with a succession of formal arguments, applying, so to speak, on a large scale the medieval form of disputation which seeks to establish a proposed thesis by a series of independent proofs. The thesis of the whole work is the immortality of the Soul, as the subtitle indicates. After a general consideration of the degrees of Being (Books I–IV), the argument proper is developed through the successive stages of *rationes communes* (Book V), *argumentationes propriae* (Books VI–XII), *signa* (Books XIII–XIV), and *solutiones quaestionum* (Books XV–XVIII).[1] The same form of exposition employed in the composition of the work as a whole is repeated in each section, book, and chapter. Any free development of broad considerations is rare: on the contrary, throughout we find groups of closely related arguments, either connected according to logical rules or set without connection one after the other.

As a result of this procedure the several philosophical doctrines do not appear in their direct form, but are modified to suit the particular ends of the argument. Repetitions and inconsistencies are consequently more difficult than usual to avoid. The form of the arguments being anything but convincing to

[1] See pp. 79, 156, 284, 326, 424. Matthias Meier (*op. cit.,* p. 237) is wrong in stating that the first five books of the *Theologia Platonica* explain Ficino's own system, while the remaining thirteen books are devoted to criticism of the opinions of other writers. Pusino (p. 510) is equally wrong in asserting that Books IX–XII are dedicated to the "divine mind." Toffanin (*Storia dell'umanesimo,* p. 212) affirms that thirteen out of eighteen books are dedicated to the polemic against Averroism (*sic*). Actually, this is true only of the fifteenth book. Montano (*La Rinascita,* No. 11, p. 76*n*), apparently following Toffanin, also asserts that the polemic against Averroism occupies the greater part of the *Theologia Platonica.*

the modern reader, the philosophical content of the doctrines becomes equally doubtful. The interpreter must therefore try to
separate the positions themselves from their logical framework
and to explain the inconsistencies between various statements by
recurring to certain more fundamental ideas. In justification of
this method one may cite the author's own procedure. For the
thesis of immortality in the *Theologia Platonica* is really no more
than a guiding principle that is lost sight of over long sections.
Beneath the formal plan of division we can recognize a rational
distribution of material. Moreover, whole arguments are repeated almost word for word in other works of Ficino that do
not deal with immortality and do not follow the scholastic
method of formal proof. In Ficino, however, the form of argument is not merely an external cloak that can be arbitrarily removed from its philosophical content; it expresses his own
method of thinking and cannot be separated from it. "All
speech," he has said somewhere, "and even all action in life and
all consideration is nothing but a process of reasoning." [2] To understand Ficino's ideas, therefore, we must first take into account
their particular logical form and connection. But on examining
more closely those forms of argumentation that seem at first
glance particularly strange, we find that they arise, not from any
sophistry or dishonesty in the author or from any lack of training
or acuteness on his part, but rather from definite ontological
premises, from which they derive their certainty and through
which they stand or fall. It is therefore the primary task of the
ensuing study to analyze the system of Ficino's ontological conceptions with respect to his logical methods. These conceptions
are frequently implied rather than explicitly developed. They belong in part to the traditional heritage of medieval philosophy;
but inasmuch as they have given form and characteristic structure
to Ficino's system as a whole they deserve fuller exposition.

[2] *Op. om.,* p. 262.

III

THE CONCEPT OF BEING

ANYTHING WE EXPERIENCE or anything that may become an object of thought may be said to exist, irrespective of whether or not we attribute special significance to this assertion and whether we assign the character of "Being" to the object itself or to its concept. The division of philosophy that deals with Being and its attributes is called ontology. If, therefore, we would understand Ficino's ontological ideas in their context, we must start with the concept of Being as the real basis of all.

The question of Being contains three elements: How is the attribute of Being related to the objects and to their other attributes? How are the objects related to each other in respect to their Being? What does it mean when we say that the individual object exists and is defined as Being? We must therefore seek to establish the function, order, and character of Being. The general problem hardly admits of an answer, but through the three specific questions we may arrive at an understanding of the concept of Being in Ficino.

The attribute of Being is, on the one hand, the most universal and common of all the attributes.[1] This means first merely that Being is inherent in all objects in general. The terms "universal" and "common," however, indicate a particular aspect, in other words, the relation between a genus and its species or between a species and its individuals. This conception of Being appears more clearly in other statements. Speaking of the concepts "ens," "essentia," and "esse," for example, Ficino says that everything

[1] "Esse universale" (*Op. om.*, p. 102). "Communissimum omnium . . . esse ipsum" (*ibid.*, p. 370; see also pp. 147, 238).

that is, is included under those terms.[2] In the same way all attributes through which an object receives a certain quality or essence are considered merely as limitations or qualifications of Being.[3] In the process of defining, thought rises from the lower and higher species to the lower and higher genera, arriving ultimately through a continual sequence at the concept of Being, from which it may descend again in a converse sequence through the genera to the species and individuals.[4] Being therefore has definitely the function of a genus, but is never called a genus— an omission that is certainly not accidental. For the Aristotelian-Thomistic tradition definitely rejected such a conception and replaced it with the theory of the *analogia entis*. Ficino never mentions the analogy of Being, but he certainly took it into account in his cautious formulation of the opposite concept.

Through the general attribute of Being even the objects as such enter into a definite reciprocal relation and so constitute a closed sphere, in other words, the world or nature, in which each object has its own definite place. The coexistence of objects in a world indicates in the first place a sort of spatial order. Referring to the sum of all objects, Ficino therefore uses the characteristic term "extent of all Being."[5] However, this order is by no means spatial in the proper sense, since it includes incorporeal, in other words, nonspatial, objects. Rather, the spatial order of corporeal objects in a physical world is analogically applied to the order of all objects in an absolute world and so loses its concrete character. This spatial conception of the order of Being and the ambiguity of the term "world" connected with it were once clearly expressed by Ficino himself.

---

[2] "Sub iis vero ea quae sunt omnia continentur" (*ibid.*, p. 217).
[3] *Ibid.*, p. 102.
[4] See *ibid.*, pp. 192 f., 201, 217, 281, *et passim*
[5] "Totam entis ipsius latitudinem" (*ibid.*, p. 238). "Latitudo" is a technical term frequently found in the literature based on Suiseth's *Calculationes;* see Pomponazzi's treatise *De intensione et remissione formarum.* However, I do not believe that this statement of Ficino refers to that tradition.

Reason tells us [he says, referring to the divine omnipresence] that what we call "everywhere" is nothing more or less than the universal nature of things . . . But phantasy, taking the nature of things simply as this corporeal machine, declares that what is called "everywhere" is nothing but the whole extent of corporeal things.[6]

Finally, if we wish to understand the significance of Being for each single object, we must start with the highest genera included under Being in its function as the most universal attribute.

The most common of all things, according to the Peripatetics, seems to be Being itself. It is divided into two classes: the one exists by itself; the other is inherent in something else. The former is substance; the latter, attribute. Substance, again, is either corporeal or incorporeal. In like manner, attribute is either quality or quantity, *etc.*[7]

Being is therefore the concept superior to substance and attribute, which means conversely: anything that exists is either a thing or the attribute of a thing, in other words, existence always includes the character of thing or substance. Here the concept of "thing," originally derived from corporeal objects, is deliberately conceived in such a way as to include incorporeal objects too.

With these concepts we find ourselves involved in Aristotelian ontology. We are now obliged to show briefly how its principal ideas handed down through Scholasticism are employed in Ficino's system.

As we have seen, the difference between substance and attribute relates to the most general possibilities of Being. Whereas substance exists by itself and is defined by its "capacity for existence,"[8] the attribute is a property of something else, in other words, of a substance, and cannot subsist by itself.[9] It therefore follows that the world as the sum of subsistent things is composed mainly of substances and thus the most universal genera of substances, namely, the corporeal and the incorporeal, indicate at

---

[6] *Ibid.,* p. 98; see also Saitta, *La filosofia di Marsilio Ficino,* pp. 91 f.
[7] *Op. om.,* p. 370.   [8] "Sufficientia subsistendi" (*ibid.,* p. 193).
[9] *Ibid.,* p. 370.

the same time partial spheres of the universe itself.[10] As to its concrete meaning, in Ficino "substance" indicates the species,[11] not the individual. It is therefore the species that determines the structure of the world as a whole, as we shall show later on. On the other hand, attributes are divided into two groups, according to the character of their intrinsic content: the properties of substance (*proprietates substantiae*) are correlated with the concept of the substance from the start, while the common qualities (*qualitates communes*) are added to the substance afterwards and not of necessity.[12] The division of attributes according to their content will be treated below in connection with the theory of categories.

The concepts of form and matter as first formulated by Aristotle originate in the consideration of a work of art in which shape and material may be clearly distinguished. This is shown by the recurrent example of the statue. These concepts are thence transferred to natural bodies in such a way that every concrete attribute is understood as form, while beyond all attributes or delimitations there is an undetermined and indefinable material, "first matter." [13] So every natural body is composed of form and matter [14]—is generated by their union and is destroyed by their separation.[15] Matter is above all attributes. It has neither quality nor quantity, and the only thing that may be said of it is that it is the same for all bodies.[16] It is the foundation of all forms, but is in itself formless and incapable of arriving at a form by its own power.[17] According to an Averroistic doctrine certain seeds or beginnings (*inchoationes*) of forms are attributed to matter to indicate merely the passive capacity of being formed.[18] Conversely, the concept of form includes all the concrete attributes that make up the essence of a natural body, and therefore the

---

[10] Cf. *ibid.*, p. 370.　　　　　　　[11] Cf. *ibid.*, p. 179.

[12] *Ibid.*, p. 107; cf. p. 1141.　　　[13] Cf. *ibid.*, pp. 140 f.

[14] *Ibid.*, p. 164.　　[15] *Ibid.*, p. 144.　　[16] *Ibid.*, p. 129.

[17] *Ibid.*, pp. 82, 136 f. See also Horbert, *Metaphysik des Marsilius Ficinus*, pp. 11 ff.

[18] *Op. om.*, p. 91; cf. *ibid.*, pp. 141, 144, 221.

Being of things resides precisely in their form: "Each thing receives from its form its own existence, its nature, and its species as distinct from others." [19] Consequently, even the general division of Being reappears in the concept of form, and there is a distinction between substantial and accidental forms.[20] In so far as form occupies the whole realm of Being, matter is, so to speak, practically expelled from it. Matter has no existence of its own. It merely has, in respect to each object, the equal possibility of being and of not being.[21] Matter, therefore, is next to Nothing and stands midway between Being and Nothing.[22] Like the conceptions of spatial order and substance, the relation of matter and form is also transferred to incorporeal objects. And in this attempt either a universal matter is conceived as underlying both corporeal and intelligible entities,[23] or there is supposed to be in incorporeal entities a particular element which has the same function that matter has in bodies. This element is called "essentia" and corresponds to intelligible matter in the Neoplatonic sense, but it is more directly related to the Thomistic tradition.[24]

The relation between act and potency is akin to the relation between form and matter, but it contains several new elements and also has a more general significance. When an object undergoes a change and so receives a new attribute, that attribute is not added to it at once and, so to speak, out of nothing. The attribute was already potentially contained in the object and is now actually received by it. "The sculptor," says Ficino employing the usual Aristotelian example, "actually makes the statue out of a stone that has been prepared for it in such a way that in a certain sense the stone possessed the statue in potency." [25] The object that appears after the change can therefore be divided into two elements: the act (*actus*), in other words, the new

[19] *Ibid.*, p. 141; cf. p. 142. See also Horbert, *op. cit.*, p. 9.
[20] *Op. om.*, pp. 165, 179, 1030.   [21] *Ibid.*, p. 146.
[22] *Ibid.*, p. 226.   [23] *Ibid.*, pp. 386 f., 1253.
[24] *Ibid.*, pp. 96, 97.   [25] *Ibid.*, p. 148.

attribute as such, and the potency (*potentia*), in other words, the object in its previous condition.[26] Since potency cannot arrive at the act by itself, it requires the action of some other extraneous object, the agent.[27] Likewise, the agent (*agens*) or acting object will generally be composed of potency and act. But in any case only by its act can the agent have effect outwardly and lead the second object, the passive one, the *patiens,* to actuality.[28] In like manner the passive object (*patiens*) may be active in respect to a third object and lead the latter by its own act from potency to act. So act and potency, considered as elements of different objects, determine the relation of activity and passivity and coincide with the concepts of active force and passive potency (*virtus activa et potentia passiva*).[29] In the degree to which each object is composed of potency and act, it is characterized by a passive element and an active element. In that sense the relation of act and potency is applicable not only to corporeal changes but to almost all objective relations as well, so acquiring a fundamental significance. "Everything that is produced is made up of . . . potency and act." [30] "The first and common distinction or composition in objects is that constituted by potency and act." [31] The relation between matter and form appears therefore as a particular case of that relation, with the result that matter is called "potency," form, on the other hand, "act." [32] In this way even the concept of Being receives an important new specification.

The general character of Being is expressed by three different terms: "ens," "essentia," and "esse." [33] *Ens* means the general character of an entity, while *esse* and *essentia* are included in the entity as partial elements.[34] The difference between *essentia* and *esse* is defined by Ficino as follows: "We call 'essence' the con-

---

[26] Cf. *ibid.,* pp. 148, 387.   [27] *Ibid.,* p. 148.

[28] Cf. *ibid.,* p. 250.   [29] Cf. *ibid.,* pp. 96, 148, 221.

[30] "Quare quicquid producitur, ex potentia et actu . . . componitur" (*ibid.,* p. 387).

[31] "Prima et communis in rebus distinctio compositiove illa est quae per potentiam fit et actum" (*ibid.,* p. 349).

[32] Cf. *ibid.,* pp. 81, 349, 386 f.   [33] *Ibid.,* p. 217.   [34] *Ibid.,* p. 270.

cept of a thing as comprehended in its definition, 'existence'
(*esse*) . . . its presence in the nature of things." [35] *Essentia* is
therefore the *quid* of an object; *esse,* on the other hand, its *quod.*
This concrete definition, however, does not clearly explain the
formal relation between *esse* and *essentia,* and for that reason the
terms "act" and "potency" are used: *Esse* is the act of *essentia,*[36]
esse, and *essentia* are related to each other as are "act" and
"potency." [37] The *quod* is therefore not a part of the *quid,* and
essentia, being mere potency, is incapable of producing by itself
esse, which is its act.[38] Since, therefore, every entity that exists
is composed of *esse* and *essentia,* act and potency, that entity requires a primary, external agent (*agens*) that confers on it act
and *esse* and that has itself the character of pure act—in other
words, all Being is dependent on God and has the character of
creature.[39] In so far, then, as this composition is valid for incorporeal objects also, we can now understand why essence
(*essentia*) was considered an intelligible counterpart of matter.[40]

The Aristotelian categories must be understood, according to
their origin, as genera of Being. If we take into account the
difference between substance and attribute, the nine remaining
categories, apart from substance, may be conceived as genera of
attribute. We can therefore expect to find them in the general
division of Being which begins with the difference between substance and attribute. But at that point, as a matter of fact, only
two of Aristotle's nine categories figure as genera of the attribute:
quality and quantity.[41] This choice is certainly influenced by the
principle of twofold division, and Ficino refers elsewhere to the
other Aristotelian categories as well. Considering his system as
a whole, he actually uses only the categories of quality and
quantity as having great importance for him. Quantity is first
conceived as spatial extension which is joined to matter as its

[35] "Essentiam quidem dicimus rationem rei quae definitione comprehen-
ditur, esse vero . . . quandam eius in rerum natura praesentiam" (*ibid.,*
p. 140). Cf. Horbert, *Metaphysik,* p. 8; Kieszkowski, *Studi,* p. 73.

[36] *Op. om.,* pp. 140, 148. [37] *Ibid.,* p. 387. [38] *Ibid.*
[39] Cf. *ibid.,* pp. 282, 387. [40] Cf. *ibid.,* p. 144. [41] *Ibid.,* p. 370.

first specification and so constitutes the difference between body and matter.[42] Its most important connotation is divisibility.[43] Quantity in the sense of extension not being applicable to incorporeal objects, divisibility can be understood in a more general way and serves indeed as a sort of guiding principle for characterizing the different spheres of Being.[44] Even more important is the concept of quality which embraces all the other specifications of matter and is almost identical with the concept of *forma accidentalis.* Quality is not in this case merely an objective attribute, but is considered as cause of all physical activity and conceived therefore as a sort of active force.

If bodies seem to have some action, they act not through their bulk . . . but through some innate force and quality.[45]

Thus action is produced . . . through a gift of quality.[46]

No creature acts directly through its substance, but through an active force which is quality or attribute.[47]

The particular concept of an infinite quality which indicates the highest grade of intensity is apparently based on the concept of a form unlimited in its efficacy.

Every quality that is free from external addition is called "infinite" by the physicists. When warmth exists in itself, unhampered by cold and humidity, unburdened by weight of matter, it is called infinite warmth, because its force is free and not narrowed by the limits of any addition.[48]

This conception of quality leads to the relation between force and action which has a basic importance for ontology and fully explains the process of acting. Each action must be referred, according to its nature, to an acting object. Now, each object having the character of a concrete entity and each form of actuality being preceded by its own particular form of potentiality, the result is the triad of *essentia, virtus,* and *operatio*

---

[42] *Ibid.,* pp. 79 f., 374.   [43] *Ibid.,* p. 79.   [44] *Ibid.,* pp. 81, 120.
[45] *Ibid.,* p. 80. Cf. Horbert, *op. cit.,* pp. 13 f. Cassirer, *Erkenntnisproblem,* pp. 86 f.
[46] *Op. om.,* p. 81a.   [47] *Ibid.,* p. 149.   [48] *Ibid.,* p. 1354.

which circumscribes the entire process and is frequently found in Ficino as a fixed ontological scheme.[49] Among these three factors, to which occasionally are added *esse* and *objectum*,[50] there is a triple relationship. In the first place *virtus* has the character of a quality or attribute (see above) and is intrinsic to the substance or essence of the acting entity. Then, *operatio* can always be referred through *virtus* to the *essentia* of the acting entity and thence derives its objective basis. Finally, the relation between *virtus* and *operatio* is, as Ficino says, like the relation between potency and act.[51] There is, however, a difference between these two pairs of concepts, a difference all the more striking since both of them go back to the Aristotelian distinction of δύναμις and ἐνέργεια. For the relation between force and action is less universal than the relation between act and potency.[52] Potency, moreover, cannot pass to act by itself, at least according to the primary concept of potency, whereas force produces action through its own activity. We are right therefore in interpreting *potentia* as passive and *virtus* as an active potency, and save for a few exceptions this terminology is generally preserved.[53] This duplication of terms which can be connected with some of Aristotle's statements,[54] is based upon the medieval tradition, whereas the triad *essentia, virtus,* and *operatio* is due to the Neoplatonists, who conceived ἐνέργεια as a function of the same οὐσία.

The ontological interpretation of the process of thinking is based upon the relationship between substance and action. For the concept of *operatio* not only is conceived in a sense of outward activity but also comprises in itself two different forms, according to its relation with the acting substance: "There is a double action: the one flows out of the acting entity like heat; the other remains inside, like knowledge and will." [55] Therefore the internal activity of an object is also considered as action, and

[49] Cf. *Op. om.,* pp. 84 f., 238, *et passim.* See also Horbert, *op. cit.,* p. 16. The source is Proclus.
[50] Cf. *Op. om.,* pp. 148, 238.   [51] *Ibid.,* pp. 148 f.
[52] Cf. *ibid.,* pp. 148 f.   [53] Cf. *ibid.,* p. 221.
[54] *Metaphysics,* ix. 6. 1048 b 8 ff.   [55] *Op. om.,* p. 148.

thought is an *operatio* intrinsic to the substance of the thinking Being and commensurate with the action of the latter on itself. This difference between internal and external action, for which Aristotle prepared the way,[56] not only is illustrated by the examples of knowledge and heat but also serves the express purpose of making the concept *operatio* applicable to incorporeal entities and of indicating particularly the contrast between thought and physical action.[57] Since both represent merely different forms of action, they cannot stand unrelated one beside the other, but must be interpreted in a connected sense. On the one hand, external action, which occurs everywhere between bodies, is by nature imperfect and is based on an impotence of the bodies which are unable to act upon themselves.[58] Conversely, internal action includes that external action as its element and is divided into two different factors; in other words, the action first emanates from the substance and then returns to it by a higher force. The first element is called the "life" of the thinking substance; the second is called "thought," in the proper sense.

Therefore, essence is called "rest" by Plato, since if it is without life, it is torpid. Life is called "movement," because it passed into act. Mind is called "reflection," because without it life would flow out in external work. But mind halts the vital movement of essence in itself and reflects it into the essence through a consciousness of itself.[59]

In this way the element of life corresponds to the emanating action, and the element of thought, in the proper sense, stops that action and fixes it within the thinking substance. The factor that provokes this return of action and constitutes the real and true act of thought is the consciousness, or awareness, of oneself. Thought is then defined as "reflection" and thus metaphorically related to a movement returning to itself. It is even called "infinite reflection" in so far as it thinks that it thinks and so repeats over and over again the act of awareness and of return to oneself.[60] It follows, then, that life and thought have a fixed

---

[56] *Metaphysics*, ix. 8. 1050 a 30 ff.   [57] Cf. *Op. om.*, p. 199.
[58] *Ibid.*, p. 199.   [59] *Ibid.*   [60] *Ibid.*

relation to one another as *actus rectus* and *actus reflexus*.[61] If we refer both of them to the objective foundation of the substance, we have as the result the triad *essentia, vita, intelligentia,* which frequently occurs as a fixed scheme and is evidently of Neoplatonic origin.[62]

Another group of concepts connected with the totality of Being is the so-called "transcendentia," namely, *unum, verum,* and *bonum.* According to the scholastic theory they do not indicate a distinction within the compass of Being, but accompany Being everywhere as accessory elements. Ficino occasionally refers to this doctrine,[63] and on one occasion he uses it explicitly in his exposition of the divine attributes.[64] As to the ontological significance of the three concepts, we must notice that they occur frequently and at important points in the argumentation. We shall deal with the concrete attributes of *verum* and *bonum* in another place. About the *unum* we need merely state that it is intrinsic to all objects and constitutes the coherence between their attributes.[65] Ficino, however, did not uphold the theory of *transcendentia* in its traditional form, and so he sacrificed even the unitary and homogeneous order of Being. While the concept *verum* is maintained in its connection with Being, *unum* and *bonum* constitute a group in themselves and as an independent principle they are placed beside and above Being. In this way they fill the whole sphere of existence along with Being, but they also include matter that no longer has a true and proper Being, as we have seen.[66] Being is therefore no longer the highest principle and supreme genus, as at first it seemed to be. Above and beyond Being is the One and Good.[67] On the other hand, we must admit that Ficino does not really change the theory of Being in its inner meaning. He merely adds the concepts of One and Good in an almost external and secondary way, and this inconsistency has its historical reasons, of which he is clearly

[61] *Op. om.,* p. 195.   [62] Cf. *ibid.,* pp. 274 f., 282.
[63] *Ibid.,* p. 233.   [64] *Ibid.,* p. 92.
[65] Cf. *ibid.,* p. 115.   [66] Cf. *ibid.,* p. 270 *et passim.*
[67] *Ibid.,* pp. 193, 248, 282 *et passim.* Cf. Horbert, *op. cit.,* p. 8.

aware. In fact, in the theory of Being he refers repeatedly to the Peripatetics, in other words, to the medieval Aristotelians.[68] On the other hand, with regard to the separation of the One and Good from Being he cites the Neoplatonists, whose system is characterized by that very doctrine.[69] Ficino even gave much importance to this point in his Platonism, though the real motives of the doctrine are no longer effective in his philosophy. Whereas Pico, agreeing with Aristotle, reasserts in his tract *De ente et uno* the coincidence of Unity and Being, Ficino criticizes that view extensively in his commentary on Plato's *Parmenides* and tries to justify the distinction of the two attributes in the Neoplatonic sense.[70]

If we consider the realm of Being as a whole and ask ourselves whether there is anything to be found outside it, we are obliged to answer that there is nothing apart from Being, and by that we indicate merely a limit of Being. But if we ask further what this Nothing is, we are driven necessarily to amplify it with attributes of Being and so invalidate its own nullity. This process has already begun when we say that Nothing does not exist, in fact even when we say "Nothing," spelling it with a capital letter. "Nothing" has acquired a philosophic significance mainly because according to the Christian doctrine God created the world, not out of matter, but through His infinite power out of nothing. The particular difficulty of this concept or rather nonconcept, appears as early as St. Augustine, who expounds that theory.[71] Ficino accepts the creation out of nothing according to the ecclesiastical tradition [72] and frequently mentions Nothing, or Nonbeing. We can clearly observe in him the passage from pure nullity to a positive and determinate Being. Above all, Nonbeing is accessible to thought, since the mind "after the concept of Being . . . also conceives that which can be imagined as farthest removed from it, namely, Nonbeing." [73] Then "that which is

---

[68] *Op. om.,* pp. 270, 370.   [69] *Ibid.,* pp. 193, 248, 282, 677, *et passim.*
[70] *Ibid.,* pp. 1157–64, with the polemical reference at the end on p. 1164.
[71] Cf. *Confessiones,* XII, 7 ff.   [72] Cf. *Op. om.,* pp. 96, 400, *et passim.*
[73] *Ibid.,* p. 677; cf. p. 201.

called 'Nothing' seems to us to be deprived of all Being," [74] and when Nonbeing is called the opposite of Being,[75] it has already been placed in a definite relation to Being. Since matter, as we have seen, is next to Nothing and stands midway between Being and Nonbeing,[76] Nothing is assigned a fixed place beside Being in an ontological sense. This pseudo-spatial relationship is most accurately expressed in the statement that Nothing has an infinite distance from Being.[77] For by means of the concept "infinite" pure negation is transformed into an extreme limit, and distance indicates precisely a concrete ontological coexistence. When finally in the creation Nothing and Being assume the relationship of potency and act,[78] the concept of Nothing is already almost raised to the function of primary matter.

The sphere of Being, therefore, is not held within its initial delimitation, but is transcended by the concepts of principle of Being and of Unity or, on the other hand, by the concepts of matter and Nothing.[79] The limiting principles, however, have a fixed relationship to Being and constitute along with Being an enlarged sphere. This sphere includes all existence, and nothing that can be thought of can escape its laws.

[74] *Ibid.*, p. 282.
[75] *Ibid.*, pp. 145 f.
[76] *Ibid.*, p. 226.
[77] *Ibid.*, pp. 148, 201, 677.
[78] *Ibid.*, p. 148.
[79] Cf. *ibid.*, p. 217.

IV

BEING AND THOUGHT

ANY ATTEMPT to determine more precisely the concept of Being leads at once to the question of the relation between thought and Being. This question owes its importance to the fact that according to Parmenides and Plato real and true Being is accessible only to thought. But the particular form of the problem is determined by the approach of modern philosophy which, since the day of Descartes, has been starting with thought as the basis of all certainty and therefore has ever been reassigning itself the task of understanding Being from the standpoint of thought and in relation to thought. For Ficino, as indeed for medieval philosophy, this relation presents itself at the outset in altogether different terms. To him Being appears as a concrete entity and admits the existence of nothing outside its own sphere. It is furthermore antecedent to all finite thought and allows the latter to entertain no doubt as to its reality.[1] By nature, therefore, Being is Being in itself, and not even a negative relation of Being to thought is directly implied by that language. Being is simply indifferent to thought. The relation between thought and Being can therefore be interpreted only in an ontological sense; in other words, there arises the problem of explaining the phenomenon of thought on the basis of and within the scope of Being considered as an aggregate of concrete entities. Here it might be well to consider first the thinking subject in itself, then the relation of thought to concrete objects, and finally the relation of concrete objects existing in themselves to a possible thought.

For Ficino the process of thought is not a logical or psycho-

[1] Dress, *Die Mystik des Marsilio Ficino*, p. 85.

logical act performed by a consciousness without substance; it is the internal action of a thinking entity, conceived by its nature as an incorporeal substance—in other words, mind or intellect. "The action of intellect is thought," [2] and "the substance of the mind is the cause of its action." [3] The thinking subject, with all its action, is therefore included in the universal sphere of Being, has its definite place therein, and is subject, like everything else, to the laws and attributes of the universe.[4] The original reciprocal relationship between thought and Being appears only in so far as intellectual substance is considered superior to corporeal substance and in so far as, conversely, all incorporeal Being is primarily conceived as intellectual or intelligible.[5]

Since the thinking subject belongs to the sphere of Being as objective reality, the relation of thought to its objects must therefore be understood in an objective sense. When the object of thought is termed "objectum," this does not indicate the particular character of thought as "meaning something." But an *objectum* is merely the objective counterpart of an action, and when a certain *objectum* corresponds to thought as to a certain kind of action, that simply means that an objective entity from without encounters the thinking substance and offers an opportunity for the act of thinking.[6] But for this encounter to be possible, thought, like any other action, must have an original affinity with its object. For "we must not believe . . . that an action can deal with any object unless similar, convenient, and congruent." [7] This principle of affinity, which we shall repeatedly discuss again, furnishes one of the most frequent arguments for the immortality of the Soul.[8] It indicates a formal and general agreement of thought with its objects, an agreement that of

---

[2] "Cum eius operatio intelligentia sit" (*Op. om.*, p. 198).

[3] *Ibid.*, p. 200.

[4] Heitzman, "L'agostinismo avicennizzante," *Giorn. crit.*, XVI (1935), 303: "La conoscenza è soltanto un caso particolare della reciproca influenza degli oggetti."

[5] Cf. *Op. om.*, p. 221.   [6] Cf. *ibid.*, pp. 218, 238.   [7] *Ibid.*, p. 238.

[8] Cf. *ibid.*, pp. 238, 703, and see below, chap. xv.

necessity must precede all acts of knowledge. On the other hand, the concrete and particular agreement of thought with its object is produced in each case by the act of thought itself and constitutes, according to the Thomist doctrine, the truth of a particular conception. "Knowledge is achieved by a correspondence (*adaequatio*) of the mind with things," [9] and "the truth of the mind is its correspondence to things." [10] The precise meaning of this correspondence is shown by the way in which the act of knowing is interpreted. Just as each action is determined by a form inherent in it,[11] so thought, being an internal action, is accompanied by a form that is inherent in the thinking substance and corresponds to the known object. "Since in knowing the mind performs an act, and acts only in so far as it is in act, and acts in the same way as it is in act, and is in act only as the result of a form, it never contemplates essences unless it be embellished with their forms." [12] In the act of thinking the mind is therefore united with the object through its inherent form, and in so far as the object as being in itself precedes the act of knowing, it follows that through this act the mind is formed by the object.

As long as the intellect is only potentially prepared to know, it is not yet united with the object potentially to be known; but when it is actually knowing, it is united with the object actually known. But it is united with it . . . since the form of that object is inherent in the mind. . . . Thus the knowing mind and the thing known become one, since the form of that thing, as such, molds the mind.[13]

The mind, nevertheless, is not entirely passive during this molding and does not allow the forms to enter from outside in the sense of the traditional image theory. On the contrary, the forms of all things are contained in the mind from the start, and on meeting the objects these forms merely pass from the potential state to the actual.

[9] *Ibid.*, p. 201; cf. Cassirer, *Das Erkenntnisproblem*, p. 90.
[10] "Veritas mentis est eius ad res adaequatio" (*Op. om.*, p. 1221)
[11] Cf. *ibid.*, p. 105.   [12] *Ibid.*, p. 191.   [13] *Ibid.*, p. 230

Therefore, neither the mind nor even the senses . . . are formed by external bodies in order to perceive something. But just as the vegetative part [of the Soul] changes, generates, nourishes, and increases through inherent seeds, so the inner sense and the mind judge all things through innate formulae that are stimulated by external objects. And this judgment is nothing but a passage of the formula from potency to act.[14]

The correspondence of the mind to an object consists in the fact that the mind brings from potentiality to actuality that particular one of its innate forms which corresponds to that particular object. So by the act of knowing the mind reproduces in itself the form of the object. In Chapter XII of this work we examine several details of Ficino's epistemology not directly related to the ontological problems.

If from a modern point of view we are inclined to consider truth solely as an attribute of propositions, we readily tend to refer to the intellect alone the scholastic definition which reduces truth to the relationship between mind and objects. Ficino considers this relation in its bilateral aspect, and therefore truth is not merely peculiar to thought but likewise and primarily to things.[15] "Truth is the correspondence of the thing and the mind," says Ficino in his commentary on Plato's *Philebus,* "and the truth of the mind is its correspondence to the objects, the truth of the things is their correspondence to the mind." [16] There is consequently a truth that belongs to the objects themselves and must be understood as the relation of the objects to thought. We must ask in what sense this truth is related to thought and what it means in itself.

Since the objects exist in themselves and outside thought, the attribute of truth also seems at first to belong to them in them-

[14] *Ibid.,* pp. 241 f.

[15] Saitta tries to prove the "immanence of truth" in Ficino and merely isolates a certain aspect of a more complicated concept (*La filosofia di Marsilio Ficino,* pp. 209 ff.).

[16] "Veritas est adaequatio rei ac mentis . . . et veritas mentis est eius ad res adaequatio, veritas rerum est rerum adaequatio menti" (*Op. om.,* p. 1221).

selves and without thought. But in so far as the mind contains the criterion of all truth,[17] and as the whole of truth is the object of its thinking,[18] the very fact that the objects are true implies a relation to thought. "The object of the intellect is Being itself under the concept of truth." [19] The attribute of truth is not placed or produced in the objects by intellect alone, but precedes all finite thought and even makes the truth of that finite thought possible. "We truly know the things, because we know them as they truly are." [20] The truth of things is therefore neither dependent on nor entirely separated from thought, but consists in an original relation of the objects to a possible thought.

What the truth of the things means concretely is indicated in the following definition: "Truth is the pure integrity and entire purity of each nature." [21] A given object therefore possesses truth in so far as it really is what it is.[22] This aspect of truth is not present in all things in the same way, but is subject to certain differentiations in the sphere of Being. The painting of a horse is merely the image of a real or natural horse, and the truth which belongs after all to the painted horse is derived from the truth of the original.[23] The same relationship subsists, according to Plato, between corporeal substances and their originals, in other words, the Ideas. "The truth of natural things consists in the fact that they are congruent with the reasons of the divine mind." [24] Apart from these differences connected with the structure of Being, the attribute of truth is peculiar to all things without exception. For one can say of each object that it is truly that definite object. Truth, therefore, is deservedly placed among

---

[17] *Ibid.,* p. 261.   [18] *Ibid.,* p. 307.

[19] "Obiectum intellectus est ens ipsum sub ratione veri" (*ibid.,* p. 236).

[20] "Ideo res intelligimus vere, quoniam ita ut revera sunt intelligimus" (*ibid.,* p. 398; cf. p. 261).

[21] "Veritas est naturae cuiusque pura integritas et integra puritas" (*ibid.,* p. 261).

[22] Cf. *ibid.,* pp. 90, 258.   [23] *Ibid.,* p. 260.

[24] ". . . veritas rerum naturalium in eo consistat ut divinae mentis congruant rationibus" (*ibid.,* p. 261). See also Dress, *op. cit.,* p. 62; Horbert, *op. cit.,* p. 23.

the *transcendentia,* in other words it is connected with the basic character of Being, fills the whole sphere of Being, and originates in God, fount of all truth as of all Being.[25] In so far, therefore, as mind has all truth for its object [26] and as the character of truth is intrinsic to all existing things can the whole fullness of Being become an object of human thought.[27] And, conversely, everything the mind knows as true is necessarily included among the existing things. In other words, as thought belongs through its substance to the sphere of objective Being and has an objective relationship to its objects, so it is also limited to the same sphere in the choice of its objects. The relation therefore of thought to Being is interpreted in all its aspects on the basis of an objective reality.

This ontological conception is made questionable by three phenomena with which thought seems to transcend the realm of objective Being: error, possibility, and infinity. Let us now see how Ficino deals with these phenomena. While the problem of infinity is solved in a developed doctrine, the two other questions are treated only in an outline, in which we can recognize the direction of the theory.

The fact that the human mind is capable of error is sometimes used by Ficino to justify the distinction between the known truth and the knowing mind.[28] But every time he comes, in the course of the discussion, to the fact that the mind transcends the sphere of truth at its own risk, he does not speak of an error in the proper sense (and that is characteristic), but of a fiction of thought. In discussing the Epicureans, for example, he says: "That mixture which is made by the mind will be true only if such a unity exists in the things themselves. For whatever the mind produces outside the nature of things is fiction rather than knowledge." [29] In the same way he distinguishes between things that really exist in nature and things merely conceived by human thought.[30] The mind either is directed toward objects that belong to the sphere

[25] Cf. *Op. om.,* pp. 92, 236, 307.   [26] *Ibid.,* pp. 236, 307.   [27] *Ibid.,* p. 238.
[28] *Ibid.,* p. 90.   [29] *Ibid.,* p. 191.   [30] *Ibid.,* p. 190.

of objective Being, and so thinks something true, or thinks without reference to a proper object and by its own imaginative potency conceives something that does not exist in nature and therefore is not true. Error, like truth, for that matter, is properly explained, not by an attitude of the mind, but by a quality of its so-called illegitimate object. If these fictitious objects did not belong to the realm of objective Being, they would contribute very little to the understanding of the universe just because of their nullity. But in reality they are part of the world, since they are intrinsic to the mind and the mind is a member of the objective order of Being. The mind "conceives many things that might perhaps exist, but that will never be, and it invents many things that can perhaps never exist. The things that the mind through itself paints in itself, however, seem to exist in the nature of things no less than those it paints in the air by the tongue or on the wall by the hand." [31] This statement might seem of slight importance but for the fact that it shows clearly with what insistence Ficino upholds the self-contained character of the real Being.

The concept of the possible, which may be defined formally as the median between the necessary and the impossible,[32] means, according to its content, that something contains in itself all the conditions of Being without, however, having a real existence. In this sense the possible is an important ontological attribute, which we shall discuss in another chapter.[33] The possible, by its own nature, involves a potential reality; but it also has a particular relation to thought. For it is peculiar to the mind to conceive possibilities,[34] and anything, therefore, that contains a contradiction is excluded from the realm of the possible.[35] But

---

[31] "Multa enim excogitat (sc. mens) quae forte esse possent, non tamen fient unquam, et multa quae esse forsitan nunquam possunt, ipsa fingit. Quanquam non minus in rerum natura esse videntur quae mens per se pingit in se ipsa quam quae per linguam in aere vel per manum pingit in pariete" (*ibid.*, p. 200). See also Saitta, *op. cit.*, p. 198.

[32] *Ibid.*, p. 146.   [33] Cf. *ibid.*, p. 709; and see below, chap. v.
[34] *Ibid.*, p. 200.   [35] *Ibid.*, p. 110.

since many things that do not exist in reality are possible, the sphere of the possible is wider than the sphere of the real. Hence the mind seems to transcend the realm of the real Being when beside the real it also conceives the possible. However, the possible also has its definite place, that is, not in the mind itself as is the case with fiction, but in God. God as principle of Being also contains all the possible and when the mind penetrates beyond the real to the possible, it is simply attaining something which, as possible, is already real in God.

In this potency of Being is included everything that does not contradict the concept of Being. . . . For nothing can be conceived that might contradict the concept of Being except its opposite, namely, what is called Nonbeing. Contradiction alone includes the concept of Nonbeing. All things therefore that do not include a contradiction . . . are included in the concept of Being, and God can produce them all. This is proved by the fact that if we exclude contradiction the mind can extend itself through the whole immense vastness of Being. But the producing power of God cannot be smaller than the conceiving power of the mind. . . . Why should that be? So that you may understand that anything that does not include a contradiction is subject to the divine power, and since there are many things that do not exist in the nature of things, which if they did exist would not include a contradiction . . . you may know that many things are contained under the divine power which, however, are never found in the order of things.[36]

The problem of infinity is solved in almost the same way, but because of its frequent occurrence it deserves more extensive consideration. The whole of real Being constitutes, as we have seen, a closed sphere in which each substance with all its parts and attributes occupies a definite place (see above, Chapter III). This structure excludes the concept of infinity in all its aspects from the realm of Being. The world is finite in size and power. It is not extended through infinite space.[37] It has an unlimited smallness, but a limited largeness.[38] By unlimited smallness is implied that each corporeal particle can be divided again, but the

[36] *Ibid.,* p. 110.   [37] *Ibid.,* p. 399.   [38] *Ibid.,* p. 98; cf. p. 660.

individual particles exist only potentially as long as the division is not yet achieved. It is considered altogether impossible for an infinite number of particles actually to exist in nature.[39] What has been said of power, size, and divisibility is valid also for all other aspects, and therefore in nature there can be no infinity of genera, of specific differences, of forms, or of acts of knowledge.[40] In all these statements there appears the common principle of finiteness that goes back to the basic conception of the real Being and is used in the argumentation without further justification.

The argument of the *progressus in infinitum,* which is frequently applied by Aristotle and is often used by Ficino, is based on the principle of the finite. It generally serves to reduce a premise *ad absurdum* by showing that that hypothesis is connected with an endless chain of conditions.[41] The postulate is obviously that such an infinite series of conditions cannot exist in reality, and therefore the *progressus* is by nature a negative argument. But it also contains a positive aspect; for, an infinite series being impossible in nature, it must at least be achieved within the arguing thought itself. "Who proceeds infinitely? . . . The mind certainly does." [42] "What prevents the mind, which in a certain sense has infinite power, from wandering around endlessly, provided that it never accomplishes this infinite course?" [43] Therefore the *progressus* shows an infinite potency of the mind and at the same time reveals a contrast between infinite thought and finite reality.

This infinity of thought appears not only in the argument of the *progressus;* it is characteristic of the essence of the mind as a whole, which by nature is capable of transcending all finiteness. "The human Soul transcends each finite thing, because whatever finite truth or goodness you might offer to it, the intellect can think more, and the will can strive further." [44] "Moreover, [the mind] divides the bodies into many parts and particles of

---

[39] *Ibid.,* pp. 168, 190.   [40] *Ibid.,* pp. 189, 190.
[41] Cf. *ibid.,* pp. 85, 163 f., 355.
[42] "Quis infinite progreditur? . . . Mens certe haec facit" (*ibid.,* p. 201).
[43] *Ibid.,* p. 355.   [44] *Ibid.,* p. 237.

parts, increases numbers over numbers without end. It invents innumerable kinds of figures and their reciprocal proportions, as well as the relations of numbers, and it draws a line above the heaven beyond any limit in all directions. It extends time into the past without beginning and into the future without end. Not only does it conceive beyond all time an earlier and later time, it also conceives beyond all space a larger space and innumerable degrees in each quality. Moreover, the mind is not content with one genus of things, as is the sense: not with colors, as is the sight; not with sounds, as is the hearing; but it runs through all things. I say through not only all things that are but also that were and will be. Not only that, but also through those things that neither are nor were nor ever will be." [45] So beyond any finite entity it finds an ever higher one, but it never reaches a limit inside the realm of the finite. In this way thought can proceed through all aspects to the infinite and can by its own power transcend the limits set for finite Being.

The contrast that seems to exist here between thought and Being is overcome, as in the problem of the possible, by the concept of God. As the cause of all Being, God has a certain connection with the other objects (see above, Chapter III). At the same time He is absolutely superior to and essentially distinct from the world as totality of all Being. Therefore God is in all

[45] "Quinetiam (sc. mens) corpora dividit in partes plurimas partiumque particulas, numeros auget supra numeros absque fine. Figurarum modos mutuasque illarum proportiones atque etiam numerorum comparationes innumerabiles invenit, lineam supra coelum ultra terminum undique protendit. Tempus in praeteritum absque principio, in futurum absque fine producit. Neque solum ultra omne tempus aliud antiquius cogitat et prolixius, verum etiam ultra omnem locum alium semper cogitat ampliorem. Innumeros quoque effingit gradus in singulis qualitatibus. Accedit quod non uno quodam rerum genere mens sicuti sensus contenta est. Non solis coloribus ut visus, non solis vocibus ut auditus, sed currit per omnia, per omnia inquam, non modo quae sunt, sed quae fuerunt eruntve. Neque id solum, sed per illa etiam quae neque sunt neque fuerunt unquam aut erunt" (*Op. om.*, pp. 200 f. Cf. Thomas, *Summa contra Gentiles*, III, 50; Cassirer, *Das Erkenntnisproblem*, pp. 90 f.; Saitta, *op. cit.*, pp. 197 ff.; Cassirer, *Individuum und Kosmos*, pp. 74 f.).

things and at the same time outside all things.[46] Though the
world is finite in all respects, God is infinite in size and potency,
in duration and perfection.[47] God is infinite "because He is
neither narrowed by any limits of a subject, nor infected with
the mixture of a quality, nor overcome by the excellence of a
higher cause, nor exceeded by intervals of time or space, nor
limited by enumerated degrees of force [*virtutis*], however many
they may be."[48] Even the distance that separates Him from the
highest among the other entities is infinite.[49] God is therefore
infinity itself; He complements the finite existence of the world.
When the human mind proceeds to the infinite by its own
power, it does not fall into the void, but ascends from the finite
object to the infinite one, from the world to God.

[God] cannot lack any degree of force that may be conceived by the
mind. Otherwise the mind, being a product of God, could reach beyond God, because the mind can imagine beyond any finite number of
degrees a still greater degree. Indeed, the mind would be disposed in
vain to an infinite progression if there were not found an infinite limit.[50]

In another passage Ficino refers to God as infinite goodness:

Our mind would exceed the nature of the highest cause by its thought
and striving, by which it proceeds without end through the degrees of
good, if there could be conceived any good which were not in that
cause and if it [that cause] were not immense.[51]

[46] Cf. *Op. om.*, pp. 97, 403.   [47] *Ibid.*, p. 399.
[48] "Quia neque subiecti alicuius limitibus ullis cohibeatur neque per-
mixtione qualitatis inficiatur neque causae superioris excellentia superetur
neque vel temporum intervallis vel locorum spatiis excedatur neque nume-
ratis virtutis gradibus quamvis quam plurimis terminetur" (*ibid.*, p. 685).
[49] *Ibid.*, p. 236.
[50] "Neque potest deesse illi [sc. Deo] virtutis gradus ullus qui mente
queat effingi. Alioquin mens quae Dei effectus est ultra Deum sese posset
extendere, quae quolibet finito graduum numero valet semper ampliorem
aliquem cogitare. Imo etiam frustra ad infinitam progressionem esset mens
ordinata, nisi inveniretur terminus aliquis infinitus" (*ibid.*, p. 96); cf.
Thomas, *op. cit.*, I, 43.
[51] "Atque excederet [op: excedere] mens nostra cogitatione et [om. op.]
affectu quibus per boni gradus absque fine progreditur principii summi
naturam, siquid boni cogitari posset quod in eo non esset ac nisi illud esset
immensum" (*Op. om.*, p. 709).

In like manner the infinite essence of God is often interpreted as
the goal and limit of the infinite movement of thought.[52] When,
therefore, the mind proceeds beyond any limit, it is directed
toward the infinite divinity—an object toward which it tends in
continual movement, but never quite reaches.[53] So thought is
always bound to the sphere of Being, and in the paradoxical
phrase "terminus infinitus" is seen the particular antinomy of
thought which transcends any finite limit, but at the same time
never reaches the infinite limit, that is, God. Thus thought,
while striving to escape the finite existence of the world, finds
its consummation in the higher, infinite existence of God.

[52] *Ibid.*, pp. 201, 411, 685; cf. Saitta, *op. cit.*, pp. 200 f.
[53] Cf. *Op. om.*, pp. 684 f., 201.

V

PERFECTION OF THE WORLD

PHILOSOPHICAL THOUGHT is first directed toward corporeal objects, but because of their mutability and changing aspects it is sooner or later forced to transcend them and to inquire into the cause of their existence. Whereas the preponderance of natural science and epistemology in the modern age has changed the original meaning of the problem, ancient philosophy has almost always tended to conceive the actual world of phenomena in terms of metaphysical causes. This conception found, perhaps, its perfect expression in Plotinus, who describes the universe as rising steadily from its higher causes, without beginning and without end. According to the doctrine of the Christian Middle Ages, which Ficino follows for the most part, the corporeal world is, on the other hand, like all existing things, created by God out of nothing.[1] The world has, therefore, in contrast to the Neoplatonic conception, not only a certain beginning but also really only one metaphysical principle—in other words, God, who uses all other principles as His instruments and so produces everything in all things.[2] The individual things outside of God are not merely existent or present, they have from the beginning the attribute of created beings—in other words, they refer directly and with all the fullness of their being to God as their creator.

If God be conceived as the one source of all beings, the further question arises, How does He manage to create and produce other things outside His own being? The answer is: by His own will God is determined to create things; His action is necessary

[1] Cf. *Op. om.*, pp. 397 ff. [2] *Ibid.*, pp. 100 ff.

only in respect to His own essence, but it is free in respect to His creations.[3] God is therefore not limited in His essence by His relation to things, but by His will He becomes all the more responsible for the quality of the creations.

A definite conception and evaluation of all Being is formulated on this basis. Because of the misfortune or injustice he suffers, the individual is easily tempted to call the world order itself before the tribunal of his own needs and desires. Prompted by a similar feeling the Gnostics considered the world itself evil and spoke of an evil principle of the universe. When one makes an effort to understand the world from an unbiased point of view and with the help of physical and metaphysical principles, events are withdrawn from the judgment of personal emotion and assume the character of an objective necessity to which the individual, conscious of his own impotence and unimportance, is obliged to resign himself. But if the world is created by God, that implies its unconditional justification; therefore it must be considered neither evil nor necessary, but the perfect creation of a perfect creator. Therefore, through the theory of creation the concepts of the good and the perfect receive a basic, ontological importance and are peculiar both to God and to the world with respect to their reciprocal relationship. Since things are created by God, He is the author of all good in the world and is therefore the totality of all perfection. And God having determined by His own will to create the things, all things are in a certain sense good and perfect.[4] We must now analyze in more detail those elements and the doctrines connected with them.

Ficino frequently refers to God as "the good itself" or "the infinite goodness." By that he does not mean so much that God has a certain moral attitude, as that He represents an unlimited perfection which includes all particular good. "The highest goodness includes whatever good can be found anywhere." [5] And the

[3] *Ibid.*, pp. 108 ff., especially p. 110; cf. Horbert, *op. cit.*, p. 47.
[4] On the divine will and the perfection of the created world cf. Dress, *op. cit.*, pp. 90 ff.
[5] *Op. om.*, p. 94.

all-embracing good would not be itself "did it not include every-thing whose existence is considered to be better." [6] This axiom not only contains a general statement about God's essence, but also serves as a premise for a series of other attributes. Liberty, for example, is shown to be an attribute of God by the following argument: "Liberty is desirable as a good. Moreover, anything that can be desired as a good is included in the all-embracing good." [7] Here "the good" is the median term that serves to connect God and liberty. The same procedure is apparent in many other ar-guments.

Since we see that all things have some function, especially at the time when they are fully evolved within a species and perfect, we must as-sert that God, the most perfect of all things, cannot be inactive, but must have some function, since action is a sign of perfection. [8]

Creation is a more excellent act than illumination. Consequently, crea-tion is more fitting to God than illumination. [9]

This free action certainly is more fitting to a more perfect animal. Of such a kind, therefore, must be especially the action of God. [10]

So each quality and each attitude that appears in some sense per-fect is in that sense fitting to God and is really attributed to God with that justification. Ficino clearly admits the basic importance of that procedure when he reports an argument of Plotinus about the internal attitude of God and then tries to make some reser-vation of his own with respect to it: "But God Himself may look after that. We always want to assert only what is worthy of God." [11] The attributes here in point, therefore, are not directly known in God, but are ascribed to him as corollaries of the postulate of His perfection. They are taken in their content from the sphere of the other things and can be applied to God just as we can know the original from the copy, in other words,

---

[6] "Nisi esset in eo quicquid melius iudicatur ut sit" (*ibid.*, p. 709).
[7] *Ibid.*, p. 109.   [8] *Ibid.*, p. 218.
[9] *Ibid.*, p. 403.   [10] *Ibid.*, p. 398.
[11] "Sed haec Deus ipse viderit. A nobis vero id tantum ubique affirmari optamus quod Deo sit dignum" (*ibid.*, p. 110).

by discarding what is bad and by adding what is better.[12] The principle of perfection makes it possible for us to define the concept of God concretely by a series of postulates, so explaining an important factor, though by no means the only one, in Ficino's theology.

The perfection of the world corresponds to the perfection of God.[13] Since the world is made up of objective substances, its goodness and perfection will first appear in the individual things. The perfection of a thing is not merely an abstract value added from without to its other attributes, it is the completion and realization of its particular essence. This meaning is indicated in the origin of the Latin word *perfectum,* which means simply "worked out," "perfected." In Ficino the original meaning of the term is still recognizable. "All things have some function, especially when they are fully evolved within their species and perfect," says Ficino in a passage quoted above.[14] Thus, to give an obvious example, an organism is perfect in so far as it is fullgrown and so brings its own species and substance to full realization. In the same sense it can be said that each thing is impelled to action by the impulse it has to propagate its own perfection [15] and that the higher entities are the very ones to gain widest distribution through the abundance of their perfection.[16] It is not mere value that induces things to action and so gains distribution, but it is the fullness of their particular Being. The perfection of things is therefore directly connected with their Being; genesis and perfection appear merely as different degrees of a single process. Consequently things must receive their Being and their perfection, in other words, the intensified form of their Being, from the same source. "It is the task of the same thing to perfect and to produce," [17] and God in particular produces and perfects all things.[18] Under the in-

---

[12] Cf. *ibid.,* p. 971.   [13] *Ibid.,* p. 689.   [14] *Ibid.,* p. 218.
[15] *Ibid.,* p. 137.   [16] *Ibid.,* p. 378.
[17] "Perficere illius est cuius est et facere" (*ibid.,* p. 1240).
[18] *Ibid.,* p. 270; cf. pp. 101, 236.

fluence of Neoplatonic doctrines Ficino also distinguishes genesis and perfection as particular acts, since each thing first proceeds from its cause and then returns to it as to its goal.[19] Consequently the perfection of a thing is not given at once along with its mere existence, but in so far as each thing tends toward the fullness of being as its natural goal, it is destined from the outset for perfection and must at some time actually reach it.[20]

Like perfection, the goodness of things must be conceived in an ontological sense. "Each thing finds itself in good condition at the time when it is united with itself and its cause and remains pure and is not mixed with lower things."[21] Goodness, therefore, is not an external value, but is contained in the unity and purity of the respective substance. However, in the relation between Being and goodness a contrast appears that was already implicit in the concept of perfection. For the universal diffusion of good in the world is essentially based on the fact that all things strive toward the good.[22] But since fulfillment comes only after desire, goodness does not accompany the existence of things, but is only prepared for. On the other hand, a share of the good already exists in the mere desire,[23] and so the good is correctly placed among the three *transcendentia,* traces of which are found in all things.[24] From the point of view of desire, the good is therefore from the outset connected with the existence of all things and confirms their origin from God, infinite good.[25]

If, therefore, everything that exists has the character of good, there then arises the question of the possibility and the origin of evil in the world. This question, which never occurs in the *Theologia Platonica,* is treated explicitly in Ficino's commentary on Dionysius the Areopagite.[26] His conclusion, agreeing with the text commented upon, is as follows: evil as such does not occur

[19] *Ibid.,* p. 270.   [20] Cf. *ibid.,* pp. 1589 f.   [21] *Ibid.,* p. 92.
[22] *Ibid.,* p. 91.   [23] Cf. *ibid.*   [24] *Ibid.,* p. 92.
[25] *Ibid.,* pp. 91 f.   [26] *Ibid.,* pp. 1071 ff.

anywhere in the realm of existing things; it is neither a substance nor part or quality of a substance. The evil that actually does occur is nothing but the limitation of a determinate good and the insufficient participation of a substance in that good—for example, blindness.[27] Evil, therefore, has no proper place in the world, and everything that exists, either substance or attribute, is in itself originally good.

Evil in the sphere of human life still remains to be explained, and for this purpose we are obliged to start from the relation between the will and its objects. As the human intellect is directed by nature toward truth, so the will is directed by nature toward good;[28] there are also many other analogies in the details. Good, too, is not produced in things merely by the finite will, but is found by itself as pre-existing before becoming the object of its desire: "We want things because they are good. But they are good because God wants them."[29] Conversely, it is not by chance that things become objects of the human will, but as the result of their own essential quality of goodness. "The object of the will is Being itself under the concept of good,"[30] and "the good concerns the will."[31] In other words, everything that exists is referred, through its attribute of good, to a possible will as an object, and conversely, the will may choose for the goal of its desire everything that exists in so far as it is good. Hence will, like intellect, is an original relation of man to Being. Most of the ontological arguments that we have met in reference to thought are therefore repeated in respect to the will and need no further analysis (see above, Chapter II).

Inquiring now into evil in the realm of human existence, we find it first in two different forms: as external evil and as a faulty attitude of man himself. External evils are not bad in themselves,

[27] Ibid., pp. 1076 ff. [28] Ibid., p. 307.
[29] "Nos siquidem res quia bonae sunt volumus. Haec vero ideo bonae sunt quia vult eas Deus" (ibid., p. 398).
[30] "Voluntatis obiectum ens ipsum sub ratione boni" (ibid., p. 236).
[31] "Bonum vero respicit voluntatem" (ibid., p. 249).

since through divine Providence everything turns out well for the good and bad for the bad.[32] Therefore evil consists for man only in his own attitude. Nevertheless, even at this point Ficino, unlike St. Augustine, avoids speaking of an evil will. On the contrary, as we have seen, will is always directed toward a good, and the right attitude and the wrong attitude differ only in the fact that the will is either directed toward God, the infinite good and the proper object of its desire, or descends to the finite, particular goods that receive their goodness from God and can therefore never satisfy the infinite desire of the mind.

Finally, men should be ashamed, I say they should be ashamed, because when they like mortal goods for no other reason than because they are good, in liking them they neglect the eternal good itself from which these things have their quality of being good. All things are in themselves good, because they are from it [the eternal good]. They are also good for us in so far as they are related to it. But they rightly become evil and hard for us because we abandon it most wrongly and follow those things that are necessarily in it and are preserved by it.[33]

A similar passage is found in the theological prayer to God: "I know that in Thee alone are, or rather Thou alone art, whatever we desire. If this or that good please us, it does so, not because it is this or that, but because it is good. In reality we desire the quality of goodness in individual things." [34] In such sentences we recognize, besides the prevailing moral issue, the basic concept that all things are good as creations of God and that the human will, even when it fails, never entirely deserts the sphere of the good.

The perfection of the world consists not only in the good of

---

[32] Cf. ibid., pp. 729, 731.

[33] "Pudeat autem quandoque mortales, pudeat inquam, dum non alia ratione nisi quia bona sunt bona (sunt bona om. op.) mortalia diligunt, in iis diligendis aeternum ipsum bonum negligere unde haec id prorsus habent ut sint bona. Bona quidem in se ipsis omnia sunt, quoniam sunt ab ipso. Bona rursus et nobis quatenus referuntur ad ipsum. At mala et aspera non iniuria nobis evadunt, quia summa quadam iniuria haec sectamur illo dimisso, quae necessario in illo sunt et servantur ab illo" (ibid., p. 730).

[34] Ibid., pp. 665 f.

objective substances but also in a universal order of nature which is based upon the divine will and which brings individual things, according to their quality, into a definite reciprocal relationship. "We must remember that God's will prefers the good of the whole to the apparent advantage of some part. For in that good appears a more explicit image of the divine goodness and that good seems to consist in some order." [35] This order manifests itself in a number of general and recognizable rules. Conversely, certain possibilities are basically excluded by these rules. Ficino may therefore maintain without further justification that "so it is always in the order of nature" [36] or that "something seems to be contrary to the order of nature." [37] The perfection of this order is taken for granted from the outset, surpasses all the requirements of human thought, and must be considered as existent even in cases where it is not accessible to observation and direct experience.

It is obvious that God creates by degrees things more-or-less similar [to Himself], in order that no rational order in degrees may be conceived by us that has not previously been conceived and fulfilled by the highest reason.[38]

In the case of the lower and less perfect things, such as elements, minerals, plants, and animals, nature has already provided for the existence of that which is better so far as concerns their organs and the rest [of their condition]; by the same token, it stands to reason that in the better things and in the highest thing of nature, whatever is shown to be better is also truer.[39]

In this way Ficino even reaches the point of making statements of fact, independently of any experience, because the order of nature requires it.[40]

By this means it is possible to determine by postulates not only God but also the world and all things therein, a procedure frequently adopted by Ficino, though the concept of the order of nature is not always explicitly shown.

[35] *Ibid.,* p. 111.   [36] *Ibid.,* p. 250.   [37] *Ibid.,* p. 332.
[38] *Ibid.,* p. 689.   [39] *Ibid.,* p. 709.   [40] Cf. *ibid.,* pp. 111, 332.

Each work which consists of several parts is most perfect when it is connected closely in its parts in such a way as to become one in all respects: to agree and to be congruent with itself and not easily disrupted. Corporeal nature proves this in the mixture of the four elements. . . . A unification of the parts is to be assumed even more in the universal work of God in order that the work of one God may be one.[41]

There can be and there must be many fullest [beings], that in the most perfect work of God the most perfect parts may be numerous.[42]

If nature must prepare the animals for their particular actions better than for common actions, and if an active thing is better prepared than a passive thing, and if nature gave animals an active power for the common acts, it certainly prepared them for their particular acts, namely, sense perception and thought, in such a way that through them they may be active rather than passive.[43]

The coherence of the world in its parts, the plurality of the angels, and the activity of animals in thought and in sense perception are postulated in equal measure as absolutely necessary. When Ficino speaks of the reward and punishment of men after death, he gives the same justification: "The good must help, and the evil must harm." [44]

A similar form of postulate, which occurs repeatedly, is the argument in which some fact is called "meet" and is therefore admitted to be real.

It is meet (deceat) that not only human minds but also all other minds that are somehow impure must be connected with purer bodies.[45]

It is meet (decet) that in all excellent bodies of the world some perpetual spirits are present as their forms.[46]

It is meet that that intellectual form, to which the whole attempt of nature tends as to a goal, be perfect and absolute to such an extent that it may be far from death. But it is not necessary that the intermediate forms also be immortal.[47]

[41] Ibid., p. 119.   [42] Ibid., p. 689.   [43] Ibid., p. 241.
[44] Ibid., p. 325.   [45] Ibid., p. 223.   [46] Ibid., p. 224.
[47] Ibid., pp. 226 f. Corsano (Il pensiero religioso italiano, pp. 23 f.) misunderstands this principle when he speaks, with reference to this point, of Ficino's "aestheticism."

Certain occasional statements show that this reasoning also has a basic significance.

God does not exist and act by chance (*ut contingit*), otherwise there would be no order anywhere at any time, but as it is convenient or, better, as it is meet (*decet*). It is meet because it is decorous. Decorum itself is God Himself, from whom and through whom all decorous things come to being.[48]

What is proved to be better in the universe is judged to be better for no other reason than that it is congruent to the true reason, that it contributes most to the order of things, and that it is most meet (*decet*) for the governor of things.[49]

In other words, everything in the world that has the character of being "meet" refers directly to God as author of the natural order and receives its reality from Him.

As "the necessary and the meet," so far as the order of nature is concerned, are at once considered real, so conversely "the unnecessary and the superfluous" are outside the natural order and may therefore be considered nonexistent—in other words, a negative procedure of postulates corresponds to the positive procedure. The justification of both methods is contained in the following basic proposition: "Nature is not lacking in necessary things, nor is it abundant in superfluous ones." [50] This thesis occurs almost literally in Aristotle.[51] Whereas in Aristotle the thesis refers to the suitable disposition of organisms, Ficino understands it in a universal and ontological sense and applies it to the quality of the universe and of all its parts. The positive postulates that correspond to the axiom of the "necessary" have been analyzed in connection with the order of nature. The negative postulates derived from the "axiom of the superfluous" have an equally

[48] "Quamobrem Deus non ut contingit ita existit et agit, alioquin nullus usquam ordo reperiretur unquam, sed ut decuit imo ut decet. Decet autem, quia decorum. Ipse vero decor est ipse Deus, a quo et per quem omnia decentia fiunt" (*ibid.*, p. 109).

[49] *Ibid.*, p. 709.

[50] "In necessariis rebus natura non deficit, supervacuis non abundat" (*ibid.*, pp. 174, 298; cf. p. 231).

[51] *De anima* III. 9. 432b 21 f.

universal character and occur mainly in discussions concerning the opinions of others. We read, for example, in the criticism of Averroism that the conception of the active intellect and passive intellect as two different substances is superfluous and hence fallacious.[52] And the Epicurean epistemology which attributes corporeal extension to the intellect is carried *ad absurdum* by the reasoning that one spatial particle should always suffice for a knowledge of the whole and that the other particles would therefore be superfluous.[53] Similarly, the return of dead Souls to earthly bodies is rejected as superfluous and contrary to nature [54] and the assumption of two gods, each of whom would produce a complete world, seems impossible for the simple reason that those two worlds would be perfectly equal and that hence one of them would be sufficient and the other superfluous.[55]

Since the superfluous has no place in the world, conversely every existing thing has its original meaning and cannot be either without purpose or in vain. This doctrine is expressed in the important "axiom of the useless" which occurs frequently and in various formulae. "Nature itself does not give or move anything in vain, since nature is guided by God." [56] "The highest reason . . . does nothing in vain." [57] "The natural inclination and tendency cannot always be vain, for that is strange to the order of the universe." [58] Good is not desired in vain by men, "for there is no temerity in the law of nature." [59] This axiom, as we see, is based directly on the order of nature and upon the will of God expressed in that order. It serves accordingly to prove the agreement of the natural substances and qualities with their particular ends. As the substances, for example, human Souls, are not created in vain by God,[60] so their potencies and capacities

---

[52] *Op. om.*, p. 348.   [53] *Ibid.*, pp. 189, 192; cf. p. 174.   [54] *Ibid.*, p. 375.
[55] *Ibid.*, p. 94.   [56] *Ibid.*, p. 916.   •   [57] *Ibid.*, p. 753.
[58] "Naturalis autem inclinatio proclivitasque inanis semper esse non debet. Id enim ab ordine universi alienissimum est" (*ibid.*, pp. 416 f.).
[59] "Siquidem in lege naturae non est temeritas" (*ibid.*, p. 312).
[60] *Ibid.*, p. 20.

cannot be useless.[61] The same is true of their movements and tendencies in so far as they derive from nature and therefore from God.[62]

God would be . . . an unjust tyrant if he imposed upon us tasks which we could never fulfill. . . . He would be an inexperienced and too-hazardous archer if he directed our desires like arrows toward Himself as a target and did not add wings to the arrows by which they could reach the target some time. He would be unfortunate if His attempt to attract us toward Himself never reached its end.[63]

The "axiom of the useless" is therefore applied even to the striving of man, a subject which we shall discuss in Chapters X and XV.

In all these postulates and axioms we recognize Ficino's tendency to arrive at a knowledge of the essence of God and of the world through the mere determination of what is perfect. This same tendency finds its direct expression in the relation between the good and the possible. When he says occasionally that infinite wisdom and good do not deny to any being any good that it could and should receive [64] and that a good possibility (*potentia bona*) cannot always be useless and is therefore actually realized at some time,[65] it appears at first as if the possible were standing independently beside the good and as if the good might need the possible to attain real existence. In fact the possible is already given along with the good and therefore, because of divine goodness, also its reality. According to Olympiodorus the life of reason, as separated from the body, is demonstrated in the following manner: "If such a life is good, consequently it is also possible. For what is impossible is also useless. But the good must not be called useless. Furthermore, if impotence belongs to

[61] *Ibid.*, pp. 709, 715.　　[62] *Ibid.*, pp. 314, 397, 681, 1209, 1581, *et passim*.

[63] "Esset autem Deus . . . tyrannus iniquus, si ea nobis mandaret appetenda quae nunquam possemus implere. . . . Esset quoque sagittarius imperitus ac nimium temerarius, si desideria nostra velut sagittas ad se ceu signum dirigeret neque addidisset spiculis pennulas, quibus quandoque signum attingerent. Esset denique infortunatus, si conatus suus quo nos ad se rapit, nunquam finem suum consequeretur" (*ibid.*, p. 306).

[64] *Ibid.*, p. 681.　　　　　　　　[65] *Ibid.*, pp. 417, 709.

evil, to good belongs power (*potentia*). Consequently each good is possible by its nature." [66] And in a general ontological discussion we find these similar statements:

Power (*potentia*) and truth are naturally desired as goods. And as what they are they are either identical with goodness itself or derived from goodness. Consequently, anything that is more possible and more true than the nature of the universe is also better; and conversely anything that is judged to be better than the universe is also more possible and more true. Moreover, anything that is better participates more in the good. Consequently, it is not impossible. For the impossible is judged to be not participating in any good.[67]

This possibility and reality are included in the good, and though this connection is ultimately based upon the essence of God, it can be used conversely to derive the reality of God and of His perfect qualities. This is clearly shown later in the same discussion.

Why do we ask curiously and stupidly whether it is possible and true or not that there is an immense good in the universe? For there is nothing more possible and more true than that thing in comparison to which nothing more powerful can be imagined. . . . If in the highest cause and end of all things . . . is the highest good, and if the highest good itself is identical with the highest power and truth, whatever is judged to be better about it will also be more possible or, rather, is already more real.[68]

[66] "Vita eiusmodi si bona est, ergo et possibilis est. Quod enim impossibile est, idem quoque inutile. Bonum vero inutile non est dicendum. Item si impotentia ad malum pertinet, ad bonum potentia pertinet. Ergo bonum omne natura sua possibile est" (*ibid.*, p. 186).

[67] "Rursus potentia et veritas tamquam bona naturaliter appetuntur. Atque hoc ipsum quod sunt, aut sunt ipsa bonitas aut a bonitate. Ergo quod universi natura possibilius veriusque est, hoc est et melius, atque converso quod universo melius iudicatur, idem possibilius est et verius. Item quod est melius, magis est boni particeps. Non est igitur impossibile. Nam impossibile nullius boni particeps iudicatur" (*ibid.*, p. 709).

[68] "Sed quid curiose inepteque quaerimus, utrum possibile verumve sit in universo esse immensum bonum necne? Cum nihil sit possibilius veriusque eo quo nihil potest potentius cogitari. . . . Si in summo principio omnium atque fine . . . summa bonitas est et summa ipsa bonitas idem est prorsus ac summa potentia veritasque, sequitur quicquid circa ipsum melius iudicatur possibilius fore, imo iam verius esse" (*ibid.*).

Therefore, while the ontological conception is here pushed to its extreme limit, it also returns to its point of departure, and what had been a premise in the beginning appears again as a conclusion in the end. After the real has found the justification of its own existence in the good, the good now reveals itself as sufficient cause of the possible and the real; and while God produces all good in the world as real, His perfect goodness is equally the cause of His own perfect existence.

VI

HIERARCHY OF BEING

THE WHOLE SPHERE of Being, as we saw at the beginning, is constructed out of substantial entities that coexist in a definite order (see above, Chapter III). The task is now to seek a systematic principle that will make the division of the world apparent in each case and will thus assign to each entity its definite place in relation to the other entities. This question—at least in this form —had no importance for ancient philosophy in its earlier periods, nor has it had for modern thought. In the modern period the concept of substantial entity has been practically eliminated by natural science, and once the physical world had lost its clear outlines, the systematic order of Being could be approached only from the standpoint of the knowing subject. In ancient philosophy, since Aristotle's day, the concept of substance prevailed, it is true, and some system of the physical world is recognizable in certain theories that were transmitted from Aristotle to the following ages, such as the theories of the celestial spheres and of the gradation of organisms according to the potencies or faculties of the Soul. But the consideration of reality was mainly directed toward principles or causes. From this point of view all phenomena formed a homogeneous whole, whereas the causes inside or outside the world were not placed in a clear and conceivable relation to the things themselves. The Neoplatonists were first to conceive the structure of Being as a continual hierarchy, so obtaining a universal principle of division which became, through Dionysius the Areopagite, a fixed element in medieval thought. This hierarchical order constitutes, so to speak, an ontological space that embraces all corporeal and incorporeal entities alike and in which all things have a definite relationship of proximity to or distance from each other. The Neoplatonic form of hierarchy, however, first developed by Plotinus, is distinguished from the medieval order by a few essential features. In Plotinus, Being is divided into a few large and homogeneous spheres: One, Mind, Soul, Sense, Nature, and Body. Each of these spheres contains the whole wealth of objective forms, and each, as active principle, produces by itself the next lower sphere.[1] The elements of medieval hierarchy, on the other hand, are no such comprehensive spheres. They are, rather, the individual objective forms or species themselves. Since each of these forms as creature is directly related to God, each form is essentially independent of the next higher form and is surpassed by it only in degree. Plotinus' hierarchy is a series of strata superimposed one above another. The hierarchy of the Middle Ages, on the other hand, is a series of degrees disposed one beside the other. In Ficino we find both the Plotinian and the medieval hierarchy of Being—a fact perfectly compatible with his historical position. But Plotinus' theory of strata occurs in its unmodified form only in Ficino's earlier works.[2] The doctrine of the five substances found in the first few books of the *Theologia Platonica* has a secondary character and is definitely modified by the concept of the grade series. In the later books of the *Theologia* merely a few elements of the Plotinian doctrine are found in connection with other concepts. On the other hand, the medieval theory of grades constitutes a general and essential premise of Ficino's philosophy and must, hence, be explained.[3]

Along with its essence and its particular attributes, an object within the sphere of Being is given a certain rank which distinguishes it from other things. So it is said, for example, that the rational nature (in other words, the human Soul) occupies its

[1] Cf. *Enn.* iii. 4. 1. In the handbooks we usually find Matter listed as the last hypostasis, which, in reality, is only the initial state of Body preceding the conversion.

[2] Cf. *De amore*, pp. 1324 f.

[3] For a treatment of the general history of the doctrine of hierarchy see Lovejoy, *The Great Chain of Being*, 1936.

particular rank in the reign of God (*gradum suum obtinet*).[4] Discussing the relation of sense perception and reason to truth, Ficino says that sense perception does not comprehend "the intimate and pure substance of the thing nor [does it comprehend] in what order each thing is placed in nature, all of which belongs to the truth of the thing itself." [5] In this way rank and place, like substance, are included in the real essence of an object and belong to the original attributes toward which all thought and knowledge are directed.

Because of its rank each object is placed in a certain relationship with the other things, since the hierarchical similarity or difference of things defines their ontological proximity and distance. Hence, in discussing the Averroistic doctrine Ficino says that the intellect "is connected with us in respect to the proximity of its nature—in other words, the nature of that intellect is by degree next to our Soul." [6] Elsewhere he says that the form agrees more with matter than with quantity in the order of genus and nature.[7] While these are only particular applications of the concept, another passage shows that the ontological distance is valid for the whole sphere of Being and is measured by its extreme limits—in other words, Nothing and the first being. "As the first matter is most distant from the first being and next to Nothing . . . so the last form is most distant from Nothing and next to the first being." [8]

The hierarchical relation of two things always indicates the superiority of one over the other, without respect to their proximity and distance, and hence the variety of Being always involves various degrees of dignity and perfection.

[4] *Op. om.*, p. 326.
[5] "Intimam meramque rei substantiam aut quo ordine in natura res quaelibet disponatur, quod totum ad rei ipsius pertinet veritatem" (*ibid.*, p. 261).
[6] *Ibid.*, pp. 346 f.   [7] *Ibid.*, p. 707.
[8] "Item sicut materia prima a primo esse distat longissime atque est proxima nihilo . . . , ita ultima forma longissime distat a nihilo atque est primo esse quam proxima" (*ibid.*, p. 226).

It is an old opinion of the theologians, oh excellent gentlemen [Ficino's early eulogy of philosophy states], confirmed by the arguments of many philosophers, which teaches and informs us that the individual things seem to be the more perfect and dignified in the nature of things, the closer they come to the perfection and dignity of the first cause of all things.[9]

We see clearly that some things in nature make and that some others are made; the first precede in dignity, the latter follow.[10]

When a higher degree approaches a lower degree, it does not receive from it, but gives to it.[11]

We see that some things are more perfect than others and that the force of perfection increases in ascending and decreases in descending.[12]

We must not believe that the mind is related to a more perfect action than that matter, except for the reason that the mind is more perfect than it [that matter]. If so, the mind is more distant from Nothing and closer to the highest act, from which all perfection originates.[13]

Perfection of a thing, as we have seen, means the fullness of its peculiar essence (see above, Chapter V). If each object is now said to have a definite degree of perfection, not in respect to its own completion, but in comparison to other things of different rank, it evidently means that each entity has a definite degree of existence and that the variety of rank concerns the essence of things itself. This conception is clearly expressed by Ficino:

All men judge [he says in a discussion of Being] that this thing does not exist at all, that this other thing exists, but in an imperfect way, and that that thing exists in a more perfect way. Such gradation in existence cannot come to being or be known but by an approach

[9] "Vetus theologorum praestantes viri sententia est, multorum philosophorum rationibus confirmata, qua sane docemur atque instruimur, eo singula in rerum natura perfectiora dignioraque videri, quo ad primi rerum omnium principii perfectionem dignitatemque accedunt propinquius" (*ibid.*, pp. 757 f.).

[10] *Ibid.*, p. 692.   [11] *Ibid.*, p. 347.   [12] *Ibid.*, p. 95.

[13] "Neque putandum est mentem respicere actum perfectiorem quam materia illa respiciat, nisi ex eo quod mens est illa perfectior. Si ita est, longius discedit a nihilo et propinquius ad actum accedit summum, unde est omnis perfectio" (*ibid.*, p. 349).

(*accessum*) to the highest existence, which is God, and a departure (*recessum*) from it.[14]

The hierarchical relation of things, ontologically considered, is fixed and clear—in other words, a higher object in comparison with a lower one is not superior in one respect and inferior in another, but surpasses it in all respects. Hence the hierarchy of substances manifests itself in a continual gradation of their qualities and attributes. This gradation not only concerns the most general attributes, like true or good, that are connected everywhere with Being itself, and so share its graded differences, but also is found in the particular attributes that are limited to certain sections or aspects of Being. The ascent in the series of natural bodies, for example, is accompanied by an increase of form and a corresponding decrease of matter:

The order of natural bodies is disposed in such a way that it descends to the first matter and ascends to the last form. And the closer each matter comes to the first matter, the better—that is, the truer and purer —a matter it becomes. The closer a form comes to the last form, the more perfect a form it becomes.[15]

The same relationship is still more explicitly developed with respect to the active and the passive powers of different bodies:

In the order of bodies we see that the sublime body, that is, the highest heaven, contains in its nature all forces of all forms to be produced, through which forces, because of their being active and effective, it prepares the lower bodies for the reception of the different forms . . . in order that it may be said that the sublime heaven contains actually or by active force the forms of the other bodies. But we can say that the following bodies are subjected to it in such a way that they possess the same forms through a receptive and passive force and receive them actually from it. But such an order is preserved that the higher a body is below it, the more active force and the less passive force it has.[16]

[14] "Nam omnes homines iudicant, illud quidem nullo modo esse, istud vero esse, sed imperfecto modo, hoc esse modo perfectiori. Talis autem in essendo gradatio neque fit neque cognoscitur nisi per accessum ad esse summum qui Deus est atque inde recessum" (*ibid.*, p. 281).

[15] *Ibid.*, p. 226.   [16] *Ibid.*, p. 221.

In this example the Plotinian doctrine is apparent in so far as the higher degree acts upon the lower one and communicates to it a plurality of forms. But, in contrast to Plotinus, the existence of the lower degree itself has not been produced by the higher one.

Whereas hitherto different degrees of the same attribute were concerned, on the other hand, groups of different attributes can be distributed among different substances according to their rank. The higher attribute can be added to the lower one in such a way that in ascending an increasing accumulation of attributes results. This, for example, is the case with regard to the famous gradation of natural entities, familiar in ancient philosophy.

The divine mind gives to the lower bodies only life like warmth; to the higher ones, also sense perception like light; to the highest ones, also intellect like lightness. . . . Thus that divine ray that penetrates all things exists in the stones without living, lives in the plants without shining, shines in the animals without being reflected in itself and without returning to its source. But in men it exists, lives, shines, and is reflected in itself.[17]

In most cases the ascent is accomplished in such a way that the lower attributes are gradually replaced by the addition of the higher ones. The lowest Souls, for example, are, so to speak, contained by the bodies; the middle ones are in a certain way contained and in a certain way contain them; the higher ones contain the bodies entirely.[18] Or, in another example, God is the form which neither is inherent, nor forms, nor is formed. The irrational Soul, on the other hand, is formed, forms, and is inherent; the angel is formed by God, but is neither inherent in matter nor forms it; and the rational Soul is not inherent in matter, but is formed and forms.[19] In the same way, there are rational and immortal animals, and on the other hand there are irrational and mortal animals, and between them are rational and mortal ones.[20] Finally, sense perception is form of the body and needs an instrument; the human intellect is form of the body, but needs no cor-

[17] *Ibid.*, p. 231.   [18] *Op. om.*, p. 332.
[19] *Ibid.*, pp. 332 f.   [20] *Ibid.*, p. 224.

poreal instrument; and the angelic intellect is independent in both respects.[21] In all these examples the qualities are ordered according to their rank and are referred to the ontological series of substances.

In so far as there is a clear relationship of rank between the individual substances and their attributes in all cases, the totality of things can be conceived as one ascending or descending sequence of grades. So Ficino can start an extensive discussion from the series of things (*series rerum*),[22] and at one time he says that the mind, which knows all, comprehends and examines the whole series of the divine work (*universam divini operis seriem*).[23] Whereas in the *Philebus* Plato speaks of all things that exist in the universe, Ficino, in his paraphrase, speaks of those entities "which are in the whole order of things that descend from the one prince of the whole order." [24] The world as a whole in relation to the existing things is taken as a hierarchical series of members distinct in grade.

Since the world as totality of all things is first divided into some partial spheres, these spheres, like the whole, must be considered as gradated series or orders. "The series of things is divided in its parts in such a way that there are many different orders of things in nature and that always the lowest parts of each higher order are somehow connected with the highest parts of the next following lower order." [25] While this passage is aimed at many smaller groups, as the context shows, elsewhere a few larger orders are clearly emphasized as main elements of the universe.

Since the order of bodies is placed below that of intellects and depends upon it, the order of bodies follows the order of intellects as the trace of the foot follows the foot and as the shadow follows the body.[26]
Three orders of things seem to belong to the human Soul—Providence, fate, and nature. Providence is the series of minds; fate, that of Souls; nature, that of bodies.[27]

[21] *Ibid.*, p. 330.   [22] *Ibid.*, p. 222.   [23] *Ibid.*, p. 218.
[24] "Quae sunt in universo ordine rerum ab uno totius ordinis principe descendentium" (*ibid.*, p. 1257).
[25] *Ibid.*, p. 222; cf. p. 1243.   [26] *Ibid.*, p. 221.   [27] *Ibid.*, p. 288.

The orders of intellects, Souls, and bodies show the influence of Plotinus even in their names. These orders are also distinguished as a whole from each other by their rank. "The whole genus of the Soul is more excellent than the whole corporeal genus. . . . Hence the lowest of the animal genus surpasses the highest thing of the corporeal genus, etc." [28] But in so far as these spheres are called "orders," or "series," they are no longer independent and real substances, as in Plotinus, but merely some limited sections within the unique continual series of things.[29]

The real elements of the universal hierarchy are, not the partial spheres or genera or the individuals, but the natural species of things. When in the *Philebus* Plato conducts thought from the indifferent unity and the indefinite infinity toward the definite plurality, Ficino understands this as a superiority of the species with respect to the genera and individuals.[30] The species thus have a particular importance not only in relation to knowledge but also in an ontological sense.

If somebody despises the concepts of genera because of their confusion and dispersion and those of the individuals because of their shadowlike nature, that may be accepted. But the species have to be honored according to Plato. In them consists the perfection of the world and the truth of knowledge.[31]

The importance of the species rests essentially upon the fact that each species is distinguished from the others through its ranking, but does not admit further graded differences within itself, in other words, between its individual members.

The species does not admit greater or lesser degrees, and it stands on a certain degree of nature to which nothing can be added or taken away without changing the species itself.[32]

[28] *Ibid.*, p. 332.

[29] Because of their general character of gradation, the series of affinity in astrology are comparable to the ontological series, but in their concrete structure they are not bound to the ontological hierarchy. The magnet in the astrological series of the bear is above the iron, although the iron occupies a higher place in the order of bodies (*Op. om.*, p. 551). The astrological series cannot be considered as real elements of the order of Being.

[30] Cf. *Op. om.*, p. 1218.   [31] *Ibid.*, p. 358; cf. p. 192.   [32] *Ibid.*, p. 192.

While they [the species] are distinguished from each other because of their own differences, they are also separated by degrees of goodness. Consequently, whoever takes away the different degrees of goodness, he also takes away the admirable fulness of various species.[33]

In addition, as those things that are equal in quantity are also one in it, so those things that are equal to each other in perfection are also one in perfection. Perfection consists in form; through the form the species is constituted. Consequently, those things that are one in perfection are one in form and one in species. Thus two species of things cannot be equally perfect.[34]

Finally, in a discussion of the Scotist doctrine we read:

The complete order is such that the higher things are arranged in respect to the lower things, the lower conversely in respect to the higher, and the equal things in respect to each other. We recognize clearly such an order in corporeal things. If incorporeal things have a fuller order, we must also conceive in them a similar, in other words, a threefold, order. But there can be no order between equal things if there are not several individuals included under the same species.[35]

The single species, therefore, constitute the different degrees of Being, and the whole universe, as a unique hierarchy, is constructed upon the different species. For this reason the perfection of the world consists in the species,[36] and the world itself, considering its content, can be called the sum of all species (*cunctarum complexio specierum*).[37]

We do not say [we read in a characteristic passage of the commentary on Plato's *Philebus*] that the genera exist primarily within the essence of the universe, because they are related to the species like potentialities, nor do the individuals exist primarily because they are infinite, without order and changeable, and because in enumerating them, one by one, the universe is perfect without any of them. Consequently, the essence of the universe consists in the species. Thus they are, so to speak, primarily real—in other words, natural.[38]

The hierarchy of things which constitutes the whole realm of Being is not spread without limits, but directed in all its members

[33] *Ibid.,* p. 1692.   [34] *Ibid.,* p. 349.   [35] *Ibid.,* p. 354.
[36] *Ibid.,* p. 358.   [37] *Ibid.,* p. 249.   [38] *Ibid.,* p. 1226.

toward the perfect existence of God, which it approaches more and more in the different degrees of its dignity and perfection.[39]

God is for us the measure of all things [says Ficino, commenting upon the famous passage in Plato's *Laws*] because He measures the ascent and descent of all things. For up to Him there is ascent, but no farther; and as far as His power extends to the external things, so far the descent of the degrees of nature goes, but no farther.[40]

God is thus called the "head of the species" (*princeps specierum*),[41] and He therefore constitutes the upper limit of the ontological series, which He produces out of Himself, being the effective cause, and to which He also belongs as the highest member.[42] The concept of God is therefore defined in a new way, and conversely His existence can be concluded from the very fact that the given hierarchy of things must start from a highest degree.

Why do we judge that the Soul is better than the body, if not because it is closer to the highest goodness? If there were no highest goodness, but an ascent from good to good without end, the body would be distant from the highest goodness by an infinite interval, and the Soul also by an infinite interval. One infinite is not larger or smaller than the other. . . . Consequently, the Soul would not be closer or more congruent to goodness itself than the body—in other words, it would not be better, and the angel would not be better than the Soul.[43]

If there is no first and no last degree among things, each middle degree will depend on infinite higher degrees and produce infinite lower degrees. . . . Consequently, it will be of immense power and full of infinite perfections. Thus all things would be equally infinite, one thing would not be more excellent than another, the cause would not be better than its effect.[44]

[39] Cf. *ibid.*, pp. 757 f. *et passim.*
[40] *Ibid.*, p. 1249; cf. Plato *Laws* iv. 715 e f.
[41] *Op. om.*, p. 93.
[42] Cf. *Op. om.*, pp. 93 f. As Dress (*op. cit.*, p. 55) rightly observes, in Ficino the concept of God is sometimes included in the world, sometimes opposed to it. Anichini (*L'umanesimo e il problema della salvezza in M. Ficino*, pp. 34 f.) sees in the fact that God belongs to the ontological hierarchy, a danger for His transcendency.
[43] *Op. om.*, p. 95; cf. Dress, *op. cit.*, pp. 35 ff.
[44] *Ibid.*; cf. Anichini, *op. cit.*, pp. 34 f.

In a similar discussion the doctrine of those who admit one cause above another without end is rejected:

Then one thing would not be more excellent than another, for where there is no highest being, there one thing does not come closer to the highest than another. But we see clearly that some things in nature are active, some passive, and that the active ones are superior in dignity, the passive ones inferior.[45]

If the series of causes continued without end, each thing would seem equal in rank to each other, and that is judged to be absurd.[46] The hierarchy of things is used here as an obvious premise, and accordingly the existence of a unique God, who determines all things in their mutual relation, being their peak and measure, and puts a finite limit to both their ascent and their descent, is necessary for the order.[47]

The gradation of substances, which we have hitherto considered in its particular aspects, is not only just an incidental attribute of things but also an essential attribute of Being itself, on which the order of nature and the perfection of the world is essentially based. "The exact order requires that all grades of things be contained in the universe." [48] And in the same sense the order of nature is frequently illustrated by a gradation of things.[49] The terms "order" (*ordo*) and "series" are used with almost the same meaning. The hierarchical structure of Being therefore becomes, like the order of nature, a universal ontological principle—its validity needs no justification and it serves to determine the individual things by postulates beyond all experience. A number of particular principles and methods of arguing are based on this fact.

When we consider two objects in their mutual relationship, the principle of hierarchy at once leads to the postulate that the higher one does not depend on the lower one in any way, or if it seems to, it does so only in a very limited manner. "That which is earlier in nature is free from that which is later," [50] and "that which is

---

[45] *Op. om.*, pp. 691 f.   [46] *Ibid.*, p. 692.   [47] Cf. *ibid.*, p. 1233.
[48] *Ibid.*, p. 111; cf. Thomas, *Summa contra Gentiles*, III, 72.
[49] *Op. om.*, pp. 219, 332.   [50] *Ibid.*, p. 254.

more excellent must depend less upon that which is less excellent than the converse." [51] This principle frequently occurs in the argument, and, especially with respect to the relation of body and mind, the existence of intellects without bodies can be derived from it.

When one thing is the result of two, and when one of them, which is less perfect, is found to exist somewhere in itself without the other, the other thing, being more perfect and less needy, can all the more readily exist somewhere without the first thing. One animal is the result of the intellectual substance, that is, the rational Soul, and the body. We see that many bodies exist and live without such an intellect. Consequently, what is there to prevent the existence of many minds not united with bodies? [52]

Since the ascent of the objective substances is conceived as a homogeneous increase of their perfection, there follows the further principle that a higher entity necessarily includes the perfect qualities of the lower entities. This principle also not only is expressed as a general doctrine but also is used in the argument for definite and particular conclusions.

If truth is above the mind, and if whatever is superior does not lack the inferior goods, truth cannot lack the perspicacity of the mind.[53] Since the superior nature includes and surpasses the whole power of the inferior nature and will therefore produce the same work as the inferior, provided that it is given the same instruments, that mind which sees within us can necessarily perform the work of nourishing and sense perception no less than can the imaginative Soul.[54] Since the superior force can perform whatever the inferior can, and even better, and since the Souls connected with bodies know the universals and the individuals, obviously the minds connected with truth itself can know both by means of one force and one intuition.[55]

These principles and arguments, however, indicate merely particular aspects of a more general logical procedure, which finds its immediate expression in a number of analogical conclusions.

[51] *Ibid.*, p. 332.
[52] *Ibid.*, p. 87; cf. Thomas, *Summa contra Gentiles*, I, 13; II, 91.
[53] *Op. om.*, p. 90.   [54] *Ibid.*, p. 331.   [55] *Ibid.*, p. 414.

In most cases these conclusions have approximately the following form: two substances are connected with each other in a certain hierarchical relationship, and observation shows that a certain perfect quality is intrinsic to the inferior substance. Consequently, this quality can and must be attributed even more to the superior substance.

Since the order of minds is more excellent than the corporeal order and since the order of corporeal things finally descends to an eternal matter . . . who is so mad as to admit that the order of minds, being more stable and more divine than the bodies, finally ends in a corruptible mind? [56]

Our Soul possesses and produces true forms. . . . Consequently, all the more does the Soul of the universe possess and generate the true concepts of forms. For where the more excellent force and intelligence is found, the conception and birth of more developed forms must take place.[57]

If the rational faculty [of art] is innate in each irrational nature, it is all the more innate in each rational nature.[58]

Since in all natural things there are certain forces that produce their movements, it is therefore unjust to deprive of force the substance of the human mind, which is the most excellent among all natural things.[59]

Besides this main form, other forms of analogical conclusions sometimes occur; but the type of argument remains essentially unchanged. For example, the analogy may also start from the higher substance and descend to the lower.

If there is distinction among the minds, there is all the more diversity among the Souls; because the human minds are much more united to each other, being more excellent, than the Souls are to each other and because if one Soul were sufficient for the government of our bodies, one mind would be all the more sufficient for the understanding of truth.[60]

Within one substance the conclusion leads from one attribute to another.

[56] *Ibid.*, p. 222.   [57] *Ibid.*, p. 250.   [58] *Ibid.*, p. 255.
[59] *Ibid.*, p. 350; cf. pp. 241, 676, 1342.   [60] *Ibid.*, p. 367.

If life precedes intelligence in origin, and if intelligence surpasses life in value, and if the human Soul is given such dignity that it has somehow an infinite force of thinking and willing, it must all the more and the earlier possess an infinite force of living.[61]

In all these arguments from an observed fact a further conclusion, not accessible to experience, is reached, and the common premise lies in the fixed hierarchy of the respective substances and in the homogeneous gradation of its attributes and perfections.

The principle of hierarchy is valid not only in the relationship between existing things but also in a number of more abstract relations that apparently are not connected with the series of Being. We must keep in mind that thought does not constitute a peculiar sphere and is hence always related to the existing things as to its objects (see above, Chapter IV). Concerning the most general types of relation, the difference of grade between their members is fixed from the beginning and so can be used in the argument at any time. The most important is the relation of causality, which has already occurred in connection with the doctrine of hierarchy and in which the cause always has an unconditioned superiority over the effect.

Anything that produces something must be more excellent than anything that is produced by it. The more something is free from matter, the more it is sublime. Consequently, the cause must always be freer from matter than the effect.[62]

In the same sense it is said of the relation between the world and its causes:

How can such an order and ornament be generated out of unordered and unadorned things, especially since the effective cause is always accustomed to be more excellent than the effect? [63]

Accordingly, the effect is usually inferior to the cause [64] and cannot receive the whole perfection of the cause.[65]

As the cause is superior in rank to its effect, so is the substance to its attribute.

---

[61] *Ibid.*, p. 202.   [62] *Ibid.*, p. 181.   [63] *Ibid.*, p. 397.   [64] *Ibid.*, p. 1352.
[65] *Ibid.*, p. 1340; cf. Thomas, *Summa contra Gentiles*, I, 8.

Since the substance is the foundation of each attribute, it is by an order of nature prior to the attribute; and since it is prior and does not lack the force of form, it can exist somewhere without attribute.[66]

Thus we can demonstrate that the Soul cannot be an attribute of the body, but that it has the character of a substance.

Since the Soul governs and moves the body . . . it is more excellent than the body. The body is a substance. No attribute is nobler than the substance.[67]

Also with regard to the relationship between the whole and its parts, the whole possesses the greater perfection, and on this principle the proof for the animation of the world is based.

The body of the world is a whole body . . . of which the bodies of all animals are the parts. . . . Just as the whole is more perfect than the parts, so the body of the world is more perfect than the body of the individual animals. It would be absurd that the imperfect body should have a Soul and the perfect body should not have a Soul or live. . . . Consequently, the whole body of the world lives, since the bodies of the animals that are parts of it live.[68]

Besides these concepts of relationship proper, we must mention two other pairs of concepts that are fixed in their hierarchical relation and so assume a greater importance for ontology: unity and plurality; rest and movement. The superiority of one over the multiple is, in Plotinus, decisive for the structure of reality.[69] In Ficino's system, also, the higher rank of an entity involves a higher degree of unity.[70] Especially in the series of substances the ascent from the angelic intellects to the divine cause is based on the relation of plurality and unity.

Since the angel is not entirely simple, but has a number, and since above the number there must be unity, because unity is the origin of the whole number and needs no union, while plurality by its nature needs union, above the angel there exists of necessity something else which is not only immobile, but entirely one and simple. This is God.[71]

Just as plurality is surpassed by unity, so movement is surpassed by its correlate, rest. "Rest precedes movement," Ficino asserts,

[66] *Op. om.*, p. 690; cf. pp. 707, 709.   [67] *Ibid.*, p. 165.   [68] *Ibid.*, p. 1342.
[69] *Enn.* vi. 6. 1.   [70] *Op. om.*, p. 367.   [71] *Ibid.*, p. 89; cf. p. 1352.

without further proof.[72] We can conclude that the movement of the world will end at some time in a state of rest.

Movement itself cannot be the real end, since it always flows from one point to another. . . . Hence the highest and last end of the universe . . . will be, not movement, but rest. For rest is more perfect than movement, and for the sake of rest the individual things are moved.[73]

Consequently, the concept of rest, along with that of unity, is used as a particular connotation in the ascent of substances.

Rest is judged to be far more perfect than movement. For movement necessarily needs rest, but not the converse. If, therefore, in our ascent from inferior things to superior things a more perfect degree of movement occurs, and if the one that is more stable is more perfect, all the more must there always be a more perfect degree of rest.[74]

The ascent from the rational Souls to the angelic intellects in particular is based upon the relation of movement to rest.

Since there must be rest before movement, because rest is more perfect than movement, there must be some stable intelligence above the mobile reason of the Soul.[75]

As the natural species appeared to be the elements of the ontological series, conversely, outside the proper order of substances, each differentiation involves a gradation of the single members and cannot be conceived without it.[76] For example, if God conceives in Himself the Ideas, He thinks the possible things not only as different images but at the same time as images of His own essence different in rank. "For God sees in Himself whatever is peculiar to each thing when He sees to what degree each thing can imitate the divine form." [77] Consequently, the Ideas themselves constitute in God a continual series (*series idearum*)[78] and are distinguished from each other through their rank.[79] When Ficino illustrates the differentiation of the Ideas in God by that

---

[72] *Ibid.*, p. 254.   [73] *Ibid.*, p. 416.   [74] *Ibid.*, p. 686.
[75] *Ibid.*, p. 1325; cf. pp. 85 f., 115.
[76] Cf. Thomas, *Summa contra Gentiles*, II, 44.
[77] *Op. om.*, p. 107.   [78] *Ibid.*, p. 268.   [79] *Ibid.*, p. 665.

of the colors in the light, the factor of gradation is again manifest.

As many species of colors are in compounded things, so there are many Ideas of colors which that light sees in itself. In so far as that light sees itself as communicable in the first degree, it is the Idea of the color black; and as it sees itself as communicable in the second degree, it becomes the Idea of the color dark brown. . . . But when that light sees the highest degree of itself, it sees also on how many following degrees the highest degree can be spread and how many species of colors it can thus produce.[80]

The different colors are interpreted as so many degrees of light, and so the metaphor itself receives a new feature, which it did not possess in its older forms, for example, in Plotinus. Similarly, the division of the basic corporeal qualities is accompanied by a difference in rank. This is responsible for quite definite conclusions such as the following: "It is certain that warmth cannot be the main cause of increase, nor any other accidental form, if warmth cannot, which is the most excellent among them." [81]

Finally, extreme contrasts, which at first seem irreconcilable, are subjected to the principle of hierarchy and thus deprived of their real force. For extreme contradiction can take place only between concepts of thought, and when the concept as such is considered to be lacking substance and is referred to the world of objective entities, it necessarily assumes the particularities of that world. The abstract contradiction is thus transformed into a concrete polarity, whose extreme limits or poles are connected with each other by a series of intermediate members. This particular relationship, which we noticed in the cases of form and matter and of active and passive force,[82] must be conceived essentially in the same way when applied to the basic contrasts of Being and Nothing, good and evil. The first being and Nothing are but the extreme ends of a comprehensive hierarchy whose intermediate members are determined by their distance from the poles and by their different share in the opposite quality of these poles.[83] Like-

[80] *Ibid.*, pp. 825 f.   [81] *Ibid.*, p. 179.
[82] Cf. *ibid.*, pp. 221, 226.   [83] *Ibid.*, p. 226.

wise, as extreme poles good and evil are connected with each other by the whole series of intermediate degrees.

Since divine Providence does not take away from things, the particular natures and actions which it gave to and preserved in them and since from their gradual decrease there results defect and evil in the work, the evil is not taken away by Providence, but rather is transformed into good.[84]

Out of the long production of degrees of goodness there finally originates evil, when something either abandons or can abandon its own good.[85]

Properly speaking, there are only degrees of being and of good, and since Nothing and evil in themselves do not exist in the series of things, they must be considered as imaginary counter-poles, to which things, so to speak, come closer in the same measure in which they really become more distant from being and from good. A world order which thus reconciles the contrasts of Being and Nothing, good and evil, must also eliminate all minor contrasts, so proving anew the limitation of thought to reality and the absolute validity and power of the hierarchical order.

[84] *Ibid.*, p. 1692.   [85] *Ibid.*

VII

UNITY OF THE WORLD

PHILOSOPHICAL CONSIDERATION which attempts to interpret things in their relation to the universe usually goes about its task in three steps. First, it asks what is common to all objects; then, what distinguishes individual things from each other; and, finally, what connects and unifies individual things into a whole. It proceeds from unity through multiplicity to a connection, that is, to a unity including multiplicity. In Ficino's system abstract unity is represented by the basic character of Being and its attributes, articulated multiplicity by the principle of hierarchy. He now has left the task of conceiving the connection of things and the concrete unity of the universe from these premises. This task, however, is not accomplished by applying one basic principle, as in the case of the principle of hierarchy. It is expressed rather in a series of individual theories, whose connection may even seem arbitrary. Only a few of these theories have a basic significance; most of them are derived formulae, whose origin can be traced in Ficino's works. The unifying and basic factor lies in the common problem which motivates all these thoughts that at the end are joined in a kind of system. In order to interpret these thoughts we must take the problem of the unity and connection of all things as a guiding principle and examine individually the theories that refer to it. Above all, we must consider three groups of theories that may be designated by the terms "symbolism," "continuity," and "affinity."

In order to understand the meaning and origin of symbolism we must proceed indirectly and begin with the use Ficino makes of metaphors. The metaphor, one of the characteristic forms of poetical expression, entered at an early date into philosophical literature, and at times it assumed such a remarkable importance that a detailed study of the history of philosophic metaphor is warranted. In the Platonic tradition, especially, the metaphor has developed into an important instrument of thought. Plato's *Dialogues* abound in their use, and, though we might attribute this fact to Plato's poetical genius, examples such as the famous metaphor of the cave in the *Republic* serve not only a literary but also a philosophical purpose. No less numerous or important are the metaphors of Plotinus, some of which—like those of the light, the rays, or the drama—contain the answers to fundamental metaphysical problems. Hence Ficino was able to profit from a long tradition, and many of his metaphors are repetitions or modifications of those of Plato or Plotinus. On the other hand, there are original inventions in Ficino's works that expressively demonstrate the character of his own thinking. To give an example: he compares the Soul which obeys the desires of the body to the indulgent mother of a spoiled child.[1] Elsewhere he illustrates the attitude of the Soul, directed in temporal movement toward the immutable God, by comparing it with the painter Apelles, who painted the picture of his immutable subject matter in a slow succession of motions.[2]

In Ficino's choice of images and in his manner of description there is a strange mixture of rigidity and delicacy that is quite distinct from Plato's clarity and majesty and from the lofty strain of Plotinus, but seems to reflect the art of his period. More important than the impression, however, is the function of the metaphor, the relation between image and idea. For Plato, as well as for Plotinus, the metaphor's primary task serves as a means of making abstract ideas evident to intuition, and since the relation of the image to the idea is produced by an arbitrary act of thinking, the metaphor can claim validity only for our thought, without stating anything definite about real entities. For Ficino, on the contrary, the relation of image to idea is not merely suggested by thinking but also corresponds to a real relationship existing among objects.

[1] *Op. om.*, p. 206.　　　　[2] *Ibid.*, p. 118.

In the example quoted in the preceding paragraph the Soul is not incidentally compared to an indulgent mother, but the love of the generating cause for its generated effect is in reality common to both entities. And the painter Apelles is not only metaphorically an image of the Soul directed toward God; in reality Apelles is induced to action by his reference to an immutable subject. In Ficino's metaphors there is evidently a new, ontological element, and underneath the external connection of concepts is hidden an internal symbolism of things.

By "symbol" we mean an object which by virtue of a similarity of character indicates another object; accordingly symbolism is the internal relation of the symbol to the object represented by it. The metaphor becomes a symbol when it is freed from its connection with thinking, transferred into reality, and, so to speak, "substantiated." While the relation of image and idea is transformed into a real relation between real objects, there appears a hidden connection between the individual objects in the world. The manner of thinking symbolically, therefore, seems to take metaphorical elements for immediate attributes of things, but in this procedure it tries to grasp the essence and internal unity of things. In Ficino the transition from metaphor to symbol is clearly observable, and in most cases the external form of comparison is maintained by simply asserting that one thing behaves like another, or in a similar way (*sicut, similiter,* and so forth). On the other hand, statements about symbolism are rather rare. We shall, however, consider only these extreme cases, since they alone concern our principal question.

Symbolism in the proper sense appears when an object in itself, independent of the thought about it, is conceived as an image or metaphor of another object. Ficino usually expresses this relationship as "copy" and "original," based on an objective process of imitation. In most cases he has in mind the famous symbolism of light, which after Plato had been developed particularly by Plotinus and Dionysius the Areopagite. In Ficino, however, it loses the form of a metaphor.[3] In one place he says that the light is "everywhere the image of the divine truth and goodness." [4] And, having considered the attributes of the supercelestial spirits, Ficino continues: "The image of them all is the splendor of the heaven, or rather it is like a shadow in relation to their clarity, since the body of the heaven can imitate the clarity of the spirit less accurately than the earth does the splendor of the heaven." [5] Likewise, he says in another context that the light imitates God,[6] and in a similar passage he associates God and the sun as exemplar and image.[7] When he calls the movements of the Soul the models of those of the body,[8] we must understand this statement in the same way.

Since the symbol and its represented object must both belong to the objective world, they are subject to the principle of hierarchy and are definitely related to each other. The character of this relationship is already indicated by the concepts of "original" and "copy," which have a clear ontological meaning in Plato and Plotinus and which Ficino applies to symbolism. The symbol is therefore inferior in rank to the represented object which is its original, and constitutes its manifestation on a lower level of existence.

If an object is considered a symbol of another object, this is for the former object not only an external and incidental attribute but something which concerns its internal essence as well. So it becomes possible to know an existing thing not only through its direct attributes but also through its relation to that higher reality of which it is the symbol. The most characteristic example of this procedure is given by the small treatise *De lumine*, which is found in its earlier and shorter version among the letters of the second book.[9] In it Ficino first tries to define the essence of light by the

---

[3] For the history of this important metaphor cf. C. Baeumker, Witelo (*Beitraege zur Geschichte der Philosophie des Mittelalters*, III, 2), pp. 357 ff.
[4] *Op. om.*, p. 719.   [5] *Ibid.*   [6] *Ibid.*, p. 981.
[7] *Ibid.*, p. 971.   [8] *Ibid.*, p. 171.
[9] *Ibid.*, pp. 717 ff.; cf. pp. 976 ff., and *Suppl.*, I, 72 f.

aid of sense perception, but he then abandons that method as insufficient and interprets light, with the help of mere thought, as a manifestation of higher metaphysical substances.

Even more important than this procedure is the contrary one: in other words, the definition of the originals themselves by means of their symbols. Because of the internal unity between the original and the symbol, the essence and attributes of a symbol can also be predicated, in a metaphorical sense, to its corresponding original. This transference, which sometimes surrounds Ficino's abstract considerations with the veil of an obscure and shadowlike concreteness, serves to complete and to enrich immediate ontological knowledge by means of symbolism. If God is frequently called "infinite light" and the Soul "an indivisible point," this is to be understood wholly in a symbolical sense.[10] The same is true of the doctrine of the direct act and the reflected act, which is applied to the relation between life and thought and which we have met in another context (see above, Chapter IV). Occasionally this symbolic aspect becomes obvious in the exposition itself. "As a whole," Ficino says in reference to the virtues, "what else is speculative virtue but a brightness (*claritas*) of the intellect, and moral virtue but a stable ardor of the appetite kindled by the brightness of intellect?" [11] In another passage, apparently imitated by Landino in the second book of his *Disputationes Camaldulenses,* we read about the movements of the Soul:

There appear in the Soul the originals of the corporeal movements: of generation when it adheres to divine things, of corruption when it refers to mortal things, of increase when it remembers, of decrease when it forgets, of change when it passes through various passions, of condensation when it contemplates something directly and concentrates upon itself, of rarification when it is occupied in discursive thought or distracted about many things, of rectilinear progression when it touches external things, of circular movement when it resolves in the objects the effect into its cause and deduces the effect from the cause or is reflected in considering itself. Again, the Soul seems to move straight when it descends to the body and sense, obliquely when it is reflected in itself or in the angel, in a circle when it turns to God, its cause and end, upward toward the universals, downward toward the particulars, to the right and left toward the opposite differences of a genus, and, finally, forward and backward when it turns to the natural causes and effects.[12]

Because of its ontological meaning the relation of original and symbol may be used in the argument itself. A demonstration for the incorporeality of the Soul, for example, begins as follows:

Food is received in such a way that it is transformed into the substance of the thing which it is to feed—for example, bread is eaten to become flesh. The food therefore must be similar to the thing which is to be fed so that it may easily be transformed into its nature. So water animals are fed by waterlike food, earthly by earthlike, aerial by airlike. In a similar way, bodies are fed by bodylike things, incorporeal entities by incorporeal ones. For a body is not transformed into a spirit, nor a spirit into a body. . . . We know that the Soul is not fed by bodies. We know that it is fed by incorporeal things. Therefore we know that it is incorporeal.[13]

The concept of food is not only transferred to the Soul in a symbolic sense here—a conception already found in Plato's *Phaedrus* [14] —but the metaphorical food of the Soul and the proper food of the body are almost united in a kind of genus, in such a way that the attitude of the one may be derived from that of the other by a direct analogy. The symbolism of the objects therefore possesses an immediate force of demonstration, the justification of which is based upon the internal unity of all things.

As a last consequence, the symbolic thought finally recognizes the particular attributes of the original in the symbol. This method, which Ficino uses especially in his later period, he calls "comparatio." Though this expression still indicates the ultimate derivation from the metaphor, in reality it is a developed form of symbolic exposition. A characteristic example is the *Orphica comparatio solis ad Deum,* published among the letters of the sixth book and written in 1479.[15] It does not contain, as we might expect, a

---

[12] *Ibid.,* p. 171.
[14] *Phaedr.* 247 d.
[13] *Ibid.,* p. 184.
[15] *Op. om.,* pp. 825 f.

detailed comparison between God and the sun, but merely a careful description of the sun and its attributes. But in that description a symbolic description of God is implicit. This is clearly emphasized toward the end as the real purpose of the whole treatise: "If we do not want to claim this Orphic mystery as true, we may at least for a moment imagine it as being true, so that, looking at the celestial sun, we may see in it as in a mirror that supercelestial One who has pitched his tent in the sun." [16] Later Ficino made a similar attempt on a larger scale in his tract *De sole* which in a different version bears the title *De comparatione solis ad Deum*.[17] This work consists chiefly of a detailed physical description of the sun's forces and effects. The symbolic application of it to God is left to the reader; but even in this case Ficino does not fail to express the leading idea of the work in clear terms in the beginning of the exposition:

Therefore, if you want to assert many angelic minds above the heaven-like lights and their relation to each other and to God the father of lights, why do you need long detours of investigation? Look at the heaven, please, oh citizen of the celestial fatherland, at the heaven which was made orderly and manifest by God for the purpose of making that clear. When you look upward, the celestial entities tell you the glory of God through the rays of the stars, like the glances and signs of their eyes, and the firmament announces the works of His hands. But the sun can signify to you God Himself in the greatest degree. The sun will give you the signs; who would dare to call the sun false? So the invisible things of God, that is, the angelic divinities, are seen and understood particularly through the stars, and God's eternal power and divinity through the sun.[18]

Therefore, though in his introduction Ficino qualifies the work as an allegorical exercise of the mind (*allegoricam . . . ingeniorum exercitationem*),[19] if we take into account the vague ter-

---

[16] *Ibid.,* p. 826; cf. Ps. 18: 6.
[17] *Op. om.,* pp. 965 ff.; cf. p. 944 and *Suppl.* I, 74 f.
[18] *Op. om.,* p. 966; cf. Jas. 1: 17; Ps. 18: 2; Virgil *Georgica* i. 463 f.; Rom. 1: 20.
[19] *Op. om.,* p. 965.

minology of the older period, we see that he refers to nothing other than the peculiar symbolic character of the exposition.

In symbolic knowledge, wh:ch is developed beyond the simple metaphor through its ontological meaning, there appears for the first time a substantial connection among different things. It is still vague and a mere tendency of thought rather than a clear philosophical doctrine. The unity of the world is presupposed and indicated, but not explicitly interpreted and justified. This is done by the doctrines of continuity and affinity, which possess great importance for the systematic structure of Ficino's cosmology.

Since particular things belong to the sphere of Being in a kind of spatial order (see above, Chapter III), there exists a concrete unity among them, since two neighboring beings everywhere agree with each other in as great as possible a number of their objective attributes. The old proposition that nature makes no leaps is thus interpreted to mean that contrasting entities in the world do not directly touch each other, but are bound together in a gradual sequence of intermediate members. The whole of Being is thus connected within itself, and the result is an ontological principle of universal continuity—a principle found in Ficino, at least in its consequences,[20] and which even Kant maintains with qualifications.[21]

According to this principle of continuity we can require a homogeneous succession of elements for whatever group is determined by beginning, middle, and end. If the beginning and the end agree in some respect, the middle cannot disagree with them in the same respect, otherwise the entire succession would fluctuate and would not proceed steadily in one direction. Hence, in Ficino's opinion, the Averroistic doctrine of a single intellect is reduced *ad absurdum* by the reasoning that the intellect "will be wholly present in two men who are far removed from each other by a great interval, but will not be present in the middle (space), a

[20] Cf. Saitta, *op. cit.*, p. 180, 192 f. Heitzman, "L'agostinismo avicennizzante," *Giorn. crit.*, XVI (1935), 297.

[21] Kant, *Kritik der reinen Vernunft*, 2d ed., pp. 685 f.

fact which nature does not admit." [22] Therefore from the quality
of beginning and end we can directly derive that of the middle, a
method which Ficino frequently uses in the argument. "If it [the
intellect] acts by itself upon itself, it also acts through itself, for if
both terms of action are in it, the middle is also in it." [23] In another passage the relation of the intellect with God is compared
to a circle. This leads to the following conclusion: "The beginning
and end of this circle is God, the intellect is the middle. If the
first and last term of this circle is eternity as such, certainly the
middle, which participates in the terms, is also eternal." [24] A similar conclusion is valid for the regions of the visible world: since
the first and the last spheres have twelve parts and are filled with
rational beings, we must also believe the same about the spheres
placed between them.[25]

While this principle of continuity in the relation of beginning,
middle, and end is only used in a general way, it gains particular
significance in the hierarchical order of Being. The whole series
of Being is divided into a number of larger sections or partial orders, as we have seen (Chapter VI). Hence it is necessary for the
connection of the universe that these sections be, not separated by
empty spaces, but directly connected at their proximities. Ficino
clearly expresses this concept on several occasions:

If someone inquires [he says in the commentary on Plato's *Philebus*]
why nature makes these animals so defective [sponges, conches, etc.],
he may understand that the series of things are distinguished by such
degrees that the lowest being of a higher order is always next to the
first in the successive order; otherwise the things would not be connected with each other, and the work of the one God would not be
one. The highest angel is next to God; the lowest, to the fiery demon.
The lowest water demon is similar to the most perfect man; the stupid
man, to the intelligent beast; the most simple animal, to the most
beautiful tree; the lowest plant, such as the mushroom, is almost
identical with the inanimate body.[26]

[22] *Op. om.*, p. 348.   [23] *Ibid.*, p. 199.
[24] *Ibid.*, p. 705; cf. p. 1324.   [25] *Ibid.*, pp. 126, 377.
[26] *Ibid.*, p. 1243.

And in a similar, more extensive analysis in the *Theologia Platonica* Ficino passes through all the individual spheres of Being and again arrives at the conclusion that "the series of things is divided into parts in such a way that, although there are many and various orders of things in nature, the lowest parts of the preceding order are always connected with the highest parts of the next following lower order." [27]

The most significant expression of this postulate of continuity is found in the important principle of mediation, which is also founded on the hierarchical order of reality. This principle states that wherever there are contrasts or sharp differences in the series of Being we must assume the existence of some intermediary elements. Ficino formulates this principle in the commentary on the *Philebus:* "From extreme to extreme we cannot proceed without some middle term." [28] In the illustration added to this sentence he refers to the exposition of the four elements in the *Timaeus,* where water and air are introduced as the necessary middle terms reconciling the contrast of fire and earth, a passage which probably occasioned the development of Ficino's entire doctrine.[29]

This principle of mediation is used frequently and in various ways in the argument. The reconciliation of contrasts by intermediary terms is first considered as a simple fact that can be directly observed in several parts of the world and can therefore be applied by analogy to other regions.

Since everything passes from extreme to extreme through some middle term—from the winter through the spring to the summer, from the summer to the winter through the autumn—so between the completely mobile quality and the completely immobile substance we must put something partly mobile and partly immobile.[30]

Similarly, the median state of children's souls after death is illustrated in another passage:

[27] *Ibid.,* p. 222; cf. p. 87. See also Thomas, *Summa contra Gentiles,* II, 68.
[28] *Op. om.,* p. 1233.
[29] Ibid., p. 1234; cf. Tim. 31 b f.
[30] *Op. om.,* p. 85.

As in man there is spirit between the thick body and the Soul, and in feeling there is painlessness between pain and pleasure, so in reasoning there is right opinion between knowledge and ignorance, and again in the universe the transparent is between the light-bearing and the dark, and among the separated spirits there seem to be those that are happily formed in the heavens through God's light and rays (*tam luce quam lumine*) and on the contrary those around the earth to which both are miserably lacking, and between them in the purer air are some median spirits that are illuminated, not by the light itself, but by its rays.[31]

But the principle of mediation is founded not only on the observation of particular facts but also on the unity and the continuity of the whole world. Discussing the degrees of spirits, Ficino therefore argues that there are spirits entirely immortal and spirits entirely mortal—in other words, angels and irrational Souls. "Moreover, there must be some middle spirits between them in order that there may be one connection (*contextus*) of all nature without interruption." [32] The four degrees of the infinite and the finite in the world are justified in a similar way: "There must be these four degrees of things in nature in order that we may descend gradually from those things that are entirely infinite through the mixed median terms to those things that are entirely finite." This gradation, however, cannot constitute a continual whole (*continuari*) if the finite and the infinite do not occur in the intelligible, as well as in the sensible, world.[33] In the commentary on Plotinus, Ficino asserts the existence of some intermediary term, "because the procession of things must be continuous and there must be no void left in such succession." [34]

Because of its general validity, the principle of mediation represents a necessary element in the perfect order of the universe and is added as a complement to the principle of hierarchy in which that order finds its visible expression, as we have seen above in Chapter IV.

It must not be held absurd [so Ficino argues against Averroism] that rational substance is bound with matter, because otherwise the order

[31] *Ibid.*, p. 423.   [32] *Ibid.*, p. 219.   [33] *Ibid.*, p. 334.   [34] *Ibid.*, pp. 1688 f.

of nature could not be preserved. There is an immaterial, rational, and immortal spirit, such as the angels. There is a connected, irrational, mortal spirit, such as the soul of beasts. These things are too far removed from one another . . . hence [we ask], What is the median term between them? [35]

And in a similar passage we read:

Let us put an order among the spirits. There is the highest spirit, which always has been and always will be—that is, God. There are the lowest spirits, of the animals, which have neither always been nor always will be. Between such contrary extremes as these there must be two middle spirits that must have part of that first spirit and part of the lowest spirits.[36]

In other words, the existence of intermediary elements belongs as an essential factor to the concept of order, and wherever the order of Being is presented as a series of grades, Ficino emphasizes the homogeneous continuity of this succession.[37] Since the world is perfect, we can always derive the existence of some intermediary being from a given contrast.[38]

Since an intermediary being is always assumed because of its concordance with the extremes,[39] and since it must have some median quality by its nature,[40] it must always be defined in such a way that it shares equally in the qualities of both extremes. In other words, the relationship between the middle term and the extremes must become manifest, as the hierarchy itself did, in a homogeneous gradation of the attributes. The form of this gradation depends upon the character of the related contrast. If the extremes are distinguished by only one pair of opposite qualities, the median form must contain both qualities, though it may possess each in a different respect. For instance, Angel is immobile, Quality is mobile, Soul, which forms the middle term between them, is immobile in its substance, but mobile in its action.[41] In the same way, angels are invariable, the beast souls are variable, hu-

---

[35] *Ibid.*, p. 337.   [36] *Ibid.*, p. 400.
[37] Cf. *ibid.*, pp. 219, 332 f., *et passim.*
[38] Cf. *ibid.*, pp. 350, 358, *et passim.*
[39] *Ibid.*, p. 214.   [40] *Ibid.*, p. 330.   [41] *Ibid.*, p. 85.

man Souls are invariable in their whole substance, but variable in some parts and potencies.[42] On the other hand, if the extremes are distinguished by two pairs of qualities, the connection takes place in such a way that the middle term agrees with each extreme in one quality. Since there may always be two different combinations for the middle, it is necessary to determine the right one in every case by a particular argument. For instance, there are immortal spirits without bodies, and in contrast to them, mortal spirits in bodies. "There must be, therefore, some middle spirits," argues Ficino further," which are either without bodies and mortal, which is impossible, or with bodies and immortal."[43] Similarly, between God, who always has been and always will be, and the beast souls, that neither have been always nor will be always, there must be middle spirits.

In what manner shall we fashion those middle spirits? Shall we say that they have always been, but will cease to be some time? Not at all. For what has always been, existed infinitely by infinite force. Such infinite force can never be lessened. If they always have been, they will also always be, and they will be equal to God, not to middle spirits. In order to have some median quality of duration they must have begun some time, but they must never cease.[44]

Accordingly, when the extremes are distinguished by more than two qualities there are more possibilities of mediation, and though the argument becomes more complicated the procedure is essentially the same.[45]

Since the principle of mediation is founded on the concept of continuity, it may be applied not only to particular conditions of individual objects but also to the structure of the universe. In other words, the discovery of an absolute median term which by its qualities connects the extreme contrasts of Being and produces the objective unity of the world is a necessity. At one point Ficino argues against Averroism:

There must be one form in the world that connects the higher forms with the lower ones. . . . And in it the particularities of all forms

---

[42] *Ibid.*, p. 219.

[43] *Ibid.*, p. 224.

[44] *Ibid.*, 400; cf. p. 402.

[45] Cf. *ibid.*, p. 337.

must be contained, so that in a certain sense the higher forms will be weakened and drawn down to the lower ones, and the lower ones enforced and raised to the higher ones.[46]

This form which connects the higher and lower things with each other and satisfies the demand for a middle term in the universe is in fact no other than the rational Soul. "The Soul is truly the mean of all things created by God," Ficino states,[47] and this conception, though in all probability derived from the creation of the Soul in Plato's *Timaeus*,[48] assumes in Ficino more-or-less independent significance and is treated at length in an important section of the *Theologia Platonica*.[49] The chapter in question makes the transition from the general consideration of the universe (in the first books) to the theory of the Soul (the subject of the following books), and on this account the author is obliged to emphasize the particular importance of the Soul in the universe. He begins with a short description of the middle position of the Soul. "We put God and Angel on top of nature, Body and Quality below, and Soul in the middle between those highest and these lowest beings." [50] In the usual way he derives from the contrast of Angel and Quality the existence of a middle being:

Quality is entirely different from Angel, because Quality is moved and Angel is permanent, and because the former is born at some time and the latter exists always. There must be, therefore, some middle term, agreeing in part with Angel and in part with Quality. What may it be? Perhaps something that stays or is permanent at some time? No! For nothing like that exists. . . . The middle, therefore, will be something that is always becoming, that is, is always moved. It agrees with Angel because it exists always and with Quality because it is moved.[51]

After other considerations Ficino continues:

Each work made up of several elements is most perfect when it is composed of its elements in such a way that it is united in all respects, agreeing with itself and not being easily dissipated. The corporeal nature shows this clearly in the mixture of the four elements, in which

---

[46] *Ibid.*, p. 348. [47] *Ibid.*, p. 388; cf. pp. 403 f.
[48] *Ibid.*, p. 388; cf. Tim. 35 a ff.
[49] Theol. Plat. Lib. III, ch. ii, pp. 119 ff.
[50] *Op. om.*, p. 119. [51] *Ibid.*

earth and fire, which are far removed from each other, are connected by water and air. In order that the work of one God be one, it is even more important that we presuppose such a connection of parts in the whole work of God. God and Body are the extremes in nature, and are entirely different. The Angel does not unite them because the Angel is entirely directed toward God and does not concern himself with the Body. . . . Also Quality does not connect the extremes because it is inclined toward Body, and abandons the higher things. . . . Hitherto all are extremes, and the upper and lower things flee from each other because they lack the fitting bond. But that third essence between them [in other words, the Soul] is of such quality that it holds fast to the higher things, but does not abandon the lower ones, and so the higher and lower beings are bound by it. For it is immobile and mobile, and in the former quality it agrees with the higher beings, in the latter with the lower.[52]

Here the position of the Soul in the universe corresponds exactly to the principle of mediation. In agreement with this also is the comparison with the elements which is repeated later.[53] This comparison is evidently derived from the passage in the *Timaeus* already quoted in this context.[54] As he states elsewhere, the Soul stands on the boundary line between time and eternity[55] and so appears as the absolute median which connects the extremes of the world and by its mere existence demonstrates the inner unity of Being.[56]

From this analysis we can now understand the characteristic theory of the five substances which dominates the structure of the first few books of the *Theologia Platonica*. Listing God, Angel, Soul, Quality and Body as the chief grades of the universe,[57] Ficino merely seems to follow the model of Plotinus.[58] Indeed, in

[52] *Ibid.*

[53] *Op. om.*, p. 119.

[54] *Tim.* 31 b ff.; cf. Ficino, *Op. om.*, p. 1234.   [55] *Op. om.*, pp. 657 f.

[56] Cf. Cassirer, *Individuum*, pp. 68 f.; Saitta, *op. cit.*, pp. 110 f.; Dress, *op. cit.*, pp. 48 ff., 148.

[57] *Op. om.*, pp. 79, 119, *et passim*. Cf. Dress, *op. cit.*, pp. 26 ff. It is not correct to consider quantity the last substance, as does Meier, *Gott und Geist*, p. 240, or to consider the *mens angelica* as part of man, as does Rocholl, *Der Platonismus der Renaissancezeit*, p. 60. The degree *animus* which Pusino, *Ficinos und Picos religioes-philosophische Anschauungen*, p. 510, puts between the Soul and the angels, does not occur in Ficino at all.

[58] Cf. Saitta, *op. cit.*, pp. 104 f.

Plotinus the following hypostases appear: One, Mind, Soul, Sensation, Nature, and Body.[59] The two schemes are quite similar, particularly since the identification of Angel with the Neoplatonic Mind had already been handed down by medieval tradition. However, some differences remain that need further explanation. In the first place, in Plotinus there are six substances; in Ficino, five. Moreover, two of Plotinus' substances, namely, Sensation and Nature, do not appear in Ficino, and in their place another grade is added, Quality. The significance of these differences becomes apparent when we examine other statements of Ficino more closely. In one passage in his earlier work, *De amore,* for example, we find a series of six substances, which corresponds exactly to that of Plotinus,[60] and in some other passages of the same work we find series of five or four elements, which differ from Plotinus only in the omission of the fourth degree, or of the fourth and fifth degrees.[61] Ficino evidently begins with Plotinus' theory of hypostases and transforms it gradually by omitting a few elements. But there is no trace of Quality in the *De amore,* and we must consider its introduction into the series of substances as a later step. This opinion is confirmed by a close examination of the *Theologia Platonica.* It is true that the definitive series of five substances, including Quality, is there consistently developed in the first few books and also is indicated in a few other passages closely connected with the opening section.[62] But in the later books we find many statements which are directly connected with the Plotinian scheme. In the thirteenth book we find a series of four elements, excluding Quality, and in the course of the exposition, *idolum* and *natura,* corresponding to the remaining two Plotinian elements, are mentioned at least as faculties of the Soul.[63] In several other passages the rational Soul is not defined as the middle term between Angel and Quality, which would correspond to the later series, but according to the older scheme it is defined as

[59] Cf. *Enn.* iii. 4. 1. The handbooks usually give a different scheme, which is not correct.
[60] *Op. om.,* p. 1361.
[61] *Ibid.,* pp. 1324 f., 1351 ff.
[62] Cf. *ibid.,* p. 388.
[63] *Ibid.,* pp. 288 f.

the middle term between Angel and the irrational Soul of the animals.[64] Even in the first book of the *Theologia Platonica* we find the irrational Soul once mentioned as shadow of the rational Soul,[65] with no reference to its relation to Quality. That is, the later form of the series is not consistently upheld even within the *Theologia;* it seems to belong only to the outermost layer of thought. If we seek the reason for this transformation, we must consult a passage in Plotinus that has evidently influenced Ficino. In the second book of the fourth *Ennead* Plotinus explains the different grades of divisibility and indivisibility and introduces Quality as the second grade between Body and Soul.[66] Since Ficino always interprets the relation of Quality with Body and Soul from the point of view of divisibility,[67] there is no doubt that he leans on this passage in Plotinus. However, this fact is not enough to explain his scheme, because Quality never appears as one of the hypostases in Plotinus. Considering, however, that in the first books of the *Theologia* Ficino seeks to present the Soul as the middle term of the world, we understand at once that his later series of substances is much better suited for this purpose than the earlier Plotinian series. For a series of five grades has a central element equally distant from both ends. And while Plotinus' Sensation and Nature are still closely connected with the Soul, Quality is clearly separated from it and can therefore constitute, along with the Body, the lower half of the universe. The transformation of the series of substances and the introduction of Quality has apparently been caused by Ficino's interest in a symmetrical construction of the world, founded on the Soul, and the inconsistencies that occur are justified by the tendency of his speculation. The scheme of the five substances therefore appears as an impressive and visible result of speculation, but it is by no means the basis or starting point of Ficino's philosophy.[68]

The principle of continuity explains the unity of the world only

---

[64] *Ibid.*, pp. 219, 400, *et passim.*   [65] *Ibid.*, p. 84.
[66] *Enn.* iv. 2. 1.   [67] *Op. om.*, p. 81, *et passim.*
[68] Dress, *op. cit.*, pp. 26 ff., and Horbert, *op. cit.*, p. 10, seem to consider this scheme as Ficino's starting point.

in a static sense; that is, it places the individual elements near each other, but it does not affect their reciprocal relation at all. By the principle of affinity (which we must now explain) the unity of the world is conceived dynamically. The similarity of things determines their reciprocal relationship, and the unity results in a lively community of action and movement.

The principle of affinity appears in Ficino's ontological doctrine of thought (see above, Chapter IV). The thinking subject being considered an existing part of the objective order of the universe, the act of thinking is a relationship between the thinking subject (the thing that thinks) and the thought object (the thing that is thought). All thinking is therefore the result of an original affinity between the mind and its objects. Conversely, the act of knowledge establishes a concrete unity between the intellect and its object whereby the truth of thought is immediately established (see above, Chapter IV).[69]

Since the intellect enters into a real relationship with its objects, it can also give them something of its own essence. So the mind that thinks the corporeal objects changes their original quality in a certain sense and lifts them up to a higher grade of being by its thinking power.

This shows the excellency of the mind [Ficino says in treating of the incorporeality of the Soul] that it conceives as true that which is in a certain sense false in matter . . . What in matter is impure, the mind distinguishes as pure . . . What in itself is multiple, the mind considers as simple . . . What in itself is mobile, the mind contemplates as quiet . . . What in itself is divided, the mind sees as united . . . the dead as alive . . . the transitory as stable. . . . From all this it may be concluded that the intellect . . . is neither impure nor infected, dispersed, mutable, or corruptible, since by its power it frees from such characteristics even those things that are of like quality.[70]

This seems to be a simple allegory, but Ficino conceives it as a real procedure. The corporeal being is really lifted to the sphere of the intellectual being by the intellect, and in this way the mind can overcome the gulf between the sensible world and the intelligi-

---

[69] Cf. *Op. om.*, pp. 238, 239, *et passim.*   [70] *Ibid.*, pp. 198 f.

ble world and in a new dynamic sense realize the unity of the universe. The human Soul appears here as the carrier of the thinking act, so creating for a second time—though in another sense—the universal connection of things. In the exposition of this concept Ficino follows the Neoplatonic analysis of the genesis of substances. The divine ray which contains all forms descends from God to matter through several degrees, thereby withdrawing farther and farther from its origin. In like measure the derived forms become more and more different from their originals, finally becoming impure instead of pure, dispersed instead of united, particular instead of universal, mutable instead of immutable. The ray must therefore be reduced to its origin, the derived forms to their originals.

Who will help? [Ficino continues.] Not the Souls of animals that look only at individual images. Not intellects superior to ours . . . because they do not have bodies subjected to all the impulses of all bodies, and they do not receive the particular passions and forms of the particular bodies. Nothing is left but the Soul of man, which is affected by the individual impulses of individual bodies through its earthly body, receives these images of the Ideas maculated by the matter of the universe through perception, but collects them through fantasy, cleans and refines them through reason, and connects them at last with the universal Ideas of the mind. So the celestial ray that had descended to the lowest things returns to the higher beings, because the images of Ideas, formerly dispersed in matter, are collected in the fantasy, and, formerly impure, they are purified in reason, and, formerly particular, they are lifted in the mind to universality. In this way the Soul of man restores the world that had already been shaken (*iam labefacta-tum restituit mundum*). For by its gift the world that was formerly spiritual and had become corporeal is continuously being purified and daily becomes spiritual (*evadit quotidie spiritalis*).[71]

As the good corresponds to the true and will to intellect, so love, as a second basic form of attitude, corresponds to knowledge. Like thought, love also follows the law of affinity. If one being loves another, there must first be some original relationship in them.

---

[71] *Ibid.,* p. 373. Cf. Cassirer, *Erkenntnisproblem,* p. 88; Saitta, *op. cit.,* pp. 159 f.; Dress, *op. cit.,* pp. 59 f.; Hak, *Marsilio Ficino,* p. 101.

Because of that relationship love is mutual. "Love is produced by similarity," Ficino states in the *De amore*. "Similarity is an identical nature existent in several beings. For if I am similar to thee, thou art also similar to me and the same similarity which incites me to love thee, also obliges thee to love me." [72] Hence love is the result of a certain similarity, a rule that concerns not only men but also all other existent beings. "Everywhere similarity is the reason for love," Ficino writes in a letter to Matteo da Forli. "We see that clearly in the stars and elements, in plants and animals." [73] And in a long discussion of the heavens and the elements in the *De amore* he shows that love always attracts like to like.[74] Yet a being not only is induced to love by a similar quality in its nature but also is joined in a concrete unity with its object by love itself. The spatial world and the individual bodies, therefore, owe their unity and consistence to the mutual love of their parts.[75] Likewise, love leads two human beings not only to a union of their bodies but also to an inner unification of their beings, a unification that transforms the lover entirely into the object of his love and makes them both one will, one Soul, and one life.[76]

While the power of knowledge is limited to the higher, rational beings, love, as we have seen, is common to all existing things. Since love always unites things that are separated, it may be considered the internal principle of some universal, dynamic connection of the world. This conception is developed in Ficino's *De amore*. Love, he says in commenting on the speech of Eryximachus in Plato's *Symposium,* is implanted in all things and extends through all things.

Indeed we consider three grades of things in nature: the higher, the lower, and the equal. The higher things are causes of the lower; the lower are the works of the higher; the equal things have the same nature with regard to each other. The causes love their works as parts and images of themselves. The works strive after the causes as their protectors. Things having their places in the same order are attracted

[72] *Op. om.,* p. 1328; cf. p. 673.   [73] *Ibid.,* p. 861; cf. Dress, *op. cit.,* p. 110.
[74] *Op. om.,* p. 1329.   [75] *Ibid.*
[76] *Ibid.,* pp. 310, 324, 660, 663 f., 889, 1327, *et passim.*

to each other by mutual love, as similar elements of the same whole. Therefore, God guides and governs the angels, the angels, along with God, guide and govern the Souls, the Soul, along with them, the bodies, with some benevolence. Here the love of the higher things for the lower becomes clear. Again, the bodies are most willingly united to their Souls and most unwillingly separated from them. Our Souls desire the felicity of the celestial beings. The celestials happily revere the majesty of the highest divinity. And here the love of the lower things for the higher appears. Likewise, all parts of the fire willingly cling together and also the parts of earth, of water, and of air. In each species of animals those of the same species always attract each other in mutual intercourse, evidence of the love for equal and similar things. There can be no doubt that all things have an innate love for all things. This is what Dionysius the Areopagite meant when, following the thought of Hierotheus, he said in his *De divinis nominibus:* Love, either divine or angelic or spiritual or animal or natural, we conceive as an innate and uniting force that drives the higher things to care for the lower ones, the equal things to some special communion with each other, and finally induces all lower things to turn toward the better and higher ones.[77]

The terms "higher," "lower," and "equal" merely mean the three-fold division of the world in its hierarchical order (cf. above, Chapter VI), and the threefold love is really a single power that draws everything to all others, thus preserving the construction of the universe from decay.

All parts of the world [Ficino concludes] are works of one artist and members of one structure which are similar to each other in their being and life. They are therefore connected with each other by a mutual love, and so love may well be called the perpetual bond (*nodus*) and juncture (*copula*) of the world, the immobile pillar of its parts and of the whole, and the firm foundation of the whole structure.[78]

The doctrine of the threefold love reminds us of a well-known and significant passage in Goethe's *Wanderjahre*. In his description of the pedagogical province Goethe says that a threefold ven-

[77] *Ibid.,* pp. 1328 f.; cf. p. 1070 and *Suppl.,* II, 168.
[78] *Op. om.,* p. 1330. Cf. Cassirer, *Individuum,* p. 140 f.; Saitta, *op. cit.,* pp. 245 f., 248 f.; Dress, *op. cit.,* p. 102; Semprini, *I platonici italiani,* pp. 54 f., 62 f.

eration is taught the boys as the essential gift of education: a veneration for what is above us, for what is equal to us, and for what is beneath us.[79] The application of the concept in Goethe is entirely different from that in Ficino, it is true, but the similarity of expression can hardly be considered incidental. We must keep particularly in mind the fact that the distinction between higher, lower, and equal no longer has any significance in the modern conception of the universe. In Goethe the distinction springs from a vague intuition, whereas in Ficino it comes directly from the strict hierarchical order of Being. It is by no means impossible that Goethe owed his inspiration to Ficino. He was not acquainted with Ficino's original philosophical writings, to be sure. But we know that Goethe used Ficino's Latin translation in reading Plotinus, and he may have done the same in reading Plato. The *De amore* is included in all the editions of Ficino's translation of Plato. We may therefore suspect that Goethe at least noticed the suggestive passage. In any case it would not be the first time that Ficino's intellectual influence, like that of Plotinus, was hidden behind the name and authority of Plato.[80]

Through the theory of universal love, Ficino gives the concept of humanity which is characteristic of the moral thought of the Renaissance a new interpretation. The term "humanity" (*humanitas*) occurs with two different meanings, indicating respectively the essence of man as a natural species and human love as a moral quality that has to do with man's relation to other men.[81] There is always an inner connection between these two meanings. Anyone who is in the habit of considering the things that are common to all men by their nature will also be inclined to treat his equals as men—in other words, in a humane manner. In Ficino this connection is given a more profound and exact motivation. The virtue of humanity is nothing but the love of men for men, in other

[79] Goethe, *Wanderjahre,* Lib. II, ch. i.

[80] Cf. St. Augustine: *De doctrina Christiana,* I. 23, a passage which may have been the direct model for Ficino, but not for Goethe.

[81] For the first meaning see *Op. om.,* pp. 140, 148, 255, 339; for the second meaning see pp. 735, 748, 797, 805, respectively. Cf. Dress, *op. cit.,* pp. 121 f.

words, the universal love of equal for equal applied particularly to humanity as one of the natural species and grades of the universal order. The more a man loves others as equals, the more he proves himself a member of the whole species, the more perfectly he expresses the essence of humanity, the more humane he is. And the more cruel and inhumane a man is, the more he removes himself from the essence and community of his species, finally arriving at a point at which he is a man by name only.

Why are boys crueler than old men? [Ficino writes to Tommaso Minerbetti.] Insane men crueler than intelligent men? Dull men crueler than the ingenious? Because they are, so to speak, less men than the others. Therefore the cruel men are called inhumane and brutal. In general those who are far removed from the perfect nature of man by a fault of age, a vice of the soul, a sickness of the body, or by an inimical position of the stars hate and neglect the human species as something foreign and alien. Nero was, so to speak, not a man, but a monster, being akin to man only by his skin. Had he really been a man, he would have loved other men as members of the same body. For as individual men are under one Idea and in one species, they are like one man. Therefore, I think, among all the virtues the sages called by the name of man himself only that virtue that loves and helps all men as brothers deriving in a long series from one father, in other words, humanity.[82]

In another letter, quoted above, we read:

He who is mostly inclined to love men is, among all, most like to the Idea of the human species according to which the divine artist created men. On the other hand, those who are most alien to love are also most unlike the divine Idea and farthest removed from the human species.[83]

Since the theory of love as connecting all things has an important place in the *De amore*, we may be surprised not to find it at all in the *Theologia Platonica*, which was written some years later. This omission may be explained by the fact that the theory of love would not be compatible with the theory of Soul as de-

[82] *Op. om.*, p. 635. Cf. Galli, *Lo stato*, p. 25; Saitta, *op. cit.*, pp. 156 f.; Cassirer, *Individuum*, p. 75; Corsano, *Il Pensiero religioso italiano*, pp. 6 f.
[83] *Op. om.*, p. 861.

veloped in the *Theologia*. Soul, in its connecting power and in its effect in the world, has taken the place of love and is characterized in almost the same words that characterized love, "bond and juncture of the universe." [84] This is not only a casual word-borrowing; on the contrary, the Soul appears in the same context as the bearer of a twofold love, which is directed upward and downward and is thus comprehensive. With perfect coherence the Soul has absorbed the attributes of the all-comprehensive love as its own new and independent qualities.[85] After discussing the position of the Soul in the center of the world Ficino continues,

If the Soul agrees with both [that is with the higher and the lower beings], it also desires both. In other words, by a natural instinct it ascends to the higher beings and descends to the lower. In ascending it does not leave the lower things, and in descending it does not leave the higher things. For if it should leave one of them, it would be inclined to the other extreme and no longer be the true juncture of the world.[86]

Though the principle of affinity first determined only the mutual relationship of two objects, further consideration led, as we have seen, to the assumption of a particular bearer of the relation which, as "bond," occupied an independent place between the other things and by its force brought them to a vital connection. The result is a new conception of the ontological medium: in other words, the middle term no longer reconciles the extremes by its objective qualities alone, but by some movement in both directions, thus transferring the effects from one extreme to the other. In his theory of the so-called "spirit" Ficino gives a clear example of this conception. According to older medical doctrines, spirit is conceived as an invisible constituent of the human body and defined as a fine lucid stuff generated by the warmth of the heart out of the finest part of the blood and from there spread throughout the whole body. This spirit is characterized as the bond and

[84] *Op. om.*, p. 121; cf. p. 1330.
[85] Cf. Dress, *op. cit.*, p. 52; Hak, *op. cit.*, p. 93.
[86] *Op. om.*, p. 119; cf. p. 219. See also Cassirer, *Individuum*, pp. 68 f.; Horbert, *op. cit.*, p. 14.

medium between the body and the Soul. Its essential tasks are to communicate life and movement to the body and, conversely, to convey the perceptions of the senses to the Soul.[87] Somewhat similar is the function assigned to light in relation to celestial and earthly things.

So strong is the power of light [says Ficino in the *De lumine*] that it connects celestial things easily and in one moment with earthly things from which they are otherwise far removed beyond all proportion. Not only does it transport the forces of the stars to the following things, but it brings the sun and the stars themselves to the lower beings, just as our spirit brings the forces of the Soul and the Soul itself to the humors and members. And as in us the spirit is the bond [connecting link] of Soul and body, so the light is the bond of the universe (*vinculum universi*).[88]

The same conception is also applied to the human Soul in its relation to eternal and temporal things. As light is the dynamic medium connecting all in the spatial world, so is the Soul in the whole order of Being, and hence it may be compared with light. Light, Ficino once says, following Plotinus, passes from the sun into the air. It gives clarity and warmth to the air, but is not separated from the sun and is even reflected into it.

In a similar way the Soul of man is sent from God to matter, penetrates it in one moment, but does not leave God. It does both at the same time, directing the body and, through intellect, attaining the truth of all things, namely, God. . . . Again, as light is reflected into the sun, so the Soul is reflected to God through its will, desiring always the goodness of all things, God.[89]

The same comparison, and with it the same concept, also occurs in the important third book of the *Theologia,* which we have had occasion to quote many times. After comparing the orders of Being with the four elements, Ficino continues:

The Soul does the same as the light of the sun. The light descends from the sun to the fire and fills the fire without leaving the sun. It always

---

[87] *Op. om.,* pp. 177, 211; cf. Saitta, *op. cit.,* p. 188.
[88] *Op. om.,* p. 981; cf. Saitta, *op. cit.,* p. 130.   [89] *Op. om.,* p. 338.

adheres to the sun and always fills the fire. It perfects the air and is not infected, whereas the air is infected. In a like manner, the third substance [the Soul] must be attached to divine things and at the same time fill mortal things. While it adheres to the divine things, it knows them, because it is spiritually united with them and spiritual union produces knowledge. While it fills the bodies, moving them from within, it animates them. So it [Soul] is the mirror of the divine, the life of the mortal and the connecting link between both.[90]

In our analysis of any type of ontological relation the human Soul has always appeared as the carrier of the relation. We may therefore suppose that the human Soul is by nature an entity that is capable of all relations with all things. This conception is largely developed in the fourteenth book of the *Theologia*. Though the question of the unity of the world and the central position of the Soul are not particularly emphasized in this context, the ontological importance of man is conceived from another point of view, giving new justification to a number of concepts we have already met. In this section Ficino tries to demonstrate the admirable greatness of the Soul, showing that in all ways the Soul desires to become God. As a guide to this consideration he introduces twelve principal attributes of God, proving the excellence and dignity of the Soul by its imitation of these attributes. The first five attributes are most interesting for our purpose, because in them the Soul's relation to the whole universe becomes fully apparent. God is the first truth and the first goodness. He is all things, author of all, above all, and in all.[91] The imitation of the first attribute means that by nature the Soul searches all truth and desires all good.[92] In other words, the whole sphere of Being is the original object of the Soul's thinking and willing. This fact has more than incidental significance, since it demonstrates the divine dignity of the Soul and its universal power. The same concept is again expressed in connection with the second attribute of God: because

---

[90] *Op. om.*, p. 119. Cf. Saitta, *op. cit.*, pp. 110 ff.; Cassirer, *Individuum*, pp. 68 f. Hak is not correct in asserting that the Soul is the middle between God and the world (Hak, *op. cit.*, p. 94).

[91] *Op. om.*, p. 305.   [92] *Ibid.*, p. 307.

the Soul is directed toward all truth and all good, and because in
thinking and willing it attains some unity with its objects, it (the
Soul) strives to become absolutely all, as God is all from all time.[93]
In this, Ficino at least indicates the unity given to things through
the thought and love of the human Soul. He also mentions incidentally [94] the position of the Soul between the higher and the
lower entities. However, the universal power of the Soul is not
limited to its thinking and willing. It also appears in the practical
conduct of man, which repeats, in its various forms and grades,
the life of all the other beings as in an image. In a discussion of
the second attribute of God we read that the Soul tries "marvel-
ously" to become all.

It lives the life of the plant when it yields to the body by abundant
nourishing; the life of the beast when it flatters the senses; the life of
man when it reflects through its reason on human affairs; that of heroes
when it inquires into natural things; that of demons when it considers mathematics; that of angels when it contemplates the divine
mysteries; that of God when it does all for God's sake. Each man's Soul
experiences in some way all these possibilities in itself, but different
Souls in different ways. And so the human species strives to become
all things by living the lives of all things. In admiration of that fact,
Mercurius Trismegistus says that man is a great miracle. . . .[95]

This analogy between the forms of human life and the grades of
Being is more than an empty metaphor. It is the necessary instrument for an allegorical interpretation of Plato's tales of the transmigration of Souls, the literal sense of which could not be reconciled with Christian dogma. Wherever Plato seems to speak of a
transmigration of the human Soul into other natural species, we
must understand by it the different forms and habits of human
life.[96] Ficino then goes on to describe how the Soul endeavors to
produce all, to dominate all, and to penetrate all.[97] The universal

[93] *Ibid.*, pp. 310 f.   [94] *Ibid.*, p. 310.
[95] *Op. om.*, pp. 309 f. Cf. Saitta, *op. cit.*, pp. 160 f.; Dress, *op. cit.*, pp.
54 ff.
[96] *Op. om.*, p. 395; cf. p. 275. See also Dress, *op. cit.*, p. 54.
[97] *Op. om.*, p. 311; cf. Saitta, *op. cit.*, pp. 162 ff.

character of the Soul is clearly emphasized here, but a more exact description of its individual qualities is found in a preceding passage in the thirteenth book, to which Ficino refers.[98] In that passage Ficino explicitly describes the different arts and faculties of man in order to prove the superiority of the Soul over all bodies and hence its divinity and immortality.[99] He demonstrates first how man invents innumerable arts, copying or perfecting the works of nature by their help. Man treats all stuffs, uses all elements, and even ascends beyond the heaven with his mind. All animals are subject to his command, and as head of the family or of the state he is able to direct his equals toward the good. Finally, when he understands the laws of the universe by his thought, he proves himself as an equal and worthy companion of the divine creator.

Not everybody can understand the artistic work of a clever artist in the manner of its composition, but only he who possesses the same artistic genius (*ingenium*). For nobody, unless he were endowed with a similar genius, could comprehend how Archimedes constructed the iron spheres and communicated to them movements similar to the celestial movements. And he who by the similarity of his genius does distinguish it would also be able to construct the same spheres, after understanding them, if he did not lack the matter. Since man has understood the order of the celestial spheres—from whence they are moved, where and in what measure they proceed, what they produce—who can deny that he is nearly of the same genius as the author of the spheres and that he could, in a certain sense, make the heavens if he could obtain the instruments and the celestial matter? Because now he is able to produce them, though of a different matter, but in a similar order.[100]

If we try to survey all the theories hitherto described, we notice that they are all directed toward one common goal: the Soul is the center of the world—static and yet at the same time mobile—connecting all existing things into a unity. This result may be

[98] *Op. om.*, p. 311.   [99] *Ibid.*, pp. 295 ff.
[100] *Ibid.*, p. 297. Cf. Gentile, *Giordano Bruno*, pp. 141 ff.; Saitta, *op. cit.*, pp. 173 ff.; Cassirer, *Individuum*, p. 101; Dress, *op. cit.*, pp. 79 ff. Nygren (*op. cit.*, pp. 454 ff.) gives a somewhat exaggerated account of Ficino's "anthropocentrism."

considered from two different aspects. Since the rank of the Soul is evidently established at the outset, we may first ask what the human Soul means at all and why it can be considered the center of the world. The discussion of this question belongs to the sphere of theology and hence must be reserved for another context (see below, Chapter XVI). On the other hand, the question of the unity of the world is a problem for ontology. I have attempted to show ontologically how a series of different solutions proceed out of that basic question, and how these different solutions finally converge into the doctrine that the Soul is the center of the universe (as in a cupola), finding in that doctrine their visible conclusion. Therefore all the essential elements that we have analyzed individually can be found in the words with which Ficino concludes his argument about the ontological position of the human Soul:

This is the greatest of all miracles in nature. All other things beneath God are always one single being, but the Soul is all things together. It possesses the images of the divine things on which it depends itself and the concepts and originals of the lower things which in a certain sense it produces itself. And since it is the center of all things, it has the forces of all. Hence, it passes into all things. And since it is the true connection of all things, it goes to the one without leaving the others. It goes into an individual thing and always deals with all. Therefore it may be rightly called the center of nature, the middle term of all things, the series of the world, the face of all, the bond and the juncture of the universe.[101]

---

[101] *Op. om.*, p. 121. Cf. Saitta, *op. cit.*, pp. 113 f.; Dress, *op. cit.*, pp. 50 f. For two other specific problems connected with this chapter see the appendices at the end of this volume.

VIII

CAUSALITY

THE QUESTION of world unity, which we have just treated, apparently finds its definite solution in a universal system of causality in which each thing is active and passive with respect to its relation to other things. In reality modern science, which considers phenomena and their inner laws, maintains the relation of cause and effect as almost the only real relation between things. Similarly ancient philosophy, at least from Aristotle's day, was chiefly concerned with the causes of things, though in a different metaphysical sense. In the conclusive Neoplatonic world system the relation of cause and effect, generating and generated, constitutes one of the essential conditions for the order of reality. For Ficino the causality relation could not assume such a universal significance, since for him individual things are directly related to God, according to the doctrine of creation, and hence exist before any mutual causal influence. However, he tries to understand the phenomena of causality and generation within the limits of the theory of creation and on the basis of objective substantial existence. It is therefore important for the understanding of his system to give a comprehensive analysis of his respective doctrines, although a great part of them are borrowed from the Neoplatonists and the different theories are not really combined into one single system.

As in many other cases, so with regard to the doctrine of causality Aristotle has had a strong influence on the later tradition. He distinguishes, as we know, four types of causes: matter, form, end, and origin of movement, having arrived at this distinction mainly by determining what conditions contribute to the genesis of a corporeal object.[1] Aristotle's distinction is always recognizable in

[1] Cf. *Phys*. ii. 3 ff.; and *Metaph*. i. 3.

Ficino, but it is expressed only once within the argument. When Ficino proves that the Soul is independent from matter, he states that natural bodies depend on four causes and so are conditioned by other things in every respect. God, on the contrary, exists by Himself in every respect and excludes all four types of cause. Between these two extremes there must be intermediary degrees which, through their attributes, reconcile the contrast between God and Body, with the reservation that the independence from a higher principle and end must belong to God alone. So Quality, which in the hierarchy of substances follows immediately after body, no longer depends on four causes, but on three, being itself a kind of form and requiring no formal cause. Above Quality there is Soul. Soul does not depend on matter and is therefore determined by two causes only: end and principle. Finally, the Angel is distinct from the Soul because it is next to God and has no tendency at all toward matter.[2] This consideration is characteristic of Ficino's thinking. He realizes that Aristotle's distinction of causes is based on the effect produced, especially on the natural body, and that therefore it cannot be transferred to incorporeal entities. However, he does not abandon the distinction and even attempts to construct a homogeneous gradation in the series of five substances with its help: Body has four causes; Quality three; Soul two; God none. The continuity of the series would now require that the Angel depend on one cause. Such a development of the theory is excluded by the doctrine of creation, according to which God is the principle and end of all things. Consequently the Angel must depend on two causes, as does the Soul, and the difference between those two substances must be determined by some other attribute.

Alongside the Aristotelian scheme of four causes we sometimes find another distinction according to three causes: efficient, final, and exemplar causes. This distinction, which goes back to the so-called "middle Platonism," still corresponds to Aristotle's view of the problem. The exemplar cause, the only new element in it, is in reality nothing but an attempt to include the Platonic Idea

[2] *Op. om.,* p. 138.

among the conditions of corporeal objects. In Ficino this theory has almost lost its original meaning under the influence of the doctrine of creation. Ficino simply defines God as efficient cause, end, and exemplar of the world, and the three kinds of objective causes are mere aspects of the divine essence.[3]

So far we have been discussing the case in which different causes correspond to a given effect. There is another distinction, however, also traditional, that has to do with the various methods of possible actions of a given cause. An object acts either through choice or reason, or through its nature or substantial potency, or finally through its sheer being. The first attitude is peculiar to the human Soul; the second is peculiar to all corporeal things and their qualities; the third is peculiar to God.[4] When Ficino compares the action of the Soul with that of corporeal substances, at first glance the latter seems to be superior, since it is achieved without fatigue and occurs more generally in the realm of things.[5] But from another and no-less-important point of view the action of the Soul is more perfect, because it acts freely, whereas the corporeal substance acts from necessity. Moreover, while the action of a quality or of an animal always produces one homogeneous effect, the action of the Soul is capable of producing varied and even opposite effects.[6] If an absolutely perfect action belongs to God, it must combine the advantages of the activities of the Soul and of the natural bodies. Consequently God is called both free and necessary.[7] And if God's action does not come from mere choice or reason, such an action involving fatigue and effort,[8] it cannot be derived from natural force either, because God's action produces diversified effects.[9] Therefore, God acts out of His mere existence, but in this existence reason and will and the whole fullness of objective attributes are included.[10]

In the above considerations Ficino has attempted to distinguish different kinds of causality and activity with the help of tradi-

---

[3] *Op. om.,* p. 437; cf. pp. 397, 1440.   [4] Cf. *Op. om.,* p. 102.
[5] *Ibid.,* p. 102.   [6] Cf. *ibid.,* pp. 127, 167 f., 207, *et passim.*
[7] *Ibid.,* pp. 108 ff.   [8] *Ibid.,* p. 102.
[9] *Ibid.,* p. 106.   [10] Cf. *ibid.,* pp. 105 ff.

tional divisions, but he also proceeds to interpret directly and comprehensively the phenomenon of action itself. The central concept is that of action (*operatio, actio*), and for its interpretation we must again start from the triad *essentia, virtus,* and *operatio* which we have already mentioned (see above, Chapter III). This triad does not express a different sort of attitude, but simply a series of connected factors.[11] *Essentia* forms the beginning of the series. This means that action does not exist by itself, but proceeds from a pre-existing substance and in this way belongs to the sphere of substantial things. In consequence, the action of each thing must correspond to its essence, and the kind of action is always determined by the particular kind of being.[12] The *essentia* is followed by *virtus* as second element. In one place Ficino states that a thing that is not God acts, not directly through its substance, but through an active force which must be called "quality" or "attribute."[13] The acting force is therefore related to action as potency is to act, being intrinsic to the substance of the thing as a determining quality. This identification of force and quality should be kept in mind in the further development of the doctrine. The factor of *virtus* also indicates that of the three types of activity, action through natural force is decisive for the analysis and conception of action in general. For this reason Ficino calls this activity the most universal and the most widely diffused[14] and chooses the greater number of the examples of objective activity from it. Action itself finally follows after substance and force as the third element, being nothing more than an external manifestation and realization of the substantial force around its own substance. This relation between the three factors is expressed in the oft-repeated principle that each cause achieves its action through some form (*omnis causa per aliquam agit formam*).[15] Here the cause is the objective substance from which action starts, and the form, constituting the middle between the cause and its action, is

---

[11] Cf. *Op. om.,* pp. 148 f., 238, *et passim.*
[12] *Ibid.,* p. 198; cf. pp. 80 f., 211.   [13] *Ibid.,* p. 149.
[14] *Ibid.,* p. 102.   [15] *Ibid.,* p. 105; cf. pp. 81, 103, 208.

equivalent to the force or quality through which the substance proceeds to act. When, for instance, the phenomenon of action is illustrated by the example of heat, the fire corresponds to the substantial cause, the warmth of the fire to the active form which determines the action of the cause and makes it possible.[16]

The phenomenon of action is not limited to the fact that action is intrinsic to a substantial cause, but it is essential that the action transcend the sphere of the cause in order to act upon another thing and so have an effect. The term "action" originally expressed the internal relationship of the act to its underlying substance. An external relationship to other things is neither expressed nor excluded. However, Ficino sometimes distinguishes explicitly between internal action and external action as different species of the same genus.[17] The examples, knowledge and heat, which he uses in that context make it quite clear that on the basis of such a distinction only the concept of external action is used for the analysis of objective activity. In addition Ficino occasionally formulates another conception, according to which the external action proceeds from the internal action, as illumination from lighting.[18] External action and internal action thus are no longer different species of a genus, but simply different elements of a unique process, and the series leading from *essentia* through *virtus* to *operatio* seems to continue in one outward direction to the *actio exterior*. In any case, through the concept of external action, which indicates both the starting point and the direction, a bridge is made from the acting cause to the other things. Hence for the first time we can seek the external correlate of substantial action. This external correlate is first expressed in the term *obiectum* which is sometimes added as the fourth element to the series *essentia, virtus,* and *operatio* and may be applied, as we have seen, even to the "internal" action of thinking.[19] But when Ficino says that the action seeks the object,[20] he merely indicates a general relationship, and the real action of the cause upon the external object remains un-

---

[16] *Ibid.,* p. 208.   [17] *Ibid.,* p. 148; cf. chap. iii, above.   [18] *Ibid.,* p. 250.
[19] *Ibid.,* p. 258; cf. chap. iv, above.   [20] *Ibid.*

determined. The proper correlate of cause and its action is the object only in so far as it has already undergone and received the action. This is usually called "work" (*opus*) or "effect." [21] With that concept of work the process of action, which starts with the acting substance, is completed. Thus we read in a passage quoted above that the work proceeds from the action, the illuminated thing from illumination.[22] Here the light which is derived from the external action of illumination and from the internal action of lighting has become an inseparable element of the illuminated object, that is, of the work, and the question as to what this external thing was before it was light is not raised. On rare occasions Ficino attempts to answer this question, for example, when he says that the external action passes into an external or foreign matter.[23] This is not a reference to the first matter, but in so far as the action is equivalent to a formation, the external object that precedes this form must appear relatively as matter.

Having distinguished the individual elements in the process of action, we must now inquire into the relationship between cause and effect. This relationship is essentially defined by the concept of participation. The concept of participation goes back to Plato. In his works it indicates the relation of the spatial things to Ideas. When two lines are called equal, they are so called because of their participation ($\mu \acute{\epsilon} \theta \epsilon \xi \iota s$) in the equal as such, that is, in the Idea of equality. Even in this case participation is not conceived as a merely logical relationship, but the ontological relationship here envisaged is primarily expressed in predication and not otherwise defined in itself. In middle and Neoplatonism only, where Plato's "Idea" is combined with Aristotle's "immanent form," does the concept of participation assume a more concrete significance. According to this conception, which is shared by Ficino, the form within things is derived from the form above things—in other words, the Idea—through participation or similarity, since the Idea communicates itself to the individual things and is the cause

---

[21] Cf. *ibid.*, pp. 105, 106, *et passim.*   [22] *Ibid.*, p. 250.
[23] *Ibid.*, p. 103; cf. p. 81.

of the intrinsic form.[24] Here participation in the Ideas is clearly understood as substantial causality. The concept of participation may therefore be separated from the theory of Ideas and transferred to all other causal relations. When Ficino says that in contrast to fire, wood is warm by participation,[25] he means that through its own warmth the wood participates in the warmth of the fire. This corresponds to the fact that the fire warms all things, that is, by its own nature produces the effect of warmth in them.[26] We see, therefore, that participation corresponds to the element of form, or quality.[27] When Ficino states that the communicated quality emanates everywhere from the absolute quality,[28] the process seems almost like a sort of material communication. However, we must examine the conditions under which the participation of a quality actually takes place.

It would be an easy matter to assume that a thing, participating in a certain form, itself made other things participate in it. This would mean that all the effects would also be causes under another aspect and would therefore form a continual causal series—a logical conception frequently expressed by Ficino.[29] But since Plato's day the concept of participation has involved the axiom that many things participate in one cause only. Ficino therefore formulates the doctrine of objective causality in such a way that many effects and secondary causes participate in one primary cause.

Each thing having a certain quality must be referred to a nature that really determines itself (*suimet agitatricem*). So the Soul really (*proprie*) is moved by itself if by participating in it other things receive the power of being moved by themselves in a certain way. . . . One must arrive at an essence which is the source and receptacle of movement and life as one arrives at some essence which is the root and foundation of light and warmth.[30]

Soul, sun, and fire appear as the active causes in which all other things participate in so far as they move, shine, or are warm.

---

[24] *Ibid.*, p. 183; cf. p. 247.   [25] *Ibid.*, p. 90.
[26] Cf. *ibid.*, p. 106.   [27] Cf. *ibid.*, pp. 81, 105.
[28] *Ibid.*, p. 202 (*manare, effluere*).   [29] Cf. *ibid.*, pp. 95, 221, *et passim.*
[30] *Ibid.*, p. 169.

The result, therefore, is an essential difference between the quality of the acting cause and the same quality as found in the participating things: the latter is communicated and therefore mixed with other elements; the former, on the other hand, is absolute and infinite so that it is never exhausted by its communication to other things.[31] It is clear that this difference has nothing to do with the content of the quality, but only with the manner of its inherence. Therefore it obviously coincides with another difference mentioned at the beginning of our study—the difference between the proper qualities of the substance, which are connected with it from the beginning, and the common qualities that are added to it afterward and not of necessity.[32] For example, for fire warmth is a proper quality of the substance and is contained in the concept of its essence, while for wood on the other hand, warmth is merely a common or contingent quality, produced in it by the action of fire or by its own participation in the warmth of the fire. The difference is sometimes described in the following manner: a thing possesses a certain quality, either by itself or through another thing; here the indicated relation becomes even more obvious. We read, for example, that the Soul does not live through another thing, but is life in itself (*per se*). "Thus the essence of the Soul is life. A sign of that is that the Soul brings life to whatever it approaches, as if the Soul were by itself that which it gives to something else." [33]

Anything that belongs to a thing by itself is never separated from it. Roundness is intrinsic to the circle by its nature; therefore no circle is ever without roundness. But roundness is occasionally intrinsic to wood, not because it is wood, otherwise all wood would be round, but because the wood receives circular form which is accompanied by roundness from the artist, and so is forced to receive roundness. The wood ceases to be round as soon as it ceases to be circular. Afterwards it remains wood, but not round. But the circular figure is round of necessity to such a degree that if it ceases to be round, it ceases also to

[31] Cf. *ibid.*, pp. 202, 1354 f.
[32] *Ibid.*, p. 107, and above, chap. iii; cf. pp. 205, 236.
[33] *Ibid.*, p. 150.

be circular. In like manner warmth belongs to fire by itself; humidity to water; light to the sun.[34]

The roundness of the circle and that of the wood are therefore related to each other as cause and effect, because the roundness is included in the nature of the circle as a proper quality of its substance, while it is added to the nature of the wood merely as a contingent quality. In the concept of being-by-itself there are two different elements. On the one hand, substance exists by itself in opposition to attribute;[35] on the other, anything that exists without cause exists by itself, whereas anything that owes its existence to a cause exists through another thing.[36] Both meanings are combined in the particular concept of absolute quality which is inseparably connected with, and almost identical to, substance, and on the other hand, may become the cause for the participating things, for the very reason that in itself it is not dependent on any higher cause. This does not mean that absolute quality is entirely free from any exterior cause. According to Aristotle, the concept of cause may be understood in four different ways. Hence, beginning with the level of Quality, all things exist by themselves as formal causes, but being-by-itself, as effective or acting cause, is reserved to God alone.[37] Ficino expresses the same idea elsewhere in different terms, when he says that the Soul also exists in itself, but that God alone exists from Himself (*in se, a se*).[38] Being-by-itself of the absolute quality must therefore be interpreted merely in terms of the formal cause. This fact is emphasized by Ficino to avoid any misunderstanding. He says that the mind exists by itself and is therefore cause of itself: "I say not effective, but formal cause, through whose power existence is given and preserved."[39] Elsewhere Ficino says that the Soul must be called life by itself, at least in its form (*certe secundum formam*).[40] In other words, the roundness of the circle, the warmth of the fire, and the life of the Soul do not exist by themselves in an absolute sense, but are

---

[34] *Ibid.*, p. 142; cf. Thomas, *Summa contra Gentiles*, II, 55.
[35] *Ibid.*, p. 370.   [36] *Ibid.*, p. 138.   [37] Cf. *ibid.*, p. 138.
[38] *Ibid.*, p. 334.   [39] *Ibid.*, p. 200.   [40] *Ibid.*, p. 150.

created by God like all other things. But once the respective substance has been created, absolute quality is given with it through itself and without the co-operation of any other cause. Consequently, each attribute may be assigned to a thing in a threefold manner: by participation, when the attribute is added afterward to the nature of the thing; by form, that is, in the sense of the formal cause, when it is included from the beginning in the essence of the thing; and, finally, by cause, that is, in the sense of efficient cause in so far as it exists beyond the acting principle, though improperly, in its higher causes.

Rational Souls are intellectual by participation; the angels by form; those reasons and Ideas finally by cause. . . .[41]
Just as the wood is called warm through some participation, but the fire through form, and finally the sun in a higher sense through the eminent power and cause of warmth, so the Soul has part of the mind, the Angel has the form of the mind, and God is the most effective origin of the mind.[42]

So far the external correlate of action has been conceived only in its neutral indefiniteness as matter, and in its complete dependence on the cause as work or effect. But in reality even before it is influenced by the cause, this correlate has its own determination and makes its own contribution, at least negatively, to the process of action and to the work produced. Each action has a corresponding receptivity on the part of the correlate. This negative action originates in a passive potency, just as positive action originates in active force, and, like positive action, it finds its last support in an underlying objective substance.[43] The three factors "essentia," "virtus," and "operatio" ascribed to the active force have thus their analogy in the analysis of passivity, and while it was asserted that the kind of action is determined by the kind of existence (see above),[44] it is now stated analogously that the kind of receiving corresponds to the previous existence of the thing.[45] This concep-

---

[41] *Ibid.,* p. 248.
[43] Cf. *ibid.,* p. 221.
[45] Cf. *ibid.,* pp. 198, 282.

[42] *Ibid.,* p. 90.
[44] Cf. *ibid.,* p. 198.

tion leads to the important and oft-repeated axiom that the degree of effective action depends on the capacity of the receiving substance.

Whatever is received by something is usually received according to the capacity of the receiving thing and is transferred to its peculiar essence.[46]
Whatever force receives something, does so according to its own nature and transfers it to its own essence.[47]
Whatever is received by something passes into the nature of the receiving thing.[48]

This axiom is already indicated by Aristotle and Plotinus.[49] If we consider that Ficino uses the terms "receiving" (*capere*) and "suffering" (*pati*) almost interchangeably [50] and that he calls the "passive intellect" of Aristotle the "receiving intellect" (*intellectus capax*),[51] we see that that axiom clearly expresses the influence of the passive substance on the effect produced. This influence of the passive substance first appears as a negative factor limiting the influence of the active cause, as indicated in the concept of participation and more clearly expressed in the proposition that an effect can never receive the whole good of the cause.[52] But it is logical to search for the cause of this negativity not only in an undetermined impotence but also in a determinate and actual quality of the receiving substance. When fire, for example, heats different materials to different degrees, such a divergence is caused, not by the fire and its warmth, but only by the various dispositions of the respective materials.[53] If we conceive of the process of action as a communication of an objective quality, it is easy to explain the limitation of action in the receiving substance by the existence of another quality opposed to the first. For it is peculiar to each opposite thing that it has no power to receive its opposite.[54] Moreover, the opposition of contrasts has its source in the realm of qualities.[55]

[46] *Ibid.*, p. 140. [47] *Ibid.*, p. 703. [48] *Ibid.*, p. 260.
[49] *Enn.* ii, 3. 11. [50] *Op. om.*, p. 221. [51] *Ibid.*, p. 240.
[52] *Ibid.*, p. 1340. [53] *Ibid.*, p. 106. [54] *Ibid.*, p. 146.
[55] *Ibid.*, p. 80.

Consequently, a passive substance will receive all the more of an active quality, the less it originally contained of the opposite quality.[56] In particular, a substance that carries with it a certain quality as necessary attribute of its own essence, that is, as absolute quality, cannot receive the opposite quality without losing its own being.[57] That this is actually Ficino's opinion is shown by the following argument: The Soul is life by itself, in other words, natural life and living form.

To life and living form death, or some quality of a death-bringing form, is called contrary in some way, as cold is contrary to warmth, dryness to humidity. But it is the nature of opposite forms that neither one can receive the other, as warmth does not receive cold. Nor does the substance to which one of those forms is peculiar receive another form contrary to its own form, as fire, to which warmth is peculiar, does not receive cold in such a way that it is at the same time fire and cold; but instead of becoming cold, warmth and fire leave or perish at the arrival of cold. Each of them is, so to speak, incapable of cold, as it cannot participate in cold. Likewise the Soul, since it either is natural life itself or has life for its natural accompaniment, cannot admit death, inasmuch as it is its opposite, as I have said. If Soul does not admit death, it is immortal just as fire, not receiving cold, is incapable of cold.[58]

Hence the absolute quality cannot have a part in its opposite, whereas each communicated quality is mingled with its opposite and therefore subject to the influence of the receiving substance.[59]

The process of action presupposes not only a substantial cause but also, as we have seen, a passive correlate of a determinate essence and quality. Action therefore appears as a secondary phenomenon in a world of pre-existing objects. The real genesis of things, at which the problem of cause originally aimed, is not indicated here and seems sufficiently accounted for by the theory of creationism. Ficino, however, makes a novel attempt to apply the theory of action to the genesis of things, so giving a specific content to creationism. As all genesis implies an acceptance of Be-

---

[56] Cf. *ibid.*, p. 93.
[57] Cf. *ibid.*, p. 146.
[58] *Ibid.*, p. 150.
[59] Cf. *ibid.*, p. 93.

ing and as Being is conceived as a quality of things, all those attributes, therefore, first observed in the process of qualitative action may now be applied to the very Being or existence of things. Being, as we have seen above, has the character of a highest genus and is common to all things.[60] All other attributes of things are therefore included, as mere particulars, in the general predicate of Being and if each specific quality intrinsic to a thing is produced in it by the action of a cause, the existence of things also is not simply given, but is communicated to them by some action and is therefore said to be the effect common to all. Moreover, if each particular quality ultimately depends on one active cause, for example, warmth on fire, Being must also be referred to one active cause, in other words, to God. And as Being includes all other attributes or effects, so all specific causes are dependent on God, the most universal cause. God and Being are therefore basically related to each other in the same way as fire and warmth or cause and effect and are distinguished from other relations of that kind only by the character of universality.

The first of all effects is Being, for the other effects are nothing but determinations and qualifications of Being. For each thing by nature first exists, then it has such and such a quality. . . . Being itself is therefore the proper effect of that active cause which is the beginning and end of all things, that is, of God.[61]

We must refer the proper effects to the proper causes, and anything that is found to be common to all proper effects, to a common cause of all things. Since Being itself is found in all things as common to all besides the proper conditions of each, we must indicate individual causes for individual conditions and qualities, but one cause common to all for Being itself, which alone is common to all. The cause common to all things is God Himself. God therefore is really the cause of Being, but other causes outside God account for a thing being this or that and having such or such a quality. Hence you have from God alone that you are, from man that you are a man, and from fire that you are warm.[62]

[60] Cf. above, chap. iii.   [61] *Op. om.*, p. 102.

[62] *Ibid.*, p. 147. Cf. Thomas, *Summa contra Gentiles*, II, 21; Anichini, *op. cit.*, p. 141; Dress, *op. cit.*, p. 131.

Once the relationship between Being and God is conceived as a qualitative action, a further development of the doctrine is indicated. The process of action is again divided into the elements of substance, force, and action and finds its completion in the external work or effect. In all these aspects the specific character of the higher and universal is maintained. The other active causes,

being inferior and of narrower range, do nothing but distinguish everywhere with the help of God that universal force and action of God that always tends toward universal Being, and they introduce modifications of Being rather than the nature of Being.[63]

As [the other causes] necessarily base their effects on the effect of the first cause, so they base their forces and actions on its force and action.[64]

Furthermore, Being in things has the character of a communicated quality, and therefore by participation it has its source in an absolute Being, which, as absolute quality, is of God Himself and coincides directly with the concept of Him. Consequently God is "the absolute Being . . . itself, in other words, pure act, cause of all existing things." [65] It is peculiar to God "to grant all things common and absolute Being itself." [66]

Whatever participates in a nature cannot produce that nature in its absoluteness, for whatever has a certain quality through participation necessarily follows that which has that quality in its absoluteness or, indeed, is whatever it is through that nature and therefore cannot produce it. . . .

But since in respect to the nature of Being each thing beneath God participates in Being and possesses Being, not in its absoluteness, but such Being as is determined by some essence and species, consequently a thing subject to God cannot produce Being itself, but can only grant to a certain matter a certain kind of existence. So it always needs a preceding basis for its effect.[67]

Being, therefore, is contained as a "proper quality of substance" in God alone. Hence it is obvious why God alone exists by Himself under every aspect [68] and why He acts outside through His mere

<hr/>

[63] *Op. om.*, p. 102.   [64] *Ibid.*   [65] *Ibid.*, p. 282.
[66] *Ibid.*, p. 148.   [67] *Ibid.*   [68] *Ibid.*, p. 138.

existence in the same way that natural causes do through their substantial force and quality.[69] As for the external correlate of divine action, the analogy of qualitative action apparently applies no longer. For if Being effected by God underlies all other attributes, it is not clear how that Being can be preceded by any passive potency, in other words, almost by a Being before Being. To be sure, Ficino occasionally emphasizes the fact that the various participations of things in Being are based, not on a difference of the substrata, but exclusively on the active power of God. And in this he sees an essential difference between God and the other, natural causes.[70] At first it appears as though this conception could no longer be reconciled with the basic doctrine of substantial action and that the given premises should lead to an entirely different solution. For as cold is the opposite of warmth, death of life, so Nonbeing is the opposite of Being; here too, therefore, the proposition that one opposite cannot receive the other is valid.[71] Nonbeing, therefore, does not participate in Being, and Being does not participate in Nonbeing.[72] Consequently, if created things participate in Being in different degrees and if they are placed in a continual series between Nothing and the first Being, or God,[73] it would be easy to assert that all things are composed of Being and Nonbeing and that their share in existence, which they receive from God, depends on their previous share in Nonbeing.[74] Though Ficino does not formulate such a solution, it seems to result from his previous conceptions and to correspond perfectly to the theological dogma of creation out of nothing. However, this conception cannot be upheld, at least in the form we have given it, because of the dialectical character of Nonbeing. For all those attributes which perhaps might belong to Nothing in its ontological function can find no hold in it because of its complete nullity. These attributes are therefore necessarily included in the all-comprehensive concept of God. This may explain why the Christian metaphysicians

[69] *Ibid.*, p. 102.   [70] *Ibid.*, p. 106.   [71] *Ibid.*, pp. 145 f.
[72] *Ibid.*, p. 282.   [73] Cf. *ibid.*, pp. 106, 226, 281.
[74] A similar view was taken by Campanella.

do not oppose matter to God as did the ancient philosophers. Instead they oppose to Him impotent Nothing.

Along with the qualitative action, the interpretation of which influenced the conception of action as a whole, a second, different phenomenon of causal process occurs within the realm of nature: organic generation. Whereas the substantial action was originally limited to the task of communicating a certain quality to a pre-existent object, generation seems to produce its "object" in an actual and unlimited sense. But since all things ultimately proceed out of nothing and through God, the process of generation is also bound by the rules and limits of a pre-existent world and cannot be considered the only sufficient cause of the generated animal.[75] Moreover, if we consider that an animal receives its substantial form from the generators, while at the same time it owes its attributes or accidental forms to the action of objective causes, the result is an immediate relationship between the two processes. Consequently, the phenomenon of generation does not receive an interpretation of its own, but is considered, with reservations, merely a particular kind of substantial action. "You have from God alone that you are, from man that you are a man, from the fire that you are warm," says Ficino without making any particular distinction, and the context shows that he merely wants to illustrate the relation of cause and effect by specific examples.[76] The concept of participation and the relationship between absolute and communicated quality is also applied, with some modification, to the process of generation. Just as each thing participating in a quality communicates it to others and is itself dependent on an absolute quality, so the father makes the son participate in the concept of man in which he himself participates and which is ultimately referred to an "absolute humanity," in other words, the Idea of man.[77]

The concept of generation, which is first associated only with the natural animals, is then understood in a larger, ontological sense and applied to the genesis of things in general. This con-

[75] Cf. *Op. om.*, p. 138.   [76] *Ibid.*, p. 147.   [77] Cf. *ibid.*, p. 148.

ception, according to which the inferior substance is always produced or generated by a superior one, was of Neoplatonic origin
and had to be slightly modified to accord with the Christian doctrine of creation. As the result of this transference the phenomenon
of organic generation becomes significant for the conception of
genesis in general. According to the principle of analogy, all those
aspects of generation directly observable in animals must recur in
the higher degrees of generation in the same way or in a similar
way. Thus the concept of organic generation assumes an ontological significance equal to that of qualitative action and in its
content and application cannot always be clearly distinguished
from it. Such an analogical consideration is first expressed in
comparisons and metaphors in which the proper ontological meaning is indicated, but not entirely revealed. In an example quoted
above we read that the Soul loves the body as a mother loves her
child,[78] and on another occasion that God loves His work as a father his son.[79] What is meant is that the Soul has generated the
body and that God has generated the world as His work and that
in consequence they must feel the same love that human parents
feel toward their children. In other cases the consideration of the
organic process at once leads to general ontological statements.
"Since we see that all things perform some act, especially at the
time when they are fully evolved and perfect in their species, we
must declare that as God is the most perfect of all things, He
must not be idle, but must perform some act, since action is a
sign of perfection." [80] In other words, when organic entities are
full grown or fully evolved and so have reached their proper perfection, they are capable of procreating. Consequently, any other
perfect substance, especially God, must arrive at some activity by
itself. Furthermore, experience teaches that children are like their
parents, and from this we derive the general principle that each
effect is similar to its generating or acting cause. Thus the continuity of the causal series is indicated, and of this we shall treat
later in our study. "Everything that performs an act is induced

[78] *Ibid.*, p. 206; cf. chap. vii, above.   [79] *Ibid.*, p. 111.   [80] *Op. om.*, p. 218.

to action by a natural appetite for propagating its own perfection in order that it may procreate another thing as like to itself as possible, a fact that is obvious in the elements, in plants, and in animals." [81] "All things, if they can, beget a descendant similar to themselves in species." [82] "In performing an act each cause has the intention of generating something as like to itself as possible." [83] The additional fact that birth is preceded by pregnancy, the plant by the seed, leads finally to the important principle that each effect first develops within the acting cause before proceeding out of it as an independent entity. "Whatever good or vital act is transferred from the cause to the effect is first developed within the cause. So warmth is first warm and burning within itself before warming another matter, and living bodies swell with germs and conceive embryos in themselves before bringing forth their fruit." [84] This axiom, valid for all active substances, assumes particular significance when it is applied to God who develops within Himself the model world of Ideas before producing the world of real things.

As all things have two acts, an internal act, I say, and an external act, and as the former is equal in life to the acting thing, the latter inferior, it is therefore meet that the creator of things Himself should contain within Himself an embryo equal in life to Himself and should produce outside of Himself an inferior fruit.[85]

This principle is extensively developed at times. In such passages it becomes obvious that though Ficino does not distinguish sharply between organic and qualitative action, he bases his concept chiefly on the organic phenomenon. "All life generates first a descendant within itself before doing so outwardly, and the more excellent a life is, the more intimate to itself is its generated descendant." In describing the way in which each degree of life produces an internal fruit before producing the external fruit and how the union between the life and the fruit becomes closer, the higher the level, Ficino passes from the vegetative life through the sentient, the

[81] *Ibid.*, p. 137.   [82] *Ibid.*, p. 196.   [83] *Ibid.*, p. 682.
[84] *Ibid.*, p. 169.   [85] *Ibid.*, p. 399.

rational, and the angelic to the divine life. The divine life first generates in itself the whole structure of the world as its offspring before bringing it forth outside itself, and is wholly identical with its internal work.[86] Through the concept of internal fruit, therefore, the relation between God and Ideas is clearly determined and a metaphysical interpretation of the trinity is outlined.

The relation of cause and effect which we have analyzed in its different forms and aspects is not found incidentally here and there in the sphere of things, but is clearly related to the order of Being and therefore subject to well-defined rules. As we have seen in the doctrine of hierarchy, a cause is always higher in degree than its effect.[87] This conception, with respect to the qualitative character of action, occasionally leads to the characteristic statement that each cause that acts through its Being forces its effect to have a like quality in the next degree to the one it has itself in the first degree (*talem sequenti gradu facit effectum qualis est ipsa primo*).[88] But another conclusion is even more significant for the ontological system: each graded relation between objects must by its nature be considered as a causal relation. Thus Ficino asserts without any particular justification that each higher degree does something to the lower degree and receives something from the degree that is still higher than itself.[89] He does not say that the lower degree is produced by the higher one, but simply that the one acts and the other receives. In this limited sense the hierarchy of things appears as a continual causal series, in which each member is passive as regards all higher grades and communicates the effects of its own force and substance to all lower grades.[90] Causality therefore becomes an essential and inseparable aspect of the doctrine of hierarchy. Finally the term "anterior" becomes almost equivalent to "superior," and "posterior" to "inferior."[91]

---

[86] *Ibid.*, pp. 18, 251; cf. Saitta, *op. cit.*, p. 147. Hak, *op. cit.*, pp. 95 f., considers this a pantheistic element.

[87] Cf. chap. vi, above.   [88] *Op. om.*, p. 249.   [89] *Ibid.*, p. 95.

[90] Cf. *Op. om.*, pp. 95, 221; Heitzman, "L'agostinismo avicennizzante," *Giorn. crit.* XVI (1935), 297.

[91] Cf. *Op. om.*, p. 90.

A cause always surpasses its effect in point of perfection, therefore conversely a thing never produces anything superior in perfection to itself. "As nothing acts beyond its own grade," says Ficino, "an attribute cannot in any way generate a substance," for the substance is by nature superior to the attribute.[92] The same concept occurs in a discussion on the incorporeity of the Soul.

Nothing acts beyond its own genus. Even those lower things never act outside their species (for a dog never begets a sheep). Much less do they act above their species. For how will a dog procreate a man? In the same way, a body cannot extend its power of action outside its own genus and still less above its own nature. Therefore it will never reach, attain, or produce every kind of body or any incorporeal thing.[93]

As the quoted examples show, this negative formula of the axiom is valid also for the procreation of organisms, though there is no hierarchical relation between cause and effect in the proper sense.

The conception of a comprehensive ontological series of causes and effects entails the necessity not only of tracing the individual effect back to its cause but also of examining the mutual relations of the various causes and of the various effects. We may easily assume a well-defined and homogeneous relation at the outset. Ficino himself clearly states as much. "Do we not set up a hierarchy of causes corresponding to a hierarchy of effects?" he asks, without supplying any further proof.[94] And elsewhere: "For the order of causes is sought in the order of their effects, since effects are congruous with causes."[95] Here the order is still conceived in a fairly abstract sense and treats merely of the difference between anterior and posterior, particular and universal causes or effects. But elsewhere the hierarchical relationship and the connection with the series of Being becomes clear. "Each cause produces its peculiar effect in the order of things, and as the causes surpass each other, so also do the effects."[96] In other words, all causes and likewise all effects, taken together, form two gradated series, and the separate members of the two series correspond the one to the

---

[92] *Ibid.,* p. 122; cf. chap. vi, above.   [93] *Op. om.,* p. 196.
[94] *Ibid.,* p. 102.   [95] *Ibid.,* p. 147.   [96] *Ibid.,* p. 95.

other in a uniform correlation. This correlation is then more clearly defined by the axiom that the sphere of activity of a cause increases in proportion to its rank and includes in a symmetrical progression ever lower and lower grades of reality. ". . . in producing effects the higher cause always extends its powers farther than the lower cause . . ." [97] "Goodness surpasses mind by at least as great an interval as the communication of good reaches farther than that of species. For the more powerful a thing is, the farther its action extends." [98] A similar relationship also exists for the communication of a given objective quality. "The measure of the potency of any agent is the remoteness from actuality of the potency for receiving action which it brings into actuality. For a greater force is needed to warm water than to warm air." [99]

These statements are completed by another dynamic axiom only indirectly connected with the doctrine of hierarchy: that the more intense force implies not only a wider zone of activity, but also a greater unity of the agent-cause itself. "Force is increased by unity, diminished by dispersion," says Ficino at the very beginning of the *Theologia Platonica*.[100] "As there is infinite weakness in the greatest dispersion, so there is infinite power in the greatest unity." [101] "Strength consists in union in the same way as weakness consists in division." [102] This theorem seems to be based on the observation that a powerful effect frequently derives from a very small point, and in fact Ficino refers to the phenomenon of the burning mirror.[103] But he is also undoubtedly influenced by the Neoplatonic doctrine of unity, which explains the connection with the theory of gradation.[104] For an entity has greater unity, the higher a place it holds in the series of things; and in the same measure its active force also increases. Therefore God, as the Supreme Being, has the greatest unity and also an infinite power which can bring even Nothing into being.[105]

[97] *Ibid.* [98] *Ibid.*, p. 91.
[99] *Ibid.*, p. 96; cf. Thomas, *Summa contra Gentiles*, I, 43, and II, 20.
[100] *Op. om.*, p. 80. [101] *Ibid.*, p. 96. [102] *Ibid.*, p. 700.
[103] Cf. *ibid.*, p. 161. [104] Cf. *ibid.*, p. 367. [105] Cf. *ibid.*, pp. 96, 148.

To understand thoroughly the mutual relationship between things we must finally seek a general teleological system of Being in Ficino's work. This concept is somewhat foreign to the modern mind, for modern science has almost eliminated teleology, except from the realm of organic being, or at least denies that it has any force of demonstration. On the other hand, the older philosophical tradition that Ficino followed has almost consistently maintained the teleological method. The end to which an object is directed is also considered as essential cause of each determinate being, and therefore since Aristotle's day it has occupied an established place in the series of causes.

In Ficino the doctrine of ends is closely connected with the basic conception of reality. Since everything that exists partakes of the nature of the created and hence does not exist by itself, the mere existence of a thing does not insure its perpetuity and perfection. Therefore producing and conserving, generating and perfecting, are always differentiated as separate acts.[106] On the other hand, in each case it is the determinate being itself in its content which is being produced and conserved, generated and perfected up to the fullness of its essence. Both acts are therefore simple gradations of one single process, and since they deal with the communication of one content alone the effective cause must always be the same too. "The cause which made the whole [effect] preserves the whole." [107] "It belongs to the same thing to perfect and to effect or the converse." [108]

Moreover, each existing thing is by nature related to itself. And, not being able to generate itself,[109] it tends at least to generate another thing and so to propagate its own essence.[110] But once a thing exists, that thing becomes everywhere and at all times intent on its own preservation. "By a natural instinct and a continual tendency all things preserve themselves as far

---

[106] *Ibid.*, p. 199, *et passim.*
[107] *Ibid.*, p. 101 (*Causa quae fecit totum conservat totum*).
[108] *Ibid.*, pp. 101, 1240; cf. chap. v, above.
[109] Cf. *Op. om.*, p. 148.   [110] *Ibid.*, p. 137, and see above.

as possible and are inherent in themselves." [111] For Ficino this axiom has such an obvious validity that the fact of human suicide, which apparently contradicts it, is even proof to him of the distinction between body and Soul. "What shall we say about that, when a Soul kills its own body . . . ? How could it ever attempt that, if the body were the origin of the Soul, since no appetite in nature can go against nature itself?" [112]

Similarly, each object tends by nature to its own perfection. This perfection, as we have seen, is based on the agent-cause of the object. Consequently each generated being necessarily tends toward its own cause in order to receive from it the perfection of its peculiar essence.

The peculiar end of a thing is its peculiar cause. For there it is perfected, and all things desire natural perfection as their end.[113]

Each appetite is fulfilled by the possession of its cause. For the same thing extinguishes the thirst of the appetite in perfecting that roused it in effecting.[114]

Every effect by natural impulse seeks its cause that it may derive perfection from the source of its being.[115]

The mind is in some way the end of its own action. But the end and the cause of each thing is the same, since all things desire their origin. . . . Consequently the substance of the mind is the cause of its action.[116]

The ultimate end of things is the same as the cause. The cause of the fire is the concavity of the moon, and the concavity of the moon is the end of the movement of the fire. . . . Hence, in an animal the cause of its actions is the nature of the body or the Soul . . . since the end of its action is the preservation of its corporeal nature and life.[117]

Therefore, God being the totality of goodness, He is the end and cause of all other things.[118]

Since the good is the ultimate end, it is also the first cause of all things.[119]

---

[111] *Ibid.*, p. 141.   [112] *Ibid.*, p. 206.   [113] *Ibid.*, p. 235.
[114] *Ibid.*, p. 236.   [115] *Ibid.*, p. 694.
[116] *Ibid.*, pp. 199 f.; cf. *Suppl.*, II, 138.
[117] *Ibid.*, p. 208.   [118] *Ibid.*, pp. 138, 270.   [119] *Ibid.*, p. 271.

The cause and end of the universe are one and the same. This is nothing but the good itself. For if it is the highest cause, certainly all things are made, preserved, perfected, and restored by it; consequently it is the highest good of all things.[120]

As all things are perfected by the good as their end, so they are effected by it as their cause.[121]

The same concept is sometimes expressed in a more dynamic form and one that is even closer to the Neoplatonic theory. "From that place to which the conversion of each thing is directed it also proceeds, and the converse."[122] "Things are converted toward their cause, as well as proceed from it."[123] Through the concepts of proceeding and conversion the individual object is first of all directed to its *causa efficiens* as its beginning and end. But as in Plotinus these terms indicate different aspects and phases of the objective process, so here they hint at a double movement of all things. For if a thing seems to withdraw from its cause in its genesis, it returns to the cause again in the conversion, and, the unilateral movement being therefore completed and balanced everywhere by its opposite movement, the result is, on a small scale and on a large scale, the figure of a universal cycle in which beginning and end coincide and where all being is united into a living unity of action.

This concept has a particular importance when applied to the relationship between God and the other things. If God is the highest cause and end of all things, God as cause produces all things out of Himself and places Himself in advance of the things as their end, so that He seems to return to Himself through the things.

God leads all things toward Himself as to their end. . . . God thus wills Himself; I say He wills Himself as the end of Himself and of all things. From the willing of the end proceeds the action that concerns those things that are directed to the end. Consequently the divine will, as Plato says in the *Timaeus,* is the origin of all creatures.[124] The divine goodness is the last end of God, for whose sake He wills

---

[120] *Ibid.,* p. 1579.   [121] *Ibid.,* p. 101.   [122] *Ibid.,* p. 203; cf. p. 91.
[123] *Ibid.,* p. 236; cf. p. 863.   [124] *Ibid.,* p. 108; cf. Plato Tim. 29 d ff.

whatever He wills. . . . Willing Himself, He wills all other things, which are God Himself as being in God, and as flowing out of God are images of the divine face and have as their end the task of reproducing and confirming the divine goodness.[125]

According to the order of active causes there follows also an order in the ends, for as the highest active cause moves the causes following, so the ends of the remaining causes must be directed to the end of the highest cause. For whatever the first cause does, it does it for the sake of its own end. But the first cause leads and performs all actions of all following causes, moving all according to its own action and therefore toward its own ends. Consequently the ends of all inferior causes are directed by the first cause itself to its own end. The first cause is God. The end of the divine will is His goodness. Consequently all other things are necessarily directed to God as their end.[126]

Considering the same relationship again from the point of view of the things, we find analogously that all things proceed from God as the origin of goodness and return to Him in their tendency toward good.

It is known that all things derive their origin from that place [from the good] as from their father and that all things are directed to that place as to their fatherland.[127]

From that place from which all things come they are moved, and to that place they tend. Hence all desire and action of all things has its source in the good and is directed and reflected to the good.[128]

[All things] act for the sake of the good. Therefore, all action in all things takes place from the good through the good to the good.[129]

The cycle of Being therefore explains the double relationship of all things with the good and at the same time confirms the unity and perfection of the world.[130] This conception therefore touches the center of the whole system. Thus it was not by chance that Ficino began the motto which he composed for the walls of his "Academy" at Careggi with the following words: "All things are directed from the good to the good." [131]

[125] *Op. om.*, p. 110; cf. Saitta, *op. cit.*, pp. 95 f.
[126] *Ibid.*, p. 306; cf. *Suppl.*, II, 139.   [127] *Ibid.*, p. 91.
[128] *Ibid.*, p. 137.   [129] *Ibid.*, p. 100; cf. *Suppl.*, II, 135.
[130] Cf. chaps. v and vii, above.
[131] "A bono in bonum omnia diriguntur" (*Op. om.*, p. 609).

IX

PRIMUM IN ALIQUO GENERE

HAVING REVIEWED the most general premises of Ficino's world system, we are now in a position to consider two particular concepts that also belong to the sphere of ontology: the doctrine of the "primum in aliquo genere" and the doctrine of the "appetitus naturalis." These seem to deserve more detailed consideration because of their peculiar character, as well as because of their frequent occurrence; and inasmuch as almost all the basic motives of Ficino's thought are united and fused in them their interpretation also serves as a test for understanding his entire philosophy.

The concept that every genus possesses a supreme element on which the quality of all the other elements depends, is expressed by Ficino in his early work *De voluptate*.

He asserts [says Ficino, referring to Mercurius Trismegistus] that in all genera of things there is one greatest and highest and that by participating in it the other things are placed in the same genus; as, for instance, all warm things become warm through the nature of fire, to which the greatest warmth is intrinsic, and all good things must be called good because they follow and imitate the highest and first good.[1]

In the late commentary on Plotinus we read a similar passage:

Whatever is first in a genus has no cause in that genus. Thus, in the genus of mobile things that thing which is mobile by itself because it is the first to be mobile has no higher cause through which it is mobile, but has some other through which it is intellectual. In like manner, the first intellect is not properly intellect through a higher cause, but it owes to a higher cause its being one and good.[2]

And in Ficino's chief work, the *Theologia Platonica,* he states the following argument without supplying any proof:

[1] *Op. om.,* p. 991.   [2] *Ibid.,* p. 1673.

The first in every genus is the cause of the whole genus. Whatever is the cause of the other members contains the succeeding members in itself. Whatever, therefore, is first in its genus lacks nothing of its genus. For example, if the sun is the first among the light-bearing things, it does not lack any degree of light. The other light-bearing things below it, like stars and elements, cannot receive the whole fullness of light. Since the first form contains all perfections of forms and so cannot be imperfect, that form which is called imperfect cannot be the first.[3]

To understand the meaning of these propositions we must examine not only the concept of the *primum* itself but also the basic concept of "genus" and the relation between the "particular" and the "universal." But first we must consider the traditional concept of genus which, foreshadowed by Plato and fully developed by Aristotle, has since remained a fixed element in the philosophical tradition.

By "genus" we commonly understand a plurality of particular elements all of which possess a common quality. According to the usual conception, aside from the particular quality which assigns them to the genus, the individual members are unrelated and indifferent to each other. Wherever a more determinate relationship is supposed to exist between some of them—for example, a hierarchical relation—this fact is without significance for the concept of genus as a whole. For, according to an axiom of Aristotle, there can be no gradation within a genus in respect to the particular essence characteristic of that genus.[4] For Ficino, on the contrary, the members of a genus, like all existing things for that matter, constitute a continuous and well-defined hierarchy. Their reciprocal relation and therefore the internal structure of the genus are fixed from the beginning, and it is very important to know in any given case whether a certain object is the first, the second, or the last member of its genus.[5]

The statement that the genus is a plurality of members involves the concept that we first find the individual objects in reality and

[3] *Ibid.,* p. 82. [4] Cf. Aristotle *Categ.* 5. 3 b 33 ff.
[5] Cf. *Op. om.,* p. 221.

subsequently add them together, so to speak, into a purely external unity. Analogously we may consider the existing genera as basic elements of the world and calculate the totality of Being from them as a sum is calculated from its given numbers. Ficino, on the contrary, has a different conception: he speaks, for example, of the first member *in* a genus and states that a given object exists *in* the order of things.[6] The individual object is contained in the genus as a more comprehensive sphere, and likewise the genus is contained as a partial sphere in the universal sphere of Being as a whole. When, therefore, we determine the genus of a given entity, at the same time we are giving that entity its right place in the order of things.

The question of the existence and origin of universal attributes then arises. This question led to two different solutions, and the contrast between them is one of the most remarkable phenomena in the history of philosophy. According to the doctrine of nominalism, which goes back to Aristotle, the universal exists only in particular things and can be separated from them only by thought. The doctrine of Plato and of the realists, on the other hand, states that the universal exists by itself, outside all particular objects, and is conceived in its own original being by pure thought. Between these contrary positions, which are basically irreconcilable, Ficino seems to take an intermediary stand. On the one hand for him, too, the universal is really accessible only in the particular objects, and though he clearly maintains the existence of Ideas and intelligible entities, they are, according to his conception, contained as real things in the sphere of Being and even included as particular members in the respective genera. So far, he seems to follow the nominalist position. But, on the other hand, there is doubtless a realistic factor in the concept of the *primum* which includes in itself the whole unlimited content of the common quality and therefore represents, in a certain sense, within the sphere of the genus the universal existing in itself. The realist and the nominalist doctrines are here replaced by an entirely new concept, which we

⁶ Cf. *ibid.*, p. 140.

may describe as a speculative identity of the universal and of the particular; for while the *primum* is a particular and a privileged member of its genus, at the same time it translates the whole fullness of the universal into reality, and conversely the universal in itself is no longer placed by thought outside the sphere of existing things, but as *primum* it is included among the real objects, without any necessary relation to thought.

Finally, the relation of the particular object to the general attribute is interpreted, according to the nominalist or realist doctrine, as a relation of inherence or of participation, respectively—in other words, the universal is either contained in the particular itself, or it exists outside the particular and forces the particular to partake of its own quality. In both cases the relation is immediate and abstract. Aside from the particular and the universal, there is no further factor concerned. Moreover, the particular sort of relation (inherence or participation) is not so much meant to indicate an objective process, as simply to explain the logical fact of predication in a justifiable way. In Ficino, on the contrary, the *primum* contains the essence of the universal and communicates it to the other members of the genus. The other members are therefore related to the universal only through the *primum,* and since the objective quality is conceived almost in the form of a material quality, the logical relation also becomes concrete and almost material. Consequently the participation of the other members in the *primum* means that the *primum* gives to them, so to speak, a piece of its own quality, and, similarly, the inherence of the universal in the particular, which is reserved to the *primum* alone, means the objective presence of an unlimited quantity of the attribute. The further question of the source from which the *primum* itself receives the fullness of its essence may be answered with a reference to God and to the doctrine of creation, and thus the theory of the *primum in aliquo genere* is well established on all sides.

Considering all these factors in their totality, Ficino, with his concept of the *primum,* seems to detach himself from the ordinary concept of "genus" and, moreover, to replace a clear and simple doctrine with a number of complicated and arbitrary reflections. His concept of the *primum,* however, has unity and is complete, and the various transformations of traditional concepts merely correspond to the known basic elements of his ontology: hierarchy of things; spatial extension of Being; limitation of thought to reality; and material and qualitative character of the causal relation. All these concepts are united in an interesting, but historically fruitless, attempt to proceed from a formal logic to a concrete and objective logic.

Ficino's theory of the *primum in aliquo genere* is to be interpreted not only in its relation to traditional logic but also in relation to certain historical premises. We must first mention Plato, whose theory of Ideas is one of the essential foundations of the concept of the *primum.* Many important attributes, such as self-existence, purity, and the relation of participation, apparently were transferred from the Idea to the *primum;* and, conversely, the Platonic Idea is explicitly called and interpreted as a *primum.*[7] Taking into consideration the fact that Plato speaks of a first friendly thing in the *Lysis,*[8] it is easy to conclude that Ficino's *primum* is only a slightly modified form of the Platonic Idea. But in spite of these undeniable congruences, the differences between *primum* and "Idea" must be recognized. In the first place, the Idea is basically distinct from the things that participate in it and is separated from them by an abyss, whereas the *primum* is contained in one series along with the other members of the genus and is distinct from them only in degree and rank, not in its essence. Above all, the Idea in Plato belongs to the sphere of intelligible beings and this meaning is also maintained by Ficino, although with modifications which are not relevant to our present inquiry. On the other hand, the *primum* may occasionally coincide with the Idea, but as *primum* it is by no means limited to the sphere of the intelligible, being a formal concept, not bound to any particular part of reality. On the contrary, the most common examples—sun and fire—are taken from the sphere of sensible things,

---

[7] *Ibid.,* pp. 247 f.   [8] Plato *Lysis* 219 c.

and it would be absurd for Plato, as well as for Ficino, to call them Ideas.

Another premise, the actual starting point of Ficino's reflection, is the Aristotelian theory of the relation of the universal to the particular, a theory on which the traditional system of logic rests. To what extent Ficino adopts this doctrine and to what extent he detaches himself from it we have already seen. But for a more exact understanding of the complete doctrine of the *primum in aliquo genere* we are however obliged to consider a characteristic point. As we know, for Aristotle there is a fixed and absolute difference between substance and attribute, that is, between that to which something can be predicated and that which is predicated to something else. Thus, while substances coincide mainly with individual objects, the genus to which something can be predicated is called a second substance. Conversely, therefore, individual things can be united into genera only in respect to their substance, not in respect to any attribute. In Ficino the lowest species on which the hierarchy of Being rests are defined, it is true, by the so-called substantial forms; but the higher genera, as the examples warm, light-bearing, and mobile show, are rather defined by accidental forms or qualities. And if the same quality is added afterward to the lower members of the genus, but is originally inherent in the *primum* and cannot be separated from its substance, the very difference between substance and quality is weakened and almost eliminated in the *primum*.[9]

It was just this latter aspect which prompted Plotinus to abandon Aristotle's viewpoint and so prepared the way for Ficino's theory. While Aristotle emphasized only incidentally the "specific" quality among the others, Plotinus, in περὶ ποιότητος, distinguishes the ordinary derived quality from the essential innate attribute which fills the substance of the respective object, and illustrates it by fire and warmth [10] (a significant point). Here the relationship be-

[9] Cf. *Op. om.*, pp. 168, 202.

[10] *Enn.* ii. 5. 1–2. On the fire as the warmest thing and as cause of warmth see also Aristotle, *Metaphysics* II 1. 993b 24 ff. To this passage my attention was called by Dr. E. A. Moody.

tween the *primum* and the other members of the genus is already clearly foreshadowed, and Ficino's interpretation of a similar passage in Plotinus makes it certain that he was aware of this connection.[11] However, Plotinus did not attempt a systematic elaboration of the concept, and the term *primum* never occurs in any of his works.

This term and its explicit formulation seems rather to originate in scholastic philosophy. In any case, the phrase *perfectum in aliquo genere,* which occurs in Thomas Aquinas and in other Scholastics, is very close to Ficino's concept.[12] The examples and the context, however, show that the Scholastics merely wished to give a general emphasis to certain objects, in particular God, and to attribute to them certain qualities of their genus. However, so far as I am aware there had been no comprehensive interpretation or application of the concept until Ficino's day.

Many of the points of the doctrine of the *primum in aliquo genere* are therefore rooted in the philosophical tradition. It is to Ficino's credit, however, that he formed a unique concept out of those scattered elements and gave them a systematic significance. The concept of the *primum* as developed by Ficino occurs later in the works of Pico, Lorenzo de' Medici, and Landino and even entered the later tradition as a supposedly Platonic concept. A vestige of this concept is found in Kant when, for example, he calls the Platonic Idea the most perfect thing in each species of possible entities.[13]

Now that we have analyzed the logical and historical premises of the theory of the *primum in aliquo genere* we must examine its particular characteristics and forms of application. In so doing we must keep in mind the basic character of the *primum,* that is, that it translates into reality and represents in itself the essential content of its genus.

Starting from the term itself, Ficino usually calls it the first

[11] *Op. om.,* p. 1555; cf. *Enn.* i. 2. 1.
[12] Cf. Anselm, *Monologium,* chaps. i ff.; Thomas, *Summa contra Gentiles,* I, 18; I, 28; I, 41; II, 15, *et passim.*
[13] Kant, *op. cit.,* 2d ed., p. 596.

thing in each genus (*primum in quolibet genere*) [14] or, even more frequently, the highest thing in each genus (*summum in quovis genere*).[15] This is, above all, another way of expressing the superiority of the *primum* with respect to all other members of the genus according to the principle of hierarchy. At the same time, through the *primum* the genus itself receives an upper limit in the sphere of Being: "Anything that holds the highest place in a genus has, so to speak, a certain limit beyond which the genus does not extend and beneath which all things are not yet the highest." [16]

The *primum* is also called "the perfect thing in its genus." This term, customarily used by the Scholastics, seems at first glance to indicate merely a difference of gradation. "Perfect things are always to be preferred to imperfect ones, for perfect in a genus are those things that have the genus quality by their own nature, while imperfect are those things that do not have it by themselves." [17] However, for Ficino, as we have seen, the perfection of a thing means not only an abstract value, but also the fullness of its peculiar essence.[18] If, therefore, we call the *primum* perfect in its genus, we mean that it realizes in itself the total fullness of the essence of its genus.

The first thing in a genus is lacking in nothing that belongs to that genus. For example, the sun, being the first among the light-bearing things, lacks no degree of light, whereas the other light-bearing things beneath it, such as the stars and the elements, do not receive the whole fullness of light. Since the first form contains all perfections of the forms and cannot be imperfect, we rightly conclude that that form which is called imperfect cannot be the first.[19]

A similar assertion is made in the *Orphica comparatio solis ad Deum* with respect to the first light (*lux*): "For the very fact that it [the first light] is the simplest, it is the first in its genus and the most common of all. Therefore it necessarily contains in itself all

[14] *Op. om.*, p. 82.
[15] *Ibid.*, p. 93; cf. pp. 100, 991.
[16] *Ibid.*, p. 350.
[17] *Ibid.*, p. 85.
[18] Cf. chap. v, above.
[19] *Op. om.*, p. 82; cf. above.

grades of its genus. For in each genus only that form is all-com-prehensive (*omniformis*) which is simplest (*uniformis*)." [20]

Thus perfection serves only as a paraphrase to the basic character of the *primum* as containing in itself the whole content of the genus. But the identity of the *primum* and the genus must be understood in such a way that the *primum* itself is entirely filled by the content of the genus and contains nothing more. It is, there-fore, as Ficino sometimes emphasizes, pure and unmixed with respect to the basic quality of its genus.

This [quality] cannot be the first form if it is not pure. For everything must first exist according to its genus before being made impure. [21]

Anything that is the highest in a genus must have the pure nature of that genus, not mixed with other things, in order that it may not be weakened by the mixture. [22]

Whatever is the highest in a genus has nothing of the opposite genus, either in itself or near to itself. [23]

The *primum,* therefore, excludes the opposite of its genus from itself, and since, for example, the Soul is conceived as first life this is at once proof of its immortality. [24] Since through the *primum* the quality of the genus is translated into reality completely and with-out any mixture of its opposite, the concept of the absolute or in-finite quality, which we have already met in connection with causality, is given a new justification. [25]

Each quality [we read in the *De amore*] is called infinite by the physi-cists when it is separated from any external addition. When warmth exists in itself, unhampered by cold or humidity, unburdened by the weight of matter, it is called infinite warmth, because its force is free and not narrowed by any limits of an appendage. [26]

And in the same sense in which the *primum* is called "pure," it also is entirely what it is, that is, entirely filled by the essence of its genus.

[20] *Ibid.,* p. 825.   [21] *Ibid.,* p. 81 a.   [22] *Ibid.,* p. 100.
[23] *Ibid.,* p. 275.   [24] *Ibid.,* pp. 150, 275.
[25] Cf. chap. viii, above.   [26] *Op. om.,* p. 1354.

Anything that has a certain quality as regards a part, possesses it through something that has the same quality as the content of its whole essence: for example, wood, being warm in a part, becomes warm through the fire which is warm in its totality. For whatever has a certain quality through its own nature, for example, warmth, is also filled as a whole by this quality, since it is as a whole filled by its own nature.[27]

In a genus, whatever first has the respective quality has nothing else but that quality.[28]

Since the *primum* embodies in itself the whole content of the genus, it is for all the other things belonging to the same genus the principle and cause of their manner of being.

The first thing in each genus is the cause of the whole genus.[29]

As each warm thing is produced and maintained by the highest warm thing, so each light-bearing thing is produced and maintained by the highest light-bearing thing.[30]

As, however, the *primum* is related to the other members as their cause, the special attributes of causality which we have noticed above [31] become applicable to it, or rather, the concept of causality receives its real content and conclusion through the concept of *primum*. Hence, while we have seen above that all warm things participate in the warmth of the fire, which for them is the cause of the warmth and is itself warmed by itself, we may now add that this fire which is warmed by itself is none other than the first thing in the genus of warm things; for since the *primum* is the cause of the genus it is also that which by itself has the respective quality (*per se tale*).

In a genus, whatever first has the respective quality possesses it through its nature: for example, anything that is first light-bearing or warm is light-bearing and warm through itself.[32]

Whatever first has the respective quality possesses it through itself.[33]

As in other genera, in addition to the thing which has the respective quality through its own nature [that is, to the *primum*] there are also

[27] *Ibid.,* p. 86.   [28] *Ibid.,* p. 247; cf. pp. 168, 259.   [29] *Ibid.,* p. 82.
[30] *Ibid.,* p. 684.   [31] Cf. chap. viii, above.   [32] *Op. om.,* p. 117.
[33] *Ibid.,* p. 211.

other things which have that quality through something else. So in the genus of eternity, in addition to God, who is eternal by Himself, there are many other things that become eternal through Him.[34]

As we have treated the doctrine of causality in our Chapter VIII, above, it is unnecessary to deal with it further here.

From the character of the *primum* as cause we derive the important axiom that each genus has a *primum* to which the other members are related in their quality.

All things that have a certain quality through something else are related to a first thing which possesses it through its nature.[35]

All things that have a particular quality through something else, are necessarily related to something that has it through its nature.[36]

And in a note on Plotinus, Ficino emphasizes that "each imperfect thing in each genus must be referred to a perfect thing placed in the same genus." [37] The existence of a *primum* is therefore assured in every case, and when the *primum* is not immediately given it can be postulated at once with the help of this principle.

We must arrive at some essence which is the source and receptacle of movement and life, as we arrive at one which is the root and foundation of light or of warmth.[38]

Above all things that have a quality in part, and impurely, there must be those that have it as the content of their whole essence, and purely.[39]

It is therefore possible to deduce from the given members of a genus the existence of a first member, the principle of the *progressus in infinitum* being also used to set a limit to the process of thought.[40]

Finally we must consider another attribute that has a certain importance for the application of the theory: in each genus there is only one *primum,* to which all the other members are subordinated.

[34] *Ibid.,* p. 237.   [35] *Ibid.,* p. 117.   [36] *Ibid.,* p. 678.   [37] *Ibid.,* p. 1731.
[38] *Ibid.,* p. 169.   [39] *Ibid.,* p. 259.   [40] *Ibid.,* pp. 163 f.

Whatever is the highest in each genus is only one.[41]

In each genus of things that which is the highest in that genus is only one; for if there are two highest lights, both coincide to the extent that each of them is the highest light, and so they are one. If at the same time they are two, they must differ through another nature rather than through light. Thus, another nature, different from light, is present, and by being infected with it, the light becomes dim and is no longer the highest. So also the highest warmth is that which is not mixed with cold or other things, because if it is mixed, it is hampered. It could become stronger only if it were purified. Therefore the highest in each genus is only one, and only filled with that particular quality, for example, the highest light is one light, not two lights, and light only—not light and at the same time something else.[42]

The fact that there is only one *primum* in a genus is here dialectically derived from its purity; but it can also be understood directly if we remember that each thing occupies a definite place in the sphere of Being and that quality is conceived in the form of a definite material quantity.[43] It therefore becomes clear that a certain quality which in its entire fullness is inherent in a certain thing, as warmth in fire, is as though totally absorbed and cannot be found again in another point of the sphere of Being.

Now that we have described the concept of the *primum* in its essential attributes, we must consider the quality of the other members as well as the structure of the genus as a whole. In this part of the analysis we must proceed cautiously. Ficino did not develop these concepts explicitly, but merely indicated the direction of his thought incidentally and not always consistently.

First: it is obvious that all attributes characteristic of the *primum* as such are denied to the other members of the genus. They are of inferior rank to the *primum,* imperfect and impure. They have the particular essence of the genus only in part, not through themselves, but through the action of the *primum.*

While perfect in a genus are those things that have a certain quality through their own nature, imperfect are those that possess it not through themselves, otherwise these imperfect things would be entirely

[41] *Ibid.,* p. 100.   [42] *Ibid.,* p. 93.   [43] Cf. chaps. iii and viii, above.

filled with this quality. So, since the imperfect things do not have the quality through themselves, they must have it through the higher things.[44]

Anything that has a quality according to a part has it through something that possesses it according to its own totality—as wood, being warm in part, becomes warm through the fire, which is warm as a whole.[45]

Whatever does not perfectly possess a quality depends on something higher.[46]

It is not necessary to develop these attributes of the lower members in detail, since they are either included in what we have said about the *primum* or can easily be deduced from our discussion. Only one of them is of basic importance, and it leads us a step forward beyond the sphere of the doctrines hitherto discussed: the inferior members not coinciding wholly with the essence of the genus as the *primum* does, they are considered impure—in other words, they contain besides the quality of the genus another element, an additional quality.

When the nature of a species exists in matter, a possibility of non-existence has at once been added. . . . After that it suffers many additions and frequently of an opposite character. For there is often something of fire in the air and always some dirt besides the essence of air. . . .[47]

Each thing, therefore, which is not the first in its genus can be divided into two elements: the quality of the genus and an addition which is not that quality.

Anything that lives through another thing, not through itself, is made up of two parts; I mean, of its proper nature which is not living through itself and of that life received from something else.[48]

Those beautiful [bodies] have two natures, the corporeal matter which comes to participate in beauty and the quality of beauty.[49]

From this point it is easy to conceive the addition or matter even as a negation or a contrast to the quality of the genus and to ex-

---

[44] *Op. om.*, p. 85.   [45] *Ibid.*, p. 86.   [46] *Ibid.*, p. 688.
[47] *Ibid.*, p. 259.   [48] *Ibid.*, p. 150.   [49] *Ibid.*, p. 247.

plain the inferior members of a genus through a mixture of two opposite qualities. Ficino expresses this opinion several times, though he does not always develop it consistently. "These bodies are partly beautiful, partly ugly," so he continues in the passage quoted above in reference to Plato. "For in respect to their matter, which is something else than beauty, they are judged to be ugly." [50]

Whenever a quality has ceased to exist in the original fullness reached at the peak of its genus, this is due to a mixture with the opposite genus.[51]

Anything that is not a perfect unity is not a perfect unity because it is infected by a mixture with plurality, as something that is not entirely warm [is so] because of a mixture with cold.[52]

Not only are the lower members of the genus opposed as a whole to the *primum,* they are also definitely related to each other. The structure of the individual genus is conceived in the same way that Being as a whole is conceived, according to the principle of hierarchy, and all the members are subjected to a fixed, continuous, graded order, in which each member is inferior in perfection to the higher one and has, correspondingly, a smaller share in the quality of the genus. For example, in the genus color Ficino distinguishes twelve grades,[53] and also four degrees in the genus light.[54] And of the genus of bodies he says:

Whatever is next to the first is receptive and passive only with respect to the first, but is active in relation to many members. Whatever is placed on the following grade is even more passive and less active, because it already is passive with respect to two members, the first and the second, and communicates to the following members what it received, until finally we come to a lowest matter which is passive with respect to all superior members and is not active in relation to anyone.[55]

In like manner the intelligences subordinated to the highest intelligence "are related to each other in such a way that the superior distributes, so to speak, to the inferior the Ideas and the light." [56]

[50] *Ibid.*   [51] *Op. om.*, p. 350.   [52] *Ibid.*, p. 1233.
[53] *Ibid.*, pp. 825 f.   [54] *Ibid.*, p. 402.   [55] *Ibid.*, p. 221.
[56] *Ibid.*

And as the hierarchical series of members ascends upward to the *primum,* in which the quality of the genus is brought to full reality, it also has at the other extreme its end in a lower or last member, in which the quality of the genus is diminished to its smallest possible degree or even entirely eliminated. For instance, the genus of bodies ends in a lowest matter,[57] and in the genus of intelligences "the lowest mind must finally be such as to be opposed to their first cause and to be passive in respect to all, active in respect to none." [58] In like manner we read elsewhere of the order of natural bodies; it descends to the first matter, "at which we must finally arrive in order that we may not descend to the infinite or be driven conversely to ascend without end." [59] In another passage, referring to Plato's *Philebus,* Ficino explains that the difference of the species within a genus must not be disregarded, and he says, among other things, that otherwise "the highest member of each genus would not differ from the lowest one," [60] apparently taking for granted that in each genus there exists a highest and a lowest member.

Each genus is therefore a definite sphere of reality, constructed according to the principle of hierarchy and limited at the upper and lower extremes by a first and a last member. The place of any given intermediary member is determined by the distance from both extremes as in a linear interval, and the share in the essence of the genus is determined by the distance from the upper limit.

Beauty itself is the measure of all beautiful things, because the following things are judged more or less beautiful according to the proximity to the first beauty and to the distance from it. . . . And we must not listen to certain barbarians who think beautiful things cannot be measured by proximity to the pure actuality of beauty. . . . They assert that this measure must be conceived according to the distance from the pure privation of beauty.[61]

[57] *Ibid.,* p. 221; cf. above.   [58] *Ibid.*
[59] *Ibid.,* p. 226.   [60] *Ibid.,* p. 1220.
[61] *Ibid.,* p. 252. This problem is discussed in Suiseth's *Calculationes;* cf. Pomponazzi, *De intensione et remissione formarum.*

The order of natural bodies is arranged in such a way that it descends to the first matter and ascends to the last form, and the closer each matter is to the first matter, the more matter it is—that is, truer and purer matter. The closer a form is to the last form, the more perfect a form it is.[62]

From this point it is easy to conceive the highest and lowest member of a genus as contrasts or opposite poles, and, the middle members having been explained by a mixture of two opposite qualities, it is easy to relate not only the quality of the genus to the *primum* but also the opposite quality to the other pole opposite to the *primum*. For example, it was said that the lowest intelligence is the contrary to the first,[63] and referring to the series of bodies, Ficino once says:

There are two limits to this series, in other words, matter is the lower limit, and that mind [the human mind], the upper limit. Since they have the greatest possible distance between them, they have opposite qualities among each other. Thus, as first matter is pure matter, by its own nature free of all form and subject to all forms and matters, so the last form—in other words, the mind—is a pure form, that is, free of all matter and superior to all forms and their matters.[64]

In like manner we also learn that in nature there is a pure actuality and a pure potency and that all other intermediary things are a mixture of act and potency.[65]

This conception seems to admit an ontological activity from the lower to the higher, or even to cancel the difference in grade between the two poles, on which the relation of the remaining members to each other essentially rests. This would contrast with Ficino's system, however, and he tries to escape the difficulty, at least formally, by defining the opposite pole and its negative quality as privation, potency, and pure passivity. Ugliness, for example, is nothing but the pure loss of beauty;[66] the pure act is contrasted with the pure potency,[67] form with matter,[68] active force with

[62] *Op. om.*, p. 226.   [63] *Ibid.*, p. 221; cf. above.
[64] *Ibid.*, p. 226.   [65] *Ibid.*, p. 349.   [66] *Ibid.*, p. 252; cf. above.
[67] *Ibid.*, p. 349.   [68] *Ibid.*, p. 226.

passive force.[69] Hence, when we descend continuously in the hierarchy of members, the opposite quality, meanwhile steadily increasing, is nothing but the pure decreasing of the essential quality itself and consequently has no conceivable content of its own. This conclusion of the genus theory has, however, only a dialectical interest.

Examining the applications of the genus theory, we must keep in mind that this theory has to do only with a formal relationship between given objects and is by no means bound to any particular sphere of Being. How fixed the conception was for Ficino and how precise a knowledge of it he could presuppose even among his friends and pupils is apparent from the humorous use he makes of it in a letter of introduction addressed to Poliziano.

Be careful, oh Poliziano, not to judge the present introduction as unimportant from the very fact that it seems to lack a cause. I should wish it rather to appear very important just for that reason. For philosophers judge highest in each genus of things whatever has no cause in that genus, but depends on nothing but itself. So the present introduction, for which there is no cause other than itself, may appear to you as the highest of all introductions.[70]

With the exception of this particular case, however, the concepts of *primum* and genus are not applicable arbitrarily, but always relate clearly to the given order of Being. The hierarchical difference between the members of a genus corresponds in each case to the more original gradation belonging to these same members in their quality as existing things. According to their relation with reality we can distinguish two groups of genera: partial genera and universal genera. We call "partial genera" those whose higher and lower limits do not coincide with the higher and lower limits of reality and consequently embrace only a limited section within the whole sphere of Being. The genus warmth, for example, is limited on the highest extremity by the fire sphere; light, by the sun; mobility, by the Soul. This limit is always the *primum*.[71] In

[69] *Ibid.*, p. 221.   [70] *Ibid.*, p. 834.
[71] Cf. *ibid.*, pp. 117, 350; cf. above.

like manner the genus of the intellectual is limited at the lowest extremity by the human intellect as its *ultimum*.[72]

On the other hand, we call "universal" those genera that extend throughout the whole sphere of reality and represent in all existing things one particular aspect of Being. True, perfect, eternal, beautiful are such genera, to which each object belongs and in whose essence it shares in the same measure in which it exists. Referring to the genus beauty, Ficino says: "Anything that lacks all beauty lacks all essence; and anything that possesses the whole beauty has the whole essence, because the first essence and the first beauty are identical." [73]

On this basis we can also definitely determine the relationship between *primum* and Idea. The *primum* of a universal genus actually coincides with the Idea of the respective genus quality. For example, Ficino explicitly defines the Idea of beauty as the *primum* in the genus of beauty,[74] and a similar conception must be assumed in other passages. In other words, *primum* and Idea are not identical in a formal sense, but in the case of the universal genera the Idea has the function of the *primum* and is defined as *primum* in its relation to the lower things. The concept of *primum,* therefore, since it is a formal concept, is entirely independent of the theory of Ideas. From a methodological point of view it is even more original than the theory of Ideas, in spite of the close relation existing between them in the history of the problem. On the other hand, Ficino's "Idea" has a fixed place in the hierarchy of things. According to the Neoplatonic doctrine it is nothing but a concept of the divine mind. But in so far as the difference between knowing and known is canceled in the perfect thought, all Ideas are identical with the essence of divine thought and therefore with each other.[75] In other words, the universal genera, representing simply different aspects of Being and each having an Idea for *primum,* converge like rays in the essence of the divine mind.

---

[72] *Ibid.*, p. 221; cf. above.
[74] *Ibid.*, pp. 247 f.

[73] *Ibid.*, p. 252.
[75] Cf. *ibid.*, pp. 259, 265 ff., *et passim.*

So we see that the system of genera is spread over reality in a manifold way. The spheres of the partial genera cross each other many times, and those of the universal genera are all superimposed one above the other. Consequently the genera do not constitute a clear division of reality. That is why Ficino occasionally speaks of a confusion of the genera, using only the lowest species for the hierarchy of reality.[76]

Knowledge properly concerns, not individuals or genera, but species. Individuals, being infinite in number and mutable, cannot be fully understood or permanently kept in mind; genera, because of their confusion, cannot be perfectly discerned in themselves.[77]

If someone despises the concepts of genus because of their confusion and dispersion and those of individuals because of their shadow-like nature, we easily agree. But the species must be honored, according to Plato.[78]

The genera, therefore, do not produce the order of things, but all relate to a previously existing reality, uniting its elements into certain groups and dynamic communities.

The theory of the *primum in aliquo genere* has its importance, however, not only for given partial spheres of reality but also for Being as a whole. As we have already shown, Ficino considers Being almost as a spatial sphere and at the same time as a kind of most universal genus.[79] It is therefore easy to apply the concept of *primum* and the accompanying attributes of the genus to Being as a whole. As a matter of fact, God is frequently represented as the *primum* in the genus of Being, and even this is one of the more important starting points for the determination of the concept of God: God is the highest of all things (*summum omnium rerum*); [80] the first Being (*esse primum*);[81] the highest Being (*esse summum*); [82] the absolute Being itself; [83] the Being itself; [84] the Being subsisting by itself.[85] The context of the quoted

---

[76] Cf. chap. vi, above.   [77] *Op. om.,* p. 192.   [78] *Ibid.,* p. 358.
[79] Cf. chap. iii, above.   [80] *Op. om.,* p. 93.   [81] *Ibid.,* pp. 259, 275.
[82] *Ibid.,* p. 281.   [83] *Ibid.,* p. 333.   [84] *Ibid.,* p. 411.
[85] *Ibid.,* pp. 1254 f.

passages clearly shows that these predicates must be understood in
the sense of the *primum* theory.

Since that which is highest in a genus is not mixed with anything of
the opposite genus and has nothing of that opposite genus in its proximity, the first Mind (*mens*) has nothing mad (*demens*) in itself or
near itself . . . nor has the first Being anything that is exposed to
Nonbeing. . . .[86]

God's existence is not determined by a certain species of existence,
through which it would become a particular Being, otherwise God
would be composed of the common nature of Being and some added
difference—in other words, some property of Being. So the absolute
Being itself is not bound by any limits, because it is entirely infinite,
the vast root that contains and produces all those things that have a
particular existence. For all composition originates from a simple
source.[87]

Since God is the *primum*, He is also the cause of all Being. The
remaining things, therefore, being existing things, not only are
created by God, but also their very existence is participation in
God's Being.

Being itself is common to all things. Wherever there is Being, it depends on God.[88]

[God is] the first origin of Being itself and the cause of Being for
all following things.[89]

Since it is peculiar to God to grant common and absolute Being to all
things, and since this Being follows immediately after Nothing, before all kinds of Being, it must be only God's task to produce something
out of Nothing into being.[90]

Reality as a whole, furthermore, is a graded and closed sphere
that tends from God as the highest Being to matter as the lowest
Being and farther to Nonbeing. Each thing has its place and grade
in the same measure in which it is distant from God and participates in His Being.

As the first matter is most distant from the first Being and closest to
Nothing, for which reason Plato places it between Being and Non-

[86] *Ibid.*, p. 275.   [87] *Ibid.*, p. 333.   [88] *Ibid.*, p. 100.
[89] *Ibid.*, p. 103.   [90] *Ibid.*, p. 148.

being, so the last [highest] form is most distant from Nonbeing and closest to the first Being.[91]

For all men assert, for example, that this thing does not exist at all, that that thing exists in an imperfect way, and that another thing exists in a more perfect way. Such gradation in existence does not happen, nor can it be known except by proximity to the highest Being, which is God Himself, and likewise by distance from it.[92]

We have previously noted all these attributes of Being,[93] but only now, through the concept of the *primum,* do they receive a more precise meaning and connection.

The importance of the *primum* quality for the concept of God is apparent in the demonstrations that are occasionally based on it, designed to prove that God is and is one only. Demonstrations of God's existence are rather rare in Ficino and are never the center of discussion. But at one point he deduces the existence of a highest cause from the gradation of causes and effects constituted by the real things. If all things depend on other things, without end, "there would be no thing more excellent than another, for where there is no highest thing, there one thing cannot come closer to the highest than another." [94] Elsewhere he concludes that the first Being cannot be a mere fiction, but must really exist and coincide with God.

Being itself shines so clearly that it cannot even be thought not to exist. For as Nonbeing itself appears to lack all Being, so Being appears to lack all Nonbeing. Thus in Being itself there is no potentiality of Nonbeing or lack of Being.[95]

Even simpler is the demonstration for the fact that there is only one God. Having proved that the highest thing in each genus is only one, Ficino continues: "God is the highest of all things. Thus He is one and simple." [96]

The doctrine of the first Being, which seems destined to crown and complete the concept of reality, is sometimes abandoned, and

---

[91] *Ibid.,* p. 226; cf. pp. 259 f.
[92] *Ibid.,* p. 281.
[93] Cf. chaps. iii, vi, above.
[94] *Op. om.,* pp. 691 f.
[95] *Ibid.,* p. 282.
[96] *Ibid.,* p. 93.

beside and above the first Being appears the absolute One or Good as the last cause of all things.

They [the Platonists] place the first Intelligible [the first Being] below the first Cause of things. For the first Intelligible is of such a character that it can be comprehended in some way; but the first Cause, in no way. The first Cause is called by them Unity and Goodness itself.[97] [God] is called Being by the Peripatetics in so far as He is the pure and absolute actuality through which all essences receive the actuality of existence. But Plotinus and Proclus place the One or Good itself above the Being. . . .[98]

In other words, with reference to the Platonists the "Peripatetic" concept of God as pure Being is subordinated to the One or Good. In another passage Ficino tries dialectically to reconcile the concept of pure Being with this duplication of causes.

When the Platonists call God the Being itself, they would not understand the Being which is essence, but the cause of this Being, that is, the Being above all that Being which is conceived with some proper concept of Being and understood by a notion. For they call the highest God Unity or Goodness, the next God . . . Being.[99]

The problem contained in this relationship between the One and the Being has already been touched upon in our Chapter III, but we must now consider it again in the present context. For this purpose we must start from Plotinus' doctrine of substances, on which Ficino bases his theory at this point. In his series of hypostases Plotinus establishes two distinct causes, One and Mind. One is the absolutely simple and transcendent cause of all things. Mind, the second cause, is unity and plurality—in other words, absolute thought and the totality of its concepts. In the interpretation and application of this doctrine Ficino used two different methods. In the first few books of the *Theologia Platonica,* in which the theory of the five substances is developed, we find God and Angel (or angelic mind) as the two highest substances. They apparently correspond to Plotinus' two hypostases.[100] God and

---

[97] *Ibid.,* p. 248.   [98] *Ibid.,* p. 270.   [99] *Ibid.,* p. 282.
[100] Cf. *ibid.,* pp. 85 ff., 115 ff.

Angel are two separated substances, defined respectively as "unity" and as the "sphere of pure intelligences." The Soul follows as third substance. But in Ficino's thought the Angel is a particular intelligence, and so the universal Plotinian Mind is replaced by something new and different. Conversely, the universal attributes characteristic of the Plotinian Mind are absorbed in Ficino by the concept of God. In other words, Ficino's concept of God contains the essential attributes both of the Plotinian One and of the Plotinian Mind. We can even say that in Ficino's description of God the features of the Plotinian Mind prevail; for in an important passage God is defined as "that which thinks itself and thinks all things in itself." [101] Even when, aiming at the Christian doctrine of the Trinity, Ficino distinguishes two aspects in God, he is relying essentially upon the relation between knowing and known.[102] Accordingly he can define God as the source of the Ideas [103] and consider the Ideas as intrinsic even to the One, though not strictly so.[104] The basic attributes of the One are absorbed, with no clear differentiation, in this concept of God, with the result that in the important second book of the *Theologia,* which is entirely dedicated to the concept of God, there is no trace of the Plotinian duality.[105]

However, in other contexts Ficino clearly distinguishes the One or Good from the first Being or highest Mind, according to the Plotinian conception.[106] In his later works especially Ficino interprets One and Mind as the absolute One and the divine Mind, or as Father and Son, in other words, as aspects within God Himself. In this way the doctrine of the Trinity receives a different justification, which, however, had long been foreshadowed in the tradition.[107] Here the universal meaning has been restored to the Plotinian "Mind." On the other hand, the sharp difference be-

---

[101] *Ibid.,* pp. 103 ff.   [102] *Ibid.,* pp. 18, 429 f.

[103] *Ibid.,* p. 268.   [104] *Ibid.,* p. 249.

[105] Dress rightly observes that Ficino's concept of God is connected with the universe and hence lacks the Neoplatonic "transcendency" (*op. cit.,* pp. 34 ff.).

[106] Cf. above.   [107] Cf. *Op. om.,* pp. 1727, 1758, 1766 f.

tween the two divine substances, which would not be reconcilable with the Christian doctrine, has been eliminated.

The double interpretation or application of Plotinus' doctrine therefore creates a dilemma. In his effort to reconcile Plotinus' concept of two universal (that is, divine) substances with Christian dogma, Ficino either had to deprive the second substance of its universal character or to eliminate the distinction between the two substances as such. Certain incidental statements show that he was aware of this difficulty. For example, we read in the commentary on the *Timaeus:*

They [the Platonists] call this divine intellect, not the Good itself, but the best Child of the Good. If we understand it [the divine intellect] to be of one substance with the former [the Good], we shall make Plato more compatible with Christian theology, but the rest of Plato's interpreters will contradict us. . . . Therefore the Christian and Mosaic truth stands.[108]

And in the commentary on the *Parmenides:*

Therefore we say with Plotinus and Parmenides that the first thing is the One above all things and that the second is One and All in order that the Child of the most perfect Father may be the most perfect. But how Father and Son are one—that we treat of in Christian theology. Plato, whom we are now interpreting, apparently considered them as two.[109]

The distinction between the first Being and the One to which we have thus returned is conditioned, therefore, by Ficino's consideration of both the Neoplatonic and the Christian doctrines. We may therefore leave unsettled the question as to whether he was brought to this distinction also by other, direct reasons of a philosophical character. In the context of the theory of Being, as it has appeared until now, this separation of the One is, not a necessary result, but a troubling, external factor. This explains the inconsistent and ambiguous character of Ficino's exposition. However, though the doctrine of the *primum esse* could not be fully developed, because of this addition, its foundations are clearly recognizable.

[108] *Ibid.,* p. 1442.   [109] *Ibid.,* p. 1169.

Therefore we may conclude that the theory of the *primum in aliquo genere* not only presupposes the various basic qualities of reality but also makes possible a clearer and more concrete interpretation of reality as a whole.

X

APPETITUS NATURALIS

LAST AMONG Ficino's doctrines that are related to Being and to the universe in an objective sense is the theory of the "natural appetite" and "natural movement," which we shall now consider. As in the case of the *primum in aliquo genere,* this seems at first glance to be a particular conception, based on several ontological premises, that later, through consistent development and application, assumes importance for the definitive structure of the whole system.

The passages in which Ficino explains the concepts of natural desire and natural movement are fairly numerous, particularly in his later works. To cite an unusually clear example, he says in the fourteenth book of the *Theologia:*

A natural movement directed toward some end is destined to that end rather than to another, for no other reason than by some disposition of its nature through which it agrees with such an end rather than with another, and because of this agreement it loves it, and because of it, it can also attain what it loves. For example, the air, agreeing in lightness with the concavity of the fire [that is, with the external part of the fire sphere], strives through lightness and is moved toward that concavity. Through lightness again it can attain that concavity and rest in it after attaining it. Therefore the human desire, directed toward God, may sometime be fulfilled. For who implanted it in our Souls but the same God Himself whom we seek? As He is the only author of species, He implants their peculiar appetites in the species. For all natural appetite is derived from the primal cause of things as from the first good and desirable thing.[1]

A similar passage occurs in the commentary on Plato's *Parmenides:*

[1] *Ibid.,* p. 305.

An innate appetite for the primal cause as the end of all things is inherent in all things; hence, before the appetite there is, so to speak, an occult sense of that cause. Through this natural sense, which is hidden to the other senses, the heavy and the light things choose their natural place on the straight line and reject the contrary one; the roots of trees choose humidity and avoid dryness; the leaves cleverly flee the shadow and seek warmth and light. Through this admirable sense and appetite all things are converted toward the primal thing, even without knowing the primal thing. In like manner, by a natural sense and tendency, through its own unity derived from that source, the Soul desires unity itself, even before any open knowledge and choice of reason.[2]

To understand the origin and purport of these thoughts we must start from the two central terms "appetite" and "movement." When we talk of tendencies in the world in a general way, we do not always clearly determine the objects that have those tendencies; and even when we ascribe a tendency to a given thing, there is always the possibility that the same thing may show successively entirely different tendencies. With the concept of natural desire developed by Ficino, the arbitrariness of tendencies receives a double limitation. For a natural desire is not only related directly to the object that has the desire but also is even based upon its innermost nature and essence. Conversely, each thing, by virtue of its original quality, has a peculiar tendency of its own, which either excludes or at least surpasses in significance any other, arbitrary tendency. In this way all tendencies are derived from substances, that is, all dynamic factors are derived from static principles.

The elimination of absolute dynamic factors is even more obvious when we consider the concept of movement. It is possible to explain processes of movement entirely, or almost entirely, without any static principles, and modern science has gone far in that direction. Yet in the history of philosophy it is an old idea, which we can trace back at least to Parmenides, that movement is something imperfect and that all mobile things have a lesser

---

[2] *Ibid.*, pp. 1187 f.

reality as compared to anything that rests in itself. This conception lives in Ficino, and it is so obvious to him that he frequently uses it without applying any proof. Reporting it as a common doctrine of Jews, Christians, and Moslems, he agrees "that rest . . . is more perfect than movement and that the individual things are moved for the sake of rest." [3] And in a small tract published among the letters of the second book he says: "Rest is judged to be much more perfect than movement. For movement necessarily needs rest, but not conversely." [4] His task therefore is to derive all movement from stable substances, and this is achieved particularly through the concept of natural movement. For since natural movement is, so to speak, simply the external continuation of natural desire, which originates directly in the nature of its bearer, the movement is no longer a condition communicated incidentally and from the outside, but the necessary emanation of its own inner substance and quality.

If we now seek the historical origin of these concepts, we soon notice that a number of important doctrinal elements were already part of the ancient tradition. The term "desire," or "appetite" (ὄρεξις), was first coined by Plato as far as I am aware, to interpret human willing, and it has remained ever since one of the basic concepts of Greek ethics. Aristotle distinguishes between natural and conventional desires, and this distinction is later elaborated by Epicurus who recognizes three species of appetites: some are natural and necessary; others natural, but not necessary; others neither natural nor necessary.[5] The term "natural appetite" appears here for the first time. It evidently inspired Ficino, though Epicurus' use of the term differs greatly from Ficino's. However, even in classical antiquity the concept of desire was not limited to the attitude of the human Soul, but was also transferred to other spheres of reality. It is sufficient to mention Aristotle, who

<hr/>

[3] *Ibid.,* p. 416. [4] *Ibid.,* p. 686.
[5] Aristotle *Eth. Nic.* iii. 13. 1118 b 8 ff., and vii. 7. 1149 b 4 ff. Epicurus, *Epist.* III (*Diog. Laert.* x. 127 f.), p. 62, Usener. Cf. Bignone, *L'Aristotele perduto e la formazione filosofica di Epicuro* (Florence, 1936), I, 396 f.

defines God as the object of desire on the part of the celestial spheres.[6] This ontological concept of desire was then further developed by the Neoplatonists. In Plotinus we find the significant doctrine that each entity is directed by its desire toward its cause and all things toward the highest cause, the One.[7] This doctrine foreshadows Ficino's theory in some important features.

While the concept of appetite belongs originally to the sphere of human attitudes, the concept of movement is taken apparently from the observation of spatial objects and events. In Aristotle's work *De coelo* we find a theory of natural movement as applied to the elementary bodies, a concept that agrees with Ficino's theory in several important points and has apparently been influential in its formation. Each element, according to Aristotle, has its natural place in its respective elementary sphere and can be removed from it only by force. The natural movement of an elementary particle is therefore nothing more than the return to its own sphere, and for this reason all heavy things, like the stone, are moved downward by nature, and all light things, like fire, are moved upward by nature.[8] This Aristotelian theory of the natural movement of elements was transferred by St. Augustine to the attitude of the Soul toward God in a significant passage. This passage, which probably had a direct influence on Ficino, we have yet to analyze. It is somewhat isolated in St. Augustine and is in the form of a metaphor. Thus it is to Ficino's credit that he developed the Aristotelian doctrine of movement into a general ontological doctrine and merged it with the Neoplatonic theory of universal desire into a systematic unity.

We can distinguish several stages of the genesis of the definite doctrine of natural appetite in Ficino's works. In the earliest works there are only a few indications of the later theory. For example, the book *De voluptate,* written in 1457, is chiefly concerned with the Epicurean division of desires.[9] A similar division is attributed to Aristotle.[10] In 1460 Ficino wrote a short treatise, *Dello appetito,*

[6] *Metaph.* xii. 7.   [7] *Enn.* vi. 2. 11.   [8] Cf. *De coelo.* iii. 2, and iv. 1 ff,
[9] *Op. om.,* p. 1010.   [10] *Ibid.,* pp. 999 f.

in which he defined the concept of appetite in general and that of natural desire in particular.[11] Yet even this work, as we shall see, contains merely a preliminary form of the developed theory, which occurs in its definite form only in Ficino's later works, especially in the commentaries on Plato, in the letters, and in the *Theologia Platonica*. At that late period Ficino could base the theory of appetite on a series of ontological premises, which we have analyzed and may summarize as follows: every existing thing is either a substance or inherent in a substance; [12] perfection of a thing is nothing but the integration of its own quality of being; [13] each thing tends toward its origin, and therefore beginning and end are always identical; [14] and because of the perfection of the world order, nothing in the world is vain or useless.[15]

Following these preliminary remarks, we can now analyze the doctrine of natural appetite and movement. We must, however, limit our consideration to the main points and partly neglect the minor details and discrepancies that are not lacking in Ficino. The concept of appetite from which we must start and which Ficino sometimes expresses by the terms "inclination" and "affection," indicates first that something is directed toward something. For each desire is necessarily a desire of something for something; thus the analysis of the mere act of desiring discloses two additional terms. This fact is of basic importance for the whole interpretation of appetite and movement.

If we would understand the concept of natural desire, we must go back to the concepts of nature and the natural. The term "nature" may assume many different meanings, but in the context with which we are concerned it indicates the stable essence of a thing, independent of incidental influences. The "nature" of a thing is thus basically equivalent to its "substance" and coincides in the case of earthly creatures with the concept of species. "Forces proceed from natures," we read in the second book of the letters, "natures are indicated by forces." [16]

---

[11] *Suppl.*, II, 158 ff.   [12] Cf. chap. iii, above.   [13] Cf. chap. v, above.
[14] Cf. chap. viii, above.   [15] Cf. chap. v, above.   [16] *Op. om.*, p. 715.

That which is inherent in all things [that is, in all individuals of a certain species] and at all times is derived from their species and nature.[17]

Whatever belongs to each thing by nature is given to it before that which belongs to it outside of its nature. For whatever belongs to it by nature, inheres in each thing by itself, and whatever belongs to it outside of nature, is added to it by some incidental factor.[18]

Therefore an attribute or capacity is natural if it is based on the essence of a certain species and consequently is intrinsic to all individuals of that species at any time.

Since [religion] is the commonest and most steady attribute [of man], it is consequently the most natural.[19]

Always and everywhere men speak and drink, since it is natural. But at different times and in different places they speak and drink in a different manner, since the order of action is based on opinion rather than on nature. In like manner, God is worshiped among all peoples at all times, because it is natural, though not with the same customs and rites.[20]

Things belonging to the same species do not differ in the natural actions following that species. Just as all swallows build their nests in the same way, as we have said, so all minds conceive in the same way those first principles of arts and morals that are known to everyone by nature.[21]

The natural desire is directly based, by virtue of its concept alone, on the nature or substance of the desiring thing. Hence it is not produced by any arbitrary circumstances, but remains unchanged in the alteration of circumstances.

Natural appetite is the necessary inclination of nature, tending from want toward satisfaction.[22]

The natural inclination always remains as long as the nature remains.[23]

Such an attempt [to become God] is natural to man no less than the attempt to fly is natural to birds. For it is inherent in all men always and everywhere and consequently follows, not the incidental quality of some man, but the nature of the species itself.[24]

[17] Ibid., p. 1209.   [18] Ibid., p. 401.   [19] Ibid., p. 474.
[20] Ibid., p. 324.   [21] Ibid., p. 209.   [22] Ibid., p. 1208.
[23] Ibid., p. 416.   [24] Ibid., p. 305.

The leader of nature gave to the Soul the desire for the universal and whole true and good, which is more natural than the desire for food and copulation, since it is more continual. For the body seldom requires food, and still more seldom copulation. But we desire the true and the good every single moment.[25]

The natural desire is therefore inseparably united with the stable substance of the desiring thing. Hence Ficino can say in reference to the totality of things: "The appetite is based on the essence and is most diffused and perpetual. For all things that exist always desire something." [26]

However, each desire and appetite is not only founded upon a certain substance but also directed toward something. Thus a determinate end is always given along with a tendency. We read even in the early *De voluptate* that according to the Platonists "end is that to which the appetite is referred as to an extreme." [27] And in the important discussion at the beginning of the commentary on Plato's *Philebus* we read:

Who will deny that the end of each nature and action is that toward which its impulse is directed by nature (*proprie*) and always?[28]

Since the corporeal force produces its effect through a necessary tendency (*intentio*), the force properly aims at the effect and desires by natural instinct what it aims at. That which is openly desired by something is the end of its action.[29]

Therefore the ultimate human goal consists in the knowledge or possession of God only, which only ends the natural appetite.[30]

The natural desire of knowledge is directed toward a definite end.[31]

However, not only is the end conceived as an internal factor of the desire, as it might appear, but also it has its own reality, independent of the desire and of the desiring substance. This corresponds to the realist character of Ficino's system, in which each act is inserted into the objective universe, but in which an existing thing is never derived from a mere act. We have considered this conception and its consequences in relation to the

---

[25] *Ibid.*, p. 308.   [26] *Ibid.*, p. 664.   [27] *Ibid.*, p. 990.   [28] *Ibid.*, p. 1207.
[29] *Ibid.*   [30] *Ibid.*, p. 307.   [31] *Ibid.*

theory of thinking,[32] and now in a similar way its influence is felt in the theory of appetite. Each end is something real in itself, and, conversely, each real thing, in so far as it is the end of a possible desire, partakes of the nature of being good. "The good and the end are entirely the same," Ficino says according to a doctrine attributed to the Platonists.[33] "The good has the function of the end, and the end has the function of the good." [34] Each desire is therefore directed by its nature toward a good, and since all good in the individual things is derived ultimately from God, who is the good in itself, each existing entity is related by virtue of its natural desire not only to a particular good but also to God.

It is obvious that the natural appetite is directed toward the good, namely, toward life, existence, and similar things, and not toward the contrary things, because that appetite, as we have said, is implanted in all following things by the highest good. . . . Consequently, all desire and action of all things originating in the good tends to and is reflected in the good.[35]

No Being tends toward a thing as its end, unless it is good. Consequently, the good as such is end. The highest good, therefore, is end more than is any other thing. Moreover, the primal good for all things is the cause of their being good, hence it is the cause of their being desired. If for its sake all things are to be desired, itself is consequently to be desired more than all other things, and by all things. It is therefore the end of all things.[36]

The basis of all these considerations becomes even more manifest when we examine the early tract *Dello appetito*. The appetite is defined in the beginning as "an impulse and inclination moving the nature to unite itself with that thing which corresponds to it," and since this appetite is interpreted as a kind of action, or operation, it necessarily proceeds from the form. There are two kinds of form, the impressed form and the perceived form (*apprehensa*). The impressed form is either substantial or accidental; the perceived form, either spiritual (that is, sensitive) or intellectual. Accordingly the appetite is either natural or animal; the natural ap-

---

[32] Cf. chap. iv, above.   [33] *Op. om.*, p. 990.   [34] *Ibid.*, p. 1209.
[35] *Ibid.*, p. 137.   [36] *Ibid.*, p. 306.

petite is either substantial or accidental; the animal appetite, either sensitive or intellectual. The natural substantial appetite has the character of remaining unchanged in all places and at all times. As it proceeds from one form, it is directed toward one object. The other kinds of appetite are analyzed analogously.[37] And right here we must emphasize two points with respect to the later doctrine of natural appetite. First, the appetite is evidently conceived as a special case of action, and the terms "form" and "object," which are in the foreground, are nothing but those factors of causal action or operation that we have already analyzed.[38] The developed theory of appetite is therefore derived from the theory of causal action, and the factors of nature and end that occur in it are merely different names for the terms of substantial form and object. As a matter of fact, later writings still show some trace of this connection. The important passage at the beginning of the commentary on Plato's *Philebus,* which we have repeatedly quoted, is entirely based on the term "action," [39] and the end of the appetite is also occasionally termed "object." [40] On the other hand, the natural appetite, which is exclusively considered in later works, still appears in the tract *Dello appetito* as one among several possible species of appetite. Furthermore, this tract considers the appetite merely as an attribute of the Soul, not as a general ontological phenomenon, and its connection with the concept of movement, which becomes very important later, is barely indicated.

The concept of movement seems on the surface to be entirely different from that of appetite. For a thing tending toward something can meanwhile remain in its given state, whereas a thing moved necessarily proceeds from one place or state to another. But as the natural movement accompanies the substance of a thing, it also appears as a direct continuation of the natural appetite in so far as the thing potentially surpasses its given state first through the appetite and then actually abandons it through movement. But since movement and appetite are both natural, appetite does

---

[37] *Suppl.,* II, 159 ff.
[39] *Op. om.,* pp. 1207 ff.

[38] See above, chap. viii.
[40] Cf. *ibid.,* p. 414.

not need an external impulse to pass into movement. This passage takes place by itself if it is not hindered by an external counteraction. The difference between appetite and movement therefore loses all importance, and consequently those factors that we analyzed in the appetite are also valid for movement. Both terms are even used interchangeably in the argument. Movement, therefore, also has a double relation: it is movement from something toward something. "There are two limits of movement according to the philosophers: namely, that from which it emanates and that toward which it proceeds . . ." [41] The limit from which the movement emanates is merely the nature or character of the respective species. "Each natural movement of any species proceeds in a certain manner. For different species are moved in a different way, and each species always maintains the same course in its movement." [42] Accordingly, the other limit into which the movement runs is the end of the movement. The movement "is directed from a certain and determinate nature toward something certain and determinate that agrees with that nature from which the movement started." [43] Similarly, we read in the commentary on Plato's *Philebus* that God leads all movements through adequate means toward their end [44] and that all things always direct their movements toward an end.[45] And since each end, as we have seen, partakes of the nature of goodness, each movement is directed toward a good.

That which is moved, as we have seen, is not moved equally toward anything, but toward something peculiar and congruous to itself. For it would not be moved toward it except because of some congruence with it. But whatever is peculiar and congruous to each thing is good for it. . . . Each movement therefore leads to a good.[46]

Movement, as we have already noticed, being a spatial concept, the end of the natural movement can accordingly be considered as the natural place of a thing. This concept was foreshadowed in Aristotle's theory of the elementary movement.

[41] *Ibid.*, p. 675.   [42] *Ibid.*   [43] *Ibid.*
[44] *Op. om.*, p. 1208.   [45] *Ibid.*   [46] *Ibid.*, p. 1209.

Nature gave to the thick bodies an appetite and inclination through which they desire the lower places, and in addition it granted them gravity and cold as the means through which they could descend to the desired place. It gave to the subtler bodies the appetite for the higher place and added lightness and warmth as the means through which they would reach the desired end.[47]

Just as the element put outside of its own place retains, along with its nature, its force and natural inclination toward its primal end, through which it may some time regain its own region, so, even after he has left the right trail, the Platonists believe man retains the natural power to regain the trail and the end.[48]

But when we are not concerned with a local movement, the end toward which a thing naturally tends is called its natural state or habit.

It must not seem absurd that after they have left their natural state the Souls should again return to it. For the plants leave and regain their natural habitations. Also elementary particles that are frequently driven out of their proper place and separated from it for a long time, tend continually toward it and finally return to it.[49]

The natural end seems to exist only in the natural state.[50]

We have considered as yet only the things in the state of appetite and movement, and it would therefore seem, to use a paradoxical expression, that they would always stay in movement and remain separated from their end. In contrast to that possibility, Ficino formulates the important principle that each natural appetite and each natural movement actually reaches its end. "Each natural movement can at some time reach its end, and each preparation that is naturally directed toward a form can at some time attain that form."[51] The proof of this principle, which has the character of a postulate, is given in different ways. First, each appetite is directed to one ultimate end, and therefore an infinite sequence of movements is completely excluded.

Something is found in the action of each cause beyond which the cause requires nothing. Otherwise the actions would proceed indefinitely,

[47] *Ibid.*, p. 308. [48] *Ibid.*, p. 681. [49] *Ibid.*, p. 417.
[50] *Ibid.*, p. 682. [51] *Ibid.*, pp. 618 f.

which is impossible. For since nothing can pass through infinite points, nothing would ever begin to act. For nothing is moved toward that at which it is impossible to arrive.[52]

The interval through which a thing passes before it arrives at its end is therefore always finite. Furthermore, the movement itself is not constant, but is accelerated at the approach to the end, in order that the actual attainment of the end may be definitely guaranteed.

We see that [the Soul] is moved more and more rapidly, as each element is moved faster, the more it approaches its natural goal. Consequently, like the element, the mind also does not always proceed in vain from one point to another without end, but at some time attains the goal which is desired for its own sake.[53]

We must not believe Panaetius, who says that we desire the divine things, but will never entirely reach them. . . . The nature of things itself teaches us the contrary. For the elements which seek their places through natural desire are moved faster, the more they approach their places and ends. Therefore Aristotle proves in the *De coelo* that the straight natural movement cannot wander infinitely, or it would not be now slower, now faster in its course. Therefore, anything that has such a quality as to tend toward something more rapidly afterward than before, does not wander infinitely, but proceeds to a definite end.[54]

This passage is of particular importance for the additional reason that in it Ficino refers explicitly to Aristotle's *De coelo,* which constitutes, as we have seen, one of the chief sources for his entire theory.

The attainability of the natural end is most frequently proved by another argument which brings us even closer to the real premises of Ficino's system. In the order of existing things, as we have seen, nothing is in vain.[55] Consequently, since the natural desire belongs directly to the respective substance, it cannot be void and vain, but must at some time arrive at its end.

The more natural the desire for the true and good is in comparison with the desire for food and copulation, the more the leader of nature

[52] *Ibid.,* p. 1208; cf. p. 678, and Thomas, *Summa contra Gentiles,* III, 2.
[53] *Ibid.,* p. 678; cf. p. 411.   [54] *Ibid.,* p. 307.   [55] Cf. chap. v, above.

has arranged that it may attain its end. . . . For if the attainment of the ultimate end is impossible, the whole species and its action are accidental, casual and vain.[56]

Since the natural appetite of each species which is directed by the universal nature cannot be wholly vain, all minds must be able to see the divine substance. . . .[57]

The natural inclination and tendency must not always be in vain. For that would be most foreign to the order of the universe.[58]

We have here, it is clear, the special application of a general postulate which is based directly on the concept of a significant world order and hence has its ultimate justification in God as creator of that order.

[God] would be too rash and inexperienced a marksman if He directed our desires toward Himself like arrows toward a mark and had not added feathers to the arrows by means of which they might some time attain the mark. He would be unfortunate if His attempt through which He attracts us toward Himself never reached its end.[59]

Consequently [the appetite is] natural. . . . Hence, from that which is the cause of the nature and species, namely, God. . . . Hence the appetite is not given in vain; hence it will rest at some time; hence it attains its ultimate end. For the wise and good king does not perceive and move in vain.[60]

Thus at some time each natural movement attains the end toward which it is directed, and in the presence of the end desire is finally satisfied and transformed into the joy and certainty of possession. But since the separation from the natural goal constituted the real cause for the movement, the thing, once it has arrived at its end, will not again leave it through its own force, but will remain in its presence. Thus movement flows, by an inner necessity, into its opposite, rest. "Whatever adheres naturally to an end is not separated from it except by violent force." [61] Accordingly, it is said that the highest power of the Soul will cease to move the Soul in

[56] *Op. om.*, p. 308.   [57] *Ibid.*, p. 411.

[58] *Ibid.*, pp. 416 f.; cf. Thomas, *Summa contra Gentiles*, II, 33; 55.

[59] *Op. om.*, p. 306.   [60] *Ibid.*, p. 1209.   [61] *Ibid.*, p. 414.

the future life, but will retain the Soul in that life, "for lightness draws the fire upward and retains it in the upper region." [62]

Since all movement is toward the good, and since the same nature which is moved toward the future good rests in the present good, rest is related to the present good in the same way as movement is to the future good. [63]

Because the upper place is good for the fire, therefore the fire is moved toward it and rests in it. [64]

As man through will is moved toward the end, so he rests in it, just as all natural things have their natural inclinations toward an end, which cease when they have arrived at the end. [65]

God gives the elementary body its natural inclination "that it may arrive through it at its peculiar place, and when this place has been reached like an end of the inclination, there follows rest." [66]

Each natural movement is thus finally transformed into a state of rest, and if we comprehend all factors hitherto analyzed, movement appears as a mere phenomenon of transition, constituting the mediation, so to speak, between two stable states: the pre-existent substance and the possessed goal. This result was foreshadowed in the double relationship of the natural desire, and thus Ficino succeeds in inserting the basically dynamic concepts of appetite and movement into a basically static world system based on stable substances.

The phenomenon of movement is therefore overcome dialectically, but not really denied, and it assumes on the contrary, according to Neoplatonic conceptions, a basic significance for the structure of the world system as a whole. For each desiring substance is directed not only toward its own preservation or perfection or toward its nearest cause but also toward God as cause of all good. The natural movement thus represents the countercurrent which brings the things emanated from God back to their

---

[62] *Ibid.*, p. 1248.   [63] *Ibid.*, p. 1251.   [64] *Ibid.*   [65] *Ibid.*, p. 1252.
[66] *Ibid.*; cf. Thomas, *Summa contra Gentiles*, III, 26.

origin, and the great cycle of the world is completed in which God
returns through the created things to Himself.[67]

In consequence of this positive significance an ontological principle results from the concept of natural appetite and movement
which comprehends the whole sphere of reality in so far as movement is possible in it. In other words, each existing thing capable
of movement possesses a certain natural movement congruous
with its essence and species. We read in a letter to Bernardo
Bembo:

Such a condition is common not only to men but also to all created
things, that they can rest nowhere but in their proper origin and that
they try for the sake of rest to place their goal in that place from which
they had their beginning. So water and earth descend downward; fire
and air ascend upward; so the moles and similar animals hide themselves in the abdomen of the earth; most other animals walk on the
back of the earth. The fish born in the water swim in the water.
Through a common and natural instinct the Souls of men continually
desire heaven and beyond it the king of heaven by whom they are
created.[68]

And the *De mente* begins with the following argument:

Each natural movement of any species proceeds in a certain manner.
For different species are moved in a different way, and each species
always maintains the same course in its movement.[69]

And after a few other remarks Ficino continues:

We do not doubt what the ends of the movement of the elements,
plants, and brute animals are. Some elements descend through gravity
to the center of the world; some ascend through lightness to the concavity of the higher sphere. The movement of the plants, which proceeds from the nourishing and generating force, has its end in the
sufficient nourishment of the plant itself and in the generation of a
similar plant. The same applies to the force which we and the animals
have in common with the trees. The movement of the brute animals,
which belongs properly to the senses, proceeds from the sensible form

---

[67] Cf. chap. viii, above.   [68] *Op. om.*, p. 753; cf. *Suppl.* II, pp. 185 f.
[69] *Ibid.*, p. 675; cf. above.

and a natural need through those things that are perceived externally toward fulfillment of the bodily need. The same happens to that nature which we have in common with all animals. All movements hitherto mentioned obviously proceed from a particular force, since they are directed toward something particular. And in the mentioned ends they find sufficient rest and are perfected as far as their nature requires it. We must now deal with the movement of the mind.[70]

Since this principle, as we see, claims a universal validity, we must now consider the details of its actual application to the different spheres and degrees of reality. If we advance in order in the series and start from the lower part, we encounter first the group of the four elements. According to the traditional conception they constitute in their main bulk four concentric spheres placed in space one above the other like layers. Sometimes a circular movement is attributed to these spheres. But the natural movement of the elements consists in the fact that individual particles of the elements, separated from their sphere, return to it on a straight line. Hence the particles of water and earth always move downward, while those of fire and air always move upward. To this movement an inner force or inclination corresponds, and as both originate in the nature and substance of the elements, they come ultimately to an end in a state of rest as soon as the elementary body has reached its natural place—its sphere. This conception is frequently developed by Ficino. He speaks especially of the movement of fire and earth because as extremes they offer the clearest example. It is essentially the same theory already described in Aristotle's *De coelo,* which in many important points, as we have seen, is the basis for Ficino's more general theory.

Nature gave to the thick bodies an appetite and tendency through which they would desire the lower places and gave them in addition gravity and cold as means through which they could descend to the desired place. It gave to the subtler ones the desire for the higher place and added lightness and warmth as means through which they would reach their desired end.[71]

[70] *Ibid.,* p. 676; cf. pp. 1207 f. An abstract of this passage is given by Galli, *La morale,* pp. 39 ff.

[71] *Op. om.,* p. 308; cf. above.

The particles of the elements, frequently driven out of their peculiar place and separated from it for a long time, meanwhile continually tend toward it and finally return to it.[72]

Because the higher place is good for the fire, the fire is therefore moved toward it and rests in it . . .[73]

Above the elementary particles are the plants and animals, whose bodies, composed of the different elements, possess in addition the faculties of nutrition and generation, and as far as animals are concerned, that of sensation. Their natural appetite is therefore directed toward nutrition, generation, or sensation.

Anything that performs an act is induced to action by a natural appetite for propagating its own perfection, in order to generate something else as like as possible to itself, as is manifest in elements, plants and animals, where it appears that the natural appetite is directed toward the good, that is, toward life, existence, and similar things, not toward their opposite.[74]

Nature "gave to the animals the appetite for food and copulation and added the members adapted to eating and copulating." [75] But when we compare these statements more accurately with each other and with other passages quoted above, we notice some obvious inconsistencies. For in one case the appetite toward sensation is peculiar to animals; [76] elsewhere that toward nutrition and generation.[77] Now like the elements they tend toward their congruous place of habitation; [78] now the desire of the individual species of animals is directed toward a characteristic activity: "The swallows, through natural instinct, are driven to build a nest; the bees to make hives; the spiders to make cobwebs." [79] The doctrine of natural movement apparently has no consistent application to plants and animals, nor is it developed in all detail in their case. This fact can easily be explained, since the theory was not originally applied to that sphere of things, but only transferred to it secondarily on the ground of a general ontological principle.

[72] *Ibid.*, p. 417; cf. above.   [73] *Ibid.*, p. 1251; cf. above.
[74] *Ibid.*, p. 137.   [75] *Ibid.*, p. 308.   [76] *Ibid.*, p. 676.
[77] *Ibid.*, p. 308.   [78] *Ibid.*, p. 753.   [79] *Ibid.*, p. 207.

The highest part of the corporeal world, above the elementary spheres and the individual substances living in them, is made up of the eight celestial spheres. The circular movement peculiar to them is again interpreted as a natural movement, in which the Soul of the respective sphere constitutes the invisible center. This theory had also been foreshadowed by Aristotle and the Neoplatonists. We read in the last book of the *Theologia* that "it is natural for the heavens to move around their Souls." [80] And in a treatise on the different degrees of movement and rest: "The celestial bodies are moved, but in a stable way, for they persist continually in their natural movement." [81]

Yet through its application to the celestial spheres the theory of natural movement assumes an entirely new meaning and also produces a radical transformation of the whole world system. As we have seen, at some time each natural movement must reach its end and pass into a state of rest. Consequently, when we say that the circular movement of the heaven must at some time have an end, we merely make a formal application of a well-known general principle to the particular case of the celestial movement. Yet when we closely examine the content of that assertion, we see that this application is essentially different from the previous cases. For if it is said, for example, that a particle of fire or earth must at some time return in a linear movement to its natural place, we presume an end to each particular movement. At the same time reference is made to a world order in which movement constitutes an essential factor and is possible at any time. But if the movement of the heaven comes to an end at some time, the whole world state in which movement takes place is not only put in question, but even ideally annihilated. So instead of the natural, ancient conception of the universe, Ficino develops a historical, Christian conception. The present state of the world represents, not an eternal order without beginning and end, but a transitory process limited at both extremes by the moments of creation and of Last

[80] *Ibid.*, p. 407.
[81] *Ibid.*, p. 686; cf. p. 129 and Kieszkowski, p. 78.

Judgment. The few passages in which Ficino draws these conclusions leave no doubt as to his opinion.

Since the immense fullness cannot attract in vain, we rightly expect
that the tendency of matter and the course of the world . . . will be
entirely fulfilled at some time by the highest fullness itself.[82]

The creation made by God will be directed toward something stable,
when the movement of the world, which has been introduced for the
sake of more perfect rest, will cease.[83]

Referring to the common doctrine of the Jews, Christians, and
Moslems, Ficino says, accordingly,

that the highest and last end of the world which the world must reach
at some time, since even the individual things that are lower than the
world reach their peculiar end at some time, will be, not movement,
but rest. For rest is more perfect than movement, and for the sake of
rest the individual things are moved. Moreover, the body of the world
will be most beautiful in that most perfect state. When the course of
the heaven through which all things are generated is finally fulfilled,
nothing will be generated anymore. . . .[84]

Every movement is therefore not only conceptually overcome by
the substance and by the end, but also actually overcome by the
beginning and end of the universe.

These eschatological theories are confirmed and completed in
the theory of the natural movement of the Souls, which we shall
now consider in concluding this section. The human Soul is the
lowest among all intelligible entities. Hence in the series of existing things it is the first degree surpassing the corporeal world.[85]
According to Plato the Soul is the cause of all movement, and
consequently to it is attributed a first and highest movement.[86]
As content for this movement Ficino usually indicates the discursive activity, namely, the continual change of thoughts and actions peculiar to the Soul. In the apparent arbitrariness of this
change the Soul is guided by one natural appetite. Ficino defines
the end of this appetite sometimes as the Idea, or the totality of

[82] *Op. om.*, p. 689.   [83] *Ibid.*, p. 417.   [84] *Ibid.*, p. 416.
[85] Cf. *ibid.*, pp. 221 f.   [86] *Ibid.*, p. 121.

things, or the true and good, but usually as God.[87] The human Soul thus possesses a natural inclination and movement toward God. We shall examine the ethical premises of this conception in Chapter XV, below. Here we shall consider it only in its ontological significance. "The whole attempt of our Soul is to become God," we read in the thirteenth book of the *Theologia*.

This attempt is no less natural for men than the attempt to fly is for birds. For it is inherent in all men always and everywhere and therefore follows, not a contingent quality of an individual, but the nature of the species itself.[88]

The ultimate end of man consists in the knowledge or possession of God alone which alone ends his natural appetite.[89]

Accordingly, in the *De mente* the consideration about the end of the human mind leads to the conclusion that the natural appetite of the human intellect and will is directed toward the infinite true and good only, that is, toward God, as its end. "Therefore, you cannot rest but in the immense true and good or make an end but in the infinite." [90]

Like each natural movement, this tendency of the Soul toward God must attain its end at some time, in other words, the Soul must arrive at the unlimited vision and the enjoyment of the divine essence. Since this cannot happen during earthly life, it must happen in the future life, that is, after death or at the end of all things. So the immortality and future beatitude of the Soul can be postulated from the natural appetite of the Soul for God, and the need for the actual attainment of the end of the movement leads, as in the case of the celestial movement, to eschatological conceptions.

The human tendency directed toward God can be fulfilled at some time. For who implanted it in our Souls but the same God whom we seek? [91]

---

[87] Cf. *ibid.*, pp. 305 ff.   [88] *Ibid.*, p. 305; cf. Anichini, pp. 46 ff.
[89] *Op. om.*, p. 307.   [90] *Ibid.*, p. 678.
[91] *Ibid.*, p. 305; cf. Anichini, *op. cit.*, p. 47.

The rational Soul can sometime reach its perfect end. For if those things which are less perfect in nature reach their perfection in the possession of the desired end, the more the Soul which is most perfect and the end of all natural things [must reach its perfection].[92]

Since the natural appetite toward God, infused in us by God, cannot be vain, in order that the highest reason which does nothing in vain may not have infused it in us in vain, the minds of men are eternal so that some time they may reach the eternal and divine good desired by nature.[93]

Once the Soul has reached this end it does not leave it any more, but remains united with it for ever.

When the Soul attains the infinite end . . . it attains it without end. For the same infinite force which had attracted it toward itself from afar, retains it within itself from nearby with an indescribable intensity.[94]

Consequently, the Souls once adhering to God will never again leave Him, since they have already transcended movement and fulfilled the natural desire. Since this desire is founded in a stable substance and naturally directed toward a stable object, it evidently desires a stable possession as its end also.[95]

The Soul's original desire is thus directed toward God, that is, upward in the series of things. Hence it is compared with the light elements, especially with fire, which always moves upward toward its natural place.

The end of fire is the concavity of the last heaven. Therefore, if there were no obstacle each flame would fly up to that place, and when it reached that concavity, if it had sufficient extension, it would extend itself throughout that whole concavity in order to enjoy entirely what is natural to it. . . . The goal and end of the mind is the true and good itself: God. There it runs by an essential instinct like fire. . . .[96]

[The Soul] desires through the same love to retain the good, through which it had striven to reach it, just as the light things try, by the same lightness through which they had tended toward the upper region, to remain there.[97]

[92] *Op. om.*, p. 678.   [93] *Ibid.*, p. 753.   [94] *Ibid.*, p. 682.
[95] *Ibid.*, p. 414.   [96] *Ibid.*, p. 99.   [97] *Ibid.*, pp. 488 f.

Because the higher place is good for the fire, therefore the fire is moved toward it and rests in it. The converse of this, that the place is good because the fire is moved toward it and rests in it, does not hold good. For if, perhaps, a stone were forced and did ascend and remain there, it would not be good for it. Likewise, felicity is the attainment of the ultimate end [that is, by the mind].[98]

This comparison, as it appears from its frequent repetition, is not chosen incidentally, but is based on the fact that Ficino has transferred the Aristotelian theory of elementary movement in all its aspects to the movement of the Soul. That this was done deliberately is seen from the quotation from the *De coelo* which occurs in the same context.[99] The inspiration for this transference had come apparently from the following passage in St. Augustine:

In Thy gift we rest, there we enjoy Thee. Our rest is our place. Love lifts us there. By its weight the body tends toward its place. The weight is not only directed toward the lowest places, but toward its proper place. The fire tends upward, the stone downward. They are moved by their weight and seek their proper places. . . . My weight is my love; by it I am moved wherever I am moved. Through Thy gift we are kindled and moved upward. . . .[100]

Here, too, the tendency of the Soul toward God is compared with the spatial movement of the elements, but what is an isolated image in St. Augustine is elaborated by Ficino into a complete theory which is of decisive importance for his world system.

Though the Soul is always directed toward God as its natural end, its attitude during life is thereby by no means fixed. On the contrary, whereas all elementary bodies and animals are by their nature limited to one form of action, the greatest variety of action is peculiar to man, and he can turn his thought and action arbitrarily toward the most diverse objects.[101] He can thus turn equally toward God and earthly things—that is, it is possible for him to follow his natural appetite, whose object is God, or to act contrary to it. The contradiction which apparently lies in this fact is resolved when we examine closely the relation between God

---

[98] *Ibid.*, p. 1251.
[100] *Conf.* xiii. 9.

[99] *Ibid.*, p. 307; see also above.
[101] Cf. *Op. om.*, pp. 207, 295.

and earthly things. For Ficino, God is the universal good, and earthly things are particular goods. Since the absolute good is the basis for any particular good, the pleasure we find in earthly things is in reality also directed toward God.[102] In this way man can never really counteract his natural appetite, since God, the universal good, is always the end of his actions; but man can follow his end by the straight and right way or by an indirect and wrong way. So the conceptual unity of the natural appetite is maintained, but at the same time there occurs the contrast between a right and wrong attitude, that is, between virtue and vice. The future destiny of the Soul rests on this difference as developed during earthly life. For the one who follows virtue here below, that is, for him who turns his appetite immediately toward God, is reserved beatitude after death, that is, the unlimited vision and enjoyment of God. But he who turns his appetite toward earthly goods and thus falls into vice, faces after death condemnation and the eternal loss of the knowledge of God. To this double correlation of the present and future state of life, which traditional theology represents by the terms "reward" and "punishment," Ficino gives a more precise conceptual interpretation. Here, also, he applies the theory of natural movement: in any case future life is merely the continuation and completion of the present life, and the Soul is moved toward the place of its final destiny by the mere weight of its inclination during earthly life.

All [virtuous Souls] are moved by a corresponding habit, like a natural lightness, toward that region which is the dwelling place of the angels after whom they have most closely patterned themselves during life. In like manner Christians believe that by their similarity, like a natural weight, damned Souls dash headlong toward the nine degrees of damned demons to which they made themselves similar during life.[103] Virtue and vice originate in the present life. With virtue, reward originates; with vice, punishment. In the future life virtue and vice are consummated. There reward and punishment are fulfilled. Virtue is incipient reward; reward is adult virtue. Vice is incipient punishment; punishment is consummated vice. . . . Just as nature, the servant of

---

[102] Cf. *ibid.*, pp. 665 f.   [103] *Ibid.*, p. 410.

divine Providence, moves the bodies internally upward by lightness and downward by gravity, so Providence guides all things by an internal law similar to some natural inclination. . . . Accordingly, through this innate law human minds guide themselves toward the places fitting to their life. As the humors in an animal have two causes of movement, namely, natural and animal, and by the natural one the light humors move themselves mostly upward, the heavy ones downward, by the animal one they move themselves primarily toward those members which need them most, according to the want of the life of the animal, so Souls possess internally two causes of movement, that is, their own impulse or judgment and the innate law of the divine Providence. Through the former they move themselves toward such and such habits; through the latter they guide themselves according to assumed habits by an intimate and occult inclination toward places, punishments, rewards fitting to their habits.[104]

Moral behavior during life is hence at the disposal of the free will of the Soul, but its future destiny is thus determined once and for all and is produced directly, so to speak, by an internal gravity of things. In this way Ficino tries to give a philosophical justification for Christian eschatology, as Plotinus had tried to give a justification for the eschatology of Plato's myths.

But the relation of the Soul to earthly things is based not only on its misguided tendency toward God. Rather the human Soul possesses, besides its inclination toward God, a second natural appetite toward its own body, originally connected with its essence and free from moral reproach. It is on the ground of this appetite that the Soul can enter the body at all and exercise in it the necessary functions during life.[105] While the desire of the Soul for God was compared to fire moving upward, the inclination which upholds the connection of the Soul with the earthly body may accordingly be illustrated by the example of the stone falling downward. We read, for example, that during life the Soul can be lifted for a moment to the immediate intuition of God.

How long does the Soul do these admirable things? How long does it remain so removed (*abstractus*)? It remains only for a short time,

---

[104] *Ibid.*, p. 418; cf. Horbert, *op. cit.*, p. 37.
[105] Cf. *Op. om.*, pp. 371, 374, 401 f.

since a natural desire of the lower force draws it back to the care of the body, as a stone is said to remain in the air for a short while between ascent and descent when it has been thrown upward.[106]

In the same way he says that this inclination toward the body remains in the Soul even after death.

After [the human Soul] has left the body it is natural that it be again reconciled with the body so that, even apart from the body, the Soul is left with a desire to return again to the same body, as the stone when placed above remains intact, but meanwhile tends downward as much as it can.[107]

These words indicate a further development of the theory. The natural tendency toward the body, which during earthly life was fulfilled by the presence of the body, remains in the Soul after death as an unsatisfied desire, since the body is then destroyed and the Soul separated from it. However, no natural appetite can remain unsatisfied forever, but must at some time attain its end. Hence the desire of the immortal Soul for the body must be fulfilled at some time, that is, the Soul must be again united with its body in the future life at the end of days, and thus the Christian dogma of the resurrection of the flesh receives a philosophical justification.[108]

First argument. Since one natural compound is made out of the Soul and the human body, and since the Soul is endowed with a natural inclination toward the body, the Soul evidently is bound to the body not only according to the order of the universe but also according to the order of its own nature, and consequently it is contrary to the universal as well as to its own nature that the Soul remain separated from the body. But the Souls remain eternal after the destruction of the body. Since that which is contrary to nature cannot be eternal, it results that the Souls will again receive their bodies at some time. Second argument. The individual Souls are naturally inclined to animate and to guide the individual bodies. . . . The natural inclination remains as long as nature remains. Consequently, the Souls separated from the bodies will always be naturally inclined toward them. But a

[106] *Ibid.*, p. 304.   [107] *Ibid.*, p. 351.

[108] Anichini (*op. cit.*, p. 131) emphasizes Ficino's doctrine of resurrection, but does not recognize its characteristic form and origin.

natural inclination and tendency must not always be in vain. For that is most foreign to the order of the universe. Hence at some time the Souls will again receive their bodies, for which they always have a natural affection.[109]

The resurrected body will then be immortal and remain forever united with the Soul in order that the natural desire of the Soul be satisfied for ever.

The body will be resurrected to become entirely immortal. For from the beginning God disposed the order of things in such a way that to the rational Soul, which is both eternal life and the natural form of the body, its matter, that is, the body, may correspond in that particular respect, that through the Soul, always living and always naturally desiring to animate, the body likewise may always live. . . . Moreover, this creation of God will be directed to something stable, when the movement of the world introduced for the sake of some more perfect rest, ceases. Therefore, the body will always remain united with the Soul.[110]

The resurrection therefore coincides with the end of the world movement, and it is significant that Ficino refers explicitly in this context to the myth in Plato's *Politicus*.

In the book on the kingdom, Plato writes that after the present fateful course of the world the Souls of men, under the order and impulse of God, will resume their bodies, which they lost during this course, and just as once the human bodies under the reign of fate fell down into the earth, so they will be resurrected and revived from the earth under the empire of divine Providence.[111]

Thus we have successively found two natural appetites of the human Soul, one directed upward toward God, and one directed downward toward the body. This co-existence of two opposite tendencies in one entity can easily be construed as a contradiction, but for Ficino it is merely the last and boldest conclusion resulting from his particular concept of Soul. For the human Soul, as we remember, is the central member in the hierarchy of substances.[112] This means not only that in its objective quality it holds a middle

---

[109] *Op. om.*, pp. 416 f.; cf. p. 715. See also Horbert, *op. cit.*, p. 38.
[110] *Op. om.*, p. 417.   [111] *Ibid.*, p. 416.   [112] Cf. chap. vii, above.

position between the intelligible and the corporeal, between the eternal and the temporal, but also that in its conscious attitude it is directed both upward and downward, and thus unites the two halves of the world. Consequently a double tendency and a double appetite to the Soul are attributed, through which it is turned equally toward the divine and the corporeal.

If [the Soul] agrees with both [that is, the superior and inferior things], it desires both. Hence by a natural instinct the Soul ascends to the superior things, descends to the inferior.[113]

Such is the nature and providence of that life which is placed between eternity and time and has a natural inclination in part toward the eternal and in part toward the temporal.[114]

Elsewhere Ficino says that the Soul "conforms on the one hand to divine things, on the other to transitory things and turns with its affection toward both." [115] In reference to this double direction, Ficino occasionally compares the Soul to the head of Janus which faces in opposite directions.

. . . the Soul, according to the nature of the third essence, looks at both like the double-faced Janus, that is, at the corporeal and the incorporeal . . .[116]

The rational Soul . . . is placed on the horizon, that is, on the borderline between eternity and time, since it possesses a middle nature between eternal and temporal things, and being middle it has rational forces and actions ascending toward the eternal, and other forces and actions declining toward the temporal. As different inclinations originate in different natures, we can know from the fact that the Soul turns both toward eternal and toward temporal things that it is made up of both natures. . . . Therefore the Soul seems to have a double face like the double-faced Janus. . . .[117]

Moreover, if the tendency of the Soul toward God can be compared to the action of fire, and the tendency of the Soul toward the

---

[113] *Ibid.*, p. 119.   [114] *Ibid.*, p. 416.   [115] *Ibid.*, p. 531.

[116] *Ibid.*, p. 375; cf. Dress, *op. cit.*, p. 54.

[117] *Op. om.*, pp. 657 f. The theory of the two faces of the Soul through the scholastic tradition goes back to Avicenna and Algazali (Heitzman, "L'agostinismo avicennizzante," *Giorn. crit.*, XVI [1935], 298, 321).

body to the action of a stone (see above), the paradox of the double tendency can finally be expressed in a fusion of the two comparisons.

Since natural affections are based upon their own natures, and different affections upon different natures, and since we see that our Souls have an affection for the eternal and an affection for the temporal things, we rightly say that they are composed of two natures, the eternal and the temporal. Likewise, if we should see a body moved by its nature almost equally upward and downward, we would say that it is almost equally composed of gravity and lightness.[118]

A similar passage is found in one of Ficino's sermons:

In each natural thing we are accustomed to investigate the proper essence of its nature through its continual and natural inclination. From the inclination toward descent, for example, we conclude that there is gravity in a given body. Accordingly, we find through the inclination toward ascent, that there is lightness. If we notice that a body possesses inclination toward both, we shall believe that it possesses both attributes. Why that? We see that the animals rush only toward transitory things. We think that the angelic intellects raise themselves only toward eternal things. Hence we conclude that in animals there is only a transitory nature, in angels only an eternal nature. Since, therefore, our Soul is commonly and continually inclined toward both temporal and eternal things, we conclude that it possesses, so to speak, both natures—an eternal nature through the intellect, a temporal nature through the senses.[119]

The system of movements is completed with the double inclination of the Soul, for the entities superior to the Soul in the series of things, namely, the Angels and God, are beyond any movement and change.[120] We can therefore state comprehensively that all natural movement will reach its end on the Day of Judgment, since the circulation of the world will stop then and the Soul will be united for eternal enjoyment with God and with its resurrected body.

[118] *Op. om.*, pp. 219 f.
[119] *Ibid.*, p. 473; cf. Dress, *op. cit.*, p. 54.
[120] Cf. *Op. om.*, pp. 85 f., 115 f.

Since the immense fullness cannot attract in vain, we rightly expect that the effort of matter and the course of the world and the discourse of the mind will at some time be entirely fulfilled by the highest fullness itself. Then the stability of the world center will communicate itself to the peripheries of the spheres as well, and the pure clarity of the periphery will spread itself up to the center. The whole machine of the world will be clothed with the innocuous flames of the empyrean. The bodies and the senses, the natural instruments of the rational Souls, will shine through the rays of the blessed Souls. The Souls will be happily kindled by the salutary and lifegiving rays of the seraphim. The whole multitude of happy spirits will infinitely enjoy the infinite fullness forever.[121]

Thus not only each individual movement of things reaches its determined end but also the universal movement of the world is transformed on the last day into the rest of eternity. God, "before whose eye a thousand years are like one day," leads the created things through their appetite and movement back to their origin. The wheel of the world which began its cycle on the day of creation will then be stopped by God's hand, and each thing will receive the place it deserves in the sight of God, that place which was destined for it from the beginning and which henceforth it will not abandon in all eternity.

[121] *Ibid.,* pp. 689 f.

Part Three

SOUL AND GOD

THE PECULIAR CHARACTER of a philosophical system can be grasped not so much in its conception of Being and the world as in the way in which it interprets the nature of man and his place in the universe. In this respect we must distinguish between two entirely different periods in the history of philosophy, associated with the names of Plato and Kant, respectively. Plato first applied the speculative thought of the earlier philosophers to the problem of the meaning of human life, a problem which had previously been the concern rather of poets and theologians. He treated of the nature of man by means of the concept of the Soul, conceived as something substantial and in definite relation to intelligible Being. This notion, which dominated the whole later tradition, was challenged and in a sense destroyed by Hume and Kant. For since, according to Kant, the category "substance" can be applied only to objects of experience, the term "Soul" loses its metaphysical significance: Kant defines it as a "transcendental idea." But Kant himself, in his concepts of transcendental apperception and practical reason, at least indicated the direction for a new definition of human nature, and post-Kantian philosophy, in its numerous attempts at a definite solution, successively coined the terms "spirit," "consciousness," and "existence." Though none of these concepts has as yet obtained general acceptance, the concept of a substantial Soul has lost all significance for us; and if we really want to understand a pre-eighteenth-century philosopher, we are forced to distinguish between two things which for him were connected in unquestioned unity: the concrete reality constituting the content of his experience and the object of his thought, which is in a certain measure accessible to us also; and the conceptual form through which he has interpreted and developed that experience, which we can still understand in its logical form, but which for us has no longer any validity or force of demonstration.

Ficino's metaphysics is the theme of the following section. Its visible center is represented by the concepts of Soul and of God, or rather by the relation of the Soul to God. This fact, whose basis and consequences we have still to examine, is expressed in the two-fold title of his chief work (*Platonic Theology on the Immortality of the Souls*), and in his Preface to Lorenzo de' Medici, Ficino clearly refers the reader to it:

Whoever . . . accurately reads Plato's works will learn everything, especially two things, namely, the pious worship of God and the divinity of Souls, which taken together constitute the understanding of things and all institution of life and all happiness.[1]

Ficino's historical position is therefore clearly defined: It is not only Platonism in general but also that Christian Platonism which replaces Plato's intelligible reality with the concept of God and was first stated in this form by St. Augustine. Indeed, Ficino makes frequent reference to the authority of St. Augustine.[2] If we remember the sublime conversation of the Soul with God in the *Confessions* and *Soliloquia* and if we compare with it not only Ficino's basic position but also specific works like the theological dialogue between the Soul and God [3] and the theological prayer to God,[4] we cannot doubt that St. Augustine's influence on Ficino has been most decisive at just this point.[5]

In examining Ficino's metaphysics we must always keep in mind the concepts of the Soul and of God as points of orientation. But we shall seek to describe first the basic experiences that constitute the starting point for all further reflection and then to explain how through the interpretation and elaboration of these experiences a speculative world system emerges by degrees. As to the traditional doctrines of metaphysics and epistemology to be found in Ficino, we must refer the reader to the handbooks for their description, although they are not always reliable even in stating his bare

[1] *Op. om.*, p. 78.   [2] *Ibid.*, pp. 78, 855.
[3] *Ibid.*, p. 609.   [4] *Ibid.*, p. 665.
[5] Cf. my article "Augustine and the Renaissance," *International Science*, I, 11 ff.

opinions. Following the plan of our analysis, we shall mention these inherited doctrines only in so far as they are really modified and transformed in the light of the living foundation of Ficino's philosophy.

XI

INTERNAL EXPERIENCE

IF WE WISH to understand Ficino's metaphysics in terms of its living center, we must start from the phenomenon of internal experience or internal "consciousness." Internal experience is a definite sphere of experience, quite distinct from the ordinary experience which includes all types of experience without exception and for which all real things may become objects. Internal experience is extremely close to what European philosophy since Kierkegaard has called "existence"; but because of the disputes connected with the latter term we shall avoid it in our analysis. By "internal experience" we understand rather a heightened state of mind, experienced independently of and even in opposition to all outward events, bearing in itself its own certainty and having in turn an influence on the form and interpretation of all our other experiences.

It is easy, therefore, to consider internal experience as merely one form of experience among many and to explain it in terms of empirical psychology. It may, indeed, be made an object of psychology in so far as it is an aspect of actual human experience; but its peculiar character of certainty and its claim to "disclosing reality" can hardly be understood in this way.

There have been frequent attempts to designate the factor of internal certainty in metaphysics by the term "mysticism." If we prefer to give mysticism a precise meaning, as we generally do not, it means clearly an internal certainty of a religious character. We need only mention St. Augustine or the medieval theologians to indicate the intellectual content of such certainty. But when we call a philosopher like Ficino a "mystic," we have usually some private axe to grind: we are either positivists seeking to discredit a metaphysical doctrine by characterizing it as "mysticism," or else we are theologians trying to transfer philosophical metaphysics to the realm of religious doctrine. It is entirely possible that there is a connection between metaphysics and theology; Ficino himself lays much emphasis on this point. It may even be possible that the internal experience of which we are speaking is always the same and thus constitutes the common foundation for both philosophical and religious interpretations. But the term "mysticism," tending to obscure the limits between religion and philosophy, is confusing rather than helpful in our efforts to understand internal experience as a philosophical phenomenon and as the basis of a philosophical interpretation.

But first we must describe the main aspects of internal experience; then we shall give its conceptual interpretation and speculative elaboration through the various stages. In this task we face a twofold difficulty. First, immediate experience can never be entirely separated from its reflective interpretation, since every verbal expression includes a conceptual formulation and for the thinker himself "pure" experience is inseparably connected with a definite conceptual structure. Second, the use of certain terms and formulae is frequently determined by tradition and they are thus divorced from the experience which was originally their basis. In particular, a thinker of a later period often says less than or something different from what the terms he uses would seem to indicate at first glance. We cannot deny or eliminate these difficulties, but can only by constant attention try to defend the results of our analysis against them.

In considering Ficino we shall frequently compare him to other thinkers and shall recur in particular to the doctrines of Plotinus. Plotinus' influence on Ficino has been generally overestimated, but there is no doubt some influence. And since by virtue of the originality of his thinking Plotinus reveals the genesis of many doctrines which later became fixed elements in the tradition, it is instructive to compare Ficino with Plotinus.

The ordinary life of men is either suffused with complete indifference or subjected to a constant alternation of joys and pains whose comings and goings do not depend on man's will, but are generally caused by outside events and impressions. However, mind begins to cast off outside impressions and to awaken to a life of its own when it feels a profound and strange uneasiness and a vague grief. Though this grief is uncertain, in that we can indicate no particular outside cause for it, it has its cause more or less clearly in the fact that man no longer feels satisfied with reality as he sees it and with a life bound up with that reality. Ficino expresses this attitude, which we are inclined to consider the starting point for all his further thinking, in an isolated but nonetheless significant passage.

It is astonishing [we read in the fourteenth book of the *Theologia Platonica*] that whenever we are at leisure, we fall into grief like exiles, though we do not know, or certainly do not think of, the cause of our grief. Thus it has come about that man cannot live alone. For we think that we can expel our hidden and continual grief through the society of others and through a manifold variety of pleasures. But we are only too deceived. For in the midst of the plays of pleasure we sigh at times, and when the plays are over, we depart even more sorrowful.[1]

Thus the grief of which we are speaking is no transitory state of mind, but a basic sentiment which accompanies man in his actual living, always hidden beneath particular impressions, but ready to emerge whenever these impressions give it any opportunity—as, for instance, when we are at leisure. This basic sentiment of grief is not merely an expression of human unworthiness and humiliation, but he who consciously feels it raises himself on this very account from mere vulgar existence to a higher and truer degree of life.

As the Pythagoreans and Platonists believe, during the whole time the sublime Soul lives in this base body, our mind, as though it were ill, is thrown into a continual disquiet—here and there, up and down—and is always asleep and delirious; and the individual movements, actions, passions of men are nothing but vertigos of the sick, dreams of the

[1] *Op. om.,* p. 316.

sleeping, deliriums of the insane, so that Euripides rightly called this life the dream of a shadow. But while all are deceived, usually those are less deceived who at some time, as happens occasionally during sleep, become suspicious and say to themselves: "Perhaps those things are not true which now appear to us; perhaps we are now dreaming." Whoever among the dreamers is so affected is in comparison to the others, as Tiresias is said by Homer to be, among the shadows. He alone is wise, the poet says; but all the others fly about like shadows, or rather fly about as shadows.[2]

The feeling of grief is thus in reality but a way to higher life and higher joy.

When [our Soul] merges with temporal things, it seems first to feel a short and false sweetness, but it is soon entirely covered by a long and true bitterness. But when it lifts itself to eternal things, just the contrary occurs. For after a short and false bitterness, a true and lasting sweetness overflows it.[3]

It is conceivable that the mind, awakened to inner life after a short transitory state of grief, should reach the continuous rest of a higher certainty. But, according to Ficino, even after the mind has been freed from external impressions it is never free from internal unrest and is constantly being driven forth by it. For the mind does not stop at any degree of consciousness until it has reached the highest end destined for itself, and once it has really arrived there, it must tear itself away again and so fall anew into its usual unrest.

The ardor of the mind is never extinguished, whether it looks at human or at divine things. If it desires human things, what mass of wealth, what fullness of empire ends that ardor? If it desires divine things, it is not satisfied with any knowledge of created and finite things. Rightly it never rests until it receives the infinite God. . . . But now it is not only not extinguished on reaching any finite thing, it burns more ardently; because the more things it receives and the more it approaches the infinite God through some preparation, the more it burns.[4]

[2] *Ibid.*, p. 317; cf. p. 837.   [3] *Ibid.*, p. 824.
[4] *Ibid.*, p. 201; cf. pp. 609 f.

The mind is therefore driven upward to the highest end through its own unrest, and until it has reached that end its dissatisfaction increases rather than decreases, even during the ascent.

Grief and unrest, however, are not the exclusive privilege of the spiritual ascent; everyday life itself is filled with them on all sides. Suffering is added to the transitory pleasures in the very sphere of external impressions. That vague sorrow of which we have spoken does not come from outside as a foreign thing, but is always near and present, and daily life is besieged by it at every moment. In addition, there is the illusion and blindness of those who do not recognize their own situation and destiny and are thus continually driven to wrong actions. So to the spiritually awakened person the ordinary existence of men appears as a spectacle of madness and folly. "On the stupidity and misery of men" is the title given by Ficino to a series of letters in which he describes the average life with pity and contempt, trying to express both the tears of Heraclitus and the laughter of Democritus.[5] Elsewhere he seeks the reason why men always lead such troubled lives on earth and compares the wrong life of the majority to a man who stands on his head with his feet in the air, so losing all sense of what is up and what is down.[6]

Thus continually and in all its degrees human life is accompanied by grief and unrest.

We are all like Tantalus [so we read in a declamation in the third book of the letters]. We are all thirsty for the true goods, but we all drink dreams. While we absorb the deadly waves of the river of Lethe through our open throats, we scarcely lick with our lips a shadowlike bit of nectar and ambrosia. Therefore, a troublesome thirst continually burns us, oh we poor Tantali.[7]

In similar terms Ficino says in the theological prayer to God that continual thirst burns the Souls on earth and can be satisfied only by the presence of God.[8] And in the sixteenth book of the *Theologia:*

[5] *Ibid.,* pp. 636 ff.   [6] *Ibid.,* p. 755.
[7] *Ibid.,* p. 749.   [8] *Ibid.,* p. 666.

As long as we are representatives of God on earth, we are continually troubled by nostalgia for the celestial fatherland, even if we are unaware of it, and in this exile no earthly pleasures can comfort the human mind, since it is eager for better things.[9]

Continual unrest has therefore, as we can see, a positive meaning, for through it all men without exception are driven to a truer life and toward the higher end destined for them. Moreover, if we may venture to use a paradoxical expression, we may say with Ficino that a man who does not recognize his miserable state becomes even more miserable by this very fact. The first step in overcoming one's own misery is a conscious knowledge of it.

If we would seek the historical origin of these conceptions, we must start from Plotinus. He also talks occasionally of the stimulus that drives the Soul toward union with the One; he also expresses eloquent laments about the miserable life of men on earth. But his conception as a whole is quite different. For Plotinus speaks from a spiritual certainty complete in itself. The painful ascent which may have preceded that certainty is almost forgotten, and the common life of men is viewed only in contrast to that higher consciousness; the bridge to it, so to speak, has been demolished. An entirely different view is found in St. Augustine. "Our heart is restless until it finds rest in Thee"; this impressive sentence at the beginning of the *Confessions* expresses the dominating idea of the entire work and is even the concrete starting point of St. Augustine's whole theology. But the "disquietude which leads us toward God," in the sense that St. Augustine gives it, involves the whole group of concepts which we have just found in Ficino, and there can be no doubt that Ficino derives this point directly from St. Augustine. The only essential difference is Ficino's milder view. He does not recognize a radical evil as such, and he makes even the deceived participate, though without their knowledge and merit, in the common tendency and task of all men.

Besides this theory of inner unrest, we find in Ficino another very particular doctrine of melancholy, not at all foreshadowed in

[9] *Ibid.*, p. 383.

St. Augustine. The ancient and medieval physicians devised, as we know, a division of four temperaments, which were conceived in a corporeal, but later also in a psychological, sense. During the Middle Ages this doctrine became connected with the astrological views in those times so widely diffused. Ficino gave particular preference to the melancholic temperament, which had not always enjoyed very high consideration among the older authors. He assigns to it a special capacity for contemplation and considers it therefore the temperament of intellectual men in general. Accordingly, a good and beneficent influence was now attributed to Saturn, which was considered the donor of that temperament and had always been judged one of the "bad" planets. So we read in the thirteenth book of the *Theologia* that the melancholic temperament facilitates a liberation of the Soul from external events and so constitutes one of the favorable conditions for prophecy.[10] In the first book of the *De vita,* Ficino develops rather extensively the view that *literati* and philosophers are by nature of a melancholic temperament and are subject to the influence of Saturn.[11] This view, which had already been indicated in the pseudo-Aristotelian *Problemata,* was widely diffused, especially in the sixteenth century. In their beautiful book *Duerer's Melencholia I,* Panofsky and Saxl have examined the whole group of these concepts, starting with Duerer's famous etching, and they are apparently inclined to believe that all later speculations of that type are directly derived from Ficino's *De vita.*[12] But even apart from the influence upon later authors, the doctrine of melancholy has a certain interest within the framework of Ficino's own system.

It would be an easy matter to explain this theory psychologically. We know from Ficino's own utterances that he was of a melancholic temperament, that he occasionally experienced deep depressions, and that Saturn played a special role in his horoscope.[13] In

---

[10] *Ibid.,* p. 294.   [11] *Ibid.,* pp. 496 ff.

[12] Panofsky and Saxl, *op. cit.,* pp. 32 ff., 49 ff.; cf. Giehlow, "Dürer's Stich 'Melencolia I' und der maximilianische Humanistenkreis," 1905, pp. 34 ff.

[13] Cf. *Op. om.,* pp. 731 ff., 871, 901.

a weak moment he even complained about the painful influence of Saturn, and his friend Cavalcanti was obliged to comfort him with the very words about the spiritual sublimity of melancholy and of Saturn which Ficino himself was accustomed to use at other times with conviction.[14]

If now we ask how the doctrines of unrest and melancholy are related to each other and on what basis each of them originally rests, it is not easy to give an answer. It is difficult to recognize a conceptual relation between the two theories. A merely subjective "state of mind" may furnish the opportunity for many reflections, it is true, but can never account entirely for the essence of a conceptual interpretation, except when the state of mind has itself an essence and possesses the character of a basic philosophical experience. In this sense the vague sorrow of the internal consciousness is a philosophical experience which constitutes the common basis for the theories of restlessness and melancholy, but is interpreted in either case in an entirely different manner and direction. For when we speak of the restlessness of consciousness, the basic experience at once is inserted into a great metaphysical or theological context and the state of mind, though it is felt at once and concretely, is merely the occasion through which that context enters our feeling and consciousness. Here we are entirely on the ground of the medieval Christian conception as given by St. Augustine. On the other hand, when we speak of melancholy, the state of mind is conceived within itself and without any metaphysical background and can be derived from empirical causes like the complexion of the body or the influence of the stars (in that sense astrology also is an empirical method). Man can therefore complain of or curse melancholy in a fit of weakness, but as a rule he will tolerate it with a certain pride as a correlate of his intellectual vocation. He will accept and also enjoy it, even when there is no prospect of future liberation. This entirely modern view, which we can trace to romanticism and even to the present day, is essentially different from the view first mentioned. We must therefore resign

[14] *Ibid.,* pp. 731 ff.

ourselves to the fact that in Ficino these two theories coexist. In spite of a common foundation and of a recognizable affinity, they lack entirely a conceptual bond. In this discord we must understand and recognize Ficino's particular historical position.

We have hitherto considered the internal experience only in the form of that sorrow which keeps the consciousness in a continual state of dissatisfaction, urging it on in a restless movement toward its ultimate definite goal. We must now examine the positive attributes which Ficino uses to describe the content of internal experience. These attributes are not numerous, and almost all of them had been established in the Neoplatonic tradition; but their use and application in Ficino show no small amount of genuine concrete experience.

At the beginning of this chapter we said that the internal experience is achieved independently of and even in contrast to all external impressions. Accordingly, we frequently read that the Soul or mind turns away and withdraws from the external, corporeal things, looking within toward the intelligible entities. In the fifth book of the *Theologia* Ficino tells us that the Soul cannot be considered as a mere attribute of the body.

For such a thing, which would have no proper nature nor would exist by itself, but be inseparably in the underlying body like a corporeal form, could not attempt to turn itself away from that same body to the perception of the intelligible things.[15]

Consequently the body is not the origin of the Soul; for the farther the Soul goes away from it, the more perfect is its state. And if the mind decreases more in perfection the more it merges into this body and increases in perfection the more it goes away from it, the mind will then be most perfect at the time when it flies away entirely from this body.[16]

Under God's guidance we shall arrive at the highest degree of nature if we separate the affection of our Soul as much as possible from matter, which is the lowest degree of nature, in order that we may approach God as much as we withdraw from matter.[17]

[15] *Ibid.*, p. 153.　　　[16] *Ibid.*, pp. 203 f.; cf. Dress, *op. cit.*, pp. 70 f.
[17] *Ibid.*, p. 424.

And in a letter explaining the famous passage of Plato's *Theaetetus* we read:

Each Soul may retire from the pestilence of the body and collect itself into its mind, for then fortune will exhaust its might in the body and not pass into the Soul. . . . Thus Plato commands us to flee there from here, that is, from the love of the body and from the care of external things to the worship of the Soul, because evils cannot otherwise be avoided.[18]

But in turning away from the body the Soul is also able to resist actively the impulses and needs of the body, and that is considered by Ficino as a new proof of the substantial independence of the Soul from the body. "The Soul opposes the excitement of the humors while it despises their impulses through the effort of speculation, restrains them through the fatigue of moral behavior, breaks them through the industry of the arts." And then he gives some examples of the successful overcoming of passions.[19] Similarly, after a long series of examples of the same type, he says in another passage:

Therefore no one may object that there have formerly been few persons and are now at present very few who resist the passions of the body; nay, we all resist them every day for the sake of health, honor, peace, justice, contemplation of God, or beatitude. Even if we never did break the impulses of the body, the fight itself which is continual in us would be sufficient to show that the Soul resists the body.[20]

The turning away of consciousness from external impressions can be easily conceived in a substantial sense as a separation of two substances; hence the well-known Neoplatonic formula of the separation of Soul and body.

Since for the mind nothing is more desirable by nature than truth, and since truth is obtained through a separation from mortal things, nothing is more natural and familiar for the mind as such than to be separated from mortal things.[21]

Through a natural eagerness for truth the mind separates itself continually from the body, and the forms from matter, and thus it desires

[18] *Ibid.,* p. 633; cf. *Theaet.* 176 a ff.
[19] *Op. om.,* p. 209.   [20] *Ibid.,* p. 205.   [21] *Ibid.,* p. 186.

and tries to live separately, though the body and the senses drive it daily to the contrary.[22]

Likewise we read in another place that youth must be careful in judging divine things

until age itself will teach it either through the above-mentioned degrees of discipline or through experience or through a certain separation of the Soul from the body, which a moderate old age carries with it, in order that the Soul in that age may see things separated from the body as from a shorter distance and so distinguish them more clearly than it was accustomed to.[23]

And in the commentary on St. Paul, Ficino says about conscience: "At the very time when [somebody] separates himself in some way from the body, he arrives at a judgment similar to that of the Souls which are separated from the body." [24] This separation of the Soul, which is by no means a mere metaphor, is conceived in its highest degree as a ravishment or rapture (*abstractio*) out of the body. In the thirteenth book of the *Theologia* Ficino describes in numerous examples the behavior of philosophers, poets, priests, and prophets and defines the essential peculiarity of that behavior again and again as a temporary ecstasy.[25]

After Plato had departed far from the body through frequent efforts at contemplation, he finally left the bonds of the body permanently during that ecstasy. His disciple Xenocrates withdrew from the body for a whole hour each day.[26]

Whoever achieved something great in any noble art did it mostly when he withdrew from the body and fled to the citadel of the Soul.[27]

In the same context, Ficino distinguishes the seven types of "vacation," among them (and this is significant) sleep, swoon, and solitude, which by interrupting the external functions facilitate and favor the internal acts of the Soul.[28]

Then the Soul collects itself in some way and is not occupied either in perceiving corporeal qualities or in guiding and moving the members

[22] *Ibid.*   [23] *Ibid.*, p. 322.   [24] *Ibid.*, p. 451.
[25] *Ibid.*, pp. 286 ff.   [26] *Ibid.*, p. 286.   [27] *Ibid.*
[28] *Ibid.*, pp. 292 ff.

of its own body or in performing external affairs, which happens easily during sleep. And the more the external act is relaxed, the more the internal one is strengthened.[29]

In this state of rapture all the lower functions of the Soul are entirely eliminated, and thus for Ficino arises even the question of why the body abandoned by the Soul does not entirely perish at that time, a question to which he does not actually find a satisfactory answer.[30]

According to that same substantial conception, the separation of the Soul from the body is like a secretion of the corporeal elements mingled with the consciousness. And with this we arrive at the further formula (which is also Neoplatonic) of the purification of the Soul, which at the same time must be understood in a moral sense.

It is the end of moral virtue to purify and to separate the Soul from the divisible body.[31]

Through action and disputation the theologian purifies the Soul from the corporeal passions and separates reason from the fallacious opinions of sensible things.[32]

Socrates believes that through a purification of the mind this investigation [of the divine things] will finally attain whatever it desires. Therefore, putting aside for some time the usual unrest of research, he took refuge in moral philosophy so that with its help the mind, dispelling the corporeal clouds, may become serene and at once receive the light of the divine sun that shines at all times and at all places. Socrates himself, first, and Plato, later, through the imitation of Socrates, seem to have achieved that.[33]

Through this purification the Soul arrives at its peculiar perfection and dignity and thus becomes capable for the first time of recognizing consciously its own value and its superiority over the corporeal things.

The petty philosophers who trust in the judgment of the senses and cannot think that the Soul is incorporeal and divine should become

---

[29] *Ibid.,* p. 292; cf. Thomas, *Summa contra Gentiles,* III, 47.
[30] *Op. om.,* pp. 303 f.   [31] *Ibid.,* p. 187; cf. Anichini, *op. cit.,* pp. 113 f.
[32] *Op. om.,* p. 270.   [33] *Ibid.,* p. 267; cf. Dress, *op. cit.,* pp. 69 f.

wise once and for all. They should finally realize that through long intercourse with the body they have become corporeal to such a degree that they cannot rightly know anything but the body and a thing born from the body. They should become pure, and they will perceive pure things. They should finally experience in themselves, and they can, if they wish to, what they have been denying (*desiderant*) in the universe for a long time. . . . And they will prove in fact Socrates' opinion . . . that there is but one way not only to reach but also to possess incorporeal things, namely, to make oneself incorporeal, or, in other words, to separate one's mind as much as possible from corporeal movement, sensation, passion, imagination. So it will become known by experience itself of what sort a pure Soul is . . .[34]

Do emerge, I beg you, oh Souls of men, now immerged in the bodies, and at once you will find your nature above the limits of the body.[35]

A great thing thou art, oh Soul, if small things do not fill thee; the best one if evils do not please thee; the most beautiful if thou dislikest the ugly; eternal if thou despisest the temporal. Since thou art of such a kind, if thou wilt find thyself, seek thyself, I beg thee, there where such things are. . . . Hence, seek thyself outside the world. . . . Hence, leave behind the narrowness of this shadow [that is, of the body] and return to thyself. So thou wilt return to largeness.[36]

Internal experience does not exhaust itself in the elimination of corporeal impressions, but for the consciousness it is the source of a particular insight, since it opens an entirely new sphere of objects for knowledge and since, on the other hand, it makes even the previously known external objects appear in a new light. The last and most important aspect, therefore, is the resulting concept of a knowledge of pure reason or contemplation and the interpretation of the internal experience as a contemplative life.

When [the body] is sick and heavy, the Soul is so much concerned in taking care of it and guiding it that it [the Soul] is not directed toward the research of truth. But when the body is quiet, the mind easily speculates, and then especially it is nourished by its peculiar food.[37]

The petty philosophers should reconsider their attitude and

---

[34] *Ibid.*, p. 159.   [35] *Ibid.*, p. 161.
[36] *Ibid.*, p. 158; cf. pp. 659 f. and Saitta, *op. cit.*, pp. 154 ff.
[37] *Op. om.*, p. 185.

should conduct an intellectual life separated from the body, and being themselves separated, they will at once attain the separated forms and prove in fact Socrates' opinion that above the forms inherent in formed substrata, being imperfect, there are forms existing in themselves and perfect, through which the unformed substrata are formed.[38]

[The Soul] acts by itself when it neither reaches the bodies through the external senses nor recollects the images of bodies through the internal sense, but when the pure and incorporeal force of the Soul itself seeks and finds something incorporeal which is neither a body nor an image of a body; and this action we call pure thought (*intelligentia*).[39]

We have intentionally disregarded this attribute up to this time, in spite of its importance. For when Ficino, like Plato and Plotinus, speaks continually of intelligible knowledge, one is inclined, under the influence of modern epistemological theories, to interpret this merely as the quest for a more perfect scientific thought and to judge the repeated appeal to internal experience connected with it either as a mystical ornament or to attribute it to an exaggerated scholarly enthusiasm and to the joy of discovery. In reality, the higher knowledge is only the last and most important aspect of a concrete spiritual upheaval and revolution of the consciousness. This fact is sometimes clearly emphasized by Ficino.

What man, looking well into himself, has not experienced the fact that the farther he could remove and withdraw the attention of the mind from the senses of the body, the more truly he has known things?[40]

When, by reasoning with ourselves or by being asked by somebody else, we perceive the truth about some liberal art, we find what we find nowhere else but in our Soul. For this very reason, in order to find these things the Soul must leave outward things and retire into itself.[41]

The third sign which all men experience in themselves is this: whenever they seek the definition and cause of something, they simply try to remove all obstacles of the sense and phantasy and to penetrate the innermost depths of the mind, in which the thing they are pursuing shines most clearly the moment they have penetrated the sanctuary of the secret mind, and as if the treasures of sciences were hidden within.[42]

[38] *Ibid.*, p. 159.   [39] *Ibid.*, p. 157.   [40] *Op. om.*, p. 153.
[41] *Ibid.*, pp. 263 f.   [42] *Ibid.*, p. 255.

This internal interpretation of intelligible knowledge is of the greatest importance for an understanding of Platonism as a whole. In its details, however, the concept of knowledge is entirely different in Plato, Plotinus, and Ficino. For Plato knowledge is essentially conceptual and dialectic, that is, the single Idea is first fixed by pure thought and then considered in its relation to other Ideas. For Plotinus, on the contrary, knowledge is concrete and intuitive; it views metaphysical entities from the outset in a related, almost spatial order, seeking to reproduce this order as accurately as possible by means of thought and language. Ficino's contemplation, finally, is merely an abstract thought which presupposes the totality of intelligible and corporeal entities as pre-existing, ascertains by degrees their mere existence, choosing and aggregating arbitrarily and by means of a merely reflective method individual aspects and relations out of the vast number of real attributes of these entities. These differences can scarcely be proved in detail. They are, however, characteristic for the type of philosophical reflection and exposition as a whole and must be understood primarily from the historical situation of the different thinkers. Plato was the first to elaborate the doctrine of the intelligible existence of the Ideas, following certain indications given by the Pythagoreans and Eleatics. After an interval of six centuries, Plotinus returned to Plato and for the first time again gave a serious meaning to the theory of Ideas. Each of Plato's and Plotinus' utterances corresponds to a creative insight and is accompanied by the signs of direct experience and inspiration. Ficino, on the other hand, is preceded by a thousand-year tradition of Christian theology, in which the existence of intelligible entities was taken as a matter of course and as a constantly reiterated truth. His frequent use of the rich treasure of coined formulae placed at his disposal by that tradition is therefore readily understood. In contrast to these formulae, direct expressions of his own concrete experience are comparatively rare.

Now that we know the most important aspects of internal experience, we must describe more accurately its concrete development as a whole and in its main stages. Inner consciousness is first distinguished by its nature from the state of ordinary consciousness, but nevertheless, as we have seen above, it is already foreshadowed in common, everyday experience. For Ficino the ascent from ordinary to internal experience is not a sudden leap; rather, it takes the form of a steady and imperceptible passage. This fact, which results directly from the above considerations, must always be kept in mind.

As to the actual course of internal experience or contemplation, it is neither the homogeneous development of a standpoint attained once and for all nor an irregular fluctuation of different conceptions, but an orderly and steady succession of definite conceptual degrees. We find the theory of different degrees of contemplative knowledge as early as in Plato: Diotima's speech in the *Symposium,* for instance. In Plotinus this theory is maintained with explicit reference to the *Symposium,* but for him the whole sphere of internal experience and contemplation is entirely separated, by two acts of sudden elevation—from the preceding realm of ordinary experience, as well as from the still higher state of transcendent consciousness. All gradual differences within contemplation have but slight importance in comparison. For Ficino, on the contrary, the clear-cut separation of internal consciousness at its upper and lower limits, has disappeared. For, as we have seen, it is connected with ordinary experience by a gradual transition; also, on the upper limit there is no longer a sudden elevation toward a transcendent consciousness, as we shall prove. The degrees within the contemplation therefore necessarily assume a greater importance. There is, moreover, another, ontological viewpoint. If from the outset thought is related to a pre-existing reality, and if reality as a whole is divided into a definite series of degrees,[43] contemplation must also pass in a continuous succession through the hierarchy of things, since it is directed toward the existing reality, and therefore must take place itself in a definite series of degrees.

By this means a hierarchy of contemplation is basically estab-

[43] Cf. chaps. iv and vi, above.

lished, but only basically. We shall seek in vain for consistent elaboration of the principle in Ficino, and the different forms in which the doctrine occurs are significant only in so far as they express a common tendency.

After it has ascended gradually through the spheres of the world [the human mind] also gradually considers the angels so that it may see one always higher than the other, and it never finds one that is so high that it could not find another one higher by one degree and again another one higher by one degree.[44]

Elsewhere we read that the Soul "ascends through the structure of the world and the orders of the angels to God" and that it uses these means like degrees "in order that the Soul itself, which once had fallen below itself, may return through these degrees to its citadel. When it has returned there, it sees God without mediation." [45] In another passage we read that knowledge ascends by several degrees from the name of a thing to its Idea.[46] Sometimes we notice that the gradual ascent of consciousness is connected with the different fields of philosophy. Philosophy, so we read in the *Praise of Philosophy,* leads the Soul up to the highest contemplation primarily through four degrees: morals, physics, mathematics, and metaphysics.

The divine Plato thinks that the celestial and immortal Soul dies in a certain sense when it enters the earthly and mortal body and returns to life when it leaves the body. It leaves it first through some effort of meditation before leaving it through the law of nature, when philosophy, the medicine of human sicknesses, purifies and revives through moral remedies the little Soul buried in the pestilent dirt of vices. Then, elevating it from the lowest place through physical instruments, it leads the Soul through all things composed of the four elements and through the four elements themselves up to heaven. Afterwards, by mathematical steps, it gradually makes the ascent to the highest spheres of the heaven possible. Finally, and this is admirable beyond all speech,

[44] *Ibid.,* p. 201.
[45] *Ibid.,* p. 236; cf. Heitzman, "L'agostinismo avicennizzante," *Giorn. crit.,* XVI (1935), 478.
[46] *Op. om.,* p. 265.

it lifts the Soul on metaphysical wings beyond the peak of heaven to the Craftsman of the whole heaven and world.[47]

Plato's metaphor of the cavern may be interpreted in the same way, and in this context Ficino says explicitly: "If we are lead through convenient degrees of morals, doctrines, and time, we sincerely recognize those who are deceived, occupied, and oppressed by false shadows and images of this world, and judge those people blind and miserable." [48]

The contemplative life of the Soul is therefore achieved in many degrees. These degrees cannot proceed to the infinite, but must be restricted in number and must also pass through a limited interval. For, according to Ficino, an infinite series of acts is entirely excluded.[49] The degrees of contemplation are related to the hierarchy of existing things, as the above examples show. The direct result is, therefore, the conception of a highest act of contemplation, having for its object the highest of all existing things. This conception first appears in the form of a mere postulate, it being still undetermined when and under what conditions such a highest act can really be experienced and accomplished. So we read, for example, that by ascending through all degrees of the angels the mind finally arrives at God and so puts an end to its movement.

It would proceed in this way without end if it did not impose a limit to itself and conclude that there is some infinite spirit which surpasses any angel . . . by innumerable degrees.[50]

That the Soul reaches this state [the highest knowledge of God] at some time, we may conclude from the fact that it separates itself from any knowledge of a created thing to such an extent as to assert that there is a divine peak, existing by an infinite interval above any concept, however sublime, of anything to be created.[51]

If the mind withdraws farther from corporeal things, the higher it is elevated to the contemplation of the spiritual things, and if the highest limit thought can reach is God's substance itself, it follows that the mind can be subjected to divine substance only when it is entirely alienated from the mortal senses.[52]

[47] *Ibid.*, pp. 669 f.; cf. p. 322.   [48] *Ibid.*, p. 160.   [49] Cf. above, chap. iv.
[50] *Op. om.*, p. 201.   [51] *Ibid.*, p. 236.   [52] *Ibid.*, p. 306; cf. p. 203.

Anything that has a quality that makes it tend afterwards more forcibly toward something than at the beginning, does not wander to the infinite, but is moved toward something definite. But we experience that in the desire for knowledge. For the more one knows, the more ardently he burns toward the rest. Hence the natural desire for knowing is directed toward some definite end.[53]

Similarly at the end of the *Theologia:*

We shall arrive under God's guidance at that highest degree of nature, if we separate the affection of the Soul as much as possible from matter which is the lowest degree of nature, so that we approach God in the degree that we withdraw from matter.[54]

After the possibility of a highest act is established in general, the question arises as to whether and in what form such an act can really be accomplished by human consciousness. In Ficino's opinion the answer is clear: man may attain direct intuition of God during the present life, but this perfect state is shared by very few individuals and its duration is limited to a brief moment.[55] This point is of decisive importance in understanding Ficino's metaphysics as a whole, and as he deals with it comparatively seldom, we must try to enumerate the relevant passages as fully as possible.

Whilst the Soul is surrounded by the dark dwelling of this body [so we read in the fourteenth book of the *Theologia*] it either never ceases its lower functions, or hardly ever, and then only for a moment. Therefore, that admirable work [union with God] is not attained in this body and is hardly ever enjoyed by an individual.[56]

Whoever lives piously with God for some time, maintains that only at that period of his life has he lived apart from evils and tasted something good, as if he had retired into his haven.[57]

---

[53] *Ibid.,* p. 307.   [54] *Ibid.,* p. 424.
[55] Dress (*op. cit.,* pp. 74 f.) rightly admits that "ecstasy" may actually be attained during earthly life and considers this an element of "Neoplatonic mysticism"; but he does not take into account the various degrees of contemplation. Anichini (*op. cit.,* pp. 47 f.), on the contrary, wrongly asserts that according to Ficino the highest knowledge of God is excluded from earthly life and reserved for the future life.
[56] *Op. om.,* p. 306.   [57] *Ibid.,* p. 307.

Up to his last old age man strives assiduously to acquire the state of happiness which he finally perceives in part and possesses in this life for a very short time.[58]

We think that we live only at that time during this life separated for a while from evils and that we taste something of the true good and rest, when we adhere for a while to Thee [God] through the attention of the mind or through the affection of piety.[59]

But on earth we share in this great joy [the contemplation of God] with difficulty and rather seldom, oh we miserable men. Now our sick minds perceive but a slight and momentary shadow of it. For their natural taste, oh grief, is infected too much by the bitter humor of this body. Hence that celestial and salutary flavor is not perceived or sometimes offends or pleases but slightly and briefly. Those among us who through the effort of morals and contemplation have obliterated more completely the dirt and mud of the body from the nature of the mind, taste it more sharply and enjoy it more strongly and longer; but they are very few whom the righteous Jupiter loved or whom ardent virtue lifted to the ether.[60]

Of men like Socrates, Plato, St. Paul, or the theologians in general Ficino says that they have really achieved the highest act of contemplation.[61] Elsewhere he compares the Soul that for a moment lifts itself to God, meanwhile interrupting its corporeal functions, to the stone thrown upward, which for a moment stays in the heights before returning to earth through gravity.[62]

The mind can therefore achieve the highest act of contemplation under certain conditions, but it is hindered from remaining in that state by the needs of the body and of external life. Hence, after a brief moment of absolute perfection it must return to the sphere of common experience or at least to the lesser degrees of contemplation. The formula for steady ascent presented at the beginning is therefore abandoned, and the course of contemplation appears as

[58] *Ibid.*, p. 316.   [59] *Ibid.*, p. 666.

[60] *Ibid.*, p. 712; cf. Virgil *Aeneid* vi. 129 f.

[61] *Op. om.*, pp. 267, 268, 425.

[62] *Ibid.*, p. 304. In his early work, *De amore,* Ficino apparently holds a different opinion: "In this life we cannot see the pure light itself and its source" (p. 1351).

a restless upward and downward motion; for scarcely has the Soul arrived at its goal, when it is again at once separated from it, to tend toward it soon again in a renewed effort.

If we keep these facts in mind, the apparent contradiction between Ficino's various statements disappears. In one place he says that the Soul reaches the state of perfect contemplation only for a moment; [63] but at other times we read that the mind, once awakened to contemplation, will never abandon it again unless temporarily distracted by the care of the body.[64] Ficino evidently has in mind at one time only the act of intuition of God, at another the whole course of internal experience, including the lower and higher degrees of contemplation. The Soul therefore achieves the highest act of contemplation only for a fleeting moment, but once elevated to the sphere of contemplation, it never again departs from it, barring external obstacles.

The fact that the highest act of contemplation can be achieved at all during earthly life is of decisive importance for the inner content of Ficino's metaphysics.[65] For if the doctrine of the knowledge of God constitutes the real center of his whole speculation, we can now affirm with certainty from the standpoint actually reached, that it is not merely an abstract conceptual postulate, but a concrete conception based on experience. For Ficino the act of highest contemplation is in a double sense the point of orientation. First, it constitutes, as we have seen, the real goal of internal experience and thus of human existence as a whole, so that all preceding grades of life and contemplation receive a new meaning and content from it. Secondly, the future life of the Soul is conceived as an eternal intuition of God. That is, the concrete attributes of future life are taken from the experience of the highest contemplation, with the sole difference that the act which is

---

[63] See above.   [64] *Op. om.*, pp. 216, 270.

[65] Dress (*op. cit.,* pp. 76 f., 143 ff.), although recognizing the existence of this doctrine, deprives it of any philosophical importance, declaring that it is in contrast to Ficino's theory of human personality. I do not see such a contrast, and even if it existed, it should not cause us to neglect the fact of contemplative experience.

achieved during the present life for a brief moment only, constitutes in the future life a lasting and imperishable possession of the
Soul. Conversely, the act of highest contemplation achieved during
the present life is considered as a metaphor and foretaste of the
future life and of eternal beatitude.[66]

It does not escape [the attention of the philosophers] of what kind the
state of the pure Soul will be after death. It will be of such a kind as is
always experienced at the highest peak of contemplation (*in summo
contemplationis fastigio*).[67]

The odor of such a life is perceived by a mind which is withdrawn
from it as much as possible; its flavor is tasted by a mind entirely separated.[68]

From that sudden ecstasy (*abstractione*) metaphysicians conclude that
the intellect may at some time think without the images of phantasy.[69]

Since the highest act of consciousness may be experienced during
earthly life, it may be asked what its content really is and what
its particular qualities are. In comparison with other thinkers, like
Plotinus, Ficino very seldom expresses his opinion on that point.
Even though he occasionally gives an enthusiastic description of
that perfect state, we can derive from his words, which are full of
sentiments and images, very little for a conceptual analysis. We
can, however, clearly recognize two main aspects which seem to
correspond to the basic qualities of internal experience. First, the
highest act is accompanied by the sensation of perfect joy and
happiness. The incessant sorrow and disquietude of the consciousness is therefore overcome, since the restless movement of the Soul
has finally reached its end. Secondly, the highest act partakes of
the nature of a perfect knowledge of God, in other words, the
contemplative attitude is here intensified to its absolute perfection,
and therefore we have repeatedly spoken of an act of highest contemplation. The achievement of contemplation in that act is presented in a double manner. First, God is superior in rank to all

---

[66] According to Anichini (*op. cit.*, p. 56), future contemplation is distinguished from present contemplation only by a gradual difference.
[67] *Op. om.*, p. 383; cf. Dress, *op. cit.*, p. 74.
[68] *Op. om.*, p. 409.   [69] *Ibid.*, p. 715.

existing things; hence the knowledge of God must also excel all other acts of knowledge. Moreover, God is also the totality of all things; consequently, the knowledge of all other objects is directly included in the contemplative knowledge of God.

It is our end to see God through the intellect and to enjoy the seen God through the will.[70]

In the knowledge or possession of God alone consists the ultimate human goal, which alone ends the natural appetite.[71]

[The state of the pure mind] will be such as they [the philosophers] experience at any time in the highest peak of contemplation, that is, calm and serene and surrounded by the formulae of Ideas like rays of the stars, and shining through the splendor of the divine sun.[72]

[In the highest degree of contemplation] the Soul not only becomes happy by the gift of philosophy, but since, so to speak, it becomes God, it becomes happiness itself. There all things, arts, and affairs of men cease; among them all sacred philosophy alone remains. There true beatitude is nothing else but true philosophy, since philosophy as defined by wise men is the love of wisdom. But we believe that the highest beatitude will consist in some affection of the will, which is love and joy around divine wisdom.[73]

With these and similar words Ficino describes the future life of the Soul and at the same time the highest act of contemplation, in which the future life is for a brief moment anticipated.

Last of all, we must ask how the act of the knowledge of God is related to the other acts of contemplation. The answer to this question lies in the previous reasonings. It is, however, worth restating in clear terms: the knowledge of God constitutes the highest peak in the gradual series of contemplation—in other words, it is superior in grade to all other acts and distinguished from them by that very fact. It is, however, in one series with them and thus not essentially different from them.

The higher the mind is elevated to the contemplation of spiritual things, the farther it withdraws from corporeal things; but the highest limit which thought can reach is the substance of God itself.[74]

[70] *Ibid.*, p. 307.   [71] *Ibid.*   [72] *Ibid.*, p. 383.
[73] *Ibid.*, p. 670.   [74] *Ibid.*, p. 306.

There is, intrinsic in us, a natural desire always to find the cause of any effect, and this research does not cease until we arrive at the primal cause. Since we desire to see the cause of any known effect, and since our intellect knows the universal Being itself, we naturally want to know the cause of Being itself, which is God Himself.[75]

The more someone knows, the more ardently he burns for the remainder. Hence the natural desire to know is directed toward some definite end. What is this end? The cause of all causes, the knowledge of which ends all natural research for causes.[76]

The knowledge of God appears here always as the keystone of an ascending series of knowledge, and instead of further examples it is sufficient to remember the formula of the highest peak of contemplation (*in summo contemplationis fastigio*).[77]

The knowledge of God is therefore not radically separated from the other acts of internal experience; in other words, the sphere of contemplation is not really transcended in it. Here we touch, perhaps, on the most important point at which Ficino's philosophy differs from that of Plotinus. For Plotinus there is in each contemplative act the distinction between the objective substance and the consciousness striving inward. This contrast is overcome only by a wholly new, transcendent act of consciousness, in which the last cause of existing things is experienced as being also the source and origin of internal life itself, and this is really the true reason for the ontological distinction between the One and the Mind. For Ficino the contemplative attitude cannot be transcended at all, but can only be perfected within itself. To him, therefore, any reason for distinguishing between One and Mind ceases, since he moves entirely within the realm of what Plotinus calls Mind. We can now understand the discordant position of the One in Ficino, a position we have frequently noticed in our analysis. The distinction between the One and the first Being is not based on Ficino's own position, but merely suggested by the Neoplatonic tradition. Therefore, when he tries to approach this tradition or to adapt himself to it, Ficino is obliged to contradict himself.

[75] *Ibid.*, p. 307.   [76] *Ibid.*   [77] *Ibid.*, p. 383; see also above.

If we consider the whole course of internal experience in a final survey, we must establish the following result: the individual acts of internal experience or contemplation constitute a continually ascending hierarchy. This hierarchy is limited at one extreme by ordinary experience and at the other by knowledge of God. It is separated from them, not by a sudden jump, but merely through an imperceptible transition. However far a given state of consciousness may be from the highest act of contemplation, it can always be considered as a preparation for it and can be interpreted in its own content through reference to it. The totality of all human states of consciousness and life thus fills a homogeneous sphere which extends in a straight line from the common experience to the highest intuition of God. Though the details of this conception may need some doctrinal clarification, the general direction for the further metaphysical speculation is at least indicated.

XII

THE KNOWLEDGE OF GOD

WE HAVE DESCRIBED the development and the original aspects of internal experience. It is now our essential task to follow its conceptual interpretation and application, so determining more accurately and reconstructing in its details, the curve drawn in the first outline. According to Ficino the whole content of internal consciousness may be summed up in the formula that the human Soul knows God. In other words, the subject experiencing and accomplishing the ascent of consciousness is man, who is conceived according to an old tradition as an objective but incorporeal substance. The process itself has a contemplative character and opens a new sphere of reality for the Soul. In consequence it is interpreted as an attitude of thinking or knowing. Since all thought is necessarily directed toward an object and since for Ficino each possible object constitutes an element of existing reality, internal contemplation is at once related to a supersensitive object, afterward defined as "intelligible world" or "God." Later we shall examine the origin and development of the concept of Soul. First we must analyze the doctrine of the knowledge of God, which actually constitutes the cardinal point of Ficino's speculation. For that purpose we must proceed first indirectly, since this doctrine is not only derived from internal experience but also includes a number of ontological and partly traditional elements.

The totality of existing things, which contains all objects of possible knowledge, constitutes for Ficino, as we have seen, a continually ascending hierarchy limited at both extremes. The real elements of this hierarchy are the species, while the individuals within one species are co-ordinated. The larger genera indicate more comprehensive spheres or aspects of the whole reality and can thus intersect and overlie each other in various ways. Of special importance are the genera of corporeal and intelligible things, which cut reality itself into two symmetrical halves. God is at the peak of the whole hierarchy, Himself a member of the series. (We have only to recall the doctrine of the five substances.) At the same time, He is basically distinguished from all other members. Moreover, as creator and cause of existence He is above and outside all things, but at the same time, He is in all things, and hence the totality of all real things.[1]

Of special importance for Ficino's epistemology is the concept of form. In contrast to matter, Aristotle had defined the given content of corporeal things, their essence and *quid,* as the factor of form and had considered it as the essence of the things, as well as the object of knowledge. This distinction of form and matter and the respective function of the form has been transferred by the Neoplatonists to the incorporeal entities also. Accordingly, in Ficino the whole of reality as regards its perceptibility appears as a system of forms. He distinguishes, as we have seen, substantial and accidental forms. Substantial forms are the concepts of the natural species of which the world hierarchy is composed, and accidental forms are the different qualities which are inherent in the existing things and are predicated to them. We remember that, through the doctrine of the *primum in aliquo genere,* each accidental form is related to a certain substance-concept to which it belongs originally, whereas all other things possess this quality only through the *primum.* The accidental forms are distributed in various ways throughout reality, partly limited to a particular sphere of things, partly filling the whole space of existence.

The whole system of these forms and their emanation from the divine cause of all things is sometimes described by Ficino by a particular metaphor. The divine ray, we read, for example, in the sixteenth book of the *Theologia,* which contains all forms, passes from God in different degrees to the angelic and human intelli-

---

[1] Cf. *Op. om.,* p. 403.

gences to which it gives the force of knowledge and at last to the matter of the corporeal world, which it fills with all objective forms. Thereby the ray which in God is entirely simple, develops, as it recedes from God, into greater and greater multiplicity and in the corporeal world reaches the highest grade of separation and differentiation.[2] At first glance it seems that this would only mean that the perceptibility of things and the knowing force of the intellects are derived from the same divine origin; as Plato already had attempted with a similar metaphor in the sixth book of the *Republic*. But the metaphor of the ray which spreads out more and more in the form of a cone directs us to determinate Neoplatonic conceptions. For Plotinus reality is divided into several spheres, placed one above another like layers, each of which contains in its own way the totality of all forms which it receives from the next higher degree and passes on to the next lower degree. Here the image of the divine ray has its original, clear meaning. In Ficino, on the contrary, the Neoplatonic doctrine of levels has been replaced by the medieval doctrine of degrees, since all existing things no longer depend on each other in essence, but are immediately related to God. Moreover, for Ficino the division of the incorporeal world is no longer given by a hierarchy of Ideas, but now by a hierarchy of angelic intelligences. Finally, the introduction of quality as one of the five basic degrees of reality has entirely destroyed the meaning of the Neoplatonic hierarchy. The image of the divine ray retains, therefore, only a slight part of its original significance. As considered in the context of Ficino's world system, it has neither a clear meaning nor a clear relationship to the other metaphysical doctrines. It is necessary, however, for the understanding of his epistemology, and it indicates at least that the totality of all forms is present in each sphere of reality and that it has its origin in the divine substance.

To understand Ficino's epistemology proper, we must start from the sense objects and from empirical knowledge. The intercourse of human consciousness with the corporeal things and the

[2] Cf. *ibid.,* pp. 370, 373.

co-operation between the respective forces of the Soul is understood essentially according to Aristotle's psychology. Compared to that, Ficino's exposition shows only a few traits of independent significance, and it is therefore sufficient for us to emphasize a few main features that appear most clearly and most explicitly in the eighth book of the *Theologia*.

The first encounter of the Soul with the outside world is the perception of a corporeal object through the five senses. According to an old conception there is supposed to be an almost material affinity between the sense organ and the perceptible objects.[3] Ficino has not clearly expressed himself about the genesis of the sense image. Sometimes, following Aristotle, he says that the form of the object sends an image into the sense organ.[4] In addition, we also find the cruder conception that there is a direct corporeal influence of the objects upon the sense organs.[5] As to the process of seeing, he says at times that the eye itself sends out a seeing ray which meets the objects and is reflected by them into the eye.[6] To Ficino the important point in the whole process is merely the independence of the Soul from the influences of the corporeal objects. Though man's passivity as regards the sense objects cannot be denied on Ficino's premises, the body only (and perhaps the spirit, a subtle stuff intermediary between body and Soul) is said to be subjected to the influences of the outside world, while the Soul receives and elaborates the accepted impressions freely and independently.[7]

The second force which contributes to the elaboration of sense impressions is the internal sense, or imagination, which corresponds approximately to the Aristotelian *sensus communis*. While the external sense perception is still divided into the different sense spheres, seeing, hearing, and so forth, taking place within the sense organs and their *spiritus,* and presupposing the actual pres-

---

[3] *Ibid.,* p. 238.   [4] Cf. *ibid.,* pp. 182, 269.
[5] *Ibid.,* pp. 177 f., 211 f., 371.   [6] *Ibid.,* pp. 241, 377.
[7] *Ibid.,* pp. 177 f., 211 f.; cf. Cassirer, *Erkenntnisproblem,* p. 91; Saitta, *op. cit.,* pp. 181 ff.; Horbert, *op. cit.,* p. 20; Heitzman, "L'agostinismo avicennizzante," *Giorn. crit.,* XVI (1935), 306 ff.

ence of material objects, the impressions of all five senses are already united in the imagination into one conception. This is brought about through an immediate activity of the Soul and not necessarily in the presence of the objects.[8] Here the activity of the Soul is already apparent. For the imagination is not simply formed by the sense images, but includes in itself their innate seeds or potential forms which are simply awakened and brought to actuality through the external impressions.

When [the internal force of the Soul] has reached colors through the spirit of the eye, sounds through the spirit of the ears, and so forth, through its own force by which it governs the bodies and possesses their seeds . . . it conceives anew in itself the entirely spiritual images of the colors, sounds, etc., or, those being conceived previously, it brings them forth and connects them into unity.[9]

After sense perception and imagination there follows, as a third force, phantasy, which Ficino does not always strictly distinguish from imagination.[10] Its task is to express a judgment upon the images received by sense perception and united by imagination.[11] While imagination is still occupied with the production of the concrete image, phantasy can already name it and predicate attributes to it—in other words, it possesses, not a concept as yet, but an anticipation and representation of substance and quality.[12] The images or conceptions of phantasy, possessing a kind of preconceptual determination, are called intentions, after the scholastic tradition.[13] In forming these intentions the Soul shows its productive force; for it forms the images of the sense impressions "through phantasy and preserves them in memory. Hence in a

[8] *Ibid.*, p. 182; cf. Heitzman, "L'agostinismo avicennizzante," *Giorn. crit.*, XVI (1935), 308 ff. Yet Ficino does not qualify the imagination *more Platonico* as *sensus communis* (Heitzman, *op. cit.*, pp. 309, 318; cf. *Op om.*, p. 292), but, rather, the converse.

[9] *Op. om.*, p. 212; cf. p. 241. There is therefore a kind of "innatism" even for the sense knowledge, a fact which Heitzman denies (*Giorn. crit.*, XVI, 308).

[10] Cf. *Op. om.*, pp. 104, 157, 242.   [11] *Ibid.*, pp. 177 f.   [12] *Ibid.*, p. 182.

[13] *Ibid.*, p. 182; cf. Heitzman, "L'agostinismo avicennizzante," *Giorn. crit.*, XVI (1935), 310 ff.

short time phantasy is full of the individual forms of individual things." [14]

The work started by sense perception, imagination, and phantasy is finally completed by thought, and only here can we speak of a real knowledge of empirical objects. Phantasy was not bound to the material presence of the objects or to the determinate elements of perception, but its images still had a particular character, while for the first time thought arrives at the knowledge of universals. For Ficino the universal is at first, as it had been for Aristotle, the common nature inherent in individual concrete objects and contained in them, for example, as humanity is contained in this or that man.[15] This universal "infuses itself into individual bodies and so exists in a different thing and in many things." [16] This universal in things is the real object of thought and is discovered in things only by thought. Yet the activity of thought is not confined to the universal, but directs itself in a further act upon individual things in their individuality.[17] Above all, it tries to discover the substance of the individual thing, the cause of its quality, and its relation to other things. So thought never ceases to apply universal concepts to individual things and, conversely, to define the individual in terms of the universal.[18] Since, therefore, the universal is contained in the individual and is part of its specification, the construction of the object-image by the Soul is complete only in thought.

The universal in things is simply the correlate of the concept, and if previously it had seemed necessary to consider the image of phantasy a product of the Soul itself, much less could the rational concept here be derived from external influences. In reality, the Soul or mind contains innate germs or forms of all universal concepts, the so-called "formulae," or "little forms," which pass from potentiality to actual consciousness in each act of thought.[19]

---

[14] *Op. om.*, p. 371.   [15] *Op. om.*, pp. 182 f.

[16] *Ibid.*, p. 183; cf. Heitzman, "L'agostinismo avicennizzante," *Giorn. crit.*, XVI (1935), 298 f.

[17] *Op. om.*, pp. 183 f.; cf. Saitta, *op. cit.*, pp. 180 f.

[18] *Op. om.*, pp. 371 f.   [19] *Ibid.*, p. 241 ff.

Just as the life-giving part [of the Soul] changes, generates, nourishes, and increases through innate germs, so the inner sense and the mind judge all things through innate formulae which are called into being by external objects. And this judgment is nothing else than the transition of the formula from potency to act.[20]

Some forms natural to the Soul and equal in number to the species of created things in the world, through which the Soul is enabled to produce the intelligible forms of those species, must lurk in the innermost recesses of the Soul prior to the forms or notions which [the intellect] is producing in itself in every moment at every age.[21]

The Soul can, therefore, produce its universal concepts by its own power. If the Soul in a given moment directs its thought toward various empirical objects, that simply means that the images of phantasy, which are being formed every moment, at the same time stimulate the intellect to activity and serve it as an occasion to conceive definite concepts.

The diversity of images is not sufficient to produce that variety [of species]; for the diversity of images contributes nothing to that production beyond a chance to act, inasmuch as by their presence the mind is induced to call forth the species. And that means nothing else than making those idle concepts more available.[22]

The mind receives the forms of things from itself, "when stimulated by images of bodies it brings to light forms that are lurking in the recesses of the mind." [23] This theory, which is predominant in Ficino, is sometimes even further restricted. The mind needs images, so we read in one passage, before it can conceive universal concepts, in order to be stimulated by them to produce concepts. Once that has been done, the concept still needs the image as a base and guide, according to the Peripatetic conception; but according to the Platonic conception, the mind then does not need the image

[20] *Ibid.*, pp. 241 f. Cf. Cassirer, *Erkenntnisproblem*, pp. 91 ff.; Saitta, *op. cit.;* p. 204; Dress, *op. cit.*, pp. 64 f.; Horbert, *op. cit.*, pp. 21 f.

[21] *Op. om.*, p. 243. Kieszkowski (*op. cit.*, p. 80) is not correct in saying that the image-forming faculty creates formula, mind, Idea.

[22] *Op. om.*, p. 243.

[23] *Ibid.*, p. 198; cf. p. 242 and Saitta, *op. cit.*, p. 205; Heitzman ("L'agostinismo avicennizzante," *Giorn. crit.*, XVI [1935], 465) tries to introduce an artificial distinction between *ratio* and *mens*. It has no place in this context.

at all.[24] Starting with the Aristotelian distinction between the active and the passive intellect, Ficino once illustrated the particular process through which the concept is awakened by the image. As the ray of the sun reflected by a mirror on an opposite wall forms a circle of light there, so a ray of the active intellect is reflected by the particular image of phantasy to the passive intellect and actually generates there the universal concept.[25] Thought, therefore, contains in itself the potential forms of all concepts and calls them into being under the influence of images. In this way it is able to know the universal in external things and to determine individual objects in their universal factors and in their relationship to the universal.[26]

However, for Ficino human knowledge is not limited to empirical objects, but rises above them to the sphere of incorporeal and intelligible things, there to consider divine things: Ideas. Here, for the first time in epistemology, we notice the influence of inner experience. For as we have seen, by a process of spiritual ascent or sublimation a new realm of objects becomes accessible to consciousness and because of that fact the higher attitude of man has been called contemplation. Ideas form the content of this contemplation, and conversely, the knowledge of Ideas is bound to inner experience as to its necessary premise.

When [the Soul] rises above itself through the mind, like the angels [it reaches] supersensitive reasons which are separated from the imaginative intentions.[27]

[24] *Op. om.*, p. 232; cf. Heitzman, "L'agostinismo avicennizzante," *Giorn. crit.*, XVI (1935), 468.

[25] *Op. om.*, p. 240; cf. Meier, *op. cit.*, pp. 243 f. Heitzman ("L'agostinismo avicennizzante," *Giorn. crit.*, XVI [1935], 299) asserts that in Ficino, God takes the place of the *intellectus agens*. But this thesis, which seems to be confirmed by an introductory lecture (*Op. om.*, p. 896) does not agree with the passage quoted above (*ibid.*, pp. 240 f.). The question is less important than may be assumed, because the theory of the *intellectus agens* has no significance whatsoever for Ficino.

[26] Heitzman ("L'agostinismo avicennizzante," *Giorn. crit.*, XVI [1935], 299 f.) says that for Ficino the universal is produced only by the intellect, but this does not result at all from the reported passages.

[27] *Op. om.*, p. 233.

Therefore the Soul must abandon external things and retire within itself in order to find these [true] things.[28]

When [the Soul] is separated from the body and purified of the dirt of the body, it is directed with all its attention to incorporeal things alone.[29]

Because only divine things have true existence, while corporeal things are mere shadows, only true philosophers who know of the existence of Ideas are awake, while all others are dreaming.[30]

We shall be filled with true forms only at that time when we [shall be] empty of dreams.[31]

[Philosophers] should conduct an intellectual life apart from the body, then being apart they will at once reach the separated forms. They will soon actually prove Socrates' opinion that above the forms lying in the formed objects . . . . there are forms existing in themselves and perfect . . . . and that there is only one way not only to reach but also to possess incorporeal things—namely, to make oneself incorporeal, in other words, to separate one's mind as much as possible from corporeal movement, perception, passion and imagination.[32]

Ficino does not go so far as do Plato and Plotinus, for whom the intelligible world was originally established on the basis of inner experience. For according to Ficino the existence of Ideas and of incorporeal reality is already given by the Platonic and scholastic tradition. However, it is clear from the quoted passages that the subjective certainty of intelligible being is entirely based on the contemplative consciousness, and so the whole sphere of incorporeal things is placed in direct relation to the concrete, inner experience. This is a factor which occurs more or less in all idealistic speculations. As a rule, it is not correctly evaluated by interpreters who are inclined to give first a merely ontological description of intelligible reality, only to discover later, apart from it, a "mystical" element in the respective thinker, without seeing the fundamental relation between inner experience and intelligible reality. In any case, for Ficino knowledge of Ideas is closely linked to the spiritual ascent or sublimation of the Soul. Conversely, the

---

[28] *Ibid.*, p. 264.   [29] *Ibid.*, p. 714.   [30] *Ibid.*, p. 628.   [31] *Ibid.*, p. 749.
[32] *Ibid.*, p. 159. See above, chap. xi.

inner affinity of the Soul with Ideas, which is manifested in that fact, is a leading argument for the immortality of the Soul, as we shall see later.

If we now inquire into the real content of Ficino's theory of Ideas, that is, into the attributes, grade, and sphere of validity of the individual Ideas, we have very little to state. There is almost nothing left in Ficino of Plato's conceptual dialectic or of Plotinus' concrete structure of the intelligible world. All he says about Ideas is confined after all to the affirmation of their existence and to the establishment of a few basic ontological relations of the Ideas with God, with the innate concepts of reason, and with the empirical things.[33] This impoverishment of the whole theory is partly due to the historical situation, inasmuch as in their significance as intelligible entities Ideas had been partly absorbed by the Christian concept of God and partly replaced by the various orders of angels. As to the act itself of the knowledge of Ideas, Ficino illustrates it with the help of innate formulae which originally proceeded out of Ideas as their images and are united in the act of contemplation with their originals whereby the Soul also receives the Ideas into itself.

Our mind would never know them [the intelligible essences] if it had not in itself their forms as images. For if it performs an act in knowing, and if it acts only in so far as it is actual, and if it acts in the same manner in which it is actual, and if it becomes actual through the form, it will never contemplate the essences if it is not adorned with their forms. Though these forms are sometimes called intelligible, they should rather be called intellectual.[34]

Through the formula of man the mind fits the Idea of man as the wax formed by the ring, when it is carefully matched to the ring, fits its original. That fitting itself is the true and distinct knowledge of man. For then [when it reaches divine reasons] the mind, being adorned with the Idea, becomes the very truth of that thing which has been created through that Idea. This is true of all those who contemplate, and, as St. John says, they receive from the fullness of divine reason,

[33] The lessened importance of the theory of Ideas in Ficino as compared with Plato is rightly emphasized by Huit, op. cit., pp. 362 f.

[34] Op. om., p. 191.

because whoever truly contemplates a species of things, has already received in himself one of the number of Ideas whose fullness is divine reason itself.[35]

We have seen above that from the standpoint of inner experience the ordinary state of life was interpreted as a preparation (though an unconscious one) for true contemplation. Accordingly, the knowledge of empirical objects is considered an unconscious preparation for the knowledge of Ideas, and an indirect share in the empirical knowledge is attributed even to the Idea itself. First, the universal in things which constitutes the object of empirical knowledge is itself derived from the Idea as the absolute universal. It is therefore only a short step for reason to ascend from the concrete universal in things to the Idea.

Rightly we ascend from individual persons, who exist in parts of space and time, to the nature common to them in itself, which exists, so to speak, throughout all space and time, and from that nature to the concept which exists above all space and time, which Plato calls Idea.[36] How could many subjects participate in one common beauty, if one common nature of beauty did not inhere in and precede individual things so that what is inherent may be dependent upon that which precedes? [37]

Since the empirical object therefore actually rests on the Idea, all empirical knowledge of the universal is to begin with an unconscious knowledge of Ideas.

No wonder we are deceived in that matter in such a way that while contemplating the spiritual models of things we often think that we are contemplating simply the corporeal natures of things. For children, also, seeing the incorporeal images of bodies in mirrors, and dreamers, thinking spiritual images, believe that they are seeing bodies.[38] The eye, being formed by the species of color, perceives the color, but does not perceive the species through which it sees. So perhaps the

[35] *Ibid.*, pp. 268 f.; cf. p. 267. See also John 1: 16; Saitta, *op. cit.*, pp. 279 ff.; Dress, *op. cit.*, pp. 65 f.; Horbert, *op. cit.*, pp. 22 f.; Meier, *op. cit.*, pp. 244 f.; Anichini, *op. cit.*, pp. 53 f.

[36] *Op. om.*, p. 183; cf. Heitzman, "L'agostinismo avicennizzante," *Giorn. crit.*, XVI (1935), 300.

[37] *Ibid.*, p. 247.   [38] *Ibid.*, p. 266.

intellect, formed by the Idea, at once conceives through it the natural species itself which was formed by that Idea, but does not yet clearly contemplate the Idea itself or rather does not recognize it even when it contemplates it.[39]

Finally, all true empirical knowledge appears simply as the referring of things to Ideas, in which act the Soul, with its innate formulae, mediates between things and Ideas.

The truth of a created thing consists primarily in the fact that it corresponds entirely to its Idea. Knowledge, on the other hand, consists primarily in the fact that the mind corresponds to truth. But [the mind] cannot fit the truth of the thing itself if it does not also fit the Idea by the congruence with which truth is defined, so that it knows the thing through the Idea which is the cause of the thing, because true knowledge is through the cause.[40]

Since that which measures is more excellent than that which is measured, so the human mind, in so far as it measures all temporal things contained under Ideas through their relation to those Ideas, is more excellent than those things. Therefore it is next to Ideas, because it measures all things that follow Ideas and so falls between the source of Ideas and the brooks flowing out of it. But although it measures with Ideas as a standard, it does not measure through Ideas themselves as if they were a means belonging to or close to itself. For universal Ideas are not a peculiar instrument of this or that human mind, nor do universal Ideas by any means fall between the particular mind and other particular things. But just as the Soul cannot measure the particular images of universal Ideas in any other way than through the formulae of the Ideas peculiar to the Soul and almost descending to particular things, so of necessity the formulae of Ideas are inherent in the mind, and through them the mind can refer the images to the Ideas—approving those that agree with the formulae, disapproving those that disagree.[41]

Empirical knowledge is therefore a co-operation between thing, formula, and Idea, and while the part played by Idea is clearly recognized by a mind that has ascended to contemplation, it is

---

[39] *Ibid.*, p. 269; cf. Saitta, *op. cit.*, p. 281.   [40] *Ibid.*, p. 266.
[41] *Ibid.*, pp. 252 f.; cf. Heitzman, "L'agostinismo avicennizzante," *Giorn. crit.*, XVI (1935), 467.

no less effective, though it is unconscious, even in the other Souls still immersed in dream.

To Ficino the highest and decisive object of human knowledge is not the Idea, but God. Since the Soul can rise to a direct cognition of God, the knowledge of God is itself an act of inner or spiritual consciousness, and even the existence of God is directly connected with inner experience. But as the knowledge of Ideas corresponds to the contemplative attitude of the Soul, so the immediate knowledge of God is given in the highest act of consciousness, which we have called the peak of contemplation.

The separation (*abstractio*) of the Soul from the body, which increases with the increasing intensity of speculation, is fully attained when that intensity is completed. Speculation is fully achieved when all other things are put aside and only the primal True or Good is loved and thought with the greatest ardor of the mind.[42]

Elsewhere we read with reference to Plato's seventh letter:

[Socrates,] putting aside the usual unrest of research, took refuge in moral philosophy, in order that the mind, the corporeal clouds having been dispersed by its benefit, might become serene and at once receive the light of the divine sun that is always shining everywhere. Socrates himself and afterward Plato, imitating Socrates, seem to have accomplished that.[43]

We shall see the pure light of God separated from all Ideas and entirely infinite in its source only when we reach that state of purest mind in which we can contemplate in one glance that light itself which shines along with the splendor of all Ideas. Then, as . . . St. John the Evangelist says, we shall see God as He is, because we shall know God as God.[44]

In like manner Ficino exhorts the Soul to seek God:

Seek His face, I beg you, and you will enjoy forever. Do not move to touch Him, I beg you, for He is stability. Do not distract yourself over various things in order to reach Him, for He is unity itself. Halt the

[42] *Ibid.,* p. 233.
[43] *Ibid.,* p. 267; cf. chap. xi, above. See also Plato, *Epistle* vii. 341 c f.
[44] *Op. om.,* p. 268; cf. I John 3: 2.

movement, unite the multiplicity, and immediately you will reach God, who has long since reached you wholly.[45]

For Ficino, therefore, God's existence is a fact derived in advance from tradition. Yet its certainty rests on internal experience, and the way to reach Him is indicated by the ascent of contemplation.

The attributes of God, which Ficino treats extensively in the second book of the *Theologia,* are essentially based on ontological considerations, as we have seen above. For God is the first of all things, the cause of all existence, the totality of perfection, and so forth. But occasionally we also find some attributes hinting apparently at the internal contemplation of God, in which He presents Himself as the immediate fullness of reality outside and above any particular objects. There is, above all, the infinity of God, which is experienced concretely by the Soul during its contemplative ascent. This infinity is first determined as eternity when referred to the temporality of finite things.

Frequently we conceive with the mind some simple duration without beginning and end and call it, so to speak, "sempiternity," which is God Himself, though we may not recognize it. For every simple infinity is God Himself. We are then hindered from recognizing it by phantasy, which soon clothes and confuses that simple and consistent "sempiternity" with some flux and plurality and so deceives us, drawing toward the accidental flux of time that which is the substantial rest of eternity. Imagination thus impels us to think that what is really God is time. Thus the eternal God offers Himself to us on that occasion, but wrapped in time.[46]

Accordingly, in relation to the spatial extension of finite things, the infinity of God is conceived as omnipresence.

We frequently conceive a purest capacity which no limits can include and which includes all things that may exist or that may be imagined. Since pure infinity itself is nothing else than God, in conceiving that capacity, we conceive God Himself, though we may not be aware of it. For phantasy soon deceives us with its tricks, introducing instead of the divine rays some set of lines in the dimensions of long, broad, and

[45] *Op. om.,* p. 205.   [46] *Ibid.,* p. 97.

deep, and so making what is really divine light appear as a dimension or a void.[47]

But in its purest form the infinity of God appears in the infinite distance which exists between itself and all finite things as a whole and which only the mind, with its infinite force, can overcome.

The Soul is reflected into God without medium, when it sees God neither in any creature nor through an image of the sense or of the phantasy, but separated and naked above all created things. But it sees Him as such when it argues that God is so infinite that He excels by an infinite interval all things that may be conceived.[48]

That the Soul arrives at some time at that state [that is, at the immediate perception of God] we may suppose from the fact that it separates itself from any knowledge of a created thing to such an extent as to assert that the divine peak exists by an infinite interval above any concept, however sublime, of anything to be created.[49]

In all these descriptions Ficino evidently refers to an internal intuition of the divine essence which cannot be deduced from merely ontological postulates.

As we have seen above, internal experience is based on an elevation and effort of consciousness. Consequently, the contemplative life has a certain continuity, for apart from the necessary acts of external existence, consciousness need not abandon the higher state once it has attained it. Yet the act of the highest perception of God is a wholly isolated act and limited to a moment. It is even achieved suddenly, as we once read, hence without any activity of consciousness.[50] Previously indicated by Plato and Plotinus, this factor acquires a wholly different significance for Ficino through the Christian doctrine of grace. For if eternal beatitude is a gift of divine grace, and if the immediate perception of God represents a kind of foretaste of the future life, human conscious-

---

[47] *Ibid.*, p. 98. This passage is considered one of the major proofs of Ficino's supposed "immanentism," but it must not be isolated from the context. Cf. Saitta, *op. cit.*, pp. 91 f.; Hak, *op. cit.*, p. 91; Kieszkowski, *op. cit.*, p. 76; Anichini, *op. cit.*, p. 35. Kieszkowski quotes Ficino's text rather incorrectly.
[48] *Op. om.*, p. 236.   [49] *Ibid.*; cf. Anichini, *op. cit.*, pp. 36 f.
[50] Cf. *Op. om.*, p. 267.

ness would consequently not be able by its own power to accomplish the act of highest contemplation; it is God Himself who attracts and illuminates the striving Soul.

The mind is not brought by its own power to assume divine substance as its own form, but is drawn by divine action. For a lower nature cannot attain the propriety and form of a higher one without an act of the higher nature itself. . . . Why is that so? So that we may understand that the mind cannot be lifted up to see divine substance in itself by an increase of its natural force and light only, for such an action differs more than "by genus" from the natural action of the mind, but that a new force is needed and a new light descending from a higher cause. They call it the light of grace and glory, and illuminated by it and kindled even more the mind assumes divine substance . . . like a flame.[51]

To determine more accurately the essence and meaning of the knowledge of God we must examine the relation of Ideas to God. To Ficino, Ideas are the thoughts of God. This doctrine, first fully elaborated by the Neoplatonists, had been a common possession of medieval theology. The new element in Ficino is merely the fact that under the direct influence of the ancient sources he discusses the theory of Ideas more explicitly and more clearly. For him Ideas are intelligible forms, that is, the archetypes of substantial and accidental forms contained in created things and known in them. Since Ideas are conceived by God and so are inherent in His mind, they are also identical with His substance and, therefore, through His substance are identical with each other. In other words, each Idea is merely a particular aspect of the divine essence, or to use a figure of speech, a particular color in the fullness of divine light.

The last shadow of Ideas appears in matter, but above matter shines the face of all Ideas, whose source is God, author of things. . . . For if the mind and nature are full of forms . . . God, who is the form-giver of nature and of the mind, cannot be without forms.[52]

[51] *Ibid.*, pp. 411 f. Cf. Saitta, *op. cit.*, pp. 80 f.; Dress, *op. cit.*, pp. 114 f.; Anichini, *op. cit.*, pp. 114 f., 143 f.; Heitzman "L'agostinismo avicennizante," *Giorn. crit.*, XVI (1935), 479.

[52] *Op. om.*, p. 249.

Since in God being and thinking are identical, the notion which God, in thinking Himself, generates as an exact image of Himself, is identical with God Himself. . . . Those germs [that is, the Ideas] agree with each other in essence in order that God may not be a manifold substance, but they differ in concept in order that whatever is born in the world may not be uniform or without variety.[53]

There are in God the particular reasons for all things, and the species of things have their distinction from nowhere except from where they have their existence. Nor is the divine simplicity less simple because of the plurality of Ideas, since it contemplates them all through one form and in one glance. And the divine essence is called Idea, not as simply an essence, but as the model of this or that species. Therefore, in so far as several reasons are thought out of one essence, so far we may speak of several Ideas. And these aspects, through which Ideas are multiplied, are not produced by things themselves, but rather by divine intellect, comparing its own essence with things.[54]

Ideas are therefore, as we see, simply partial elements or aspects of God, and each knowledge of Ideas is in reality a knowledge of God, though the identity of the Idea with God and hence the presence of God in the Idea may not be consciously noticed. This insight is of such basic significance to Ficino that he dedicates an entire chapter to the reason why we do not perceive the presence of God in the perception of the Idea.[55]

When [the Intellect] continues to contemplate and becomes more congruous, it perceives and recognizes more clearly the Idea itself, but does not yet discern where it perceives it [the Idea]. Just as boys, seeing their images in the splendor of the sun over the surface of the water, think they see them, not in the external light, but in the depths of the water, so the untutored mind, when it sees the concepts of things in the sublime God, thinks that it sees them in itself or in other things, especially since the concept of a natural thing in God—for example, the concept of air—does not reproduce God as God or as the separated and free cause of the universe, but as the model of air. Consequently, when the mind is surrounded by the concept of divine air itself, it thinks God not as God, but as air. For it sees God as air-like, that is, as confined to the nature of air.[56]

[53] *Ibid.,* p. 251. [54] *Ibid.,* p. 107; cf. Saitta, *op. cit.,* p. 90.
[55] Ficino, *Theol. Plat.* xii, 3. [56] *Op. om.,* p. 269.

Almost all of us are deceived in this [matter], like ordinary people who, when they look at the moon during the night, say that they see by the light of the moon, though it is the light of the sun by which they see even at night. So ungrateful men assert that they see true things through their own and natural light, whereas they really see them in the common and divine light.[57]

In other words, just as after the discovery of the Idea the knowledge of the concrete universal was defined as unconscious knowledge of Ideas, so the knowledge of Ideas appears now, after the elevation toward God, as an unconscious knowledge of God.

Immediate knowledge of God, as we have seen above, is achieved, not by the Soul's own force, but by an active intervention of God. Since the Idea is a partial aspect of the divine substance, and the knowledge of Ideas an indirect or unconscious knowledge of God, the perception of the Idea is also conceived, not simply as an arbitrary act of thought, but rather as an active influence of God on the mind. And because the Idea partakes of the nature of a form and enters, so to speak, human thought during contemplation, Ficino arrives at the strange formula that the human mind in the act of thinking is formed by God.

That sublime mind which was going to form our mind daily through Ideas prepared and marked it once for that formation through the characters of Ideas [that is, the formulae].[58]

Likewise the human mind [Ficino continues, referring to Avicenna] is often prepared by the images of bodies received through the senses and phantasy to direct itself toward divine thought and to be daily formed by it in so far as it [the mind] is directed toward it. And what we call thinking is only being formed by divine thought.[59]

By these and similar reasons Plato has apparently been convinced that nothing can be really learned except through God's teaching.[60]

---

[57] *Ibid.* Cf. Horbert, *op. cit.,* pp. 23 f.; Anichini, *op. cit.,* p. 55.

[58] *Op. om.,* p. 265. Cf. Cassirer, *Erkenntnisproblem,* pp. 94 f.; *op. om.,* p. 274; and Heitzman, "L'agostinismo avicennizzante," *Giorn. crit.,* XVI (1935), 462.

[59] *Op. om.,* p. 265. Cf. Dress, *op. cit.,* pp. 66 f.; Horbert, *op. cit.,* p. 24.

[60] *Op. om.,* p. 267; cf. Meier, *op. cit.,* pp. 245 f.; Heitzman, "L'agostinismo avicennizzante," *Giorn. crit.,* XVI (1935), 473 ff.

[God], shining especially in the sanctuary of the mind, purifies, sharpens, illuminates, kindles continually its sight, and animates the formulae innate in the mind. Thus when free of care we apply our mind to the investigation of truth, those formulae that are animated by God come forth more openly, and the sight of the mind kindled by God sees more clearly and more ardently. God is related there to the act of thinking as the primal and common cause; the formula as the proper and second cause; the image as incitement; and the mind holds the place of matter.[61]

The relation between the knowledge of Ideas and the knowledge of God leads us back again to a question which we have encountered repeatedly in the course of our analysis: is God placed according to Ficino beyond the sphere of Ideas, or does He belong with them in one common sphere of reality? The question assumes a special significance in reference to the Neoplatonists, who have always distinguished strictly between the divine cause and the intelligible sphere of the mind and of the Ideas. We have noticed how many factors would tend to make Ficino abandon that distinction entirely. The Christian concept of God categorically excludes any substantial division of several degrees within God. The concrete analysis of internal experience has also shown us that the level of contemplation is not surpassed in Ficino even in the highest act of consciousness. If we observe now that Ideas are identical with the divine essence and that God is called the source of Ideas,[62] this opinion is entirely confirmed. However, it could not be Ficino's intention simply to cancel the concept of the One as coined by Plotinus from his system, but rather he was obliged to try to gather the essential attributes of that concept into his own concept of God, even though the latter may have been basically determined by Plotinus' concept of Mind. We have seen above to what extent this tendency was favored by the Christian doctrine of the trinity.[63] So we find occasionally in Ficino, as in Plotinus, the Good and the Intelligible distinguished as two aspects within God. This distinc-

[61] Op. om., pp. 271 f.; cf. Heitzman, "L'agostinismo avicennizzante," Giorn. crit., XVI (1935), 464.
[62] Cf. Op. om., p. 270.   [63] Cf. chap. ix, above.

tion, however, loses its meaning at once in so far as Ideas are inherent in the Good also.[64] As a matter of fact, it has never been elaborated by Ficino systematically. Here, however, we are interested in the particular coloring which the act of the intuition of God receives from the theory of the One. For Ficino speaks repeatedly of a union of the Soul with God, and it is obvious that he has in mind the so-called "ecstasy" of Plotinus.

[Plato] establishes the highest degree of beatitude in the *Epinomis,* where he says that when all mutability is stopped and all multiplicity collected the purified Soul retires into its own unity, superior to intellect, and transfers itself through that unity into the divine unity superior to the intelligible world, living through God rather than through itself, with whom [God] it is connected in a way admirable beyond all knowledge.[65]

Trismegistus likewise says that out of pure mind and God one spirit results in some way. And all Platonists agree that in the contemplation of reasons, divine reason is touched by a substantial rather than an imaginary contact of mind and that the unity peculiar to mind is joined with God, the unity of all things, in an ineffable manner.[66]

In another context he says, referring to Plotinus, that human intellects "through their centers, that is, their unities superior to their intellects, join with divine unity as with the center of the universe." [67] After all that, it might seem as if Ficino were assuming as possible a concrete act of unification apart from and beyond contemplation. But it is not by chance that the passages quoted are all from ancient authors, for in a similar context we see quite clearly how Ficino separates himself from his predecessors just at the decisive point, that is, on the distinction between One and Mind. The Platonists say "that the contemplating mind is formed by the highest God through unity, which is the peak of the mind, but by the second God through the intellect. But about that they may look themselves, for us it is sufficient to know that the Soul is formed by God." [68] Another circumstance makes this even clearer. In Plotinus the concept of unification serves to distinguish sharply the

[64] *Op. om.,* p. 249.
[66] *Op. om.,* p. 269.
[65] *Ibid.,* p. 409; cf. *Epinomis* 992 b.
[67] *Ibid.,* pp. 273 f.
[68] *Ibid.,* p. 282.

relation with the One from the contemplation of Mind and of Ideas. In Ficino, on the contrary, the relation with the Ideas is also explicitly called "union."

The formula, being a ray of the Idea, returns into the Idea easily and by a natural instinct and, along with itself, elevates the mind in which this ray is infused. When [this ray] is led back again into the Idea, it flows back into it as into its source, like a ray reflected into the sun, and through a bond of this kind one thing is made out of the mind and God.[69]

The Apostle Paul also says that the mind, contemplating divine things, is daily renewed and transformed into the same shape with God and becomes one spirit with Him.[70]

[And according to Plato] the Soul, perfected by contemplation, becomes entirely one in the vicinity of divine unity.[71]

Hence for Ficino the unity of the Soul with God is not a particular act distinguished from contemplation, but merely an attribute of the contemplative act itself and as such realized not only in the perception of God but also in the knowledge of Ideas.

Through the knowledge of God which is given to man in rare moments in this earthly life we may define analogously that knowledge of God which is given to the Soul in the future life and to the angels.

It does not escape [the philosophers] what the state of the pure Soul after death will be. It will be such as they experience at almost any time at the highest peak of contemplation. Namely, calm and serene and infused with the formulae of Ideas like rays of the stars and shining with the splendor of the divine sun.[72]

Accordingly it is said that when the Soul has ascended to the highest knowledge of God it is like the angels.[73] However, as the quoted passage shows, the substantial knowledge of the angels and Souls is directed toward God and Ideas. For since Ideas are contained in God, any perfect knowledge of God must also include Ideas. But notwithstanding the basic analogy that subsists in this way between the knowledge of God given to the angels and that

[69] *Ibid.*, p. 267.   [70] *Ibid.*, p. 269; cf. II Cor. 4: 16.
[71] *Ibid.*, p. 269.   [72] *Ibid.*, p. 383.   [73] Cf. *ibid.*, p. 159.

given to the Souls, Ficino places definite emphasis on the attempt
to express in the theory of knowledge the difference in rank between God, the various orders of angels, and human Souls. He does
so with the help of a characteristic theory. The divine intellect and,
following its example, the other intellects contain the totality of all
Ideas or forms. The communication of these forms, as we have
seen above, is illustrated by the image of the divine ray which,
starting from God, passes through the orders of angels down to the
human Soul, spreading in its course from a perfect unity in God
to a more and more increasing multiplicity. This transition from
unity to plurality is expressed, according to Ficino, in the number
and order of inherent Ideas or forms. God thinks Himself and all
Ideas through the one most universal Idea of Being. The highest order of angels needs two less universal forms, through which it comprehends all Ideas—namely, substance and accident. The second
order of angels needs four forms in order to think all Ideas, and so
the multiplication of basic forms proceeds down to the human
Soul, which, being the lowest intellect, represents the extreme
measure of multiplicity and already contains as many forms as
there are natural species of created things.[74] The object of contemplation is therefore the same for all intelligences, but the instruments and hence the metaphysical value of knowledge differ according to the grade of the respective intellect. The pyramid-like
order of inherent forms, which is here correlated to the hierarchy of
intelligences and cannot be clearly explained in itself, is easily
understood from its historical origin: it is the Plotinian pyramid of
Ideas which was first replaced by the hierarchy of angels and reappears here again in a rather indirect way.

We have seen how the knowledge of God is included in that of
Ideas and that of Ideas in that of empirical things. Ficino infers
that empirical knowledge is also an unconscious knowledge of
God and that all knowledge as a whole is directly or indirectly related to God. He develops this doctrine, following Plato, with the
help of the metaphor of light. God is the sun which gives all things

[74] *Op. om.*, p. 370.

the light in which they can be known by the mind, and though the mind may ignore the origin of the light, in any case it owes to it the possibility of all thinking.

As in seeing there is a threefold act, namely, the movement of color, the glance of the eye, and the splendor of the light connecting the other acts together, it is the same with knowing, where the act of intelligible things is called "truth" by Plato, the act of the mind "knowledge," and the act which is the link between the two, according to Plato, God, who brings it about that the mind knows wisely and things are known truly, or rather that He is known Himself.[75]

When our mind is illumined by the ray of God, it thinks in Him the concepts of all things whose source is God and which are God Himself, and therefore [the mind] thinks through the light of God and knows only the divine light itself. But it seems to know different things, because it thinks it [that is, divine light] through different Ideas and concepts of things emanating from there.[76]

[God] illuminates each man who enters this world in such a way that anybody thinks in God and through Him whatever he thinks, though dark minds may not comprehend Him, because they do not recognize that they see all things through Him.[77]

Accordingly, the Preface to the *Theologia* begins with the following words:

Plato, the father of the philosophers, oh generous Lorenzo, understanding that all minds are related to God like sight to the light of the sun and that hence they cannot know anything at any time without the light of God, rightly thought it to be right and pious that the human mind should refer all things to God since it has all things from God.[78]

Since all knowledge is implicitly directed to God, it is easy to consider thought in general as a way of the Soul toward God. For all indirect knowledge of God must be considered essentially as preparation for the pure and direct perception of God. This way of the Soul, according to Ficino, develops through a continual series of grades, since the acts of inner consciousness, as well as the totality of existing things, constitute a hierarchy. There is, however,

---

[75] *Ibid.*, p. 267.   [76] *Ibid.*, p. 268; cf. Dress, *op. cit.*, pp. 67 ff.
[77] *Ibid.*, cf. John 1: 9.   [78] *Op. om.*, p. 78; cf. Meier, *op. cit.*, pp. 241 f.

no clear correlation between the series of the acts of consciousness and that of real objects. Consequently, Ficino frequently speaks of a gradual ascent of the knowing Soul, but he describes that ascent in its details in very different terms. At one time the way leads from the objective form through the innate formula to the Idea and from there to the divine essence;[79] elsewhere the mind ascends from the lowest causes through intermediary causes to God as the highest cause,[80] or from the lowest species to highest genera;[81] finally the mind passes through the real grades of Being, from the spheres of the world through the hierarchies of the angels to God.[82] This last way is sometimes described as that followed by philosophy in the succession of its individual disciplines.[83] In all these utterances we can recognize a common element, but on the whole it is a schematic program rather than an elaborated doctrine.

The ascent of the Soul to God is not even fixed in a manner common to all men. Since God, as unique center, produces the plurality of existing things out of Himself, it must be possible to reach Him from each point of the universe, that is, by different paths.

We can enjoy the divine mind through various Ideas, seek it through various traces (*vestigia*), travel toward that goal by various paths. . . . [God] so disposed the intellectual eyes and the tendencies of various Souls in different manners, in order that we may approach the different possessions of the manifold divine goods by different paths.[84]

This doctrine is still based on a pyramid-like conception of reality, and while it was used in the quoted passage to explain the substantial diversity of the Souls, it is introduced elsewhere to justify the hierarchical order of angels and of eternal Souls who contemplate God as it were through dissimilar Ideas.[85]

The doctrine of the ever-present knowledge of God finally finds its most explicit expression in the ontological theory of truth. For Ficino, as in the scholastic tradition, truth is an aspect associated with existence. Hence it has its origin in God as the totality of all

---

[79] Cf. *Op. om.*, pp. 265 ff.   [80] *Ibid.*, p. 218.
[81] *Ibid.*, pp. 192 f.   [82] *Ibid.*, pp. 201, 236.
[83] *Ibid.*, pp. 669 f.   [84] *Ibid.*, pp. 353 f.   [85] *Ibid.*, p. 415.

truth and spreads from Him over all existing things. Since all things in respect to their truth may become objects of knowledge, all thought is necessarily directed toward God as the primary source of truth and finds its definite fulfillment in Him.

Since true things move the intellect under the concept of truth, therefore truth itself moves the intellect through truth toward truth itself, and the intellect does not think anything but truth itself.[86]

Our Soul [so we read in another passage] conceives . . . the common concept of truth [I omit here the parallel analysis of the good], through which it seeks the common truth. . . . All true things . . . are contained in the common truth. Hence it [our Soul] naturally seeks all true things. . . . This becomes obvious from the fact that we do not rest when we have known the truth of a certain thing, but seek another and again another as long as we believe that any truth is left to be known. . . . But all truth . . . is God Himself, who is the first truth. . . . Hence we desire God Himself.[87]

Hence we know all things in God and through God who constitutes the intelligible sun and, so to speak, the medium of all thought.

Ficino's whole epistemology therefore converges, as we see, into the knowledge of God. All thought is a steady ascent of the Soul toward God, in whom even particular and empirical knowledge unconsciously has a part and whom, in the supreme act of contemplation, the Soul finally perceives by intuition in His fullness of essence, face to face. It is the same structure and context that we have met before in the analysis of inner consciousness, now applied and transferred to the doctrine of knowledge. In reality the doctrine of the knowledge of God is nothing but the conceptual interpretation of the inner or spiritual consciousness, where "pure experience" enters necessarily into a union with different, ontological concepts, but just on this account acquires a strict conceptual form. It is the first and essential step from the original "metaphysical orientation" toward the speculative philosophical system.

[86] *Ibid.*, p. 267.   [87] *Ibid.*, p. 307.

XIII

WILL AND LOVE

THE THEORY OF the knowledge of God which we have characterized as a conceptual interpretation of the inner processes of consciousness really expresses only one aspect of inner experience. The ascent of the Soul, as we have seen, is characterized chiefly by two elements: the unrest of consciousness, which drives man from his connection with the surrounding world upward to higher and higher degrees of certainty; and the contemplative attitude, which brings the Soul at each level attained into relation with the sphere of objects then made accessible to it. Through the theory of the knowledge of God the element of contemplation in its different degrees is reunited in one single conceptual system, but the more dynamic element of unrest which really accounts for the ascending movement of the Soul is either forgotten or silently presupposed in that theory. Hence, if we start from the basic phenomenon of internal experience, Ficino's theory of knowledge needs an essential complement. This is achieved mainly by means of the theory of will and love, which we must now consider. It occupies a specific double position in relation to the theory of knowledge, being conceptually dependent on it in many points, poor in doctrinal elements of its own, and often completed through analogies in an almost artificial way. However, the real essence of inner or spiritual consciousness is revealed more deeply and more directly by the theory of the will than by that of knowledge.

The concept of will, as others have occasionally pointed out, is not really of Greek origin.[1] Aristotle examined the "choice preced-

---

[1] Cf. G. Gentile, *Sistema di logica* (Bari, 1922), 2d ed., I, 29 ff.; Ernst Benz, *Die Entwickelung des abendlaendischen Willensbegriffs von Plotin bis Augustin* (Stuttgart, 1931).

ing action" (προαίρεσις), and later, in an isolated treatise, Plotinus
discussed the human and divine will power. However, no doctrine
of will was elaborated. When St. Augustine for the first time placed
the concept of will as independent beside the intellect and so put it
in the center of philosophical and theological speculation, he perhaps accepted the Plotinian concept, but expressed essentially a new,
Christian motive. For the new manner in which the relation of man
to God and of God to the world was now conceived, could not
find its place in the merely "intellectualistic" system of ancient
philosophy. Speculation about will has remained a fixed element
of the philosophical tradition down to Kant and Fichte, and even
later. During the Middle Ages it was particularly elaborated by the
Franciscan Scholastics, who generally based their conception of
will on St. Augustine. In all probability Ficino also went directly
back to St. Augustine.

In order to understand Ficino's theory of will in its conceptual
character, we must start from the definition of will. Will is "an
inclination of the mind toward the good," [2] "an effort of the
thought" (*nixus intelligentiae*).[3] "As the irrational appetite follows
sensation, so the will, which is rational appetite, follows the intellect." [4] The last formula is especially instructive, because the
scheme of the parts of the Soul becomes apparent. The will, for
Ficino, is not an independent part of the Soul, in so far as the
scheme of the parts of the Soul is determined from the beginning
by grades of knowledge, that is, sensation, phantasy, and reason.
But the Soul possesses, in addition to the knowing attitude, the
power of appetite, which is also divided into several grades, correlated to the grades of knowledge. In this way Plato's and Aristotle's concepts of appetite (ἐπιθυμία, ὄρεξις) are reconciled with
each other and developed into a regular system, and the will is
henceforth the rational appetite or that part of the appetitive power
which corresponds to the intellect. That is, the will contains a new
element in respect to the intellect, but from the beginning it is
related to the intellect and, so to speak, leans on it. Considered in

[2] *Op. om.*, p. 108.   [3] *Ibid.*, p. 219.   [4] *Ibid.*, p. 313.

itself, however, it is nothing but a particular kind or grade of appetite.

In its conceptual elements the will can therefore be derived in part from the theory of appetite which we have already studied in another context.[5] All human willing in particular has a certain object which partakes of the nature of good with respect to the appetite that is directed toward it. For Ficino the terms "good" and "object of appetite" are interchangeable.[6] The will is the propensity of the mind toward the good, as we have read in the definition quoted above.[7] "For the will [it is natural] to want those things which have been judged good. . . . Whatever is offered under the concept of good is naturally desired by the will." [8]

The will, however, is distinguished from all other forms of appetite by the manner in which it determines its object. All irrational appetite, so we read in the ninth book of the *Theologia,* is determined once and for all by the nature of the desiring thing and is always fixed upon the same actions and objects, as may be seen in the attitudes of the elements, of the beasts, and also of the lower forces of the human Soul. Reason, on the contrary, has the power of deliberation (*consultatio*). It can review successively the most various objects and make a choice (*eligere*) among them according to its *arbitrium,* and in this consists the liberty of human action.

In our mind we have a common archetype of good which we use as standard for rejecting or more or less approving individual objects, in which judgment we are not drawn by the objects or by the body, but rather we draw the objects to the archetype and the body to the mind.[9]

The will can therefore determine the object of its own appetite by its own choice, and in this sense the will is clearly opposed to any "natural" appetite. But freedom of the will is by no means conceived as an inner decision or as an intelligible character, but, according to Aristotle's concept, simply as the choice of a particular, concrete object. Yet in accomplishing this choice the will needs the help of the intellect. For the archetype of good by which all things

---

[5] Cf. chap. x, above.   [6] *Ibid.,* p. 1214.   [7] *Ibid.,* p. 108.
[8] *Ibid.,* pp. 312 f.   [9] *Ibid.,* p. 208; cf. Semprini, *op. cit.,* p. 59.

are measured is originally contained in the mind, and the application of the standard to a particular object, which precedes the
decision of the will, partakes of the nature of a logical subordination so that in the end, again according to Aristotle, the act of will
appears as the result of a syllogism.

Man acts rationally [says Ficino, refering to the definitions of Platonists
and Aristotelians] in so far as he reasons before acting. First he accepts
a universal rule; then he adds a particular opinion; thirdly, he infers
the conclusion, in this way: every good is to be chosen, this food is
good, consequently, this food is to be chosen.[10]

Accordingly, any particular action is nothing else than the special
application of a most universal rule to the objects offered to it,[11]
and the will always appears on the heels of intellect.[12] "The will
desires the good to that extent to which the intellect offers it." [13]

But the act of willing is not limited to the determination of its
object or to its direction toward this object. For a desire is not satisfied by having its goal always before it, but is naturally destined to
find fulfillment, that is, actually to reach this goal and to cease
its inherent movement and come to rest. Accordingly, the willing
leads at last to a unification of the willing person with the desired
object, and the movement of will and action ends in the state of
joy or pleasure in which the mind directly enjoys its object, desired
and now attained.

[The pleasure of the mind is] the expansion of the will into the good
and the rest of the will in the good.[14]

[Our will] always desires to enjoy all goods. But while it enjoys
things, it unifies itself with the things which it enjoys.[15]

What does the will desire? What else but to enjoy all things in their
manner and so to transform itself into all things? [16]

Now that we have described the formal elements of the will, we
must also examine the object toward which it is directed. This
object has been qualified so far merely in a general way as a good,
and since the good, according to its concept, is something that is

---

[10] *Ibid.*, p. 343.   [11] Cf. *ibid.*, pp. 206 f.   [12] Cf. *ibid.*, pp. 312 f.
[13] *Ibid.*, p. 236.   [14] *Ibid.*, p. 108.   [15] *Ibid.*, p. 310.   [16] *Ibid.*, p. 677.

to be desired, this merely expresses the formal relation of the object to the will. But for Ficino's conception it is important that the good, which constitutes the object of the will, should also be an existing thing and belong to the realm of real things. This means, conversely, that an existing thing, in so far as it has the quality of being good, also represents a possible object for the human will.

Good things move the will under the concept of goodness.[17]

[The intellect] knows all things under the concept of truth and desires all things under the concept of goodness.[18]

As Being itself under the concept of truth is the object of the intellect, so Being itself under the concept of goodness is the object of the will.[19]

In these formulae the realism of Ficino's system, which we have already described in another context with respect to thought, becomes apparent.[20] The will, then, cannot produce its goal or objects by itself, but is always directed to real things and is confined in the choice of its goals to the sphere of existing things.

On the other hand, an extension of the will over the totality of all existing things corresponds to this limitation, in so far as goodness is connected with all Being, and therefore everything that exists can become an object of the will. Hence the intellect, which seeks the good in things, expands infinitely, "since goodness can be communicated to innumerable things in infinite ways. If the will desires the good to that extent to which the intellect offers it, and if the intellect offers infinite goodness and infinite goods, consequently the will desires so many." [21] From this we can understand another point. The will, as we have seen, is not fixed upon this or that particular object, but can choose between the offered objects according to its *arbitrium*. Yet in a general sense the will is determined, in so far as it always has the good, and in a certain sense all good, for its object. The will may therefore be qualified as a natural appetite so far as good in general is concerned,[22] without its liberty

---

[17] *Ibid.*, p. 267.
[18] *Ibid.*, p. 677.
[19] *Ibid.*, p. 236.
[20] Cf. chap. iv, above.
[21] *Ibid.*, p. 236; cf. Cassirer, *Individuum*, p. 75.
[22] *Ibid.*, pp. 312 f. This is also the position of Thomas Aquinas.

being questioned with respect to the choice of its particular objects.

However, the various things do not stand unrelated beside each other in their goodness, but constitute altogether a homogeneous order of good which is based upon one principle. For as the Being of things proceeds from God as from the origin and totality of all Being, so their goodness is derived from God who is the source and fullness of all good and allows all other things to have a part in His own goodness.[23] The human will, which is directed toward any particular object because of its goodness, is therefore always indirectly and unconsciously related to God as to the totality of good.

Good things move the will under the concept of goodness, and therefore goodness itself moves the will through goodness toward goodness, and we desire nothing in individual things but goodness itself.[24] For all things the primal good is the cause of their being good. Therefore it is the cause of their being desired. But if for its sake all things are to be desired, consequently itself is to be desired more than all things and by all things.[25]

Similarly we read in the theological prayer to God: "I know that in Thee alone are, or rather Thou alone art, all that we ever desire; if this or that good pleases us, it does so, not because it is this or that, but because it is good. For we desire the quality of goodness in individual things." [26]

But the human will not only is referred to God by an indirect path through individual objects but also has an original and direct tendency toward God. First, the individual objects are different in grade, and this difference corresponds not only to the ontological hierarchy of things but also to the inner or spiritual ascent of consciousness, so that in the higher object the will also finds a more genuine and more perfect satisfaction. "When we live apart from the infection of the body, not only does the intellect see many things more clearly but also the will is fulfilled and no longer

---

[23] Cf. chap. v, above.   [24] *Op. om.*, p. 267.
[25] *Ibid.*, p. 306.   [26] *Ibid.*, pp. 665 f.

afflicted by any troubles, but highly enjoys the divine things as most like unto itself." [27] The satisfaction of the will through the objects is therefore not always equal, in spite of their goodness, but it is more-or-less perfect, according to their grade. Indeed, the will can never be completely fulfilled by any finite object. It hastens unceasingly from one object to the other until it finally finds rest in union with God, the infinite totality of goodness. All human willing is therefore essentially a will toward God. This is the point which Ficino emphasizes again and again and to which all other elements of his theory of will are subordinated.

The will can be fulfilled only by the possession of the infinite good. . . . But since every force can be content only with that thing in which the entire concept of its object is found, intellect and will can be satiated by God alone, in whom alone lies the entire concept of truth and goodness. And since the intellect passes always from one true thing to another, and the will moves from one good thing to another, it is quite clear that they can attain rest only through that which comprises all such things.[28]

We proceed from one truth to another, so we read in another passage. Likewise do we with the acquisition of good things. "But all truth and all goodness is God Himself, who is the primal True and the primal Good. Hence we desire God Himself." [29] The will rests in the first and infinite good alone," namely, in God.[30] With these statements we find ourselves in the realm of inner experience which receives a new and conclusive interpretation through the theory of will. For the Soul, as we have seen before, is driven in its inner ascent by a profound unrest and proceeds to higher and higher grades of consciousness until it attains its end in a final act of direct intuition of God.[31] In this highest act, so we can now say, the knowledge of divine truth coincides with the enjoyment of divine goodness. But on the way to this end the acts of knowledge indicate the state of the ascending consciousness as attained on each level, while the will corresponds to that unrest which moves the

[27] *Ibid.*, p. 203.   [28] *Ibid.*, p. 236.   [29] *Ibid.*, p. 307.
[30] *Ibid.*, p. 325.   [31] Cf. chap. xi, above.

Soul and really produces the ascent toward God. Once the peak is reached, all specific acts of human will must appear as mere preparations or aberrations of the unique desire for God, which constitutes the true content and destiny of man.

The theory of love, which we must now consider, is quite different from that of will in its concrete and historical origin. For the concept of will concerns human action and its internal possibility; the concept of love signifies an emotional attitude, a sentiment the original meaning of which lies in the affection of one person for another. The concept of will was foreshadowed in Aristotle, but was developed to philosophical significance by St. Augustine. The concept of love received its classic form in Plato. In spite of these basic differences, however, will and love are closely connected in Ficino, as in the medieval tradition, and it will be our task to make clear the meaning and possibility of this union. For this purpose we shall limit ourselves now to the doctrinal nucleus of Ficino's theory, which concerns love as a human attitude, leaving aside the concepts of the physiological genesis of love, inherited from the tradition of the *dolce stil nuovo,* as well as the cosmological theories about love, though both occupy quite a large space in the important *De amore.*

For the interpretation it is again useful to start from Ficino's own definition of love. "When we say love," so we read at the beginning of the *De amore,* "one must understand the desire for beauty, for this is the definition of love among all philosophers." [32] "Love has the enjoyment of beauty as its end." [33] In this definition love is not related to the scheme of the faculties of the Soul, in which scheme the will was still included, but Ficino attached no importance to the question of that relation. However, the term "desire" which occurs in the definition is equivalent to "appetite" and "tendency," so that the interpretation of love may be related directly to the doctrine of appetite. From this we at once derive certain attributes of love that necessarily coincide with attributes

[32] *Ibid.,* p. 1322.   [33] *Ibid.,* p. 1323.

of the will in so far as the latter had also been defined as a particular form of appetite.

First, since love is a form of appetite, it is not limited within itself, but is always directed toward some object. In the definition this object is indicated by the general term "beauty." We still have to determine what that means. At present we shall consider only the relation, as such, with an object. For love, through its desire, not only is directed toward its object, but also tends to bring the loving subject to a real union with the beloved object, or, as Ficino says, to transform the loving subject by virtue of this union into the beloved object.

Love unites the mind more quickly, more closely, and more stably with God than does knowledge, because the force of knowledge consists more in distinction, that of love in union.[34]

Oh, too happy are those whom the beauty of the universe, the splendor of the Good itself, transforms through love into the Good itself, especially since while transforming into the Good, it also reforms into One, and so unites in one with the Good itself.[35]

Not the appetite that follows the action of the mind, but that which precedes it as cause of motion enjoys the end of the movement when it achieves a substantial bond and therefore alone fulfills the wish entirely.[36]

Only love of goodness transforms the Soul into God.[37]

But when the loving subject is united with its object, the movement stops, and love finds satisfaction in the enjoyment of its attained object. "Love has the enjoyment of beauty as its goal," so we read in the definition of love.[38] In the last book of the *Theologia* Ficino says even more plainly:

Since pleasure corresponds to love as its goal, those Souls that loved more ardently adhere [to God] more closely, as it is the habit of love, and are more intimately transformed into the Good, since the state of love itself brings that with it, and enjoy it more sweetly.[39]

Likewise we read about the future life that various intellects enjoy the good in various degrees,

[34] *Ibid.*, p. 324. [35] *Ibid.*, p. 271. [36] *Ibid.*

[37] *Ibid.*, p. 410. [38] *Ibid.*, p. 1323. [39] *Ibid.*, p. 413.

in so far as they love various degrees of the whole good and travel by various roads toward the Good itself. . . . Moreover, in that place where everyone attains fully what he has loved and in the way he chooses and to the extent to which he desires it, everyone lives wholly content and replete—without envy and far removed from any impulse.[40]

As we have seen, the definition indicates beauty as the object of love, and this concept, which had previously been expressed by Plato in the *Symposium,* involves from the outset a spiritual interpretation of love which is quite different from the common concept. For the concept of beauty, even if considered only in the field of external things, is not confined to human bodies, wherefore in a preliminary consideration Ficino distinguishes three kinds of beauty: beauty of bodies, beauty of sounds, and beauty of Souls.[41] Moreover, the concept of beauty itself contains a contemplative element which leads beyond mere sensual enjoyment. Hence, Ficino says consistently that love and enjoyment of beauty are attained only through seeing, hearing, and thinking.[42] The lower senses have no part in beauty. Their appetite and enjoyment cannot therefore be called love, though they may be necessary for the constitution of the universe and for human society.

As for the essence of beauty, Ficino first refers to the ancient Greek conception which understands beauty as proportion—that is, as a symmetrical relation between the parts of a whole.

Beauty is charm, which originates for the most part in the conformity of several elements . . . Charm originates in corporeal objects in the harmony (*concordia*) between several colors and lines, and likewise charm in sounds in the consonance of several voices.[43]

Ficino seems to abandon this classical concept of beauty in a later passage in the *De amore,* hinting, as did Plotinus, at the beauty of simple colors, sounds, and bodies, which beauty can by no means be explained through the relation between several parts.[44] Yet in

[40] *Ibid.,* p. 415.   [41] *Ibid.,* p. 1322.   [42] *Ibid.,* pp. 1322 f.; cf. pp. 631 f.
[43] *Ibid.,* p. 1322; cf. pp. 631 f., 275 f. See also Saitta, *op. cit.,* pp. 235 ff.
[44] *Ibid.,* p. 1336. Cf. Ferri, *Filosofia delle scuole italiane,* Vol. XXIX, pp. 271 f.; Saitta, *op. cit.,* pp. 236 f.

that section he is only interested in proving the incorporeal origin of beauty; within the sphere of corporeal beauty he does not make any progress beyond the concept of proportion. This result is disappointing, since we might expect from Ficino, the philosophical mouthpiece of the Renaissance, a doctrinal justification of that age's worship of beauty and an explicit analysis of its artistic ideals. It is even more surprising when we consider that his theory of love and beauty determined the thought of the following generations. However, we may excuse him if we recognize the fact that he did not intend to formulate a real aesthetics or theory of art and that he did not plan to analyze sensible beauty in itself, but only to insert it into the framework of a metaphysical system.

For according to Ficino beauty is not limited to the empirical world, but is diffused in different grades throughout the whole realm of Being and has its real origin in God Himself. In his book *De amore,* using Plotinus' theory of hypostases, he states that God as the totality of goodness is the center of the universe and that beauty is the reflected splendor of this goodness diffused in four gradated circles—Mind, Soul, Nature, and Matter.[45]

The goodness of all things is the one God Himself, through whom all things are good, but beauty is the ray of God infused into four circles, which are moved in some way around God.[46]

The good is called the highest existence of God; beauty, some act or ray penetrating all things from that source, first entering the angelic Mind, secondly, the world Soul and the other Souls, thirdly, Nature, fourthly, the Matter of the bodies. It adorns the Mind with the order of Ideas, fills the Souls with the series of concepts, strengthens Nature with germs, and extols Matter with forms.[47]

Some trace of this theory is still found here and there in the *Theologia Platonica,* though the Plotinian theory of hypostases has really been replaced there by the doctrine of the five substances.[48] So in the twelfth book, for example Ficino speaks of the Good "whose splendor is the beauty which is nothing else than a rational order

[45] *Op. om.,* pp. 1324 f.   [46] *Ibid.,* p. 1325.
[47] *Ibid.,* p. 1326.   [48] Cf. chap. vii, above.

of many forms in the Mind, in the Soul, in Nature and in Matter." [49] Similarly, in the fourteenth book: "As we have discussed in *De amore,* the splendor of the highest Good shines in individual things." [50] In the eleventh book, however, the metaphysical theory of beauty receives a somewhat different and more precise definition by means of the theory of Ideas. There beauty in individual things is derived from the "Idea" of beauty, which is the first and pure beauty and identical with the first and pure Being, that is, with the divine substance.[51] In that context, however, beauty appears simply as an arbitrarily chosen example for an "Idea," and hence it loses the particular metaphysical significance it possesses in the *De amore.*

Just as the beauty of individual things is derived from God, so all human love, in so far as it is directed toward a beautiful object, is related at least unconsciously and indirectly to God. So we read in the De amore: "Whoever contemplates the ornament in those four [circles], that is, Mind, Soul, Nature, and Matter, contemplates and loves in them the splendor of God and through that splendor God Himself." [52] Similarly, we read in the same book that divine beauty infuses itself in things and reverts to itself through love in a kind of circular movement.[53] We find the same conception again in the *Theologia:* "Oh, too happy are those whom the beauty of the universe, the splendor of the good itself, transforms through love into the Good itself." [54] And still more clearly in another passage: .

The splendor of the highest Good itself shines in individual things, and where it shines more fittingly, there it especially allures him who contemplates it, excites him who looks at it, enraptures and takes possession of him who approaches it. . . . There it is apparent that the Soul is inflamed by the divine splendor, glowing in the beautiful person as in a mirror, and secretly lifted up by it as by a hook in order to become God.[55]

[49] *Op. om.,* p. 271.   [50] *Ibid.,* p. 306.
[51] *Ibid.,* pp. 247 f., 252.   [52] *Ibid.,* p. 1326.
[53] *Ibid.,* p. 1324; cf. Saitta, *op. cit.,* pp. 239 ff.
[54] *Ibid.,* p. 271.   [55] *Ibid.,* p. 306.

This metaphor of the hook shows the real meaning of Ficino's theory of beauty. The beauty of things is the lure by which the Soul of the lover is led to God.

But from that we may derive a direct and essential relation of the loving Soul to God. For love is not satisfied with the enjoyment of a determined object, but is always impelled forward until it finds rest in the sight of God, its true goal and object. So we read, for example, in the passage just quoted, that the loving Soul "is not satisfied with the sight and touch of the beloved person and frequently cries out: this person has something, I do not know what, which makes me burn, and I do not know what I wish," and so the Soul is driven upward to God.[56] Likewise we read in *De amore:*

Hence, the impulse of the lover is not extinguished by the sight or touch of any body. For he does not desire this or that body, but admires, yearns for, and wonders at the splendor of the higher light shining all over the bodies. The lovers do not know what they wish or desire, because they do not know God Himself, whose secret flavor infused some sweet odor of Himself in His works.[57]

Likewise, in the theological prayer to God:

What penetrates my innermost being? What elevates my highest being? Certainly it is the admirable rays of Thy admirable goodness and beauty diffused everywhere in an admirable way throughout minds, throughout Souls, and throughout bodies. With them reachest Thou me even without my knowing, with them Thou allurest, forcest, and inflamest me . . . oh Thou unique beauty.[58]
Thou oh God, Thou alone wilt extinguish this ardent thirst.[59]

In this conclusive form the theory of love clearly manifests its close connection with the basic phenomena of internal experience: the love of the Soul for God is only a conceptual expression for that basic unrest which moves the consciousness inwardly and drives it upward from grade to grade, until at last it reaches its goal and finds rest in the highest act, the contemplation of God.

[56] *Ibid.*   [57] *Ibid.,* p. 1326.   [58] *Ibid.,* p. 665.   [59] *Ibid.,* p. 666.

But as love always has beauty for its objective correlate, a contemplative element is also included in the movement of love, which we could not discover in the movement of the will, even though the will is analogous in other respects.

Now that we have followed to the end the conceptual elements of the theory of love, we are prepared to define more precisely its relationship to the theory of will. Love and will, as we have seen, are at first glance two different concepts, having also different historical origins and being related to the different objective spheres of the beautiful and the good. Further consideration has uncovered a series of important congruences. First, both will and love fall under the more general concept of "appetite," from which we have been able to derive a number of common qualities. Secondly, the metaphysical systems of the good and the beautiful show the same order inasmuch as they comprise in different degrees the whole sphere of Being and can ultimately be derived from God Himself as their origin and peak.[60] Thirdly, will and love toward God are both conceptual symbols for one and the same basic phenomenon, the inner or spiritual unrest of consciousness. We understand, therefore, why for Ficino the two systems of will and love, good and beautiful are closely connected, if not identical. Their characteristic attributes are frequently used almost interchangeably in a single passage. So we read that the Soul is reflected back upon itself through the will in so far as it desires and loves itself.[61]

Just as, not he who sees the good, but he who wills it becomes good, so the Soul becomes divine, not from considering God, but from loving Him.[62]

Love is not satisfied with human knowledge, because this knowledge is created and finite. The will rests only in the first and infinite good.[63]

Although the intellect does not discern the immense light in an infinite way, he [man] is, however, filled with immense love and enjoyment when the will enjoys infinite good.[64]

---

[60] Cf. Saitta, *op. cit.*, p. 238.   [61] *Op. om.*, p. 202.
[62] *Ibid.*, p. 324.   [63] *Ibid.*, p. 325.   [64] *Ibid.*, p. 704.

In a letter posterior to the *De amore* and to the *Theologia* Ficino goes a step further and defines love explicitly as a disposition of the will. "What is more voluntary than love? It is the first, highest, perpetual disposition of will and so operates that we cannot desire not to love *(primus summus perpetuus est voluntatis affectus)*." [65] The intimate conformity between the theory of will and the theory of love, which as a matter of fact was clear from the outset, is unmistakably expressed here in a conceptual formula.

Now that we have followed the metaphysical theory of will and love to the end, we must define more precisely its relation to the theory of knowledge. For will and knowledge are both acts of the human Soul, referring to the whole order of Being and having God Himself as goal and object. At first Ficino did not see any difficulty in this coexistence of knowledge or intellect and will or love, but postulated a kind of indifferent parallelism between them, a parallelism foreshadowed in the medieval tradition. Nor did he abandon it, in spite of the conceptual duplication of many simple phenomena resulting therefrom. This parallelism of will and intellect occurs frequently as a general theory, the validity of which is unquestionably presupposed within the argument. The Soul, says Ficino, is reflected into itself, twice through the intellect and twice through the will.[66] Or, the human Soul has not only intellect but also will in common with divine things.[67] Once he says: "Until now we have proved our purpose mainly through the intellect; now we can prove it again mainly through the will." [68] Elsewhere, in support of a Platonic proposition, he gives first five arguments based on the intellect, then one based on the will.[69] It would be easy to collect further examples of the same kind; the co-ordination of erudition and morals or of speculative and moral virtues belongs to the same context. But more important than these trite formulae are the passages in which Ficino presents this parallelism at length and with reference to the core of the doctrine of knowledge and will.

[65] *Ibid.,* p. 741.   [66] *Ibid.,* p. 202; cf. p. 200.
[67] *Ibid.,* p. 218.   [68] *Ibid.,* p. 236.   [69] *Ibid.,* pp. 266 f.

While we live far away from the contagion of the body, not only does the intellect see many things more clearly, but the will is also satisfied and not afflicted by any troubles, but greatly enjoys divine things as like unto itself.[70]

Just as the object of intellect is Being, under the aspect of truth, so that of will is Being, under the aspect of goodness. But since each faculty is satisfied only by that thing in which the whole concept of its object is found, therefore intellect and will are satisfied only by God in Whom alone the whole concept of truth and goodness exists.[71]

Our Soul conceives the common concept of truth and goodness through which it seeks the common truth and desires the common good. In the common truth all true things are contained; in the common good, all good things. Consequently, [our Soul] naturally seeks all true things, naturally desires all good things. . . . All true and all good is God Himself, who is the first True and the first Good, hence we desire God Himself. . . . Hence, our goal is to see God through the intellect and to enjoy Him through the will. . . . Our highest powers are the mind, including the peak of the mind, and the will. Their highest object is the common true and the common and whole good, namely, God.[72]

Intellect and will, however, are not just any two distinct powers of the Soul, but the knowledge of God through the intellect and the love for God through the will are after all only two conceptional formulae indicating the same concrete fact—in other words, the inner or spiritual ascent of consciousness to the highest grade of contemplation. So the question necessarily arises as to which of the two formulae is a more genuine expression of the basic fact and which of the two forces is more effective in the ascent toward God. For the most part Ficino tries to escape this dilemma by using the device of parallelism, as we have seen; but sometimes he has to face it and to answer it, in other words, to admit the superiority of one power over the other. The problem occurs first in the early commentary on Plato's *Philebus,* where Ficino clearly states the superiority of intellect. "The intellect is more excellent than the

---

[70] *Ibid.,* p. 203.   [71] *Ibid.,* p. 236.
[72] *Ibid.,* p. 307; cf. pp. 310 f. See also Saitta, *op. cit.,* pp. 217 ff.; Dress, *op. cit.,* pp. 89 ff., 104 ff., 129.

will." [73] And "the substance of beatitude concerns the intellect more than the will." [74] Out of the great number of arguments which Ficino brings forth for this thesis, we emphasize only a few essential points.

The former [the intellect] draws things toward itself; the latter [the will] is drawn by things. For the former does not conceive things as they are in themselves, but [conceives them] in its own way, many things in one species—mobile things in a stable way, particular things in a universal way, etc.—and makes upright, through its formulae, whatever is lame in the things. The latter [the will] is inclined toward the things, to possess them as they are in themselves, and is impelled toward them after their notion is conceived, and does not change them, but is itself changed from rest to movement. [75]

That is, the intellect assimilates the objects to itself; the will assimilates itself to the objects. Moreover, the will tends through movement toward rest; the intellect accomplishes the act in which the will finds rest, namely, knowledge. For the desire of the will is a movement which comes to rest when the goal has been attained. It is true that this rest can still be considered as an act of will. But it is not itself the goal of the preceding movement, only an accessory aspect of the goal actually attained. [76] The superiority of intellect, as we see, is therefore essentially based on its independence and on its static character, and the old ontological contempt for movement apparently still has some influence.

Ficino did not hold to this solution in his later works, however, and in the *Theologia Platonica* and the tract *De felicitate* he arrives exactly at the opposite conclusion.

In this life human love for God is more excellent than human knowledge. [77]
Enjoyment is more excellent than vision (*visio*) in that felicity [of the future life]. [78]
The enjoyment of the highest good seems to concern the will rather than the intellect. [79]

[73] *Op. om.*, p. 1251. [74] *Ibid.*, p. 1252.
[75] *Ibid.*, p. 1251; cf. Thomas, *Summa contra Gentiles*, I, 77.
[76] *Op. om.*, pp. 1251 f. [77] *Ibid.*, p. 324. [78] *Ibid.*, p. 663. [79] *Ibid.*, p. 664.

Among the numerous arguments with which Ficino justifies this thesis, we shall again mention only a few essential points. "Nobody in this life achieves a real knowledge of God, but he achieves a real love for God, in whatever way He may be known, who despises the other things for God's sake." [80] As we see, Ficino is more skeptical here about the possibility of the knowledge of God during earthly life and about the independent actual power of the human intellect. "Therefore, love unites the mind with God more quickly, more closely, and more firmly than does knowledge, because the force of knowledge consists more in distinction; that of love, more in union." [81] So union with God, which is the goal of the Soul, seems to be accomplished primarily through love.

Since the force of knowledge, as we have said above, consists in some kind of distinction and that of love in union, we are united more closely with God through the joy of love, which transforms us into the beloved God, than through knowledge.[82]

Furthermore, recognizing God, we contract His amplitude to the capacity and concept of our mind; but loving Him, we enlarge the mind to the immense amplitude of divine goodness. There, so to speak, we lower God to our level; here, we lift ourselves to God. For we know as far as we comprehend; but we love both what we see clearly and what we expect as the remainder of the divine goodness beyond our clear sight.[83]

These beautiful words are repeated literally in Lorenzo de' Medici's poem *L'altercazione* and quoted with emphasis from Lorenzo by Burckhardt at the end of his famous book, though he did not know that their source was Ficino. The words also have a special importance for our problem. For we see that the same concept used in the commentary on the *Philebus* to prove the superiority of intellect serves the opposite purpose here. The fact that love assimilates itself to its objects is used here to prove that love leads the Soul to union with God, whereas the intellect, being confined to its own limits, cannot contain the infinity of God. The attitude of the intellect, which appeared to be an asset as long as the human

[80] *Ibid.*, p. 663; cf. p. 324.   [81] *Ibid.*, p. 663; cf. p. 324.
[82] *Ibid.*, p. 663.   [83] *Ibid.*, p. 664; cf. p. 325.

mind was practically over and above all objects, appears as a defect as soon as the object itself excels the capacity of human thought. In the tract *De felicitate* Ficino emphasizes this point. The intellect, he says in another passage in this tract, remains within itself; while the will stretches out toward its object and tries to join it. Consequently, when the Soul's goal is outside itself, the will can contribute much more to the real attainment of that goal than can the intellect.[84] Finally, the other principal argument which we know from the commentary on the *Philebus* is now also used in the opposite sense.

The end of movement—in other words, felicity—rightly belongs to the will, since the beginning of movement belongs to it. For since the intellect knows the things themselves not so much according to the nature of the things as according to its own nature, it seems in some way to attract the things toward itself, and so cannot really be said to move the Soul. Since the will desires to attain things as they are in themselves, it draws the Soul toward the outside things, and hence the will is the beginning of movement.[85]

In other words, the will is really the principle which puts the Soul in motion and leads it to its end. So, as we see, Ficino has become aware of the dynamic character of the will, and for his theory of the Soul and of God, which at the outset was based on the concept of knowledge, he has now found an even more solid foundation in the theory of will and of love. Afterward he always maintained this new conception, and in his *Theologia* and in his letters he returns to it repeatedly, though less extensively.[86]

Several years later, when for the first time Ficino printed his commentary on the *Philebus,* he noticed the difference in the evaluation of will between this early work and his later tracts, and

[84] *Ibid.,* pp. 663 f.

[85] *Ibid.,* p. 664. Cf. Saitta, *op. cit.,* pp. 221 ff.; Dress, *op. cit.,* pp. 105 ff.; Semprini, *op. cit.,* p. 55.

[86] Cf. *Op. om.,* pp. 309, 409, 658, 704, 710, 862, 863. Corsano (*op. cit.,* p. 25) knows only the passage last quoted on the superiority of love and therefore speaks of a lyrical exaltation, etc. But that makes no difference, since Ficino's thought is mediocre, and the *Theologia Platonica "un'esercitazione letterariamente frondosa,"* according to him.

he tried to justify it. First of all, at the end of the argument quoted above he added a passage, which is still lacking in the manuscripts, that serves to reconcile the thesis of the commentary with that of the later works.

The above-mentioned arguments within the happy Soul established the superiority of the act of intellect over the act of will. But the reasons why the opposite may be reasonably believed, we have treated in a letter, *De felicitate*. Finally, if we consider, not so much the will as it is distinct from the intellect, but rather that aspect which within the intellect itself is like the will and pleasure, then our attempt will be safer.[87]

Here Ficino merely limits the previous argument of the commentary very cautiously and at the same time indicates a solution, when he conceives the will as an element of intellect itself. He evidently means that such a consideration shows the superiority of the will, whereas the will, which is distinct from the intellect and hence irrational, must be subordinated to the intellect. He treats more clearly and more amply the same difficulty in the accompanying letter to Paolo Orlandini, added to the printed edition of the commentaries on Plato, devoting it entirely to this question, which apparently had provoked numerous objections on the part of others to Ficino's doctrines.

After discussing yesterday with me very subtly, as is your habit, many things concerning divine matters [so he writes to his friend and student] you finally asked me why in the *Philebus* I prefer intellect to will, apparently following Plato, and then in the letter *De felicitate* the will [to the intellect]. I might answer that in the *Philebus* I am expressing Plato's opinion; in the letter, my own. But I do not wish to affirm a difference between Marsilio's opinion and Plato's opinion.

Here we already notice that the superiority of will corresponds to Ficino's real opinion. However, he does not wish to abandon entirely the exposition in the commentary, and therefore he continues as follows:

Hence I shall answer summarily that there is a double process of our mind—one natural, and the other supernatural which we properly

---

[87] *Op. om.*, p. 1252; cf. *Suppl.*, I, 79.

call ecstasy (*excessum*). In the former the intellect, through some innate light, guides the will as its companion and finally, having guided it rightly, fills it and hence is given superiority. In this latter ecstasy a new light and force infused by God does not fill the intellect with divine splendor until it has kindled the will with admirable love.

The first viewpoint is said to be given in the commentary on the *Philebus;* the second in his other writings.[88] This explanation also gives more emphasis to the later interpretation. For the supernatural process, which consists in the unification of Soul and God through love, either includes the natural process of knowledge or degrades it to a mere shadow, but in any case contains in itself the higher truth.

However, it is not necessary to take these explanations of Ficino literally, for they were obviously added subsequently. It is sufficient for us to recognize in them an admission of the difficulty and of the change of doctrine. Therefore we must accept the superiority of will and love over the intellect as Ficino's more mature and conclusive theory. The inner or spiritual ascent of the Soul toward God, which had received its first systematical interpretation in the theory of knowledge, is now really caught, in its dynamic element, in the theory of will and love. So the concept of love, especially in the later works of Ficino, really becomes the heart of his philosophy.

So far we have analyzed love only as a relation between the human Soul and God; now we must consider it as a concrete relationship between two persons. This order of exposition is contrary, of course, to the natural conception, but it was made necessary by the systematical context in Ficino. For Ficino the love for a person, as we already have seen, is a simple preparation, more-or-less conscious, for the love of God, which is the true and real content of human desire and is only deflected toward persons and things by the reflected splendor of divine beauty and goodness in them. Since this love always has beauty as its object, it is not sensual, but limited to eye, ear, and thought. When one person loves another,

[88] *Ibid.,* pp. 1425 f.

this love is, so to speak, lost in nothing if the beloved person does not return the love. For one-sided love concerns only the lover, while mutual love surpasses the sphere of a single Soul and constitutes a real and concrete communion between several persons. Recognizing such communion of persons as essential, Ficino consequently is forced to consider mutual love as the true and perfect form of love. In the *De amore,* therefore, he marshals many arguments to prove that the beloved is obliged to love the lover.[89] But even there he goes a step further and states that mutual love is not only a moral obligation but also an objective necessity. Among the arguments he uses, the following is the most important one: love is based on the likeness of the lovers and therefore must rise in both for the same reason.[90] Likewise, we read in the fourth book of the letters that when love is kindled through the influence of the divine spirit, the love of the one person always encounters a corresponding love in the other.[91] Reciprocity is therefore contained in the concrete concept of love, as such.

Since love between two persons is conceived as a mutual love, although free from any sensual element, the difference between the two sexes, which actually determines erotic relations in the ordinary sense, loses its basic importance in Ficino's theory of love. Not only man and woman but also two men or two women may be united by a sentiment of love. Consequently, the concept of love can absorb the essence of two other concepts which differ from it in origin and meaning, namely, friendship and charity. Charity is the religious sentiment embracing all fellow men as brothers for the sake of God and of celestial beatitude and expressing itself concretely in active assistance to one's neighbor. This was contained in the Bible as a general command, but was developed into a clear concept by St. Paul, thence passing into the common theology of the Christian Church. Ficino identifies this charity with his concept of love derived from the Platonic tradition, uses both terms

---

[89] *Ibid.,* pp. 1327 f.
[90] *Ibid.,* p. 1328; cf. pp. 672 f. See also Dress, *op. cit.,* p. 110.
[91] *Op. om.,* pp. 771 f.

interchangeably—preferring, especially in his later period, the term "charity"—in order to emphasize his accord with the Church doctrine on this point. In a letter to Bernardo Bembo, for instance, he praises "divine charity," quoting St. Paul and St. Augustine, but in the title he uses the term "divine love." [92] In another letter to the same he uses the term "charity" in the title, while the text discusses "divine love," again referring to St. Paul.[93] Likewise, in a brief declamation he celebrates charity as the way of the Soul to God,[94] and in a prayer and in a short letter he states explicitly the superiority of this charity over knowledge.[95] "Charity" is used here along with love and with the same meaning, or it has in the context the function which is elsewhere given to love.[96]

On the other hand, the concept of friendship is also closely connected with that of love and sometimes cannot be distinguished from it. The concept of friendship originates in Greek philosophy and was first made the object of philosophical inquiry by Plato and even more by Aristotle. The speculation about friendship and the cult of friendship, however, were particularly developed in the Hellenistic schools of philosophy, especially among the Stoics and the Epicureans. This whole body of ideas found its expression in Cicero's *Laelius,* probably the starting point for Ficino as well. In any case, for Ficino friendship again becomes the focal point of consideration and is closely connected with the theory of love. The common distinction according to which love unites a man and a woman and friendship unites men or women to each other has lost its importance for Ficino. In those passages in which he still distinguishes between friendship and love he defines "friendship" as habitual love and derives friendship directly from love, also using the linguistic affinity of the two terms in Latin (*amor, amicitia*).

[92] *Ibid.,* p. 772.
[93] *Ibid.,* p. 794.
[94] *Ibid.,* pp. 862 f.
[95] *Ibid.,* pp. 881 f., 887.
[96] I cannot agree with Nygren (*Agape and Eros* II [Part II], 449 ff.) that in Ficino the medieval synthesis of Eros and Agape has been destroyed. At most we may say that under the direct influence of Plato the element of Eros has been reinforced in that synthesis.

Friendship as no one doubts [so he writes to Alamanno Donati] derives its power and name from love, because it is nothing but mutual love strengthened by a stable, that is, virtuous relationship. Hence, it is manifest that friendship always has the same quality as love, from which friendship is derived and after which it is named.[97]

Accordingly, in another letter Ficino calls love the true foundation of friendship.[98] We have, therefore, a unique human relationship, which manifests itself in love as a sentiment and in friendship as a continuous communion.

Now friendship and love between two persons, according to Ficino, do not arise incidentally. As a genuine relationship it is necessarily a communion founded on what is essential in man and therefore presupposes in both lovers the highest form of love. In other words, true love between two persons is by nature a common love for God. In both of them it is based on the original love for God, which constitutes the essence of human consciousness.

Since friendship [so he writes to Giovanni Cavalcanti] strives by mutual consent of the lovers to cultivate the Soul through virtue, it is apparently nothing but a perfect concordance of two Souls in the worship of God. Those who worship God with a pious mind, however, are loved by God. Therefore there are not two friends only, but always necessarily three, two human beings and one God. . . . He unites us into one; He is the insoluble bond and perpetual guardian of friendship.[99]

Similarly, we read in another letter that friendship is necessarily based upon the common relationship to a good and precisely to an infinite good.

But even that seems to me not to be sufficient for affection (*benivolentia*); for all by a natural instinct desire such a good, therefore we all want to be happy; but we do not all love each other. Where shall we find pure affection in itself, which is nothing but a willing of the good, if we do not find it around the good itself, which is all good, namely, God? Certainly nowhere else. Moreover, the human will can be affected toward God chiefly in two ways as far as our purpose is

[97] *Ibid.*, p. 716; cf. Dress, *op. cit.*, p. 120.
[98] *Op. om.*, p. 861.   [99] *Ibid.*, p. 634.

concerned. For it desires either to receive from Him or to give. The first instinct is common and natural to all, for we all desire and want many things from God, but we do not love God or man on that account. The other instinct apparently does not belong to everyone in the same degree, for there are very few who give, or more correctly, return (*reddant*) themselves, and, along with themselves, all things to God. . . . Whoever returns himself to God, that is, turns every inclination of thought and every effort and effect of action to Him, he loves God for God's sake alone and likes the other things because of God. . . . Therefore, such minds are moved by an ineffable ardor and sweetness of love toward God and each other while they return themselves spontaneously to Him as to their father and give themselves most willingly to each other as to their brothers. All other friendships, so called, among men are nothing but robbery.

He alone is a true lover who loves the other man solely because of God.

Only among these there is true friendship, that is, a friendship which is true from and in one unique God. For a true and stable union between several persons cannot be established except through the eternal unity itself. But the true and eternal unity is God Himself.[100]

In other words, the foundation of all true love and friendship is, not the unconscious relation to God, which is natural for all men, but the conscious turning toward God based on the inner and spiritual ascent of the Soul, and therefore, true love and friendship is based on God Himself.[101] This conception, which is explicitly developed in the two quoted letters and presupposed everywhere else, has a decisive significance for the philosophical understanding of Ficino's theory of love. True love and true friendship which unite several persons with each other are directly derived from the love of the individual for God and are, therefore, reduced to the basic phenomenon of inner or spiritual ascent, the essence of Ficino's philosophy. Conversely, the inner certainty which found its conceptual expression in love for God is enabled in this way to

---

[100] *Ibid.,* pp. 777 f.; cf. Anichini, *op. cit.,* p. 94.

[101] I cannot agree with Nygren (*op. cit.,* pp. 460 ff.) that for Ficino our love for God is based on self-love. I would rather say: Our true self-love consists in our love for God.

find its concrete confirmation in a real communion with other persons.

Love between friends, the inner essence of which is derived from the relation to God, is a favorite topic in Ficino's correspondence. The love letter (*epistola amatoria*) is even elaborated into a kind of literary genus of its own.[102] The conscious cult of love and friendship is expressed in a language of fixed formulae and images, taken in part from the old Tuscan poets, but developed by Ficino to conceptual clarity. The first indications are found in the *De amore,* but the majority of the examples occur in the letters. The concept is frequently modified by wit and jokes, but a common conceptual structure is always recognizable. We shall call attention to a few characteristic features. The point of departure is the concept which we already know: that love produces a union between the lover and his object. So Ficino writes that Filippo Valori and Filippo Carducci are one with each other and with himself through their friendship, explaining in this humorous fashion why he had addressed by mistake a letter to Carducci that was intended for Valori.[103] Similarly, he writes in fun to Bernardo Bembo, who had studied at Padua, that their close friendship, producing in them one will, seems almost to be a living proof of the Averroistic doctrine of the unity of intellect in all men.[104] And he considers the friends Lotterio Neroni and Giovanni Nesi as almost one person, because he himself embraces them in one feeling of friendship.[105] The notion that each lover has lost himself in the other and given himself to the other is developed in the *De amore,* probably after the model of the old Tuscan poets.[106] A friend therefore exists in his friend and is dependent on him, as Ficino writes in a letter to Francesco Bandini.[107] In other words, he who loves his friend no longer belongs to himself, but has given himself and everything he possesses to that friend.[108] But although

[102] Cf. *Op. om.,* pp. 621 ff.

[103] *Ibid.,* p. 859.

[104] *Ibid.,* pp. 803 f.

[105] *Ibid.,* p. 832.

[106] *Ibid.,* p. 1327; cf. Saitta, *op. cit.,* pp. 236 f.

[107] *Op. om.,* p. 859.

[108] Letter to Cavalcanti, *ibid.,* p. 626; to Corsini, p. 672; to Guicciardini, p. 754, *et passim.* Cf. Lorenzo to Ficino, p. 621.

the lover has lost himself, he finds, in compensation, the image of his friend in his own Soul.[109] As a result of the unity of the two friends, therefore, their Souls are always present to each other even during a separation in space. This is a favorite motive by which Ficino sought to prove the uselessness of correspondence and to excuse himself to an absent friend for an occasional silence. "You must remember," Ficino writes to Lorenzo de' Medici, "that Marsilio is not absent from your place if Lorenzo is not absent, in whom Marsilio is, if the Soul is everywhere at the same time." [110] Likewise when he writes to his Hungarian friends that he is unable to join them: to come to them, he adds, he would first have to separate himself from them, and he could not separate himself from those with whom his Soul had been united for so long a time.[111] Finally, love has the power to transform the lover into the figure of his beloved object.[112] This concept is sometimes given a humorous significance, as, for instance, when Ficino gives Filippo Valori a letter for Pico and writes that he was himself transformed by *Amor,* the artist of transformation, into the figure of his young friend.[113]

In all these examples, to which we could add many others, there is a strange mixture of serious and comic elements; but we can clearly recognize the continuous intent to give a strong and precise expression to Ficino's personal relations with his friends. This consciously "erotic" coloring of Ficino's correspondence has sometimes been given a bad interpretation in modern times. It is, however, a case neither of fantastic and exaggerated sentimentalism on Ficino's part nor of more-or-less veiled homosexualism, as might be thought. The great number of his correspondents, their social position, and the fact that many of them were merely his acquaintances absolutely excludes such an interpretation. In his own day Ficino's letters were never understood in that light. The fact

[109] Letter to Giuliano, *ibid.,* p. 638; to Cardinal Riario, p. 811.
[110] *Ibid.,* p. 623.
[111] *Ibid.,* p. 782; cf. the letter to the Cardinal of Siena, p. 791.
[112] *Ibid.,* pp. 658, 830, 843.   [113] *Ibid.,* p. 889.

must be explained in another way. Ficino did not consider his "Academy" a simple institute of teaching, but a living community of friends, after the model of the Hellenistic philosophical schools. In his letters, which from the outset were written with an eye to publication and served his philosophical mission, he explicitly emphasizes friendship as the spiritual tie of the circle of his pupils, making it, so to speak, a visible point of his program.[114] His correspondence abounds in expressions and allusions that confirm this fact. In the beginning of his letter to Martinus Uranius, which is known as the catalogue of his pupils, he announces that this is

a catalogue of friends drawn together, not by any kind of social intercourse or comradeship, but by a communion in the liberal arts. . . . You must know that they are all distinguished by intelligence and morals, because I decided to have only those friends who were experienced to unite . . . culture with honesty.

For Plato had considered those two qualities as the central prerequisites for philosophy and true friendship.[115] The numerous pupils that Ficino lists in that letter are therefore all considered as his friends. In like manner Ficino writes to Buoninsegni that Plato is the founder of their friendship and spiritual affinity.[116] And to Piero Compagni: "Now I am going to join other people, because I love them less. I do not go to meet members of the Academy, because I love them too much and I embrace them in such a way that I do not let them go away." [117] The membership of the Academy therefore involves a moral and intellectual communion of the individual members with each other and with their common master, Ficino. This fact is clearly emphasized when Ficino receives into the community of his Academy initiates whom he scarcely knows or never personally saw and celebrates this act solemnly by a love letter (*epistola amatoria*). In such cases there

[114] This function of friendship as a spiritual tie uniting the members of the "Academy" is indicated by Semprini (*op. cit.,* pp. 66 ff.) and Kieszkowski (*op. cit.,* pp. 45 f., 56 f.).

[115] *Op. om.,* p. 936.   [116] *Ibid.,* p. 842.

[117] *Ibid.,* p. 864.

can certainly be no question of a sentimental affection. For instance, he writes to Panezio Pandozzi:

> Our Poliziano recommended his Panezio today to the Marsilian, or
> rather Platonic, doctrine. Though I am accustomed to sing a comedy
> to new friends, a satire to old friends, I will sing a satire to Panezio,
> because I want to begin and to perfect our friendship at the same
> moment.

He then adds a short philosophical declamation.[118] To Giovanni
Altoviti he writes in similar terms:

> So many things about your elegance and constance sounded in my
> ears through the words of our Giovanni Cavalcanti that I could not or
> would not restrain myself from liking and loving you very much. For
> the present let this letter be the sign of our love.[119]

In the same sense, after his first meeting with Bernardo Bembo
he praises their ardent mutual love,[120] and he writes similarly to
Girolamo Donà, whom apparently he had never seen, that the
greetings brought him by Antonio Pelotti transformed their love
into friendship.[121] Love and friendship are nothing here but the
conscious and as it were, technical expression of an intellectual
communion; the same intention is obvious when Ficino assures
several Cardinals of his intimate love [122] or inserts in his correspondence the pathetic love letters sent him by men like Lorenzo
de' Medici or Carlo Marsuppini.[123] He was bound to only a few
friends by a real personal sentiment—to Giovanni Cavalcanti, in
particular—but he explains even this friendship by the analogy of
friendships among ancient philosophers,[124] considering it merely
as the highest grade in the hierarchy of possible relations.[125] For
when he puts his friendship with Cavalcanti as a modern example
beside that of Plato with Dion and Xenocrates,[126] he obviously
inserts it consciously in the wider community of his Academy, of
which Cavalcanti is also listed as a member.[127]

[118] *Ibid.,* pp. 640 f.   [119] *Ibid.,* p. 650; cf. letter to Corsini, pp. 672 f.
[120] *Ibid.,* p. 652.   [121] *Ibid.,* p. 907.
[122] *Ibid.,* pp. 791, 811.   [123] *Ibid.,* pp. 621 f., 638.
[124] *Ibid.,* p. 634.   [125] Cf. *ibid.,* p. 778.
[126] *Ibid.,* p. 634.   [127] *Ibid.,* p. 936.

The expression of Ficino's cult of love and friendship may sometimes approach the ridiculous and may frequently offend our taste, but the phenomenon itself, considered in itself, is most serious and important. Ficino is the only thinker in modern times who has tried to found a philosophical school as an intellectual and moral communion between master and pupils. And in so far as love and friendship between men are based on the individual's love for God, in other words, on the spiritual wakefulness of the individual friends, the school, as a field of activity and as a community, is directly connected through its bond of friendship with the essence of the philosophical system and with the basic phenomenon of inner experience. Conversely, the inner certainty of consciousness and the metaphysical doctrine acquire a concrete form in the philosophical communion of friends and so are realized not only as a propagated doctrine, but as a living part of reality.

This love between friends, which is the foundation for the communion of the Florentine Platonists and is itself based on the love of the Soul for God, is called "divine" love (*amor divinus*) by Ficino, in opposition to the vulgar concept of love.[128] And since he develops this concept essentially in accordance with Plato's *Symposium,* he states explicitly that he is following the model of Socrates and Plato on this point,[129] and occasionally he speaks of Socratic or Platonic love, that is, of love conceived in the sense of Socrates and Plato. For instance, one of the last chapters of the *De amore* is entitled: "How Useful Socratic Love Is." It begins with the following words: "You ask what the utility of Socratic love (*amor Socraticus*) is." [130] In the Preface to Plato's *Phaedrus* he mentions "Socratic and Platonic love." [131] The most explicit passage is found in the important letter to Alamanno Donati from which we quoted the definition of friendship.

What kind [of friendship] will ours be called, oh Alamanno? Since it began from nothing else than from Platonic love (*amore Platonico*),

---

[128] Cf. *ibid.,* pp. 613, 795.   [129] *Ibid.,* p. 632.   [130] *Ibid.,* p. 1362.
[131] *Ibid.,* p. 1363 (*amoris Platonici et Socratici castitatem*); cf. Meylan, *op. cit.,* p. 426.

we must call it nothing else than Platonic [friendship]. For when we recently explained our commentary *De amore* composed on Plato's *Symposium,* we began meanwhile to love each other, so that apparently we have realized and perfected in ourselves that Idea of true love which Plato formulates in that work. From this Platonic love therefore a Platonic friendship arises. . . . So why do you doubt, oh Alamanno, whether Plato believed that there were several Souls in one body? There are not several in one, but the contrary seems frequently to be true when we see that one Soul exists in the bodies of several friends as the result of the Platonic love.[132]

This remarkable passage, which has no analogies in Ficino's works, deserves our full attention. Here for the first time in the history of philosophy and literature, as far as I am aware, we have the term "Platonic love." That this term later lost its precise meaning and finally became ridiculous, need not restrain us from interpreting it here, in its historical origin, in its given and precise sense. Every term that becomes an empty slogan as the result of fashion or of repetition is born at some time from a definite concept, and its significance must be interpreted from that point of departure. And every linguistic expression that did not exist from the beginning in the living language is not developed by chance, but is coined in accordance with a given intellectual need. So the term "Platonic love" in Ficino has its clear and precise meaning: it is intellectual love between friends; love which unites the members of the Academy into a community, which is based on the individual's love for God, and is called, with reference to Plato's *Symposium,* "Platonic love"—that is, love conceived in the sense of Plato. Not only is the expression found for the first time in Ficino but also we see that in Ficino's thought there are all the conceptual elements which logically should lead to its formation. Therefore, we may consider Ficino as, so to speak, the "inventor" of Platonic love. However, he is not responsible for the deformation which the term suffered subsequently.[133]

[132] *Op. om.,* p. 716.
[133] Compare the meaning of words like "Platonic," "Stoic," "Epicurean," "skeptic," and "cynic" in modern colloquial speech.

With the concept of Platonic love Ficino enters into a large historical perspective, comprising not only philosophy and theology but also poetry and literature. In his concept of love he combines the will of St. Augustine, the charity of St. Paul, the friendship of Aristotle and the Stoics with love in Plato's sense of the term into a new and fertile idea. Moreover, Ficino's speculation on love was foreshadowed (as has been repeatedly observed) by the old Provençal and Tuscan lyric to which he himself consciously refers.[134] In this respect the explicit quotation of Guido Cavalcanti in the *De amore* is of great importance,[135] and in other points also the influence of the old poets is clearly visible in Ficino. The physiological theory concerning the genesis of love which makes the so-called spirit pass from the heart of the beloved person through its eyes to the eyes and the heart of the lover [136] and the whole technical language of love which exchanges the Souls of the lovers and transforms them into each other (see above) are evidently taken from poetry and developed into a more precise system. But it is not exact to speak of Platonic love in reference to the poets of the *dolce stil nuovo* or to Petrarch.[137] These poets tried to give a spiritual interpretation to love and to formulate in concepts the beauty of their beloved lady and their own sentiment of love. But the term "Platonic love" and the direct knowledge of Plato denoted by this term are lacking in the works of these men, as well as the essential element of the concept, in other words, the derivation of the love uniting two persons from the love uniting the individual with God. Ficino, with his interpretation of Plato, was the only one to develop this concept, and so he coined the term. Ficino's theory is therefore a turning point in the history of love speculation. He enriched the heritage from the old poetry with new and essential features before passing it on to the poetry and

---

[134] Cf. Moench, *op. cit.,* pp. 69 ff.

[135] *Op. om.,* pp. 1355 f.; cf. *Suppl.,* II, 257.

[136] *Ibid.,* pp. 1357 ff.

[137] For the difference between the meaning of "love" in the ancient poets and in Ficino cf. A. Buck, *Der Platonismus in den Dichtungen Lorenzo de' Medicis,* pp. 44 ff. Festugière, *op. cit.,* pp. 399, 433.

literature of the successive period. For there is visible evidence of Ficino's theory in the erotic poetry of the following century, from Lorenzo de' Medici and Girolamo Benivieni on and in the prose speculations on love since the commentaries of Pico and of Lorenzo. Moreover, its influence may be traced up to the end of the Renaissance, although the concept of Platonic love became flatter and closer to the vulgar conception, the farther away it grew from its historical origin.[138] Yet the Renaissance speculation on love remains an important historical phenomenon, and it is one of Ficino's most obvious merits that he started this speculation and gave it direction for about one century.

On the other hand, this speculation on love is just that part of Ficino's doctrine which had the widest and most lasting effect in history, and considering the totality and the real content of Ficino's philosophy, we must admit that this influence is justified. For Platonic love is that concept on which Ficino tried to base his school as a living intellectual community, and therefore it expresses the essence of his historical existence and activity. But since this love goes back to the spiritual love of man for God, it is directly connected with the center of Ficino's metaphysics, which is indicated by the love for God, and indirectly connected with the starting point of his philosophy—that is, with the restlessness of ascending consciousness, a restlessness which finds its conceptual expression in the love of God and its concrete confirmation in the love of friends. At the same time, in these concepts, with all their historical limits, a deep and beautiful conception lies hidden, a conception that dominates implicitly the whole structure. True human relationship does not mean an abandonment of our own inner or spiritual existence, but rises precisely from the wakefulness of consciousness which finds its fulfillment and realization in that very relationship.

[138] Cf. Saitta, *op. cit.*, pp. 265 ff.; Buck, *op. cit.*; Nesca A. Robb, *Neoplatonism of the Italian Renaissance*.

XIV

MORALS, ART, RELIGION

Now THAT we have considered inner or spiritual experience, both in its manifest elements and in its conceptual interpretation as knowledge of God and as love, we must try to determine its concrete application to particular aspects of human life. We can show that for Ficino a number of important phenomena, especially in the spiritual activity of man, are related to the concepts of *abstractio animae, contemplatio Dei,* and *amor divinus* and therefore are interpreted in terms of inner experience.

If we start with the phenomena of moral life, we must keep in mind from the outset that Fincino has no real system of morals. We are therefore obliged to interpret the basic tendency of his doctrine from a number of scattered sentences and opinions.[1] The perfection of the human Soul, as we have seen, is entirely bound up with its spiritual ascent and with the contemplative attitude.[2] "The deeper the mind is merged with this body, the more defective it is; and the farther it withdraws from it, the more progress it makes." [3] Consequently, the empirical distinction between the various virtues, as developed by Ficino in his early treatise *De magnificentia,*[4] loses all significance in the light of a more accurate philosophical analysis. Hence the particular virtues in the *Theologia Platonica* are directly related to the two "genera" of speculative and moral virtue, which express the dualism of intellect and will and are consistently defined as their perfect attitudes.

[1] We are not speaking of Ficino's doctrine from the standpoint of practical morals. This has been treated, though somewhat trivially, by Galli in his two articles. Galli also admits that there is no close connection between these moral opinions and Ficino's metaphysical position.

[2] Cf. chap. xi, above.   [3] *Op. om.,* p. 203.   [4] *Suppl.,* II, 1 ff.

What else is speculative virtue but the clarity of the intellect? What else is moral virtue but the stable ardor of appetite kindled by the clarity of the intellect? . . . What is the end of virtue? The end of moral virtue is to purify and to separate the Soul from the divisible body; that of speculative virtue, to grasp the incorporeal and universal concepts of things, whose locus is far from divisible bodies.[5]

Virtue is therefore equivalent to the spiritual ascent of the Soul. This idea corresponds to the doctrine of the four degrees of virtue, which has belonged, since Porphyry, to philosophical tradition and is explicitly restated by Ficino as follows: passing through the civic virtues, the purifying virtues, the virtues of the purified Soul, and the exemplar virtues, the Soul arrives at the union with God.[6]

No less clearly does Ficino identify the second important doctrine of ancient ethics—that of happiness and the highest good—with the inner or spiritual ascent of the Soul and with the knowledge of God. The idea is briefly developed in the *Argumentum de summo bono* and at somewhat greater length in the *Epistola de felicitate,* which was written as a result of a discussion with Lorenzo de' Medici who on the same occasion composed his poem *L'altercazione.* Ficino starts with the well-known distinction between external, corporeal, and spiritual blessings, and he tries to reach the concept of happiness by gradually eliminating all imperfect blessings. So external and corporeal blessings are first rejected as defective, then among the blessings of the Soul those belonging to the irrational Soul, afterward the natural blessings of the rational Soul and the moral virtues which are fatiguing and so cannot represent the goal of our desire. Happiness, therefore, can consist only in the speculative virtue—that is, in contemplation. Above all, it consists in that knowledge of God which the Soul attains after separation from the body and in the joy connected with it.[7]

The contemplative attitude not only receives a kind of moral in-

[5] *Op. om.,* p. 187.
[6] *Ibid.,* p. 618. Cf. Saitta, *op. cit.,* p. 269; Anichini, *op. cit.,* pp. 113 f.
[7] *Op. om.,* pp. 662 f., and *Suppl.,* II, 96 f. Cf. Galli, *La morale,* pp. 43 ff., and Trinkaus, *Adversity's Noblemen,* pp. 101 ff. For the relations between Ficino and Lorenzo see my review of Buck, *Giorn. crit.,* XIX (1938), 148 ff.

terpretation in such abstract reasonings about virtue and happiness but it is also directly offered to men as a valid norm and goal of their life in a series of exhortatory treatises.

Separate the Soul from the body [we read in a letter to mankind] and reason from the passions of the senses . . . Seek yourself outside of the world, but in order to seek and to find yourself outside, fly outside, or rather look outside. . . . Leave behind the narrowness of this shadow and look within yourself.[8]

And in a similar exhortation:

If you want rest, do not seek rest through movement, but halt the movement; if you want domination, command yourself through reason; if liberty, serve reason; if you wish to avoid pain, flee pleasure, the lure of the evils.[9]

Accordingly, Ficino exhorts his friends to take refuge in God alone.

O Friends, let us stay in that which never leaves, and we shall remain. Let us serve only the Lord of all things, who serves no one, that we may not serve anyone, but may command all. Let us enjoy Him if we can, and we can if we wish . . . let us enjoy, I say, only that which spreads itself throughout the infinite; only so shall we be entirely fulfilled, only so shall we truly and fully enjoy.[10]

Cast off earthly passions, and at once you will enjoy divine ardor in a salutary way.[11]

Nowhere is there a sufficient remedy for earthly sicknesses save love and divine worship.[12]

And in another *Exhortatio ad moralem et contemplativam religiosamque vitam,* addressed to his friends, Ficino closes with these words:

When through moral discipline the mind is purified from all disturbances of the body and is directed by a religious and ardent love toward divine truth, namely, God Himself, suddenly, as the divine Plato says, divine truth flows into the mind . . . and as it overflows the mind with light, so does it happily overflow the will with joy.[13]

---

[8] *Op. om.,* pp. 659 f.; cf. p. 158.
[9] *Ibid.,* p. 738.   [10] *Ibid.,* p. 785.   [11] *Ibid.,* p. 887.   [12] *Ibid.,* p. 753.
[13] *Suppl.,* II, 65; cf. *Op. om.,* p. 509. See also Plato *Epistle* vii. 341 c f.

Since the contemplative attitude is considered the real content and measure of human life, the ordinary existence of men in the carelessness of their acts and in the external character of their motives must appear imperfect and even contemptible. Conversely, the literary type of the *Declamatio,* which occurs frequently in Ficino's collection of letters and reveals the utterly dubious and desperate character of earthly existence, is merely an indirect exhortation to the contemplative life and must be understood with all its rhetorical form in terms of this exhortatory purpose.

We are all like Tantalus [we read in one of these declamations]. We are all thirsty for true goodness and we all drink mere dreams. . . . So a tiresome thirst burns us continually, oh we miserable Tantali. . . . O miserable lot of men, more miserable than misery itself. Where may we poor people flee? Certainly nowhere if we do not flee from the lowest to the highest things, if we do not flee toward those things which do not flee anywhere. What may we do, therefore, so that we may watch and be healthy in the right way? Our life must be converted into its contrary. We must unlearn those things which we have learned; by learning them we have hitherto not known ourselves. We must learn those things we have neglected; without knowing them we cannot know ourselves. We must like what we neglect, neglect what we like, tolerate what we flee, flee what we follow. We must cry about the jest of fortune; jest about its tears.[14]

In similar terms Ficino writes to a young disciple:

O Panezio, consider how perversely we live. We do not easily listen to infamous people, but we hope to be listened to by God; yet we live in an evil and unjust way, oh we mad people! We try to change God, but not our habits. We wish to convince others of goods, but do not convince ourselves.[15]

This paradox of outward life, which can be overcome only by a complete change of attitude is expressed in another declamation with a characteristic metaphor:

When I sought today the chief reason why men should continually lead so troubled a life on earth, I remembered a certain play in which people have their legs extended upward and walk on their hands and head—trying to look with one eye at all earthly things, with the other

---

[14] *Op. om.,* p. 749.   [15] *Ibid.,* p. 640.

at things celestial; attempting to grasp with nose, lips, and fingers whatever is going on below, but to touch with their feet whatever hangs above them. . . . O ugly spectacle! O miserable monster! Those are not men, not animals; they seem to be Stygian trees. . . . What thing more monstrous can be imagined? What more troublesome and burdensome? Oh friends, of such a kind are we almost all of us, almost all, oh we miserable people! We stupidly make reason, which is the head of the Soul, subservient to the senses, which are the feet of the Soul. Moreover, with a mind so immersed in the depths, we have faith that we shall know both celestial and earthly things. With the lowest soles of the Soul we try in vain to touch the highest parts of nature. . . . Change, I beg you, this play, oh Soul! Reverse this figure of yours.[16]

Accordingly we read in the *De religione:*

Plunge yourselves, therefore, into the filth of the body, O miserable Souls! Do you think in this way to see celestial miracles? O, how stupidly you desire to see sublime things with a head bowed to the earth; you desire to be lifted upward by miracles, not to ascend through the grades of virtues.[17]

These ideas are most clearly stated in the three declamations, *De stultitia et miseria hominum,* which Ficino inserted in the first book of his letters and then again, in the Italian version, among the *Sermoni morali.*[18]

Who will deny that men are stupid who care about foreign matters and neglect their own? They appreciate absent things and new things and despise the present and usual ones. Because of a continual desire for the future, they do not enjoy the present. And while movement has to be stopped in order that one may rest, they are always starting new and different movements so that they may rest from time to time.[19]

Men daily ask God for goods, but they never ask that they may use them well. They want fortune to heed their desires, but they never take care that the desire heed reason. They work to make even the smallest belongings beautiful, but they almost never work to make the Soul beautiful. . . . O grief, we seek the greatest in the smallest, the sublime in the lowest, the good in evil, rest in flying things, peace in discordant ones, fullness in want, life in death.[20]

[16] *Ibid.,* p. 755; cf. Galli, *La morale,* p. 61.
[18] *Ibid.,* pp. 636 ff.; cf. *Suppl.,* I, xx f.
[20] *Ibid.,* p. 637.

[17] *Op. om.,* p. 15.
[19] *Op. om.,* p. 636.

O you mad and miserable people, since you cannot grasp foreign things through anything but yourselves, how will you ever grasp outward things, when you have lost the inner ones? Why do you seek goods far away, as foreigners, when they are near, or rather within yourselves? . . . Oh what a miserable animal is man if he does not soar above man from time to time and recommend himself to God, love God for God's sake, and love the other things for His sake. That is the only solution of those problems and relief from evils.[21]

This criticism on the stupidity of outward life, which only a mind spiritually awakened can make, is clearly symbolized in the figures of the laughing philosopher and the crying philosopher, well known to ancient tradition.

Why did Democritus laugh so much? Why did Heraclitus mourn? One at the stupidity of men, I believe, the other, at their misery. Stupidity seems to be ridiculous, misery lamentable.[22]

Since we exercise virtues falsely, but vices actually, we shall become falsely happy and actually miserable in so far as we ourselves are concerned. This is what Democritus laughed at, what Heraclitus deplored, what Socrates desired to cure, and what God can cure.[23]

This symbol of the two philosophers seemed to Ficino so significant that he had it painted in his villa in Careggi for the exhortation of his friends and disciples, and the three declamations quoted above seem to refer to just that figurative representation.

You saw in my studio the sphere of the world and on each of its two sides Democritus and Heraclitus—one laughing, the other crying. At what is Democritus laughing? At the thing that Heraclitus is mourning, namely, at the average man—a monstrous animal, mad and miserable.[24]

Laughter and tears are merely different expressions of the same insight through which the wise man rises above the outward world and above the ordinary people who are bound to it.[25]

---

[21] Ibid., p. 638.   [22] Ibid., p. 636.   [23] Ibid., p. 638.   [24] Ibid., p. 637.
[25] According to information which I have received from Dr. Otto Brendel, a painting representing the same subject matter and attributed to Bramante is preserved in the Brera Gallery in Milan. Cf. A. Venturi, Storia dell'arte italiana, VII (Part II), 113.

The contrast between the contemplative and the sensuous life is reflected in a characteristic way in the notion of time. The corporeal world, in so far as it has movement, is bound to the attribute of time, while the intelligible world is superior to time and movement and characterized by the attribute of eternity. "The theologians measure rest by eternity; the natural philosophers measure movement by time." [26] Consequently, the human Soul, located midway between corporeal and intelligible things, participates equally in time and in eternity. "The rational Soul . . . is placed on the horizon, that is, on the borderline between eternity and time, since it possesses an intermediate nature between eternal and temporal things." [27] This relationship finds concrete expression in human life. The sensuous life, dedicated to the outer world, is subject to the rule of time. So long as man always turns toward new ends and gives up the present for the sake of the future, he never really comes to rest and the perpetual loss of time is the mark of his worldly and inwardly empty existence. On the other hand, the contemplative life has a part in eternity; and since eternity is nothing but a pure present, without past and future, time is overcome in any moment of real fulfillment as in a pure actual present, and the ascent to eternity is accomplished. In this sense Ficino exhorts men to ascend from tomorrow toward today, from the flux of time to the pure present. "Learn well," he writes to Antonio de' Pazzi, "and please learn today; he who learns tomorrow, never learns." [28] And to Cavalcanti:

Tell [your friend] to seek the remedy in reason, not to expect it from time. Time is an unwholesome physician, for it deceives the patient daily with the expectation of the future, and before expelling the old pains, it adds new ones to the old and accumulates daily so many evils that through the fallacious hope of life it leads to death. We must live today; he who lives tomorrow never lives. If you want to live today, live for God, in whom yesterday and tomorrow are naught but today.[29]

In similar terms he writes to Lorenzo de' Medici:

[26] *Op. om.*, p. 639.
[28] *Ibid.*, p. 617.
[27] *Ibid.*, p. 657.
[29] *Ibid.*, p. 632.

Please, my dearest patron, in the name of the eternal God, spend the precious money of this short time sparingly and prudently, that you may not some day repent in vain your prodigality and irreparable loss. . . . Free yourself, please, from this miserable prison [of unnecessary affairs] while you can; and you can only today. Belong to yourself today for the first time. Believe me, it is not fitting for a wise man to say: I shall live. The life of tomorrow is too late, live today. . . . But do not promise me tomorrow any more; you promise what you do not possess and what you do not know you will possess. If you will eat and drink only tomorrow, will you not perish within three days, O friend? That tomorrow must perish today; it must perish as early as possible that you may not perish. Nothing is more fallacious than that tomorrow; it has deceived all the men the earth has produced. . . . We all suffer heavily from this sickness: this will be done tomorrow. We hardly possess the present time, for we have it so lightly that we cannot hold it even for a short while. But the future is nothing, hence nobody possesses the future. O, we mad and miserable people, we throw our hopes into nothing and always misuse the treasure we possess, but we desire to use well that which we do not possess. So we are all sick unto ruin.[30]

The connection with the contemplative life is even more evident in a letter to Antonio Serafico:

So we shall flee outward actions, which are in movement, are scattered, and serve a foreign reward. Meanwhile we shall be content with the innermost act of the mind. This action does not depend on anything else, but lives with itself; it does not expect any reward, for its own pleasure is reward. Finally, only he who acts in this way does not lead the Soul in such a way that he may be happy some day; he is already living in happiness.[31]

Now we can understand what the notion of the present means in the motto which Ficino had written on the walls of his "Academy": "All things are directed from the good to the good. Rejoicing in the present (*laetus in praesens*), you must not prize wealth or desire dignity. Flee excess, flee affairs, rejoicing in the present." [32] This formula of present joy is an echo of the Epicurean doctrine, which deeply impressed Ficino in his youth; but if "joy" was not used in

[30] *Ibid.*, pp. 646 f.; cf. Martial *Epigr.* i. 15. 11 f.
[31] *Op. om.*, p. 880.   [32] *Ibid.*, p. 609; cf. *Suppl.*, I, 60 f.

the ordinary sense even in Epicurus, Ficino gave it a still more contemplative, "Platonic" content.[33]

The moral relation of man to the world, however, is not limited to the simple contrast between sensuous and contemplative life. The man internally awakened is still subject to the outward course of events. Although he can free himself from it in a spiritual sense and with the higher part of his self, he is in fact forced by his lower self to compromise with it. Ficino discussed these problems in connection with the idea of fortune. The idea of the blind goddess of fortune who according to her arbitrary caprice guides men from nothing up to the peak of power and wealth and throws them back again into misery occupied a large space in the popular thought of the Renaissance and found expression in many mottos and allegorical pictures.[34] Ficino did not entirely accept this conception, but he discussed it. It is consistent with his system for him to assign to fortune a certain power over the outward life of men and at the same time to require that the spiritual man shall inwardly overcome this power and with the essential part of his self withdraw from its sphere of action. A preliminary discussion of the problem, in which the solution is but vaguely indicated, is found in the early letter *Della fortuna,* occasioned by a question of Giovanni Rucellai.[35] Experience teaches, Ficino concludes, that, not the ordinary masses, but only the wise man is able to resist changes of fortune. Prudence, however, cannot be acquired by human effort; it is a gift of nature, or rather of God. For whatever is natural in us depends on nature; whatever is spiritual in us, on God. So it is really God Himself who

[33] For Ficino's Epicureanism cf. *Suppl.,* II, 81 ff., and *Op. om.,* pp. 618, 933. See also the article by Gabotto (who confines himself almost entirely to the concept of pleasure as developed in the tract *De voluptate*), and my review of Buck (*Giorn. crit.,* 1938, pp. 152 f.).

[34] Cf. Aby Warburg, *Francesco Sassettis letztwillige Verfuegung* (*Gesammelte Schriften,* Leipzig–Berlin, 1932, I, 145 ff.); A. Doren, *Fortuna im Mittelalter und in der Renaissance* (*Vortraege der Bibliothek Warburg,* Leipzig–Berlin, 1924, II [Part I], 71 ff.); H. R. Patch, "The Tradition of the Goddess Fortuna in Medieval Philosophy and Literature," *Smith College Studies in Modern Languages,* Vol. III, No. 4, 1922; Cassirer, *Individuum,* pp. 77 ff.

[35] *Suppl.,* II, 169 ff.

gives man power against fortune. And as so-called "good fortune" in reality goes back to nature and God, so the human force of resistance comes from the same source. Ficino therefore arrives at the following rule of life:

It is good to fight against fortune with the arms of prudence, patience, and generosity. It is better to withdraw and to flee from such a war, in which but a few achieve victory at the cost of insufferable trouble and extreme sweat. The best thing to do is to make peace or a truce with it, adjusting our will to it, and to go willingly where it indicates, in order that it may not drag us by force.[36]

Ficino does not attribute an unlimited power to fortune, but from the outset subordinates it to nature and God. Moreover, he gives human prudence, which affirms itself in the active life, a certain sphere of action, apparently compromising on that point with the views of his correspondent. But at the end he indicates the contemplative solution, suggesting that we conclude internal peace with fortune and withdraw from the hopeless struggle. This solution is then elaborated in a letter to Cavalcanti, which refers to a famous passage of the *Theaetetus*. Our Souls are dependent on God and his providence alone.

But our body is attracted in a violent attack by the body of the world through the forces of fate, just as a particle is attracted by the bulk of its whole, and the power of fate does not penetrate our mind if our mind has not previously immersed itself by its own will in the body subject to fate. So no one should trust his own intelligence and strength enough to hope he can wholly avoid the sicknesses of the body or the loss of things. Every Soul should retire from the pestilence of the body and withdraw into the mind, for then fortune will spend its force in the body and not pass into the Soul. A wise man will not fight in vain against fate, but rather resist by fleeing. Misfortunes cannot be hunted down, but can only be fled from.[37]

In other words, the wise man must accept the action of fortune as a matter of fact; but by retiring into his inner self, he has spiritually

[36] *Suppl.* II, p. 172. Cf. Warburg, *op. cit.;* Doren, *op. cit.,* p. 121; Cassirer, *Individuum,* pp. 81 f.
[37] *Op. om.,* p. 633; cf. Plato, *Theaet.* 176 a f.

overcome fortune and morally escaped its influence. Therefore Ficino emphasizes again and again that the moral value of life and therefore genuine happiness do not depend on the power of fortune.

Those men seem to me to be most blind of all who consider fortune blind because it does good to the bad, for whom in reality nothing is good, or does evil to the good, for whom nothing is evil. For as everyone is in himself, so for everyone are the things he receives.[38] No one is more miserable than he who places true happiness in fortune. No one is happier than he who does not judge an incidental prosperity to be real happiness. He who laughs with Democritus at the ridiculous crying of fortune or cries with Heraclitus at its tearful laughter is judged prudent by Hippocrates. . . . Whatever is done, any fortune must be overcome by tolerating it.[39]

The moral situation expressed by man's inward overcoming of fate is discussed at length by Ficino in his consideration of patience. He writes to Cavalcanti, referring to injustice done to a friend:

He who receives an injustice, receives it, not from the doer, but from himself. For the rational Soul, which is man himself, is not offended unless it thinks that that injustice is an evil for [the Soul] itself. This belief is subject to our will. . . . In comparison with his own greatness a magnanimous person must hold as little that which is little. All temporal things are little and very short. . . . He is not strong who submits to injustices, but he who overcomes them. But he overcomes them who resists them in such a way that he may not be moved from his state by their attack.[40]

And under the impression of the Pazzi plot Ficino writes to Antonio Cocchi:

I think that patience prescribes mainly three things. First that you may be willing to suffer gladly evils which nature itself commands you to be unwilling to suffer. Secondly, that those things which fate has decided to be necessary you transform into voluntary ones. Thirdly, that you turn all evils into goods, which is God's task alone. [Patience]

[38] *Ibid.*, p. 778; cf. Galli, *La morale*, p. 70.
[39] *Ibid.*, pp. 748 f. Cf. Virgil *Aeneid* v. 710; Saitta, op. cit., pp. 157 f. For the relation between prudence and fortune see also Galli, *Lo stato*, p. 22.
[40] *Op. om.*, p. 632; cf. Galli, *La morale*, pp. 65 ff.

commands us on the first point to contradict nature; on the second to overcome fate; on the third to make ourselves equal to God. . . . For only impatience causes misfortunes, which might be confined to external things and to the body alone, to pass into the Soul as well. Moreover, it causes us not to enjoy the goods prepared by nature or fortune. But patience, by bearing them well, transforms evils into good and happily enjoys goods by using them well.[41]

Another letter addressed to Bastiano Salvini is also dedicated entirely to the praise of patience.

All other virtues consist in doing well; patience alone in suffering well. What is suffering well but not to increase the passion caused by evils? What is that but to be willing to suffer what you will suffer even if you are unwilling? If you do not suffer it gladly, you will suffer it anyway unwillingly; and if you do not allow yourself to be led, you will be drawn and pulled by force. Oh admirable power of patience! Other virtues fight against fate in some way; patience alone or chiefly among them overcomes fate. For those things which fate has decided to be unchangeable and necessary, patience, agreeing with the will of divine Providence, changes in such a way as to make them voluntary rather than necessary. Just as he who acts badly converts for himself goods into evil, so he who suffers well turns for himself evils into good, for in enduring evils he becomes good himself.[42]

Ficino's moral theories, as we see, are based essentially on the experience of contemplation. We may now understand why he connects philosophical knowledge so closely with the moral life. For him philosophy is no mere theoretical doctrine whose truth can be learned and understood solely by reason. Instead he follows the true Platonic tradition, according to which knowledge can be acquired only by a profound moral and spiritual regeneration of the entire person. Ficino therefore ranks the philosopher first among those who arrive at a higher insight through a temporary separation of the Soul from the body (*abstractio*), and he mentions several examples of this contemplative rapture.

After Plato had frequently withdrawn far from the body through the effort of contemplation, he finally left the bonds of the body entirely

[41] *Op. om.*, pp. 802 f.   [42] *Ibid.*, p. 788.

in this rapture (*abstractio*). His disciple Xenocrates was separated from the body for a whole hour each day. . . . Porphyry the disciple of Plotinus writes that Plotinus was accustomed to be freed from the body frequently, to change face and at that time to discover admirable things which, afterwards, he wrote down.[43]

There are some persons, though very few such are found, who, subduing their pleasures and neglecting public affairs, conduct their life in such a way that they burn with eagerness to attain truth; but they do not have faith that it can be investigated through its human traces, in which the ambiguous minds of most natural philosophers are accustomed to trust. Therefore they give themselves to God and do not attempt anything by themselves. With open and purified eyes they wait for what may be shown by God, and this is what Socrates is said to have taught and to have done.[44]

Not only is the inward rapture in contemplation peculiar to the philosopher, but also the moral purification achieved in the inner ascent is, according to Ficino, the necessary condition for any philosophy. In a letter to philosophers and sophists he develops this requirement very fully.

The Soul will not reach the true concepts of things which are separated from bodies, if it has not separated itself from the body through purification of habits and effort of speculation. . . . You will exclude from wisdom those persons whom you discover serving the body stupidly. But those whom you know to be wise you will judge to be, not slaves, but lords of their slave, the body. . . . As a dirty vessel makes dirty by its contagion whatsoever fluid, even the sweetest, you may pour into it, so a bad mind when receiving knowledge produces malice, not wisdom. Moreover, as the air is related to the light of the sun, so is the mind to the light of truth and wisdom. Consequently, neither the air nor the intellect ever receives its rays [of light] while clouded, and each receives them directly so soon as it [the air and the mind respectively] becomes pure and serene. . . . Purify the eyes of reason from all dirt of this unwholesome body; turn away the glance of the mind from the shadow of the lowest matter; direct the sight of inner intelligence toward the light of the higher form. By that same source from which matter when sufficiently prepared is first suddenly shaped into corporeal forms, the mind when sufficiently disposed is at once endowed

---

[43] *Ibid.*, p. 286.　　　　　[44] *Ibid.*, pp. 292 f.

with incorporeal forms. And as it is illumined by the clear rays of truth, so its cup runs over with true joy.[45]

Not only is philosophy dependent upon the inner or spiritual ascent of the Soul, since both are closely connected with each other, but also, conversely, philosophy may be considered as that which really favors and produces that ascent.

What else do we do through moral philosophy but separate the Soul from the passion of the body? What else through speculative philosophy but separate reason from the senses? This whole effort of philosophy, as Plato says, is a meditation on death. For death is the liberation of the Soul from the body. Nor is death frightful for philosophers and their like, since it is familiar and customary to them.[46]

Ficino emphasizes this aspect in a few short treatises written in praise of philosophy.

Through its own eye and through the finger of dialectic, sagacious philosophy shows men this [contemplative] life, which is placed on the highest peak of things and is without contradiction most happy.[47]

There [in the sight of God] the Soul, through the gift of philosophy, not only becomes happy but also in becoming, so to speak, God it becomes happiness itself. There all things, all arts and affairs of men, cease; of them all, only holy philosophy remains. There true beatitude is nothing but true philosophy. . . . But the fact that through the benefit of philosophy the Soul can some day become a kind of God, we conclude from the knowledge that while under its guidance [that is, of philosophy] [the Soul] through thought gradually comprehends the natures of all things . . . it becomes in some way all things.[48]

Since it is impossible to approach the celestial seats with a corporeal bulk, the Soul, taking thought as its guide, by the gift of philosophy, transcends through contemplation the nature of all things. So says Aristotle. Finally, to speak comprehensively, since philosophy is a celestial gift, it drives earthly vices far away, bravely subdues fortune, admirably softens fate, safely uses mortal gifts, abundantly offers immortal gifts. . . . O sure guide of human life, who first defeats the monsters of vices entirely with the club of Hercules, then with the

45 *Ibid.,* pp. 786 f.   46 *Ibid.,* p. 383; cf. Plato, *Phaedo* 64 a ff.
47 *Op. om.,* p. 669.   48 *Ibid.,* p. 670.

shield and spear of Pallas avoids or overcomes the dangers of fortune, and finally takes human Souls upon the shoulders of Atlas, frees them from this earthly exile, and returns them truly and happily to the celestial fatherland.[49]

To sum it up in a few words, philosophy is the ascent of the Soul from lower to higher things and from darkness to light; its cause is the instinct of the divine mind, its means and faculties the disciplines we have mentioned, its end the possession of the highest good, its fruit at last the right guidance of men.[50]

Philosophy is here conceived as an active and living force guiding men by means of knowledge toward their real goal. We must go back to antiquity to find such a sublime yet concrete conception of philosophy. Ficino also tries to illustrate the connection between philosophy and inner experience by arranging the individual philosophical disciplines and their objects in a fixed hierarchical order and identifying the gradual course of knowledge through these disciplines with the gradual ascent of the mind toward God. In the *Laus philosophiae* he describes this ascent: the Soul is first purified by morals from the dross of sensible things, then ascends with the help of physics from the lowest bodies to heaven, afterward passes, under the guidance of mathematics, through the celestial spheres, and finally, under the guidance of metaphysics, elevates itself to God Himself.[51] The same four degrees are listed in the fourteenth book of the *Theologia*.[52] In the treatise on the nature of the philosopher he gives a similar, but slightly different, version, mentioning the same four disciplines, but putting mathematics, with its partial fields, in the second place and uniting physics and metaphysics into one discipline under the name "dialectics." [53] This difference, probably originating in the desire to reconcile different traditional schemes, makes completely clear (what is in any event obvious enough) that the correlation between the philosophical disciplines and the grades of contemplative ascent by no means corresponds to inner experience itself, but comes rather from a secondary

[49] *Ibid.*, p. 758.

[50] *Ibid.*, p. 763; cf. p. 780.

[51] *Ibid.*, pp. 669 f.

[52] *Ibid.*, p. 322.

[53] *Ibid.*, p. 762.

need of speculation. This need arises from the identification of philosophical knowledge with contemplative experience.

If we pass now from moral phenomena to a consideration of art and artistic creation, we must again confess that there is no real system of aesthetics in Ficino; so the task of interpretation is confined to a significant collection of isolated passages. Moreover, in order to understand the particular character and limitations of Ficino's conception we must keep in mind that the idea of "pure art," as opposed to science, handicraft, and practical activity, has been developed only in comparatively recent times. Classical antiquity and the Middle Ages made no such clear distinction; they understood by "arts" any kind of human activity. Ficino also conceives "art" in that broad meaning when he sees in the variety and free exercise of the arts one of the essential privileges of man. For the animals either live without art or possess only one art each, prescribed to them by nature. For example, the swallows build their nests, the bees their hives, the spiders their cobwebs. On the contrary, by his own power man invents the most diverse arts and so proves himself the master of nature. For he works with all materials, dominates all elements and natural creatures, elevates himself through his spirit to the heavens and even beyond the heavens, and finally gives his own life a rational order in the family and in the state.[54] For Ficino this whole system of arts is based on the contemplative experience, since every creative work in an art is made possible by an act of internal concentration and elevation. Only when the Soul has freed itself from the body can it approach the inwardly accessible sphere of truth and then bring to reality in the corporeal world the contemplated object or communicate it in words to other men.

All those who have invented anything great in any of the nobler arts did so especially when they took refuge in the citadel of the Soul, withdrawing from the body. . . . Therefore Aristotle writes that all outstanding men in any art were of melancholy temper, either born so or having become so by continual meditation. I think this comes from

[54] *Ibid.*, pp. 295 ff.; cf. p. 207.

the fact that the nature of the melancholy humor follows the quality of earth, which is never spread widely like the other elements, but always withdrawn closely into itself. So the melancholy humor invites and helps the Soul to gather itself into itself.[55]

Why should we wonder that Homer and Didymus and many other persons who were blind by nature or from their childhood could write in such a way that they seem to have seen everything clearly? Why should we wonder that Zoroaster and other inventors of wisdom have produced a knowledge of all things merely by long solitude and by the conversion of the whole Soul toward the mind alone? [56]

Among the arts those called "arts" in the modern sense constitute a particular group, recognizable, it is true, but not clearly separated from other activities. If we try, however, to describe briefly Ficino's "aesthetic" position and begin with the fine arts, we must not expect too much. For what the leading thinker of the early Renaissance, who was a personal friend of men like Alberti and Pollaiuolo, has to say about painting and architecture is surprisingly insignificant. The notion of visible beauty, which has some importance for Ficino and might have been a starting point for aesthetic analysis, is entirely orientated toward the theory of love, as we have already noted in another connection.[57] The essence of that beauty, as illustrated primarily in the human body, but valid for works of art as well, consists for Ficino, according to the ancient doctrine, in proportion—that is, in the symmetric and pleasant relationship of the individual parts.[58] For example, the round figure is considered pleasant; likewise in buildings the quadratical ground plan, the equality of the walls, the disposition of stones, the opposition of angles, the figure and disposition of windows.[59] Accordingly, two windows placed beside each other must be of equal size, while two windows placed above each other may have a different size. This difference is a matter of choice when there are only two windows; in the case of three, the eye

---

[55] *Ibid.,* pp. 286 f.   [56] *Ibid.,* p. 255; cf. pp. 294 f.
[57] Cf. chap. xiii, above.
[58] *Op. om.,* pp. 255, 275 ff., 631 f., or somewhat differently p. 1336; cf. chap. xiii, above.
[59] *Ibid.,* p. 255.

requires a homogeneous gradation of size.[60] These and similar views are especially effective in judging given works of art. Ficino tries to show explicitly that human reason finds such a measure of equality in itself and through it is related to the divine mind. In other words, in the case of the aesthetic approval of a visible proportion, the external object is related to the inner conception and through that to the divine Idea of equality. Ficino took many of these sentences almost verbally from St. Augustine, and therefore it is sufficient to have indicated them briefly. The length of the quotation is in any case a sign that the quoted exposition may be incorporated without difficulty into Ficino's own thought.[61] These passages deal mainly with already existent works of art. Ficino's conception of artistic creation, on the other hand, is entirely confined to ancient doctrines. The artist, who is not distinguished from the craftsman, achieves his product by giving a certain form to a given material. This form is originally a concept or Idea in the mind of the creative artist.

What is human art? A certain nature, treating an external matter. . . . Although human art is outside matter, it agrees with and approaches the work to be produced to such an extent as to achieve certain works through certain Ideas.[62]

We have such Ideas of works of art in the mind, I say united, as well as distinguished, that following the model of a single Idea we can talk and fabricate something corresponding to it, even though we may not produce anything on the model of another concept.[63]

None of these observations come from an immediate interest in the fine arts; they simply serve to furnish a human analogy for divine creation and to prove the inner congruence between art and nature. This is a conception which played a role in so-called Middle Platonism. Ficino probably learned it from Cicero and Seneca. He did not utilize it as a theory of the fine arts or develop it further in a metaphysical sense, and the precise relationship

[60] Ibid., p. 275.
[61] Ibid., pp. 275 ff. Cf. August. De vera religione ch. 29 ff. See also Op. om., p. 255; Cassirer, Individuum, pp. 67 f., and Erkenntnisproblem, p. 94.
[62] Op. om., p. 123.   [63] Ibid., pp. 187 f.; cf. pp. 149, 249.

between the "Ideas" of the artist and the divine Ideas is left entirely undetermined.

Ficino certainly had a deeper interest in music than in the other arts. We know that he played an instrument himself and gave frequent performances before large circles of friends.[64] In the *De amore* he places the beauty of sounds on an equal plane with that of visible forms and thoughts; [65] he speaks with great conviction about the effect of music on the Soul and even dedicates several short treatises to the praise of this art. Even here, however, he does not develop any genuine aesthetic theory, but simply voices a few isolated thoughts, most of which go back to tradition. The essence of the beauty of sounds consists in consonance, which he analyzes in a special treatise and which he relates explicitly to the concept of proportion.[66] It is a remarkable fact that he recognizes the third interval as consonant, which is contrary to classical tradition.[67] Consonance is a criterion almost analogous to the principle of optic symmetry or equality, and Ficino consequently relates the judgment of vocal harmony through a cause inherent in the Soul to God Himself, again following St. Augustine almost verbally.[68] However, music consists not only in the corporeal phenomenon of the sound; it has its origin in the Soul of the musician and can therefore act on the Soul of the listener.

Since song and sound come from the thought of the mind, from the impulse of the imagination, and from the passion of the heart and, together with the broken and formed air, move the air-like spirit of the listener, which is the bond of Soul and body, it easily moves the imagination, affects the heart, and penetrates the innermost sanctuary of the mind.[69]

Serious music preserves and restores the consonance of the parts of the Soul, as Plato and Aristotle say and as we have experienced frequently.[70]

[64] *Ibid.*, pp. 608, 609, 673, 823; cf. *Suppl.*, II, 230.
[65] *Op. om.*, pp. 1322 f., 631 f:
[66] *Suppl.*, I, 51 ff.   [67] *Ibid.*, p. 51.
[68] *Op. om.*, pp. 278 ff. Cf. August. *De musica* VI. 2 ff.; Cassirer, *Erkenntnisproblem*, pp. 95 f.
[69] *Op. om.*, p. 651.   [70] *Ibid.*

But to say something about your Marsilio, I frequently dedicate myself to the more serious strings and songs after the study of theology or medicine, in order to neglect the other pleasures of the senses, to expel the troubles of Soul and body, and to elevate the mind as much as possible to sublime things and God.[71]

To emphasize the metaphysical meaning and origin of music, Ficino sometimes reverted to the Pythagorean doctrine of the harmony of the spheres. The celestial spheres, attuned to each other according to the rules of consonance, produce a divine music imperceptible to us; and human music, being an earthly imitation of the celestial sounds, through its admirable effect induces the Soul to elevate itself into the realm of celestial harmony. "Through the ears the Soul perceives certain sweet harmonies and rhythms, and through these images it is exhorted and excited to consider the divine music with a more ardent and intimate sense of the mind." [72]

Ficino treats of poetry in close connection with music, since poetry also appeals to the ear and, in addition to using words, often incorporates melody and always has rhythm. But poetry is superior to music, since through the words it speaks not only to the ear but also directly to the mind. Therefore its origin is not in the harmony of the spheres, but rather in the music of the divine mind itself, and through its effect it can lead the listener directly to God Himself.[73] For a more profound interpretation of poetic creation in comparison with the other arts, Ficino used Plato's theory of divine madness and inspiration. The true poet does not follow the arbitrary impulse of his human thoughts, but is inspired by God—in other words, he composes on the basis of what he has seen in a state of inner or spiritual elevation and rapture. Hence, in the thirteenth book of the *Theologia,* Ficino puts the poet in second place, following the philosopher, among those who separate themselves from the body during life. For the theory of divine madness he quotes Plato's *Ion* and *Phaedrus* and gives

[71] *Ibid.*
[72] *Ibid.,* p. 614; cf. *Suppl.,* I, 54 ff.
[73] *Op. om.,* p. 614; cf. pp. 278 ff.

three arguments: first, poets, in their works, reveal a knowledge of all the arts, whereas men as a rule acquire the individual arts slowly and with effort.

Secondly, in their madness they sing many admirable things which afterward, when their fury has lessened, they do not well understand themselves, as if they had not themselves made the utterance, but God had announced it through them as through trumpets. Moreover, the great poets were often insane and uneducated. Consequently, poetry is a gift of heaven. In the *Phaedrus* Plato gives as a sign of it that no one was ever outstanding in poetry, though most industrious and erudite in all the arts, if to these qualities there was not added that more ardent excitement of the Soul which we feel when God is in us. We become warm because of His incitement. That impulse contains the germs of the sacred mind.[74]

Poetry originates in the inner or spiritual elevation of the mind. Therefore it is consistent to say that true poetry is given only to a pure mind [75] and that the true poet who receives his art from God must also return to God and take Him as the object of his poetry.[76] All these considerations, it is true, make no new contribution to a theory of art; but the interpretation of poetry shows once more that artistic activity, like other manifestations of spiritual life, is based upon the certainty of contemplation.

Passing from the arts to the consideration of religious life, we shall analyze first the special phenomena of prophecy and of supernatural influence. The phenomena of prophecy have had an important part in the tradition of all religions, and a philosophical interpretation of "mantics" was attempted again and again, especially in late antiquity. Ficino continued this tradition, not by chance or caprice, but because he was convinced of the reality and significance of predictions through personal, direct experience. He relates that his mother, Alessandra, frequently foresaw a death or an accident among her relatives [77] and that his father, Ficino, was called in a dream to heal a hitherto hopeless patient.[78] Ficino

---

[74] *Ibid.*, pp. 287, 634 f.; cf. p. 614. See also Plato *Phaedr.* 245 a.
[75] *Op. om.*, pp. 790 f.   [76] *Ibid.*, p. 673.
[77] *Ibid.*, pp. 616 f.   [78] *Ibid.*, pp. 644 f.

himself apparently inherited the gift from his mother, and during a grave illness he received the announcement of his recovery in a dream.[79] In 1477, a miracle having occurred in connection with some relics, he prophesied the war and pestilence of the following year;[80] in 1480 he warned Lorenzo de' Medici against a dangerous constellation;[81] in 1489 he indicated to Filippo Strozzi the right hour for laying the cornerstone of his palace;[82] and he repeatedly read the horoscope for his friends.[83]

If we would understand the philosophical theory behind these predictions, we must distinguish astrology from all other forms of prophecy, since it pretends to be a definite science, based on rules verified by experience. Ficino's attitude toward astrology was somewhat wavering and uncertain. In his unfinished *Disputatio contra iudicium astrologorum*, written in 1477, he attacked astrology with a number of arguments,[84] and in 1486 he inserted part of these arguments almost literally into his commentary on Plotinus.[85] But in the third book of his *De vita*, written in 1489 and originally intended as a chapter of the same commentary on Plotinus, he uses astrology in a positive way for the purposes of medicine.[86] Finally, in 1494, when Pico wrote his huge work against astrology, Ficino announced his agreement in a letter to Poliziano and then tried to make his previous statements in the *De vita* seem consistent with his (and Pico's) view.[87] However, his justification was somewhat artificial and was received with

[79] *Ibid.*, p. 644.   [80] *Ibid.*, p. 813; cf. *Suppl.*, I, lxxxvi.
[81] *Op. om.*, p. 831.   [82] *Suppl.*, II, 307.
[83] *Op. om.*, pp. 857, 894, 918; cf. p. 901.   [84] *Suppl.*, II, 11 ff.
[85] *Op. om.*, pp. 1609 ff.   [86] *Ibid.*, pp. 531 ff.

[87] *Ibid.*, p. 958. Pico (*Opera*, Basileae, 1572, p. 418, cf. *Suppl.*, II, 274) mentions Ficino among those authorities against astrology. The meaning of this passage has been entirely distorted by Pusino (*op. cit.*, pp. 505 f.) and others. Also a version by Baron (pp. 148 f.) is not entirely correct. The error is based on a mistake in Liebert's translation of Pico's passage and has been corrected by Lynn Thorndike, "Marsilio Ficino und Pico della Mirandola und die Astrologie," *Zeitschrift fuer Kirchengeschichte*, XLVI (1928), 584–85. The point is important for a proper evaluation of the relations between Ficino and Pico in general.

skepticism by Poliziano.[88] In reality Ficino's own practice during his whole lifetime, especially in his later period, shows that he was not at all opposed to astrology. This uncertain attitude of Ficino toward astrology certainly constitutes a problem that deserves a more accurate re-examination.[89] Meanwhile, it is better not to assume inconsistency or weakness in Ficino. We should try rather to understand the contrasting intellectual motives which drove him in various directions. On the one hand, the professional astrologers upheld the complete dependence of all human destiny upon the course of the stars, a thesis which Ficino could not accept and rejected consistently at all times. For since the human mind excels the whole corporeal world, it cannot be subject to the influence of the stars; and just as we are superior to the play of fortune, through our real selves, so we are superior to the fate imposed by the stars.[90] This is the real and ultimate reason why Ficino attacked astrology in the *Disputatio* and in the commentary on Plotinus. On the other hand, he never denied that the stars have a natural influence upon earthly creatures and hence upon the human body, since each higher entity in the world can act upon the lower entities.[91] This "contradiction," which in reality merely reflects the difference between nature and spirit, is stated in a remarkable formula expressed in the ninth book of the *Theologia* and repeated in the *Disputatio:* "The heavens do not move our will through the instinct of nature, but they do move our body." [92] The view of the *De vita,* in which the care of the human body itself is treated, is therefore fully justified. But Ficino, following the example of Plotinus, took still another step toward astrology, stating that many facts may be predicted by means of the stars in their character of divine signs, without being caused by the stars.[93]

[88] *Suppl.,* II, 278 f.

[89] Cf. Saitta, *op. cit.,* pp. 150 f.; Dress, *op. cit.,* p. 130; Cassirer, *Individuum,* pp. 105 f.; Baron, *op. cit.,* pp. 148 ff.; Thorndike, *History of Magic,* IV, 562 ff.; Heitzman, "La libertà e il fato"; Garin, "Recenti interpretazioni di Marsilio Ficino," *Giorn. crit.,* XXI (1940), 312 ff.

[90] Cf. *Op. om.,* pp. 209 f.; cf. Cassirer, *Individuum,* pp. 119 f.

[91] *Op. om.,* p. 221.   [92] *Ibid.,* p. 209.   [93] *Ibid.,* pp. 210 f., 850 f.

This device helps to justify astrological practice in spite of all basic objections, and so astrology is conceived as a form of prediction, characterized by a particular method and "scientific" procedure.

While astrology rests on art and experience, prophecy proper, to which a divine origin is attributed, is based on inspiration and hence referred, as in the case of poetry, to an inner or spiritual elevation of the Soul. Consequently, in the thirteenth book of the *Theologia* Ficino, speaking of those who withdraw temporarily from the body, mentions last the soothsayers and prophets and states explicitly that their predictions are made without reflection and art, whereas those of the astrologers, augurs, and so forth, require an experienced mind. In defense of these prophecies he refers to the ancient seers and sibyls, to the prophets of the Bible, to the testimonials of Platonic philosophers, and to the experience of dreams.[94]

The minds of all these [prophets] searched through many places and comprehended the three parts of time in one when they separated themselves from the body. . . . Or rather such a Soul by its nature is almost everywhere and always. It is not obliged to go outside itself in order to look at many and distant places and to recall the whole past and to anticipate the future. Its achievements are won by leaving the body behind and by returning into itself, either because its nature is everywhere and always, as the Egyptians believe, or because when retiring into its own nature it is at once united with the divinity which includes all limits of places and times.[95]

Likewise following Olympiodorus, Ficino tells how Apollonius of Tyana, in a state of internal rapture, could perceive from Rome what was happening at the same time in Egypt.[96] And from the prophetic gift of his mother Ficino concludes that "the Souls of men which in some way are separated from the body because of a moderate complexion, purity of life, and rapture of the self,

[94] *Ibid.,* p. 288; cf. Anichini, *op. cit.,* pp. 71 ff. Anichini finds this conception not exactly orthodox and emphasizes the fact that Ficino expresses himself elsewhere more moderately. Unfortunately, he quotes for this purpose chiefly from the commentary on Asclepius, which belongs, not to Ficino, but to Faber Stapulensis, cf. *Suppl.,* I, cxxx f.

[95] *Op. om.,* p. 288.   [96] *Ibid.,* p. 405.

anticipate many things, since they are divine by their nature and exercise their divinity when returning into themselves." [97] Ficino explains at length the phenomenon of inspiration in terms of a theory of the three orders of the universe which he calls nature, fate, and providence, to which man belongs through his body, lower Soul, and mind, respectively. Since our mind lives in perpetual contact with the divine intelligences, it is moved by them by a kind of sympathy, but this impulse penetrates our consciousness only when received by the middle part of our Souls, which is called reason.[98] Among the other forms of prophecy dreams are especially emphasized by Ficino. Since sleep is a form of *vacatio,* that is, a state in which the Soul withdraws from the body, during sleep the Soul is immediately accessible to divine influence, particularly the Soul of a man who has been previously purified and directed toward God. "While these men are awake their Souls are freer [from the body] than those of all others, and while they sleep, [their Souls] are completely free, therefore the higher impulse is easily perceived by them." [99] A genuine dream, therefore, is also a divine inspiration, given only to those who have already elevated themselves above the body while awake. All dreams which do not fulfill this condition cannot pretend to be true or of divine origin, but are derived from the influence of the senses, of the imagination, and of finite thought.[100] But genuine dreams, like all predictions, need interpretation, and in general the prophet and the interpreter are two different persons. For the gift of prophecy and prophetic dream is superior to reason, but interpretation requires art and acuteness.[101]

Just as in the case of predictions, Ficino did not take the doctrine of supernatural influences merely from the religious tradition: he attached it to his personal, immediate experience. He mentions repeatedly the miracles performed by a relic of St. Peter

[97] *Ibid.,* p. 616.

[98] *Ibid.,* pp. 288 ff.; cf. Heitzman, "La libertà e il fato," *Rivista di filosofia neo-scolastica,* XXVIII (1936), 350–71; XXIX (1937), 59–82.

[99] *Ibid.,* p. 293.   [100] *Ibid.,* pp. 292 f.

[101] *Ibid.,* pp. 293, 873 f.

on Christmas, 1477, in Volterra,[102] and in the *De religione christiana* he reports a miraculous cure accomplished in 1470 in An-
cona.[103] Ficino himself made two real exorcisms, in 1493 and in
1494, as he reports with a certain self-conceit in his commentary on
Plato's *Timaeus*.[104]

In his theory concerning these extraordinary phenomena we
must distinguish between various kinds or groups with Ficino,
since the supernatural effect, produced with or without human
co-operation, is due to natural forces, to demons, or to God. So-
called "natural magic" consists merely in "conveniently subjecting
to natural causes natural matters which are to be formed by them
in a miraculous way." [105] In other words, the expert can conduct
certain hidden forces of nature into an object and so produce talis-
mans or effective remedies. This type of magic is a kind of art,[106]
and Ficino makes extensive use of it for medical purposes in the
third book *De vita*.[107] Another type of magic is connected with
the activity of demons. Since demons have a certain influence over
men and things,[108] through a special ritual man may obtain their
help and so perform miraculous works.[109] Ficino basically rejects
this kind of magic as incompatible with the Christian religion:
but he does not deny its possibility.[110] The exorcism of demons as
he practiced it is directed against demons, but obviously belongs
to the same type of action.[111] The truest and most perfect form of
supernatural influence, which is a miracle in the proper sense, consists in the power of a man as the instrument of God to change the
natural course of things. In this sense Ficino considers the miracles
of Christ and of His disciples as a genuine proof of their divine
mission,[112] and in the thirteenth book of the *Theologia* he gives

[102] *Ibid.*, p. 813; *Suppl.*, I, lxxxvi.
[103] *Op. om.*, p. 15.   [104] *Ibid.*, pp. 1469 f.
[105] *Ibid.*, p. 573. Cf. Saitta, *op. cit.*, pp. 150 f.; Cassirer, *Individuum*, p. 160;
Thorndike, *History of Magic*, IV, 562 ff.
[106] Cf. *Op. om.*, p. 288.   [107] Cf. *ibid.*, pp. 548 ff.
[108] Cf. *ibid.*, pp. 382 f., 1469 f.   [109] *Ibid.*, p. 573.
[110] *Ibid.*   [111] *Ibid.*, cf. pp. 1469 f.
[112] *Ibid.*, pp. 13 ff.

a remarkable philosophical explanation of miracles.[113] The human Soul, which by its nature is superior to the body, may become an instrument of God and perform miracles when it frees itself inwardly from the body and ascends toward God.

When reason is fixed upon God with the whole intention of the Soul to seek a benefit, it sometimes gives a benefit to its own body or to a foreign body toward which it is turned. . . . But let us return to those Souls through which God performs miracles as through instruments. How does the temperate state of the body help them in that privilege? Because their reason is freer, not being disturbed by any trouble of excessive humors. How does moderate and pure living help them? Because the Soul is not aggravated by the burden of its body. How does honest and pious education? Because [the Soul] desires goods for men and being similar to God is helped by God, or rather is guided by God as an instrument.

The Soul can therefore free itself from its own body and act upon others.

What Soul does this? That which stills the imagination and, while burning with desire for the higher divinity, does not trust the usual procedures of natural reason, but lives through the mind alone, becomes an angel, and receives God with its whole breast.[114]

Among religious activities that do not transcend the natural sphere, Ficino emphasizes especially prayer, which constitutes, so to speak, the intellectual element of worship, and which may be considered as a kind of miracle when it is heard by God and so indirectly produces the desired effect. To Ficino, following a Neoplatonic conception, prayer is nothing but an inner conversion of the Soul toward God. Prayer is heard when the Soul becomes unified with God and so participates in His activity.

The prayers of a saintly man, especially when the prayers of the people concur with him, connect Souls with God in such an admirable way that the action of God and that of the Soul become one in a certain

---

[113] *Ibid.,* pp. 298 ff.; cf. Anichini, *op. cit.,* pp. 85 ff. Hak (*op. cit.,* p. 96) asserts quite arbitrarily that there is no theory of miracles in Ficino.

[114] *Op. om.,* p. 301.

sense, but that of God after the manner of an artist, that of the Soul after the manner of a divine instrument.[115]

I should explain prayer as a strong conversion toward God so that the Soul does not notice the impulses of demons and demons do not hope that they can conquer the mind dedicated to God.[116]

The highest God hears their [of men dedicated to God] prayers as those of divine men, for their will concurs with the divine will, and God frequently uses the Souls so affected as instruments or subjects to perform miracles.[117]

God Himself implanted in Souls the instinct through which they are converted toward God in prayer, and this instinct is not vain.[118]

In that union [of the Soul with God] lies the whole force of prayer.[119]

This [divine unity] leads Souls to prayers through which we implore union with God. . . . But the prayer so born attains our restitution in God.[120]

Accordingly, we read in the Preface to the translation of the Psalter that the Soul seeks and finds liberation from earthly evils in its intercourse with God. "For this reason there is no sufficient remedy against these earthly sicknesses of ours except frequent and ardent prayer." [121] The letter to Bernardo Bembo, which up to this passage agrees verbally with the Preface to the Psalter, differs here, saying that the only remedy is the love and worship of God.[122] This difference is not incidental, for apparently Ficino wrote the Latin letter first and later modified it to make it the Preface of his Psalter, introducing in this passage the notion of prayer. But the fact that he could do so shows again that for him the special act of prayer is related in substance to inner conversion toward God; and so the contemplative experience appears as the concrete foundation of every religious phenomenon.

Having considered the phenomena of prophecy, miracle, and prayer, we must turn to the theory of religion. Though Ficino has no systematic philosophy of religion, just as he has no ethics or aesthetics, religion has a basic significance for his world system.

---

[115] *Ibid.*, pp. 304 f.; cf. Anichini, *op. cit.*, p. 86.   [116] *Op. om.*, p. 383.

[117] *Ibid.*, p. 915.   [118] *Ibid.*, p. 916.

[119] *Ibid.*, p. 1439.   [120] *Ibid.*, p. 1440.

[121] *Suppl.*, II, 186.   [122] *Op. om.*, p. 753.

Religion in all its forms is equivalent to the worship of God (*cultus Dei*).

Nothing displeases God more than to be despised, nothing pleases Him more than to be worshiped. . . . Therefore divine Providence does not permit any region of the world at any time to be entirely without religion, though it does permit different rites of worship to be observed in various places and at various times. This variety ordered by God does, perhaps, produce admirable beauty in the universe.[123]

We must notice two aspects in particular in this concept of religion. First, any given form of religion, however primitive, is related, though unconsciously, to the one, true God. Secondly, all rites and ceremonies of religion are but different expressions of an internal relation to God which is called worship and coincides essentially with divine love.[124]

If we examine these aspects in detail, it appears, first, that religion, based on the worship and love of God, has its source directly in the certainty of inner experience. Speaking of Plato's *Phaedrus,* Ficino calls religious enthusiasm a form of divine madness and defines it as "a stronger excitement of the Soul in performing those things which belong to the worship of the gods, to religion, expiation, and the sacred ceremonies." [125] And in the thirteenth book of the *Theologia* he mentions among the privileged Souls who can be temporarily freed from the body, in addition to those of philosophers, poets, and prophets, the Souls of priests. After reporting several examples of religious rapture he concludes with the following quotation from the *Phaedrus:*

. . . he who rightly uses the divine meditations and is always imbued with perfect mysteries, he alone really becomes perfect. But while cut off from human affairs and adhering steadfastly to God, he is considered by the common people as being out of himself; they do not know that he is full of God.[126]

---

[123] *Ibid.,* p. 4; cf. pp. 2, 317, 680. See also Saitta, *op. cit.,* pp. 97 ff.; Cassirer, *Individuum,* p. 76; Dress, *op. cit.,* p. 125; Pusino, *op. cit.,* pp. 508 ff.; Anichini, *op. cit.,* p. 66.

[124] Cf. *Op. om.,* p. 325.   [125] *Ibid.,* p. 615.

[126] *Ibid.,* pp. 287 f.; cf. Plato *Phaedr.* 249 c f.

The other aspect, that any given form of religion has for its object, at least indirectly, the one true God, is elaborated into a theory of "natural religion" which is of remarkable interest for the history of religious thought. Everything that accompanies the essence of a natural species is natural and therefore is found in all individuals of that species without exception.[127] In this sense religion is natural for man, because it is common to all men; and since religion means worship of God, this natural religion is basically the same as the natural desire of man for God.

Divine worship is as natural for men almost as neighing is for horses or barking for dogs.[128]

The human mind is led by its divine nature to feel and to worship and to fear God. . . . But by a free choice of reasoning, it changes the rites of worship. . . . From the above argument it may be concluded that the common religion of all nations, having one God as its object, is natural to the human species.[129]

Religion, as Plato shows in the *Protagoras,* is given to man as the first of all things—not only before all arts necessary for living but also before speech and commerce. But since it is most common and stable among all gifts, it is the most natural of all.[130]

Religion is not only natural for man and therefore common to all men but also a privilege which distinguishes man from all other animals. Artistic ability, as Ficino shows in detail, is not peculiar to man, for beasts also share in it. Likewise, beasts possess at least a substitute for language. If we consider reason the privilege of man, we have to distinguish its individual parts. For active reason and the rational contemplation of natural things is not entirely absent in beasts. Only the contemplation of divine things,

---

[127] See above, chap. x.

[128] *Op. om.,* pp. 319 f.; cf. p. 2. See also Saitta, *op. cit.,* pp. 77 ff.; Semprini, *op. cit.,* p. 59; Dress, *op. cit.,* pp. 125 ff.; Anichini, *op. cit.,* pp. 63 ff. Pusino (*op. cit.,* pp. 508 ff.) explains at length this concept of natural religion, but reaches exaggerated conclusions, since he identifies universal or natural religion with the philosophical religion aimed at by Ficino and therefore considers it the sole subject and goal of the *Theologia Platonica* and of Ficino's other works.

[129] *Op. om.,* p. 324.   [130] *Ibid.,* p. 474; cf. Plato *Protag.* 322 a.

that is, religion, remains peculiar to man, and in it beasts have no share.[131]

If man is the most perfect of the animals, as is confirmed by many reasons, he is perfect especially because of that part and potency which he has as peculiar to himself and not in common with other animals. But this is in religion alone. For the more clever beasts seem to have some traces of reason, but no sign of religion.[132]

Since, therefore, religion is peculiar to man alone, and since it has God for its object, there is a particular link between man and God, and it is this participation in God which distinguishes the existence and life of man from that of beasts and compensates him for the many defects and weaknesses of his nature.

I think if we take away divine worship, the human genus will be unhappier than all the animals.[133]

It is impossible that man, who through the worship of God comes closer than any mortal creature to God, the author of happiness, should be the most unhappy among them all.[134]

It is not right that the human genus, which through divine worship comes very close to God, who is highest happiness, should always be unhappier than brute animals, which are very far removed from God, since they are deprived of such worship.[135]

Though Ficino bases his considerations on natural religion, a concept which seems to place Christianity on the same level with other cults, since he is a convinced Christian he upholds the superiority of the Christian religion to all others. In fact, if the natural or common religion is considered a kind of genus, comprising the Christian religion and the other positive religions as species, this does not exclude a hierarchical difference between these species and a resulting superiority of Christianity. We have only to recall the hierarchical order of genera and the concept of the *primum in aliquo genere*,[136] to understand perfectly why Ficino starts from

[131] *Op. om.*, pp. 319 f.; cf. p. 2. See also Saitta, *op. cit.*, p. 77; Dress, *op. cit.*, p. 126; Anichini, *op. cit.*, p. 64.

[132] *Op. om.*, p. 474.   [133] *Ibid.*, p. 647.

[134] *Ibid.*, p. 79.   [135] *Suppl.*, I, 11.

[136] See above, chap. ix.

the genus of religion, passing afterward to Christianity as a special case of it.[137] For, as he states explicitly,

Those above all others, or rather only those, worship God sincerely who revere Him through goodness of action, truth of the tongue, clarity of the mind as they may and through charity as they must. Such, as we shall show, are those who worship God in the way that Christ, the master of life, and His disciples have taught.[138]

From this conviction Ficino comes to believe in the possibility of constructing a Christian theology upon his premises. He himself made this attempt in the apologetic *De Christiana religione* and in the fragmentary commentary on St. Paul. An accurate interpretation would be needed to show to what extent he actually succeeded in reconciling his philosophical doctrine with traditional Christian theology.[139]

In any case, Ficino raised the question of the relation of philosophy to religion and believed that he could answer it by establishing an inner congruence and harmony between them. It cannot be denied that there may be conflicts between particular philosophical and religious doctrines and that there have been such conflicts in history. But true philosophy and true religion, in other words, Platonism and Christianity, must necessarily agree, since they both have their origin in the same source: in contemplative experience or the inner relationship with God. The co-existence of

[137] *Op. om.*, pp. 872, 1537; cf. pp. 12, 849. Pusino (*op. cit.*, pp. 512 ff.) rightly observes that Ficino considers Christianity a "species" of natural religion. But there is no reason authorizing us to assert with Pusino that because of Ficino's concept of natural religion he was first opposed to the revealed religion of Christianity or to claim, with Giuliano, that Ficino was always fighting against the orthodox religion of the Church.

[138] *Op. om.*, p. 4. Cf. Saitta, *op. cit.*, p. 98; Anichini, *op. cit.*, p. 67.

[139] This is the purpose of Anichini's book. Such a research is useful and even necessary if one would understand a certain aspect of Ficino's thought. But we cannot admit that "the problem of salvation" is the essence of his thought (pp. 7, 24 f., *et passim*). This assertion is based in part on the fact that the title of the *Theologia Platonica* bears the addition *"de aeterna felicitate"* (Anichini, *op. cit.*, p. 20). However, this addition is not found in the editions of the *Theologia*, but only in the Preface to the *De vita* (*Op. om.*, p. 493).

philosophy and religion may be explained on the basis of the dualism of intellect and will or of knowledge and love: they are two manifestations of the same internal process. Philosophical doctrine is therefore destined to prove the truths of religion by rational means and thus to make it convincing even to the unbelievers. Ficino, the renewer and reviver of the Platonic doctrine, believing himself to be an instrument of divine Providence, considered participation in this task as his life work.[140] He states these facts clearly in the prefaces to some of his principal works. Among ancient peoples, we read in the Preface to the *De religione*, the same men were both philosophers and priests:

And that was right. For since the Soul, as our Plato believes, can fly back to the celestial father and fatherland only on two wings, namely, intellect and will, and since the philosopher depends mainly on the intellect, the priest on the will . . . it is obvious that those who by their intelligence were the first either to find divine things by themselves or to attain them with divine help were also the first to worship rightly divine things through their will and to spread their right worship and their way of worshiping among others.

Not till much later, to the great disadvantage of mankind, did the separation of faith and knowledge begin, whereby religion was profaned by ignorance and philosophy by impiety.

O men, citizens of the celestial fatherland and habitants of the earth, let us at last free philosophy, the sacred gift of God, from impiety . . . and let us redeem the sacred religion from detestable ignorance as much as possible.[141]

Accordingly, in the Preface of the *Theologia*, Ficino says:

I believe, and this belief is not vain, that it was decided by divine Providence that even the perverse minds of many people who do not easily give in to the authority of divine law should at least acquiesce to the Platonic reasons which come to the aid of religion and that all those who too impiously separate the study of philosophy from sacred religion shall recognize some day that they are going astray, just as if

[140] See above, chap. ii.
[141] *Op. om.*, p. 1. Cf. Saitta, *op. cit.*, pp. 76 f.; Dress, *op. cit.*, pp. 136 f.

someone should separate love of wisdom from the honor of wisdom itself or true intelligence from right will.[142]

And in the Preface to the translation of Plotinus:

We must not think the acute and philosophic minds of men can ever be gradually allured and led toward perfect religion except by a philosophical lure. For acute minds for the most part trust themselves only to reason, and when they receive it from a religious philosopher they at once willingly accept the common religion, and when imbued with that they are more easily brought to the better species of religion contained in the genus. . . . But it pleases Divine Providence in these times to confirm the genus of its religion through philosophical authority and reason, until at a certain moment it will confirm the truest species of religion through manifest signs among all peoples, as it once did. Guided by divine Providence, we have translated divine Plato and great Plotinus.[143]

Ficino, therefore, emphasizes again and again the union of philosophy and religion, using especially the example of the old wise men.[144] To emphasize the congruence between Platonic philosophy and Christian religion, he collected in short treatises analogies of the doctrines of Plato and Moses and of the life of Socrates and Christ.[145] With open satisfaction he gave his philosophical lectures in a church.[146] In a letter to Pico he praised the Platonic doctrine as a fish net with which the incredulous minds are caught and converted to the Christian faith.[147] This program also explains the title of his principal work, *Theologia Platonica,* taken from Proclus. Since, according to Ficino, Platonism is the true philosophy, Platonic theology is equivalent to a philosophical theology and is the complement of the religious, Christian theology with which it agrees in content, but from which it is distinguished by its form.

This alliance with religion is essential for philosophy in so far as it is based on the original inner or spiritual relation of man with God. If philosophy is defined by all as the love and study of truth and wis-

---

[142] *Op. om.,* p. 78; cf. p. 855.   [143] *Ibid.,* p. 1537; cf. pp. 871 f.
[144] Cf. ibid., pp. 268, 321, 686.
[145] *Ibid.,* pp. 866 ff.; cf. Stein, *op. cit.,* pp. 139 ff.
[146] *Op. om.,* p. 886; cf. *Suppl.,* II, 233 f.   [147] *Op. om.,* p. 930.

dom [he says in the *Laus philosophiae*] and if truth and wisdom itself is God alone, consequently legitimate philosophy is nothing else than true religion, and legitimate religion is nothing else than true philosophy.[148]

Ficino expresses this relation emphatically in the title of a letter: "Philosophy and Religion Are Sisters." [149] One is reminded just here of the scholastic formula that calls philosophy "the handmaid of theology," and though we must not overestimate the value of that formula, since the Scholastics did not always apply it, the comparison indicates Ficino's intellectual purposes and tendencies. Ficino obviously abandons the subordination and dependency of philosophy as it was upheld throughout the Middle Ages. Philosophy stands free and equal beside religion, but it neither can nor may conflict with religion, because their agreement is guaranteed by a common origin and content. This is no doubt one of those concepts with which Ficino pointed the way to the future, clearly announcing, if not actually determining, the course of later developments.

[148] *Ibid.*, p. 668. Cf. Galeotti, *Arch. stor. ital.* IX (Part II), 59; Dress, *op. cit.*, p. 136; Anagnine, *op. cit.*, pp. 42 f.
[149] *Op. om.*, p. 853.

XV

THE THEORY OF IMMORTALITY

WE BEGAN this second part of our analysis with the basic phenomenon of inner experience and considered first the contemplative ascent of consciousness in itself. Then we saw that the contemplative attitude was interpreted as an act of intellect and will and that the object of contemplation was identified with God. From this interpretation of the basic phenomenon there followed not only the doctrines of the knowledge of God and of divine love but also a number of speculative conclusions and applications. When Ficino defines the subject of contemplation as Soul, he obtains a new and final element for his metaphysics. It will be our task to show how the phenomena and doctrines hitherto considered undergo a further transformation and are developed in their systematic consequences under the influence of this precise concept of the Soul. Above all, there will be the doctrine of the immortality of the Soul, which, as is well known, holds a privileged position in Ficino's system. It is not our intention, however, to repeat in detail the numerous arguments that Ficino adduces for immortality. Rather we shall consider a few main arguments and on this basis try to explain the connection between the theory of immortality and the basic premises of Ficino's philosophy.

Throughout all the ages and probably among all peoples the processes and origin of human thought and consciousness have been attributed to a supposed "Soul." This Soul was originally considered a corporeal or body-like entity, as many myths and symbols testify. This is not difficult to understand, for human thought always starts by considering concrete things and frees itself slowly and with effort from spatial objects as it proceeds toward a proper understanding of abstract entities. This primitive conception of the Soul was accepted and developed by the earliest Greek philosophers.[1] Plato finally made of it a precise metaphysical concept, defining the Soul as a "substance," that is, as an entity existing in itself. This Platonic concept of Soul has dominated the entire subsequent tradition down to Hume and Kant. Aristotle's doctrine was somewhat different. He defined the Soul as the form of the body and attributed an existence independent of the body to the active part of the mind only. This doctrine had a modifying effect, but it did not really supplant Plato's conception. Ficino's doctrine of the Soul is peculiarly dependent on the philosophical tradition. He frequently uses Aristotle's reasonings and, especially in his polemic against Averroism, insists clearly that since the Soul is the form of the body it cannot be outside of all individual existence.[2] On the whole, however, he tends rather to adopt the Platonic concept of the Soul without explicitly discussing the relation between the two different definitions. So he says, for instance, that the Soul "subsists by itself" [3] and that it is "an individual existing in itself." [4]

Moreover, from the very fact that we form really simple concepts and conceive true simplicity the Platonists concluded that whatever it is that carries on this process in us is not composed of intellect and its corporeal instrument or of Soul and body, but exists as a simple and unique mind.[5]

The Soul, it is true, needs the co-operation of the body for part of its activity—for example, in sensation—but in other functions, especially in pure thought, it seems to be quite independent of the body and to raise itself above all spatial objects. The Soul, therefore, is not only an independent substance, existing in itself; if two kinds of objects are distinguished, corporeal (or sensible) and incorporeal (or intelligible), the Soul must be placed among the incorporeal substances. This point, which was clearly stated

---

[1] Cf. Erwin Rohde, *Psyche,* 4th ed., Tübingen, 1907.
[2] *Op. om.,* pp. 330 ff.   [3] *Ibid.,* p. 84 b.
[4] *Ibid.,* p. 120.   [5] *Ibid.,* p. 214.

by Plato, became part of the whole later tradition, and it was a simple matter for Ficino to take it from this tradition. So he says that when the Soul truly knows itself, "it will assert that it is entirely incorporeal." [6] Elsewhere he reaches the conclusion that the Soul is a substance, but not a body.[7] However, it is unnecessary to quote further examples, since three books of the *Theologia Platonica* (VI–VIII) are devoted to the task of demonstrating that in its three functions, the vegetative, the sensitive, and the intellectual, the Soul is not a body and is not subject to the modifications of the body.[8]

Since, therefore, the Soul is a substance existing in itself and since, further, the universe is to be considered a hierarchy of existing things, it is easy to assign to the Soul a determinate place and grade in this hierarchical order. This doctrine, which Plato barely indicated, was first clearly elaborated by Plotinus. It occurs also in Ficino under the influence of the Neoplatonic tradition. In the first books of the *Theologia,* in which Ficino presents the external scheme of his metaphysics, the Soul appears in the series of five basic substances and is called the "third essence," since it follows God and the Angel and is superior in perfection to Quality and Body.[9] According to this doctrine Soul is the lowest in the series of spiritual beings and so is the immediate neighbor of the corporeal world, of which Quality is considered a part.[10]

Ficino thus took from tradition the conception of the Soul as an incorporeal substance occupying a certain place in the world hierarchy. However, he was neither perfectly free nor entirely dependent in respect to this tradition: he did not simply accept the traditional doctrine; he sought to demonstrate it by explicit arguments. On the other hand, those arguments alone would not be sufficient to restate and to establish the concept of Soul, if they were not at least directed by the traditional conception. This concept of the Soul as an object existing in itself is, however, of the

[6] *Ibid.,* p. 159.

[8] *Ibid.,* pp. 162 ff., 173 ff., 182 ff.

[10] Cf. 119 ff., 221 f.

[7] *Ibid.,* p. 165.

[9] *Ibid.,* pp. 81 a ff., 115 ff.

utmost importance for the development of metaphysics and for the speculative interpretation of inner experience. With the help of this concept it becomes possible to consider all acts of consciousness and all internal attitudes as objective qualities of a substantially existing Soul; this conceptual procedure, which we may call a substantialization or objectification of the acts of consciousness, recurs on several occasions. The mere formulation of the concept of Soul, according to Ficino, is already the result of just such a substantialization, since the mere transcending of the corporeal world by the internal ascent of consciousness explains and establishes the incorporeal existence and perfection of the Soul.

If our Soul is superior to the world by its knowledge, it will also be superior by its life. Through its power, which is separable from the body, it can be detached from the body by action and can transcend the world itself by the force of a so-called "overworldly" life.[11]

You must question the pious mind [Ficino exhorts man], but only by presenting to it the Soul as pure as you received it—not enslaved by the body; not soiled with the taint of vices. The mind will then answer that the Soul is not only incorporeal but also divine. A great thing thou art, O Soul, when small things do not fill thee; the very best when evils do not satisfy thee; beautiful when thou dislikest the ugly; eternal when thou despisest temporal things.[12]

[The way toward knowledge of the incorporeal is to] make oneself incorporeal, that is, to separate the mind from corporeal movement, sensation, passion, and imagination. So it will become clear by experience . . . what a pure Soul is: reason living with itself and circulating around the very light of truth.[13]

In this case the incorporeal existence of the Soul is not derived primarily from the inner ascent of consciousness, as in Plato and Plotinus, but is evidently related to inner certainty and receives a new justification from it.

We must emphasize another point in this connection. Since internal experience is essentially conceived as a process of knowledge, the incorporeal existence of the Soul is based primarily on the

---

[11] *Ibid.,* p. 318.   [12] *Ibid.,* p. 158; cf. p. 659.
[13] *Ibid.,* p. 159; cf. pp. 380, 610.

phenomenon of thought as the quoted passages show. Ficino seems to make no clear distinction between the Soul as subject of thought and the mind proper. In this point he follows a principle which shows effects which may be observed elsewhere: he determines the essence of a thing from its most perfect element or from its highest function and mode of existence. Consequently, the mind empirically considered is simply a part of the Soul, but since pure thought constitutes the highest activity of the Soul, the essence of the Soul must be understood from pure thought and from the mind. The same relationship reappears between the concept of the Soul and that of man. Referring to a Plotinian definition, Ficino tends to identify these two concepts with each other. "Man Is the Soul" is the title of a philosophical letter,[14] and in the sixteenth book of the *Theologia* he says that Plotinus proves "that man is the rational Soul itself, which remains in itself and generates the animal under itself." [15] Ficino does not overlook the real difference between Soul and man, as he did not overlook that between mind and Soul; but when it is a question of determining the essence of man or of the Soul, these differences become insignificant. Hence, we can understand why Ficino uses the terms "man," "Soul," and "mind" almost interchangeably wherever he is concerned, not with real functions and their distinction, but with essential definitions.[16]

After the mere fact of the existence of the Soul has been established, the concept of Soul receives a further determination through the principle of affinity. In a world system based on a hierarchy of substances it is easy to reduce every kind of causality or relationship between two objects to some objective equality or similarity in their attributes. The assertion that love is based on a similarity between the lover and his beloved object has been made in another context (see Chapter XIII). Corresponding to it is the

---

[14] *Ibid.*, p. 626.

[15] *Ibid.*, p. 384; cf. Plotinus *Enn.* i. 1.

[16] On the use of the terms *mens, anima,* and *homo* cf. Dress, *op. cit.*, p. 59. Matthias Meier (*op. cit.*, p. 239) rightly observes that the terms *mens* and *anima* are not clearly distinguished in Ficino.

principle of similarity between the knower and the known, which since Empedocles' day had enjoyed an outstanding place in philosophical tradition (see above, Chapter IV). But when the Soul is taken to be a self-existing substance, such affinity denotes a metaphysical similarity between what knows and what is known. The objects of pure thought are intelligible entities, namely, God and Ideas. The application of the principle of affinity to pure thought therefore leads to a metaphysical affinity between the Soul and intelligible entities, and so it can be argued that the Soul in its pure thought thinks intelligible entities; that it must have an affinity with its objects; that hence the Soul is itself an intelligible, incorporeal entity.

[The mind] is outside and above all corporeal things. Otherwise it could not distinguish them from incorporeal things, and the converse.[17]

[The intellect] separates corporeal forms from the passions of matter, the entirely incorporeal forms from the corporeal ones, as it itself is separated from the passions of matter and from the conditions of a corporeal form.[18]

We admit that the intellect thinks many incorporeal things. . . . As we cannot perceive invisible things with the use of our sight, so we cannot think incorporeal things with the use of a corporeal instrument or seek, inquire, find, and preserve things separated from matter, space, and time with the use of a nature bound to body, place, and time.[19]

If the thinking intellect and the intellectual species or the concept indicated by this species become one thing, and if that species or concept as such is separated from space, time, and the other passions of matter, the intellect, therefore, will also be separated from them in that act. This act is peculiar to the intellect itself. The peculiar act follows the peculiar essence, and the converse. Hence, the intellect will be separated from any contact with matter not only through its peculiar act but also through its peculiar essence.[20]

The immateriality of the Soul and intellect, which we have up to now considered a basic quality, is therefore again confirmed and demonstrated with the help of the principle of affinity. And in

---

[17] *Op. om.,* p. 195; cf. Dress, *op. cit.,* pp. 63 f. [18] *Op. om.,* p. 679.
[19] *Ibid.,* p. 627. [20] *Ibid.,* p. 239.

like manner certain other attributes of the Soul are derived from
the objects of pure knowledge.

If concept, notion, and perception are simple, the intelligible forms
from which they originate are also simple. Therefore the mind is simple, too, since it is the subject of simple things.[21]

That the Soul is simple and individual results from the fact that it comprehends simple and individual things.[22]

If [the mind] becomes adequate to the highest equality, it is not
stricken by any iniquity of unequal qualities.[23]

If [the intellect] attains the highest form of perfection, it does so
through the greatest affinity to it. Therefore the intellect is not only
more perfect than sensation but also almost the most perfect thing
after perfection itself.[24]

The most important of all the metaphysical attributes of the
Soul is immortality, and Ficino frequently uses the principle of
affinity to demonstrate it. If the intelligible entities which form
the objects of pure thought are eternal and immutable, the Soul
which conceives them must likewise be eternal and immortal in
its essence.

The Soul neither derives its origin from matter nor is mortal. For by
itself it executes the work of thinking, in which it leaves matter completely and ascends to the incorporeal and eternal reasons.[25]

The intellect is eternal, since it unites itself with the eternal reasons
and is perfected by them. If the intellect receives these reasons, and if
what receives is always in proportion to what is received, the intellect
must have a congruence with these reasons. They have neither beginning nor end.[26]

The Soul of man will always exist, because it strives toward eternal
things.[27]

Because [the human mind] is separated from mortal things in the same
way as divine minds, it must be immortal in the same way, especially
since it restores to eternity the forms descended from eternity to time
and to the parts of time [that is, thinks them as eternal].[28]

This argument from affinity, which Plato emphasized in the
Phaedo, is in Ficino one of the pillars of the whole theory of im-

<hr>

[21] *Ibid.,* p. 193.   [22] *Ibid.,* p. 194.   [23] *Ibid.*   [24] *Ibid.,* p. 679.
[25] *Ibid.,* p. 184.   [26] *Ibid.,* p. 240.   [27] *Ibid.,* p. 391.   [28] *Ibid.,* p. 373.

mortality. It occurs in several passages of the *Theologia,* either in its immediate form, in a changed form, or as an element of more complicated reasoning, and it constitutes the leading idea for certain continuous sections of the exposition—for example, the eighth and following books of the *Theologia.* In the short epilogue which Ficino added to Plotinus' book on immortality it is listed second among four arguments: "Second, because [the Soul] frequently conceives many things separated from corporeal objects, either reaching these things which are separated by themselves or separating these things itself." [29] The importance of this argument from affinity can be easily understood if we remember how closely it is connected with the very concept of the Soul itself. But we must also emphasize that it points, at least indirectly, to internal experience. For the eternity of the Soul is doubtless derived from the eternity of the objects of knowledge; but the existence and immutability of these intelligible objects receives its certainty, as we have seen, from the inner or spiritual ascent of consciousness (see Chapter XII). The analysis, therefore, accomplishes a cyclical movement as it proceeds first from the subjective experience of consciousness to the establishment of the metaphysical object, and conversely establishes the metaphysical attributes of the subject itself conceived as an objective entity.

Having considered the abstract concept of Soul and the formal function of pure thought, we must now examine the concrete experience of inner consciousness and its speculative development within the framework of the theory of the Soul. For this purpose we must recall a few basic elements of internal experience which we have described at length. Inner experience consists in a continuous ascent of consciousness, which, driven by a profound unrest, leaves the field of external activity and rises to higher and higher degrees of contemplation by which means the higher intelligible fields of Being are opened to it. This process finds its end and final achievement in the supreme act of contemplation, in which consciousness reaches a direct perception of God. This

[29] *Ibid.,* p. 1754; cf. p. 908.

highest act of contemplation, being the most perfect among all possible acts of man, is also the starting point for a philosophical interpretation of the whole of human existence, since that act itself is considered the final goal of life and since compared to it all other kinds of knowledge and action appear as mere preparatory degrees. "It is our goal to see God through the intellect and to enjoy the seen God through the will." [30] But the final goal, in which the meaning of the whole of human existence is represented, is reached, as experience teaches, only by a few persons and even by them only for a short time.

The Soul, included in the dark dwelling of this body, never, or rarely and for a moment only, relinquishes all lower forces. Therefore that admirable work is not achieved in this body and is hardly ever enjoyed by anyone.[31]

But in this great joy we participate, O we miserable people, hardly and seldom on earth. Now our sick minds perceive only a weak and instantaneous shadow of it, because their natural taste is too much infected by the bitter humor of this body, oh grief. Thus that healthy celestial flavor is either not tasted or sometimes offends or is vaguely and for a short time enjoyed. Some among us taste it at times more strongly and longer, that is, those who more definitely remove the dirt and filth of the body from the nature of the mind by an effort of morals and of contemplation; yet but a few are those whom the righteous Jupiter loves or whom ardent virtue raised to the heavens.[32]

Since direct knowledge of God is seldom or never attained during earthly life, it is easy to expect its real and definite achievement in a future life and to consider the highest act of contemplation not only as the perfection of human knowledge but also as the foreshadowing of a higher perception and existence. We must now follow this conception in detail.

The conception of survival of the Soul after death arises from a religious need which has found more or less explicit expression among almost all peoples. This conception is the basis for the philosophical doctrine of immortality which has played an im-

---

[30] *Ibid.*, p. 307.   [31] *Ibid.*, p. 306.
[32] *Ibid.*, p. 712; cf. Virgil *Aeneid* vi. 129 f.

portant role in the Platonic and Christian tradition. When Ficino speaks of the immortality of the Soul and attributes to the individual an existence after death, he is simply following this tradition. However, the position which this doctrine occupies in his system requires special explanation, as we shall see. But the chief interest in the doctrine of immortality does not lie in the purely abstract concept of the eternal existence of the Soul, as expressed in the argument from affinity. It is important to fill in this existence with a definite kind of life; and even if this future life is conceived to be as perfect as possible and superior to all earthly existence, it will necessarily be conceived according to the analogy of certain earthly experiences. Since for Ficino, as for Plato, the pure contemplation (or knowledge of God) represents the highest activity of the human Soul, to be consistent, he must consider the knowledge of God and the enjoyment connected with it the real content of the future life. And if this future contemplation is to be conceived as perfect, it must be conceived according to the analogy of the highest contemplative act—that is, it must possess all the positive qualities whereas it must remain free from all the limitations. Pure contemplation must no longer be reserved to a few persons and confined to a passing moment. It must be communicated to as large a number of Souls as possible as a permanent, eternal possession. Conversely, the highest act of contemplation, accessible to men only for a moment during this life, must be considered an image or anticipation of the future life.

The quality of the state of the pure Soul after death does not escape the attention [of the philosophers]. It will be such as they experience at any time in the highest peak of contemplation—that is, calm and serene and filled with the formulae of Ideas as with rays of the stars and shining from the splendor of the divine sun.[33]
[The Soul] could never imagine that these [separate reasons] exist in the order of things, if it could not drive the clouds of fancies from its sight for a short time at least. But soon the clouds gather again, because of the nature of this earthly region and because of habit, and hinder the clearness of celestial things. From this sudden abstraction meta-

[33] *Op. om.,* p. 383.

physicians conclude that the intellect sometimes thinks without imagination; and so it follows that it can live and think clearly without the body.[34]

The odor of such a life is perceived by a mind separated as far as possible; its flavor is tasted by one entirely separated.[35]

Not only have the earthly and the future contemplation a kind of analogy with each other but also the inner or spiritual ascent of consciousness is considered as an immediate preparation for future existence. Death, therefore, is no longer an interruption of life, but a phase in a continuous passage from a less perfect to a more perfect degree of existence and knowledge, and the present and the future life are almost united in a unique, gradual progression of the Soul.

A thing which grows can at some time be entirely perfected, namely, when another thing is perfected whose growth is the condition of the former's growth. So the abstraction of the Soul from the body, which increases with the increasing intensity of speculation, will not be perfected until the latter is perfected. Intensity of speculation will be perfected when, apart from all other things, only primal Truth and Goodness is loved and thought with great ardor of mind; then only will abstraction be perfected. And the end of this abstraction which separates us from mortal things will be, not separation from life, but arrival at the primal life. For things which are connected with each other on the way are also connected at the goal. So, the same port that receives the speculating Soul receives the Soul which flees from the body.[36]

If the farther the mind goes from corporeal things, the higher it raises itself to the contemplation of spiritual things, and if the highest goal which thought can reach is God's substance, the mind can only receive divine substance when it is entirely free from the mortal senses. So when the Soul leaves the bonds of this body, freed and pure, in a certain sense it becomes God.[37]

[The Soul] judges how much better the eternal life is, freed from the mortal body, than the present life or privation of life; and it desires a free and eternal life. But it could not judge and desire in this way if it had not already experienced in itself such a life. If a free life is very different from a servile one, and if even the Soul bound to the body

---

[34] *Ibid.,* p. 715.   [35] *Ibid.,* p. 409; cf. pp. 407 ff.
[36] *Ibid.,* p. 233.   [37] *Ibid.,* p. 306.

can experience and exercise it, how much more can the Soul which is free from the body attain it.[38]

Still another element which corresponds to a basic fact of inner experience is contained in the quoted passages: contemplative knowledge is always essentially connected with an inward overcoming of outward things, that is, with a separation of the Soul from the body. Since death is nothing but a complete and definite separation of Soul from body, according to a formula already expressed in Plato's *Phaedo,* we can consider the contemplative or philosophical life as a preparation or exercise for death.

What else do we do in moral philosophy but separate the Soul from the passion of the body? What else in speculative philosophy but divide the reason from the senses? All this effort of philosophy, as Plato says, is a meditation on death (*meditatio mortis*). For death is the liberation of the Soul from the body.[39]

So far as the contemplative separation of the Soul is, so to speak, completed by death, a slight change of thought brings a new argument for immortality. If during its earthly life the Soul is able to free itself from the body, to overcome its influence, and so to ascend to a higher knowledge, the complete separation of the Soul by death will accordingly involve a more perfect knowledge; and this requires the future existence and immortality of the Soul as a necessary condition.

Since nothing is more desirable to the mind than truth, and since truth is reached by a separation from mortal things, nothing is more natural and familiar to the mind, as such, than to separate itself from mortal things. But from what is most natural there cannot be a lessening, but only an increase, of life. So, the mind will live most fully at the time when it has left this life.[40]

The more the mind is plunged into this body, the more deficient it is. And the farther behind it leaves the body, the more perfect it is. The mind will therefore be most perfect when it leaves this body entirely. But anything that gives highest perfection, cannot give destruction, but rather life so complete as to be eternal. For by what change can

[38] *Ibid.,* p. 385.   [39] *Ibid.,* p. 383; cf. Plato *Phaedo* 64 a ff.
[40] *Op. om.,* p. 186.

the Soul ever perish if it does not perish in leaving the body, which is for it the greatest change? [41]

Ficino attaches great importance to this argument, placing it first in his short epilogue to Plotinus. "First, because the Soul can dominate transitory things and resist corporeal impulses." [42] It occurs several times in the *Theologia Platonica*,[43] and it cannot be denied that it is closely connected with the basic facts of internal experience. But Ficino uses it only occasionally, and it is not developed into a clear conceptual form as it is not in Plato.

The conception of death and a future life and the whole theory of immortality receive their definite conceptual form only with the complete substantialization of internal experience, as it is attained through the concept of "natural appetite." We have already analyzed at length the theory of the *appetitus naturalis* in its general ontological significance, and we have also noticed its application to the human Soul and its immortality (see Chapter X). We must now understand conversely how this ontological doctrine is applicable to human consciousness, using subjective experience and the concept of Soul as our points of departure. We have only to begin with the basic facts of internal experience, which we have just recalled. For the highest act of contemplation, which has God Himself for its object, constitutes, as we have seen, the real goal of human consciousness, a goal in which the original unrest finds satisfaction, and in relation to which all other thoughts and actions of man appear as more-or-less remote degrees of preparation. When the human Soul is conceived as the substantial basis for all acts of consciousness, it is easy to attribute to it a natural appetite as an objective quality—that is, a desire, based on its essence, for God and for divine things. This doctrine, which must therefore be interpreted as an objectification of the basic experience of the inner or spiritual striving which precedes the highest act, is very frequently and emphatically asserted by Ficino.

[41] *Ibid.*, pp. 203 f.; cf. p. 476.   [42] *Ibid.*, p. 1754.
[43] Cf. pp. 185 f., 203 ff.

The goal and end of mind is Truth and Goodness itself: namely, God. Toward God it moves like fire, with an essential instinct.[44]

The entire effort of our Soul is to become God. This effort is as natural to man as that of flying is to birds. For it is inherent in all men, everywhere and always; therefore it does not follow the incidental quality of some man, but the nature of the species itself.[45]

Since we wish to see the cause of every known effect and since our intellect recognizes universal Being, we strive to know the cause of Being itself, which is God. And we have not reached the ultimate goal until the whole natural desire has come to rest. Therefore the final human goal consists only in the knowledge or possession of God, which satisfies the natural appetite.[46]

The Souls of men, by a common and natural instinct, continually desire the heavens and in addition the King of Heaven by whom they have been created.[47]

Natural appetite, however, is based directly upon an objective quality of the striving substance, and therefore it is possible to form a retroactive conclusion about its nature and essence. "Forces proceed from natures, and natures are revealed by forces." [48] Consequently we must suppose an objective affinity between the striving substance and its goal, and this is a new argument for the incorporeality and eternity of the Soul.

A natural movement, being directed to some goal, is destined to this goal rather than to another for no other cause than some disposition of its nature, by which it is congruent with one goal rather than with another. And because of the congruence it loves it . . . as the air, being congruent by its lightness with the concavity of fire, strives and is moved to it by this same quality.[49]

According to the principle that "natural tendencies are based on respective natures," in another passage Ficino assigns the Soul, which has a natural desire toward the eternal, an eternal nature.[50] So we return indirectly from the concept of natural appetite to the principle of affinity and to the abstract qualities of the Soul.

[44] *Op. om.*, p. 99.   [45] *Ibid.*, p. 305.   [46] *Ibid.*, p. 307.
[47] *Ibid.*, p. 753; cf. pp. 677 f.
[48] *Ibid.*, p. 715.   [49] *Ibid.*, p. 305.   [50] *Ibid.*, p. 219.

However, this consideration has little importance for Ficino's theory of the Soul as a whole.

In addition to the concept of natural desire, we have to consider a similar formula, which is also the direct result of the objectification of contemplative consciousness. As the inner unrest of the Soul is directed toward God as its goal from the outset and as, moreover, religion may be called any kind of relation with God, the resulting proposition is that religion is natural to man.

The worship of God is as natural to man as is neighing to the horse and barking to the dog.[51]

When I say religion, I mean the instinct common and natural, to all peoples, by which a Providence is always conceived and worshiped everywhere as queen of the world.[52]

Among all peoples, in all times, God is worshiped because it is natural to do so, though not with the same rites and methods.[53]

[Religion] is more common and more constant than all things, and so it is more natural than all things.[54]

But religion is natural because it is based on the essence of man; and this conception, which is closely bound up with inner experience, is made the basis for the theory of natural religion which we have briefly analyzed (see Chapter XIV).

This objective interpretation of inner or spiritual consciousness, which was first expressed in the theory of natural appetite, leads to further ontological consequences. For since this natural tendency originates in the essence of the Soul, and since the Soul, according to the theological tradition, has been directly created by God, God Himself must be considered the author of that natural instinct. Therefore this instinct acquires, apart from its concrete internal meaning, a connection with the objective structure of the universe.

For who implanted in our Souls this [tendency toward God] but God Himself, whom we seek? As He is the unique author of all species, He implants in them their peculiar appetite. For from the primal cause of things, as from the highest good and goal of desire, all natural desires are derived.[55]

[51] *Ibid.*, pp. 319 f.   [52] *Ibid.*, p. 320.   [53] *Ibid.*, p. 324.
[54] *Ibid.*, p. 474.   [55] *Ibid.*, p. 305.

Men seek God's form, therefore this appetite is given by God.[56]
This will be shown to us by natural appetite, which draws us toward the infinite and can therefore be implanted and moved only by the infinite itself.[57]

But since direct knowledge of God constitutes the real goal of human life, and since the Soul must have been created by God for a definite end and task, this knowledge is explicitly considered the goal of creation and, consequently, the real cause of man's existence. We read, therefore, at the end of the *Theologia Platonica* that to be deprived of divine sight is the greatest punishment for the damned, "because God is the goal for which we are born and for Whose sake we all desire and do all things." [58] And the same thought is brought out in the *De Christiana religione*:

But human minds had to be resurrected some time in order that they might not have been created by God in vain, since they were created by Him for the purpose of reaching Him.[59]

And in the commentary on St. Paul:

That the enjoyment of God is the end of the human mind we can easily conclude from the fact that all desire this by nature and do not come to rest anywhere else.[60]

Therefore, not only is the direct knowledge of God the goal to which consciousness tends in its spiritual ascent, but also this goal is given to it by God along with its existence and, ontologically speaking, constitutes the very cause and end of human existence. Therefore the "destiny of man," first experienced merely as a spiritual task, enters into a broader metaphysical perspective.

From these objective attributes of consciousness we get a series of important new arguments for the immortality of the Soul. The first and most remarkable among them is based directly on the central concept of natural desire; we may call it the "appetite argument." We recall the general ontological principle that nothing in nature is superfluous or in vain, a principle that is connected

[56] *Ibid.*, p. 306. [57] *Ibid.*, p. 413. [58] *Ibid.*, p. 422.
[59] *Ibid.*, p. 20. [60] *Ibid.*, p. 430.

with the postulate of a perfect world order created by God (see Chapter V). As we have seen in another context, this principle may also be applied to the natural appetite, which is considered an objective attribute of the desiring subject (see Chapter X), and so Ficino can state in general that a natural desire cannot be useless and must therefore actually reach its goal some time.

The natural appetite of every species, directed by universal nature, cannot be entirely in vain.[61]

Every natural movement is able to reach its goal at some time, and every preparation related by nature to a form is able to acquire that form at some time.[62]

[Good itself] constitutes in the movements of nature a similar rule and faculty of inclination and consummation.[63]

If this rule is applied to the natural movement of the Soul toward God, there follows immediately the immortality of the Soul, as we have already indicated.[64] For since the striving of the Soul toward God cannot be in vain, but must at some time reach its definite goal, and since during earthly life this happens never, or only for a moment and then imperfectly, it must be realized in a future life; so survival of the Soul after death is necessary.

As the ascent of fire has a certain goal that it can reach—in other words, its rest in its own sphere—so the ascent of our mind, directed continuously toward God, has its definite goal, which it reaches at some time; this goal is nothing else but rest in God, which the Soul will not reach before it departs from here.[65]

A natural movement directed toward a goal . . . loves it because it agrees with it, and for the same reason it is capable of reaching what it loves—as air, which is congruent by its lightness with the concavity of fire, strives and moves toward it by the same quality. And by the same characteristic it is capable of reaching it and of resting in it, after having reached it. So human striving toward God can be fulfilled at some time.[66]

Man alone is a foreigner in these earthly regions, and he cannot find rest in his voyage so long as he desires the celestial fatherland, which

[61] *Ibid.*, p. 411.   [62] *Ibid.*, pp. 618 f.
[63] *Ibid.*, p. 916; cf. above, chap. x.   [64] Cf. *ibid.*
[65] *Ibid.*, pp. 231 f.   [66] *Ibid.*, p. 305.

we all seek . . . If the things inferior to us find rest at some time, when they have reached their natural condition and fatherland, we also must be able . . . to reach it at some time and to rest in it. In the present life it [the goal] is not given to us.

For as our natural condition and goal we desire a good which is pure, perfect, and perpetual; but during the earthly life none of these qualities is attained.

In order that the state which we have attained in part may be achieved at some time and that that which was a long time growing may remain a long time, it is necessary for the Soul to survive the body.[67]

Since the natural appetite toward God given us by God cannot be in vain, that the highest Reason which makes nothing in vain may not have given it to us in vain, human minds must be eternal, that they may eventually arrive at the eternal and divine Good, which they desire by nature.[68]

Because God does not move in vain and the common and continuous instinct of the mind must not be entirely in vain, faith, hope, and charity persist strongly and finally reach their goal.[69]

Religion, so far as we understand it as basic relation to God, is natural to man, and this concept of natural religion is closely connected with that of the natural desire toward God. Therefore, when we consider the real union with God as the goal of all worship of God, a similar argument for immortality results from the concept of natural religion.

Among all peoples and at all times God is worshiped because it is natural to [worship Him], though not with the same rites and methods. Speech, being natural, reaches its end—that is, to explain one's will to another person. Drinking reaches its end, which is to replace the humor of the body. There is no reason why religion should not reach its end. Its end is to enjoy God; its desire to enjoy Him forever.[70]

This argument receives another modification in so far as the fact of future life is considered to be the content of religious conviction.

[67] *Ibid.*, pp. 315 f.; cf. Thomas, *Summa contra Gentiles*, III, 48.
[68] *Op. om.*, p. 753.
[69] *Ibid.*, p. 469; cf. pp. 305 ff., 67℅ f.
[70] *Ibid.*, p. 324.

Here we derive the objective truth of this belief from its universality and "naturality."

> [Man] is most perfect through religion. If religion were void, he would be most imperfect through it . . . But with respect to the same part of his nature, he cannot suffer such contradictory things as to be most perfect and most imperfect through it. Religion is therefore true. . . . It is therefore true that there will be another life, since the most natural judgment of the most perfect species of animals must be true.[71]

Ficino also applies this argument to the concept of natural appetite itself, not only deriving from the desire for God the fact of immortality as an objective necessity but also attributing to the Soul a natural desire for immortality and proving the certainty and truth of this desire by formal criteria.

> Though some people distrust [immortality], the majority of them trust. And even those who seem to distrust, hope, at least, that they will live eternally. And this kind of hope cannot be eradicated at any time from our Soul, since it is implanted by nature. Hopes that spring from the senses by chance or habit are usually vain, which is not true with respect to the belief in immortality. . . . So the hope for immortality follows a natural instinct of reason.[72]

> The will for immortality is natural because it is a direct act resulting from the pure nature of intellect and will. For as soon as eternal Being is offered to the mind, it is judged desirable without discussion and is desired without previous reflection. . . . And just as by nature we always detest the eternal privation of life, so by nature we crave eternal life. But the artist of nature made knowledge proportional to essence, appetite to knowledge, consummation to appetite. . . . Just as Being itself is recognized as perpetual by human nature, so it is naturally desired as perpetual; hence that which is known according to our own intellectual nature is also naturally desired according to that nature. Moreover, according to that same nature we shall reach what we desire. For it is reasonable to believe that we are related [to an end] in the act of attaining it through the use of the same faculty through which we are related to it in knowing and willing it, so that the goal of movement may be natural to the same thing to which the

[71] *Ibid.*, p. 320.   [72] *Ibid.*, p. 384.

movement itself is natural. If through knowledge and will one attains eternity, I see no reason why he may not attain it through life. . . . Moreover, since no natural desire is in vain, the Soul of man will reach the eternal existence which it naturally desires.[73]

This more reflective consideration, which presupposes the subjective belief in immortality, leads to another argument, which may be called the "sacrifice argument." Convinced of survival after death, man renounces many earthly advantages and pleasures, since he is certain to be rewarded later by God. If this belief were idle, all those sacrifices would be in vain and man would be frustrated by God with respect to the meaning of his whole life. This assumption cannot be reconciled with the perfection of the world order and is therefore an indirect argument for immortality.

Eternity must be granted to a mind that transcends time and despises temporal things for the sake of the eternal God. Not only do religious people do this, but the impious also. For those who are not allured by love for God are at least frightened by fear of Him. And those who are not frightened by fear are at least troubled by misgivings. Therefore many people sacrifice all, and all people sacrifice at least many advantages of temporal life, out of love for or fear of God or out of misgivings regarding Him. God must therefore grant eternal things rather than temporal ones. But no other animal renounces present blessings because of a desire for future blessings. Man is therefore the most stupid and unhappy of all animals if he enjoys neither present nor future life. And this unhappy stupidity and stupid unhappiness would result from the fact that he trusts himself to the wisest and happiest God.

But this is impossible, and therefore man's hope of immortality is certain.[74] A similar position is found in the Theological Prayer to God: "Deception must be absent from the highest Truth. But Thou deceivest us . . . if Thou askest us to abandon temporal things for the sake of Thy worship and dost not grant us eternal things in place of the temporal things."[75] And in another brief tract we read that Souls "manifest their immortality more clearly

[73] *Ibid.*, p. 313.   [74] *Ibid.*, pp. 318 f.; cf. Dress, *op. cit.*, p. 123.
[75] *Op. om.*, p. 666.

when they despise mortal things, as unimportant, for the sake of eternal things." [76]

Another argument, which we may call the "beasts' argument," results from the fact that man is superior to all other animals and that this objective perfection of man is based (characteristically) on his internal relation to God. But the earthly life of man is full of care and sorrow and therefore is unhappier than that of the beasts. If the more perfect being shall have a happier life, man must surpass the life of the beasts in a future life and achieve there that happiness which is denied him during the present life.

Since the human race [these are the opening words of the *Theologia Platonica*], because of the uneasiness of the Soul and the weakness of the body and the want of all things, leads a harder life on earth than do the beasts, no animal would be unhappier than man if nature had established the same limit of life for him as for the other animals. Through the worship of God, man is closer to God, author of beatitude, than are all other mortal things. He cannot therefore remain the unhappiest of them all, though he can become happier only on the death of the body. It would seem to follow, therefore, that some light should continue to shine in our Souls after they leave their earthly prison.[77]

And in the Preface to the *Della religione cristiana* we read:

If the human genus, which can understand the degrees of good and evil in the light of the intellect and can sometimes distinguish true felicity from true misery and false felicity, did not expect a true life after this shadow of a life, man would be more miserable than any animal born. For whoever carefully considers the order of things in the world truly finds that the destiny and condition of man on earth is much harder and more difficult than that of the other animals. . . . It is not reasonable that reason, which proves us to be more excellent than the irrational animals and more similar to the rational celestial spirits and closer to the latter in seeing and willing, should remove us farther from them in our condition of life and our degree of goodness than are the beasts. It is not right that the human genus, which draws close to God, the highest felicity, through divine worship, should be forever unhappier than the animals that are deprived of such worship and are far removed from God.

[76] *Ibid.*, p. 817.
[77] *Ibid.*, p. 79; cf. p. 660. See also Gentile, *op. cit.*, pp. 122 f.

[Man is, therefore, capable of felicity,] but being unable to attain it in this mortal life, he must be able to enjoy it in the eternal life.[78]

Moreover, as man comes closer to the happy angels than do the beasts, through his use of reason and contemplation, and closer to God, the source of beatitude, through his divine worship, he must at some time be much happier in the possession of the desired goal. . . . Now, in this body, he is much unhappier because of weakness of the body, want of all things, and the continuous anxiety of the mind. It is therefore as easy for the celestial and immortal Soul . . . to reach felicity . . . when it is free from the body, as it is difficult . . . for it to follow its felicity continuously when it is in the earthly body.[79]

The last arguments for immortality, of which the most important is the one founded on appetite, constitute a unique group and are based on a common conception, well expressed by the following verse of Hoelderlin: "Was hier uns fehlt, wird dort ein Gott ergaenzen." (What is lacking to us here, a God will complete there.) The great importance that Ficino attached to these arguments is clear from the frequent use he makes of them, especially in the *Theologia Platonica.* The passage in the epilogue to Plotinus which we have already quoted is further testimony. In this epilogue he mentions as his third point the modified argument of appetite and that of sacrifice. "Thirdly, because it [the Soul] desires by nature eternal things and frequently neglects temporal things for the sake of eternal ones." [80] And as his fourth and last point he mentions the argument drawn from natural religion and closely connected with the preceding argument. "Fourthly, because it [the Soul] worships the eternal God for the sake of the eternal life. The whole of natural religion is for man a solid basis for immortality." [81] To what extent all these arguments are related to inner or spiritual experience we have already attempted to show. The special importance of the appetite argument is clear from the fact that large, continuous sections of his writings, such as the thirteenth book of the *Theologia* and the tract *De mente,* are es-

---

[78] *Suppl.* I, pp. 10 f.; cf. *Op. om.,* p. 647. Pusino (*op. cit.,* p. 521) considers this argument proof of the eudaemonistic character of Ficino's concepts of religion and immortality.

[79] *Op. om.,* pp. 681 f.   [80] *Ibid.,* p. 1754.   [81] *Ibid.*

sentially based on it. Moreover, it has this advantage over all other arguments: it combines original, concrete meaning with conceptual clarity and inserts the theory of immortality into a comprehensive ontological system (see Chapter X).

The appetite argument and the basic idea it expresses help us to understand more profoundly Ficino's doctrine of immortality. If we take the traditional thesis of immortality and then examine individually Ficino's arguments to see what force of demonstration they contain and how far he has modified and enlarged the concepts of earlier philosophers, we may be able to make a contribution to the history of this problem, but we shall also withdraw from any real philosophical consideration and investigation. Here we are trying to understand the "problem" of immortality in an entirely different sense. As we have seen, the doctrine, as such, is frequently treated in the philosophical tradition: Plato, Plotinus, and St. Augustine made it the subject of special treatises, to mention only a few of the thinkers whom Ficino actually knew and utilized. The new and distinctive feature in Ficino is that he devoted his most important and most extensive work to the problem of immortality, a work which bears the subtitle *De immortalitate animorum*. In other words, Ficino gave his principal work, which he dedicated to the expression of his entire philosophical doctrine, the outward form at least, of a *Summa* on the immortality of the Soul, thereby subordinating all other doctrines and problems to that of immortality. The question is therefore raised: Why does the immortality of the Soul, a problem recurring frequently in the history of philosophy as one among many metaphysical problems, become for Ficino the central problem, and why does it occupy a more important place in his system than it does in the thought of any other thinker before or after him? This question has never been raised by Ficino's interpreters—at least in this form. But the answer seems basic for any real understanding of his philosophy.[82]

[82] Saitta (*op. cit.*, p. 173) barely touches on the problem, but he states rather vaguely that the argument in the *Theologia* "mirando specificamente a provare l'immortalità personale dello spirito, elevava su basi solide un monumento eterno alla personalità umana intesa come autocoscienza."

In the light of previous conceptions and considerations we may now arrive at a satisfactory solution of this important question.

First we must consider a historical factor. We know from Ficino himself that in his day the Averroistic and Alexandrist tendencies in Aristotelianism, with their Italian center at the University of Padua, were increasing in numbers and influence. Ficino took up the task of defending the Christian dogma, which was threatened by those theories, by using the Platonic philosophy.[83] The most important product of that discussion is the long fifteenth book of the *Theologia,* which Ficino devoted entirely to the refutation of Averroism.[84] Needless to say, the Averroistic thesis concerning the unity of the intellect led to a denial of the immortality of the individual Soul. As a result the problem of immortality obviously assumed special importance in the discussion with Averroists.

In the following century a violent polemic was waged on this subject between the still more radical "Alexandrist" Pomponazzi and his opponents; and the Lateran Council of 1512, which took a definite position against the Averroistic theses, proclaimed for the first time the traditional ecclesiastical doctrine of immortality in dogmatic form. We cannot decide whether the theologians of the council, Giles of Viterbo, among others, were directly influenced by Ficino's work or whether they were led to similar conclusions by the nature of the situation.

These historical reasons are, after all, secondary. To understand the philosophical reason for the pre-eminence of the doctrine of immortality in Ficino's thought, we have only to refer to the appetite argument and to the basic conceptions underlying it. Above all, we must remember that for Ficino the direct knowledge of God or the union with God, which is momentarily achieved in the highest act of contemplation, constitutes the very end of human

[83] *Op. om.;* cf. pp. 655, 1537 f.

[84] Toffanin (*Storia dell'umanesimo,* p. 212) is wrong in asserting that thirteen out of eighteen books of the *Theologia Platonica* are dedicated to the polemic against Averroism. So is Montano (Rinascita, No. 11, p. 76n) in stating that this polemic occupies the greater part of that work.

existence. All other acts of consciousness he evaluates as merely preparatory stages, defining the essence of man and the whole of human existence in relation to it. This direct knowledge of God is attained during the earthly life but imperfectly, because it is vouchsafed to only a few, and to them for only a brief time. Therefore it can attain satisfactory realization, if at all, only in a future life. The question as to whether or not the Soul survives after the death of the body is therefore equivalent to the question as to whether human life as a whole has meaning or is, metaphysically speaking, without meaning. For if the Soul is immortal, man is assured of attaining the goal to which human life is more or less consciously directed in all its activities. If, however, the Soul perishes with the body, the inner striving of human consciousness is hopeless and doubt is thrown on Ficino's whole interpretation of human existence. The entire conception of human existence, which is derived from inner or spiritual experience and its speculative interpretation, stands or falls with the postulate of immortality, which it requires from the outset as a necessary complement. We can therefore state that the argument from appetite is not merely one among many arguments designed to give an abstract proof of a thesis of immortality which is already taken for granted, but that it reveals the philosophical roots of Ficino's theory of immortality, clarifying its premises and the reason for its central importance. Conversely, it becomes clear that the immortality of the Soul, which at first glance seems to be a derived, speculative thesis, is related in meaning and importance to the fundamentals of Ficino's thought.

From this point of view we may proceed to resolve another important problem in Ficino's metaphysics. For Ficino, the concepts of Soul and of God, or the theses of the existence of God and of the immortality of the Soul, are often so closely connected that they seem to constitute nearly the same thought. This particular connection is expressed in the full title of his principal work: *Theologia Platonica de immortalitate animorum*. It is also frequently emphasized in the course of the exposition. In the Preface to the *Theologia* we are told that every reader of Plato may from the outset deduce two things in particular from his works: "a pious worship of the known God and the divinity of Souls." [85] In the seventeenth book of the *Theologia* Ficino says that Plato expressed in his own name only a few doctrines concerning divine things, namely, "that God cares for human concerns and bestows on the immortal Soul rewards and punishments for its deeds." [86] A brief philosophical introduction ends with the following words: "We must first recognize our Soul, through which, as in a mirror, we can happily contemplate the revered face of our Father." [87] And in the summary of the tenth book of Plato's *Laws,* Ficino concludes from the fact of natural religion that "it is necessary for divine beings worshiped by religion to exist and for Souls to survive their bodies, which is the main foundation of religion." [88] This particular connection between immortality and the existence of God is the more astonishing since it is based neither on the philosophical tradition nor directly on the facts. But we can understand it by recurring to the basic phenomenon of inner or spiritual experience, the knowledge of God, and by referring the two metaphysical doctrines to that experience. The existence of God being philosophically important chiefly as a possible object of contemplation, and the immortality of the Soul being important only as the subjective condition for the perfect knowledge of God, the existence of God and the immortality of the Soul are therefore related to each other as two aspects of the same unique act of contemplation. Ficino himself clearly emphasized this fact at times. In discussing natural religion he says, for instance: "For all men always worship God everywhere for the sake of the future life." [89] And in the epilogue to Plotinus, quoted above, he asserts that the Soul "worships the eternal God for the sake of eternal life." [90] In an introduction we read: "How does it help you, O theologian, to attribute eternity to God, if you do not attribute it to yourself in

[85] *Ibid.,* p. 78.   [86] *Ibid.,* p. 394.   [87] *Ibid.,* p. 886.   [88] *Ibid.,* p. 1516.
[89] *Ibid.,* p. 320. Dress (*op. cit.,* pp. 116, 124) considers this statement a proof of Ficino's eudaemonism and speaks of a "theology *sub specie animae.*"
[90] *Op. om.,* p. 1754; cf. pp. 908, 1516.

order that you may enjoy divine eternity through your own eternity?" [91] Hence, having begun this analysis with the fact that the concepts of Soul and God are the two foci of Ficino's metaphysics, we can now understand its basic premises, those two concepts being nothing but the subject and object of contemplation transformed into substances: in other words, the two aspects of inner or spiritual consciousness, developed and made independent. We may note finally that though Ficino makes use of many familiar ontological concepts in his metaphysical doctrines and is frequently dependent upon philosophical tradition, even his highest speculative doctrines as he formulates and proves them show a close connection with the living foundations of his philosophy.

[91] *Ibid.*, p. 885.

XVI

EVIL AND OUTWARD LIFE

WE HAVE SEEN that all Ficino's speculative doctrines are dependent on the central phenomenon of contemplative experience. But contemplative experience obviously does not include all the facts of human life and consciousness, for man may give up the contemplative attitude, follow the stream of outward life and let himself be influenced by different impulses and goals. Moreover, aside from the contrast between the contemplative and the outward life, the very fact of human existence involves a number of objective functions, such as sense perception and nutrition, that are necessary for the physical maintenance of man, but cannot be derived from contemplative experience. Inner consciousness, considered in the light of the facts, is therefore doubly limited: by the possibility of an outward, that is, an imperfect or bad life, and by the fact of the empirical or objective functions of consciousness. Ficino clearly understood these facts and even saw that the contemplative attitude occupies only a small place in comparison to the other acts of consciousness, because of its rarity and limited duration, and that it remains, empirically speaking, in the minority against them. Nevertheless he persisted in defining the essence of human life in terms of contemplative experience and tried consistently, if not to derive from it all other acts of consciousness, at least to interpret them with reference to it. The related doctrines, which we shall now analyze briefly, constitute the conclusion of Ficino's doctrine of the Soul and of his metaphysical system as a whole.

To understand the imperfect, or bad, life, it is necessary to recall Ficino's ontological concept of evil, which we have already considered in connection with the perfection of the universe (see

Chapter V). For Ficino the good is directly connected everywhere with existence and, in accordance with a Neoplatonic conception, the realm of the good extends even beyond that of Being. Evil, therefore, has no place at all in the sphere of existing things and, like Nonbeing, is a mere limiting concept with a negative meaning. Consequently, Ficino neglects the ontological concept of evil in his discussion of metaphysical problems, and even in other connections he rarely mentions it, confining himself essentially to the negative assertion of its nonreality. Evil has no effective cause, he says in the main passage in the commentary on Dionysius the Areopagite. Evil is itself not an effective cause. Nothing is evil in essence, and nothing is evil in so far as it exists. Hence evil is only a defect of existence, inherent in something existing and therefore good.[1] Ficino expresses this conception most clearly in a letter to Francesco Sassetti:

Where does evil dwell if it cannot be with the good and if the good itself occupies the universe? Evil, therefore, has no true seat anywhere, but an imaginary one, not in nature itself, but in that mind which lies about the divine goodness to such an extent as to believe that things can be disposed under the infinite good otherwise than well.[2]

In addition to this ontological conception of evil, there is evidence in Ficino's letters of the common conception of evil as the outward misfortunes and unpleasantnesses of human life. Referring to the famous passage in Plato's *Theaetetus,* he says that evils are necessarily connected with our earthly existence.[3] These evils we are unable to destroy in fact, but we must strive to overcome them inwardly by patience and contemplative conversion toward God.[4] The perfection of the divine world order is not to be doubted because of these evils, for the evils are always subordinated to the higher good.[5] However, the concepts of good and evil, in the common meanings of the terms, cannot withstand any serious moral criticism and therefore have merely a preliminary character.

[1] *Op. om.,* pp. 1072 f.
[2] *Ibid.,* p. 800; cf. Galli, *La morale,* pp. 69 f.
[3] *Op. om.,* pp. 633, 961 f.
[4] *Ibid.,* pp. 633, 753, 788, 803.
[5] *Ibid.,* pp. 961 ff.

For a man who is good himself and has the right insight, so-called evils lose their noxious force and are conceived as a means in the service of a higher end. Hence, for the good man God turns all things into good,[6] and all things must be taken in a good sense.[7] Conversely, so-called "blessings" are noxious for the bad man, since he makes wrong use of them. "For perverse Souls all things are unfortunate," [8] and "all blessings of the world are evils for him who lives impurely in the world." [9] Ficino sums up this criticism of the ordinary conception in a paradoxical formula: "For bad men good fortune is bad; for good men bad fortune is good." [10]

The ontological concept of evil and the ordinary conception of misfortune are both replaced, as the quoted passages show, by the moral concept of "badness," which applies only to man and his personal attitude. "Evil has no true seat anywhere, but an imaginary one, not in nature itself, but in that mind which lies about the divine goodness to such a degree as to believe that under the infinite good things can be disposed otherwise than well." [11] Accordingly, the bad man is termed "the greatest evil on earth." [12] Yet for Ficino the bad man and the bad mind are simply the opposite of the contemplative attitude. For if, as we have seen, the way of inner or spiritual ascent is the real access to the good and perfect life, all outward life which is directed away from contemplation must be qualified as bad and imperfect. Conversely, a man's "badness" is determined, not by his overt acts, but by the negative and outward basic tendency of his attitude, which makes the bad actions possible. This interpretation of evil as negative with relation to contemplative knowledge is clearly expressed in Ficino's letter to Lotterio Neroni. Happiest are those men, we read, who never withdraw from the good; less happy, those who elevate themselves from evil to good.

Lowest and unhappiest must be judged those who have closed their eyes to the rays of the highest good shining everywhere so that they

---

[6] *Ibid.,* p. 731.   [7] *Ibid.,* p. 640.   [8] *Ibid.,* p. 729.
[9] *Ibid.,* p. 738.   [10] *Ibid.,* p. 748.
[11] *Ibid.,* p. 800, and see above.   [12] *Ibid.,* p. 752.

cannot see in that very light, outside of which nothing good is seen, how great an evil it is always to be without that thing without which any visible thing is evil.[13]

Ficino sometimes reverts to strong rhetoric to paint the picture of the bad man "whose dog and horse are better than his Soul," [14] and he draws a comparison between the crude wilderness of the corrupt Soul and the cultivated land of the good mind.[15]

In a letter to Lorenzo Franceschi, Ficino explains at length that man's inner wickedness is the source of all moral and outward evils. "Just as the greatest light attracts all lights to itself, so the greatest evil on earth, the bad man, attracts all evils from all sides toward himself. He brings much more [evil] to himself than he receives from elsewhere." We are insatiable in evils, perceiving them in the present, the past, and the future, making misfortunes worse by our attitude, and even converting good fortune into an evil by our misuse. Therefore we sow nothing but evil and must not be surprised if we reap evil.[16] It is in the light of this doctrine that we must understand the second *Apologus de voluptate,* in which Ficino allegorically derives individual evils from absolute evil itself and then shows how one evil destroys the other and at last destroys itself.[17] This reasoning, though not justified by the ontological concept of evil, becomes understandable even in its ontological cloak when we think of man and of his moral attitude.[18]

The apologue leads us a step further. How is it possible, we ask with Ficino, that man, having a natural instinct toward the good, nevertheless descends to evil and even produces a number of evils through his own attitude? The solution is given by the concept of pleasure, the lure of evil, which by its attractive appearance seduces man into accepting as good what is in reality bad. This doctrine is developed at length in the *Apologi de voluptate* [19] and also occurs here and there in the letters.

[13] *Ibid.,* p. 822.   [14] *Ibid.,* pp. 747 f.   [15] *Ibid.,* p. 835.   [16] *Ibid.,* p. 752.
[17] *Ibid.,* pp. 921 f.; cf. Saitta, *op. cit.,* pp. 252 ff.
[18] Cf. *Suppl.,* I, 85 f.   [19] *Ibid.,* pp. 921 ff.

By nature each appetite chooses and follows good, but flees from and drives away evil. Pleasure seems to present the image of good; pain, that of evil. Consequently, when pleasure affects us, we not only do not resist, but we even follow it like a friend—yield to and obey it. And . . . caught by this hook, we are then killed by the foes—namely, by the evils hidden beneath pleasure. . . . Therefore . . . let us recall that the nature of evil, being insidious, offers itself to us daily under the guise of good, that is, of pleasure, in order to deceive and to destroy us miserable people. Otherwise evil itself, and vice in particular . . . would be promptly shunned.[20]

If [you wish] to avoid pain, flee pleasure, the lure of evils; pleasure bought with pain is noxious.[21]

Ficino seems to speak of evils in an objective sense in connection with pleasure, but as a rule he generally prefers a view that agrees more nearly with the theological tradition. There is no evil in any substantial sense, as we have seen; therefore the wickedness of man consists merely in the fact that he allows himself to be misled by inferior blessings and for their sake abandons the highest and true good, God. Men must recognize

that this is evil, namely, to yield to evils; they must recognize that they yield to evils only at the time when they themselves desire that the higher blessings should yield to the lesser blessings; they must recognize that only there, where the blessing of all blessings is found, do we also find the remedy for all evils.[22]

Men must be ashamed, I say ashamed, for no other reason than that they love mortal blessings. For in loving them they neglect the eternal good itself, from which these others derive their goodness. All things are good in themselves, because they are derived from it [that good]. They are also good for us in so far as they are related to it. But they [these things] rightly become evil and bitter for us, because while neglecting it [the highest good] we follow, with the greatest injustice, those things that necessarily have their existence in it and are preserved by it.[23]

If this or that good pleases us, it does so, not because it is this or that, but because it is good. In all things we desire the quality of goodness.[24]

[20] *Ibid.*, pp. 800 f.   [21] *Ibid.*, p. 738; cf. Horace *Epistle* I. 2. 55.
[22] *Op. om.*, p. 822.   [23] *Ibid.*, p. 730.   [24] *Ibid.*, pp. 665 f.

Nothing can be found which is not good through the presence of good itself. . . . It is this which all things desire.[25]

The apparent contradiction contained in these statements, and even the intentional play on the various meanings of the word *malum* are solved in the formula already quoted: "For bad men, good fortune is bad; for good men, bad fortune is good." [26] Or, to be more precise: "Just as he who acts badly converts blessings into evil for himself, so he who suffers well [bears suffering well], converts evils into good for himself." [27] In other words, in the ontological sense there is nothing but good. In the ordinary sense there are blessings and evils. Only that human attitude that produces all evils by converting blessings and evils into moral evils is bad; conversely, the good attitude can elevate so-called "evils" to moral goodness.

Ficino obviously enjoys the dialectical paradoxes of *malum,* and though at certain periods he was really convinced of the wickedness of men, his own attitude was far from that of a moral preacher. Consequently, he did not so much reproach men for their wickedness as describe its consequences and try to combat its causes. A consequence of the "bad" attitude is the misery of earthly life, from which men can free themselves only by a spiritual conversion to God.

Just as everyone is in himself, so are the things he receives. We can complain not so much of our destiny as of our choice. We think continually of evils, and evils trouble us everywhere. We follow evils daily, and evils rightly follow us.[28]

The miserable [mind], sick because of its passions, never comes to rest, but wanders restlessly everywhere in vain. . . . Oh miserable fate of men, more miserable than misery itself.[29]

But the cause of evil is the stupidity and ignorance of men; hence evil can be overcome only by a genuine knowledge of the higher truth. Negligence and ignorance and, moreover, lack of confidence

[25] *Ibid.,* p. 785.
[26] *Ibid.,* p. 748. Cf. Dress, *op. cit.,* pp. 133 f.; Galli, *La morale,* pp. 60 f.
[27] *Op. om.,* p. 788.   [28] *Ibid.,* p. 754.   [29] *Ibid.,* p. 749; cf. p. 752.

in the immortality of the Soul and in the grace of God are among
the most important causes of sin, Ficino writes to Cavalcanti.[30]
It is therefore necessary to recognize the stupidity of men and to
ascend toward true knowledge.[31]

Know yourself [Ficino exhorts mankind]. O divine race clothed with a
mortal vestment; make yourself naked, separate [yourself] as much
as you can . . . O minds too ignorant of yourselves, O blind hearts!
Please arise from this deep sleep; please come to reason at last. For if
you come to reason, you will breathe happily.[32]

This inner vigilance as contrasted with the sleep of earthly life is
peculiar to the Platonists.[33] Both motives are therefore combined
in the famous discourses *De stultitia et miseria hominum,* which
we have previously mentioned.[34] In all these exhortations and
meditations Ficino is not trying to combat the particular weaknesses and sins of men; he is demanding a radical rejection of an
outward life and a return to the inner life—a rejection which
would automatically eliminate particular defects, since they are
possible only because of the general attitude of man.

What is to be done that we may watch and live well? Our life must
be converted into its opposite. We must unlearn what we have learned,
for by learning it we have hitherto not known ourselves. We must
learn what we have neglected, for by ignoring it we cannot know ourselves. We must like what we neglect, neglect what we like, endure
what we flee, flee what we pursue.[35]

Again we must recall the metaphor of the man who stands with
his head on the earth and his feet sticking up into the air, a metaphor which Ficino uses to describe the situation of an average,
outward life, using it as the base for his demand for a radical
change in the human attitude.[36] The imperfect and bad attitude
always appears as the negation of the inner life, and hence it is to
be overcome only by the contemplative elevation of the mind.

Ficino occasionally uses, as an illustration of the different human

---

[30] *Ibid.,* p. 630.   [31] *Ibid.,* pp. 640 f.   [32] *Ibid.,* p. 659.   [33] *Ibid.,* p. 628.
[34] *Ibid.,* pp. 636 ff., 747 f.; cf. chap. xiv, above.   [35] *Ibid.,* p. 749.
[36] *Ibid.,* pp. 380, 755. See above, chap. xiv. See also Galli, *La morale,* p. 61.

attitudes, the traditional scheme of the three forms of life, whose struggle for the Soul of man is allegorically expressed in the judgment of Paris. There are three forms of life: the contemplative, the active, and the voluptuous, says Ficino in the dedicatory letter to the commentary on Plato's *Philebus*. The poets called the first Minerva, the second Juno, and the third Venus. Paris gave the prize to Venus, and as a result of his stupid choice he fell into misfortune. Hercules had to choose between Venus and Juno only and decided upon Juno, who gave him the deserved reward after his death. Philebus was appointed judge between Minerva and Venus and seemed to favor Venus. But Socrates rightly chose Minerva, and with his death he paid the price to Venus and to Juno. Lorenzo de' Medici (so the brief Preface concludes) may favor all three goddesses and receive his due reward.[37] Ficino here seems to place the three different kinds of life on the same level, foregoing any moral contrast and renouncing any claim of superiority for the contemplative life. But in the appendix to the *Philebus* he takes up again the same idea and gives it a different turn. Paris, symbol of the Soul, is obliged to choose between three forms of life and decides upon pleasure. Most people actually choose pleasure, many choose domination, but few choose wisdom. The active life is farthest removed from the goal of man, because of its restlessness; the voluptuous life is closer; the contemplative life is closest.[38] Here Ficino's tendency becomes more apparent. He clearly grants superiority to the contemplative life and, by placing the active life on the lowest plane, prepares the situation of the *Philebus,* which no longer deals with three, but only with two forms of life.[39] Minerva becomes the symbol of the true, contemplative life, Venus the symbol of the imperfect, outward life. This consistent conception is elaborated in the third *Apologus de voluptate,* in which he introduces Pallas and Venus, who are quarreling before the tribunal of Jupiter, and gives the prize to Pallas.[40] In another apologue Ficino characterizes Minerva as the

[37] *Op. om.,* pp. 919 f.
[39] Cf. *Op. om.,* p. 920.
[38] *Suppl.,* I, p. 80.
[40] *Ibid.,* pp. 929 f.

mother of philosophy and demands that philosophy exclude Venus, Pluto, and Juno, symbols of pleasure, wealth, and power.[41] The scheme of the three forms of life is here enlarged into a scheme of four forms, but we perceive that Ficino was concerned solely with the contrast between contemplation and all other forms of life and that among these other forms pleasure occupies the first place as the counterpart of wisdom. This is understandable if we remember that pleasure, the lure of evil, seduces man from his destiny by its resemblance to good (see above). There are other allusions to this allegorical interpretation of the three goddesses, and Ficino praises Minerva especially, the symbol of contemplation, claiming her as his own divinity.[42] At times he modifies the basic motive of the allegory, and, refusing to acknowledge even Pallas, the symbol of "haughty" philosophy, as a leader on the road to felicity, he expects to find salvation in God alone.[43]

The theory of imperfect life is consistently applied in eschatology. The abstract attribute of eternal duration, being connected with the substance of the human Soul (see Chapter XV), is therefore independent of the moral conduct of the individual. But eternal life as a real existence is the fulfillment of that which man tries to attain in the earthly life through contemplation, but can realize only imperfectly. It is therefore reserved for those who have prepared themselves for it by spiritual meditation and a turning toward God and have made themselves worthy of it. On the contrary, to those who lead an imperfect life, turning away from contemplation, a lower form of existence is assigned after death, which Ficino describes in terms resembling those in Plato's myths and, even more, those in the theological tradition of the Middle Ages. Here we shall touch upon only a few major points in Ficino's conception of hell, attempting at the same time to show to what extent he has modified the traditional conception.

When the impure Soul leaves its body after death, its descent to its prescribed place of purification and punishment is not the re-

---

[41] *Ibid.,* p. 847.   [42] Cf. *ibid.,* pp. 675, 780, 847 f.
[43] *Ibid.,* pp. 784 f.

sult of the arbitrary act of a superhuman Being, but of a natural instinct inherent in the Soul itself. This instinct Ficino compares to the force of gravitation, a conception we have already met in the ontological theory of the appetite (see Chapter X). Future reward and punishment are nothing but the direct continuation and increase of virtue and vice and are related to them as the fruit is related to the seed.

Just as nature, the servant of divine Providence, inwardly moves bodies upward by lightness and downward by gravity, so Providence leads all things by an inner law similar to a natural inclination. . . . Through this innate law human minds lead themselves to the places suitable to their life.

During his temporal life man is free to choose his moral conduct, but after death "the Souls, according to the habits assumed, are led by an inner and secret inclination to the places, punishments, and rewards appropriate to their habits." [44]

In this strange conception Ficino reveals his tendency to replace traditional mythical concepts with more strict, ontological concepts. The same tendency is noticeable in the description of the punishments in hell proper. During life the impure Soul is entirely filled with outward imaginings and even after death, being unable to free itself from them, is continually tormented and terrified by the images of its own phantasy.

The Souls of those men, infected by corporeal passions, fell into such madness during this life that they preferred blindly the shadows of blessings to the blessings themselves; they loved and feared shadows. After this life they are forced to continue their madness in like manner.[45]

The fallacy of terrible images is given to impious people during and after death. For then cease the various duties of nourishing, the manifold acts of the outward senses, the occupations of human affairs, and the comforts of things; and there is left in the impious man, as the Platonists believe, only the domination of furious imagination or of imaginative reason, which, moved by hate . . . and fears, brings a long series of sad images in its train.[46]

[44] *Ibid.*, p. 418.   [45] *Ibid.*, p. 420.   [46] *Ibid.*, p. 421.

And just as he who followed true things during life attains the highest truth after death, in the opinion of the theologians, so he who followed false things is tormented by extreme delusion; therefore the former is delighted by true things, the latter worried by false images.[47]

In this way Ficino eliminates all material punishment and by an allegorical interpretation attempts to reduce the mythical concepts of Plato and of the other ancient philosophers to the same, spiritual meaning. The Furies are simply bad passions to which the impure Soul is subject; [48] the tortures of Tantalus, Sisyphus, and others indicate the painful images of the sick imagination persecuted by its own products.[49] Tartarus itself is the place where the Soul sleeps and is frightened by its dreams.[50] The transmigration of the Soul into the bodies of beasts must also be understood allegorically. In its passion the Soul reverts to the body and generates a gaseous body which is able to assume the shape of different beasts, according to the attitude of the Soul.[51]

However, the phantoms of imagination are but a partial aspect of the future punishment, which Ficino mentions primarily in connection with the Platonic and Christian myths of hell. Another, even more important, aspect is directly connected with the center of his doctrine of the Soul. The goal and end of the human Soul is, as we have seen, knowledge of God. During life the pure Soul is directed to that goal through contemplation; after death it finally attains the perfect fulfillment of its desire. Accordingly the impure Soul is deflected from that goal during life and after death is excluded from the knowledge of God. This fact in itself, as well as the consciousness of its eternal duration, is the greatest punishment for the Soul that sees itself deprived, by its own fault, of the real meaning and goal of its existence. Ficino emphasizes this idea at the conclusion of his description of hell.

The Christian theologians will not deny these [punishments of hell], but they will add, I think, another punishment, which is the true judgment of the damned Soul, since it will think of itself as being deprived

[47] *Ibid.*, p. 422.   [48] *Ibid.*, pp. 420 f.   [49] *Ibid.*, p. 421.
[50] *Ibid.*, p. 420.   [51] *Ibid.*

forever of divine sight. This is the greatest punishment, since God is the end for whose sake we are born, for whose sake we all desire and do all things . . . Although we may in some way realize during life that we are far away from God, yet we are seldom aware of it while we are occupied with the comforts of life. When we become aware of it, we hope to return soon to the Father. There neither comfort nor hope delights the miserable Souls, and this condition may be called Acheron. The punishment is increased by the fact that they think they are deprived of such a blessing by their own fault, and are therefore continually indignant with themselves. And this can be called by the name Styx.[52]

The essence of hell consists in the lack of divine knowledge and in the pains of impure imagination; the material punishments are sometimes indicated, but they have comparatively minor importance.[53]

Now that we have briefly considered the Soul's passage to the future life and the quality of the punishments in hell, we must inquire what Souls actually do incur this fate. From the outset we discover in Ficino a tendency to limit as much as possible the number of those damned or simply deprived of divine sight. For example, he dedicates the last major section of the *Theologia* to the children who died before baptism and to imbeciles, to whom theologians usually assign an intermediary state between beatitude and damnation. He tries to prove that they may finally ascend to beatitude after a period of examination and with the active help of God.[54] Led, perhaps, by his personal sympathies, he emphatically upholds the salvation of Gentile philosophers in a letter added at the end of the second edition of his *Della religione cristiana*.[55] At the end of the *Theologia* he uses a scheme (derived from Aristotle) of four grades of moral conduct to illustrate in a general way the fate of Souls after death. Man is temperate, continent, incontinent, or intemperate.[56] The temperate man's senses obey reason voluntarily; the continent man's, only reluctantly. In the incontinent

---

[52] *Ibid.*, p. 422.   [53] *Ibid.*   [54] *Ibid.*, pp. 422 ff.

[55] *Suppl.*, I, 12 ff.; cf. *Op. om.*, p. 806. See also Saitta, *op. cit.*, p. 270; Anichini, *op. cit.*, p. 124.

[56] Cf. Aristotle *Nicomachean Ethics* vii. 11. 1151 b 32 ff.

individual passion overcomes right judgment of reason; in the intemperate individual, reason itself is corrupted or lulled to sleep by the senses. After death the temperate man ascends directly to beatitude; the continent man ascends after a brief purification. The incontinent and the intemperate are left after death to the pains of their sick imagination, from which the former is freed only after a long trial, the latter, never.[57] Of the four classes of men, three finally reach the goal: knowledge of God. Though some men need a long period of purification, only the men in the fourth class are for ever excluded from this knowledge. Therefore Ficino maintains the concept of eternal punishment, which he emphasizes in another context.[58] However, his method of characterizing the intemperate shows that to him the immoral person and eternal damnation are merely extreme cases far removed from the ordinary conditions of human life. We must not forget that "bad habits are wont to cast into misery those Souls in particular in which love of God is entirely extinguished." [59] "Even while the intemperate Soul was leading the life of man, reason was either fast asleep in him or subject to passion, wherefore it [the Soul] carries with it an indestructible habit tending toward corporeal things almost as its own nature." [60] Thus eternal damnation results only from the complete extinction of the love for God. Ficino considers such a state exceptional, since the desire for God is by nature peculiar to all men and can be observed in all their actions and thoughts. Hence, it is true, he does not uphold the final salvation of all Souls as does Origen, and he submits openly to the authority of the Church in the doctrine of the Beyond, as well as in all other questions.[61] However, the small space he allots to the concepts of hell denotes the mildness of his position. Though he does not develop his opinion fully, we can recognize his natural inclination to spiritualize the conception of future punishment and ultimately to lead as many persons as possible to eternal beatitude, the true goal of earthly existence and human life. In contrast, eternal damnation, which

[57] *Op. om.*, pp. 419 f.   [58] *Ibid.*, p. 325.   [59] *Ibid.*, p. 419.
[60] *Ibid.*, p. 420.   [61] *Ibid.*, p. 424.

is radically opposed to the real destiny of man, merely represents an extreme: it is reserved for those who during earthly life have removed from themselves the last traces of their higher being.

Now that we have followed the conception of the imperfect life through its final developments, we must consider the empirical functions of consciousness, which are associated with the fact of earthly existence. Aside from their possible misuse and considered only in themselves, these functions are morally neutral. Men, good and bad, contemplative and active, all share in them, so long as they live in the world at all. However, the simple fact that there are other activities of consciousness besides knowledge is in itself an objective limitation of the contemplative sphere. This limitation assumes a more definite form in so far as consciousness can exercise only one function at a given moment, so that the function of knowledge and the empirical functions, considered as mere capacities, coexist indifferently and peacefully, but exclude each other in their actual application.

Our Soul often plays with the body in the pleasures of the body. In its diseases it governs and cures it. In both states the sublime consideration of reason is interrupted or abated because it [the Soul] is either temporarily at leisure or too anxiously busy about inferior things. But when all is settled, it rises again. So it is arranged by nature that, with regard to human powers, we are not capable of different works at the same time.[62]

When one nature, containing two dissimilar active forces, is directed too much to the act of one force, it almost stops the act of the other. Hence, the guests of a party cannot listen attentively to a lyre and taste a meal at the same time. . . . The intensified acts of nourishing and sense perception hamper thought, and thought hampers them. That means that the intellect is a force of our same Soul to which the forces of nutrition and sense perception belong.[63]

The force of imagination "is all the more weakened, the more the speculation of the mind is strengthened, and the converse." [64]

Because of the contrast between the various functions of con-

[62] *Ibid.,* p. 215.   [63] *Ibid.,* p. 345; cf. Horbert, *op. cit.,* p. 35.
[64] *Op. om.,* p. 365.

sciousness the Soul can attain pure contemplation only at that
moment when it succeeds in eliminating the other acts of consciousness as much as possible.

When [the body] is ill and burdened, the Soul is so busy curing and
governing it that it is not directed to the inquiry of truth. But when
the body is quiet, the mind speculates easily.[65]

[When the function of sense perception is interrupted,] then the Soul
collects itself in some way and is not occupied either in perceiving corporeal qualities or in governing and moving the members of its own
body or in treating external affairs, which easily happens in sleep. Yet
the more the external act is lessened, the more the inner act is increased. Inner acts are the visions of imagination and the discursive
procedures of reason.

In this way we can explain prophetic dreams and all higher knowledge and capacities which the Soul acquires through *vacatio,* that
is, through the inner separation from the body.[66] But outward
functions are necessary for the preservation of the body and for
the continuation of empirical life. Hence, we can understand why
the Soul cannot continue long in pure contemplation during its
earthly existence and, consequently, why it cannot attain its highest
goal, the direct intuition of God, before death.

Even if [the intellect] dispels the clouds of imagination temporarily
for as long as it can, it is meanwhile drawn to the difficult task of
governing the body and distracted at the same time by the continual
recurrence of sense images and by the perception of intelligible things,
and thus it scarcely perceives the higher influences or almost misses
perceiving them . . . or perceives them as through a sudden gleam
that vanishes immediately. Hence it must not seem strange to anyone
that here on earth we do not perceive the clarity of divine things nor
taste even for a while that sweetness which is enjoyed from them.[67]

In this body the Soul has two chief obstacles: one, that it is torn between several actions and troubles, and different actions hamper and
weaken each other, for it is very difficult to attend to different things
at the same time; the other, that because of the condition of this
lowest habitation and because of this corporeal duty which is temporarily assigned to men by God [the Soul] exercises the lower actions

[65] *Ibid.,* p. 185.   [66] *Ibid.,* pp. 292 ff.   [67] *Ibid.,* p. 408.

much earlier, more attentively, and more frequently than the higher actions. Consequently, when we wish to contemplate incorporeal things, we act for the most part very weakly and perceive them blurred as in a fog.[68]

This hindering effect of the lower functions finally explains why man arrives at the full use of his higher, spiritual powers only when he becomes an adult. For as long as the body is growing, it absorbs all the forces of the Soul for its own nutrition and preservation, so that no space is left for the activity of thought. Following Avicenna, Ficino therefore imagines a grown man without senses.

The mind of such a man will have some thoughts, since he is of adult age, when the growth of the body does not hinder thought.[69]
From the very outset, three such forces—vital force, senses, imagination—begin their work, and with such intensity, because of building a new body, that the Soul can give almost no attention to reason until it abates the intensity of that work when the body is fully evolved and the senses are purified. But when reason awakens, it weakens the realm of imagination, which is entrenched in the Soul as an enduring habit, only with the greatest difficulty.[70]

The tendency of objective metaphysics to interpret all attitudes of consciousness as objective qualities of the Soul leads us from the observation that consciousness can accomplish various acts exclusive of each other to the theory of a number of distinct potencies, forces, or parts of the Soul. Hence, knowledge, which was at first considered the peculiar and essential activity of the Soul, is placed on almost the same level with the other acts of consciousness; the intellect can no longer be absolutely identified with the Soul, but constitutes merely a part, though the highest part, of the Soul. This conception, which was first formulated by Plato, has been maintained ever since in the philosophical tradition, though the scheme of the individual parts of the Soul has received numerous modifications. In Ficino the doctrine of the parts of the Soul is obviously influenced by various ancient theories—by the Neoplatonic theory in particular. The result is not only that there are

[68] *Ibid.*, p. 627.   [69] *Ibid.*, p. 159.   [70] *Ibid.*, pp. 381 f.

numerous inconsistent details but also that Ficino's own opinion cannot always be clearly distinguished from his account of the ancient doctrines. Hence, we are obliged to approach this doctrine cautiously and must be alert against explaining away existing contradictions. On the other hand, we should not neglect to analyze these conceptions, because Ficino touches upon them frequently and even bases some of his more general, speculative theories upon them.

Though Ficino occasionally quotes Plato's distinction between the rational, the courageous, and the appetitive parts of the Soul, he does not assign any systematic significance to it. As a matter of fact, this first attempt at a schematic division of the Soul had a rather meager influence even in classical antiquity. Much more significant was Aristotle's division, which dominated all later speculation on the Soul. Another scheme which in its nucleus also goes back to Aristotle appears in several of Ficino's passages. This scheme distinguishes between the vegetative, the sensitive, and the intellectual Soul,[71] or, in other terms, between natural potency, potency of sense perception, and potency of thought.[72] This scheme has a certain importance for Ficino; he even bases on it the construction of his exposition in Books VI through VIII of the *Theologia*. In comparison with Aristotle's, this is a simplified scheme. Imagination has an important place in Ficino's epistemology, as we have seen in Chapter XII, and we shall meet it again among the potencies of the Soul; but it is not mentioned here. The moving force, which Ficino considers, not as a peculiar potency, but as a general quality of the Soul, is also omitted. So is the appetitive power, which Ficino never inserted into the vertical series of the parts of the Soul, but always treated as a parallel branch of the Soul, having an analogous division within itself.[73] Finally, the distinction between the active and the passive intellect, which occupies an important place in Scholasticism, is omitted.

[71] *Ibid.*, p. 404.
[72] *Ibid.*, p. 162; cf. p. 157. See also Dress, *op. cit.*, p. 58.
[73] Cf. chap. xiii, above.

Ficino does mention it occasionally,[74] but he does not give it a central place in his thought. On the other hand, this simplified Aristotelian scheme is sometimes augmented by a fourth force, which goes back to the Stoic doctrine. Just as men are characterized by intellect, beasts by sense perception, and plants by nutrition, so inanimate things, the so-called *mixta,* are characterized by a purely objective unity derived from a comprehensive force. Since each higher form includes the lower forms, the human Soul contains, besides the intellect, sense perception, nutritive power, and finally the comprehensive force peculiar to inanimate things.[75] In one section Ficino uses this concept for a somewhat strange argument. When the Soul withdraws entirely from the body, in its highest rapture, it takes with it all lower forces also. The question then arises as to why the body is not entirely dissolved at that moment. At least the unifying function must work even then, so that the continuation of the body may be guaranteed. However, the lower part of the Soul which usually performs that function accompanies the Soul in its ascent, so Ficino turns to the substitute device of attributing the unity of the body at that moment to the highest power of the Soul, the so-called *unitas.*[76]

However, the scheme Ficino prefers is a different one, and it goes back, essentially, to Neoplatonic conceptions. Since it occurs rather frequently and is also closely connected with the basic motives of his own philosophy, we must analyze it more closely. Starting from the upper limit, we find that Ficino distinguishes two potencies of knowledge, *mens* and *ratio,* which constitute, respectively, the higher and the middle part of the Soul and may be translated approximately by "mind" and "reason." [77] The reason for this distinction and the meaning of *ratio* will be discussed later on. In addition to *mens* and *ratio* Ficino frequently mentions a still higher element of the Soul, which he calls "unity," the center of the Soul or head of the mind. The unification of the Soul with God in the highest act of contemplation is primarily at-

[74] *Op. om.,* pp. 240 f.   [75] *Ibid.,* p. 336.
[76] *Ibid.,* pp. 303 f.   [77] Cf. *ibid.,* p. 290.

tributed to this element. It is never considered a particular part of
the Soul, but simply a privileged element within the *mens*.[78] If we
pass now from the cognitive powers to the empirical functions, we
see that Ficino distinguishes mainly three, which he calls the three
lower forces of the Soul: phantasy, sense perception, and nutritive
power.[79] Imagination, which in epistemology is distinguished
from phantasy and corresponds to the Aristotelian *sensus communis*, is not listed as a particular power. The nutritive power,
more generally called "vital force," comprises at once generation,
growth, and all lower functions required for the cure and preservation of the body.[80] The three lower forces, taken as a whole, constitute the lowest part of the Soul, which is opposed to *mens* and
ratio. Borrowing a term from Plotinus, Ficino called it *idolum*.

The rational Souls not only possess that power of thinking . . . but
also that animating power governing the body which nourishes the
body in the body, perceives corporeal things through the body, moves
the body through space, and guides it in space—a power which the
Platonists call *idolum,* that is, image of the rational Soul.[81]

All rational Souls have . . . an intellectual head, a rational center, and
an animating lowest part.[82]

Besides the three parts of the Soul, the lowest of which includes
all the so-called lower forces, there is assumed by Ficino a further
quality inherent in the living body itself, which he calls "vital complexion" or "nature." This nature is no longer an element of the
Soul, but is like a shadow which the Soul throws upon the body
and through which the body is distinct from an inanimate entity.

In each living body there is a certain effective and vital disposition or
complexion of it, which the animating force of its Soul grants to the

---

[78] *Ibid.*, pp. 132, 249, 271, *et passim.* This *caput mentis* is not a supernatural faculty, nor is it identical with love or a compound of innate
formulas, as Anichini believes (*op. cit.*, pp. 114, 128).

[79] *Ibid.*, pp. 374, 381; cf. Dress, *op. cit.*, p. 58.   [80] Cf. *Op. om.*, p. 381.

[81] *Ibid.*, p. 289. Anichini (*op. cit.*, p. 44) wrongly defines the third part
of the Soul as *sensus.*

[82] *Ibid.*, p. 298; cf. pp. 132, 273, 304. See also Dress, *op. cit.*, pp. 58 f.

body. The Platonists say that this is the nature of the bodies, like a trace or shadow of the Soul in the body.[83]

The corporeal life is an image of the rational Soul. . . . Above the corporeal life there is the lowest part of the Soul, which is the power of nourishing.[84]

The Platonists believe that the irrational life of the body is irradiated as light from the substance of the rational Soul as from the sun.[85]

Elsewhere Ficino often speaks of the irrational Soul which follows the rational Soul as its image, and, following the Neoplatonic example, he occasionally even considers this irrational Soul a particular degree of reality, a conception which he renounced in his final theory of the five substances.

The irrational Soul accompanies [the rational Soul], as the shadow does the body.[86]

The irrational [Soul] proceeds from there [that is, from the Idea of life] through the rational one and so lives at some time by itself.[87]

The irrational power follows the rational substance of our Soul like a shadow.[88]

The relationship of this irrational Soul to the parts of the Soul, considered above, appears at first glance to be rather indefinite. But from other statements of Ficino we can see clearly that he identifies the so-called "irrational Soul," at least in the case of man, with the nature or complexion of the body.

Nature cannot be the highest reason and cause of things . . . since it is irrational, as is obvious in our nature.[89]

The intellect of the Soul belongs to itself, because it possesses its existence in its own essence, and it belongs to something else, because out of its own rational life it pours into the body another life without reason, like an image. The nature, that is, the vital complexion which is produced in the body itself like a shadow because of the life poured from the Soul, belongs only to something else, that is, to the body along with which it is extended and divided.[90]

[83] *Op. om.*, p. 289.　　[84] *Ibid.*, p. 273.　　[85] *Ibid.*, p. 206; cf. p. 304.

[86] *Ibid.*, p. 84 b.　　[87] *Ibid.*, p. 149.　　[88] *Ibid.*, p. 401; cf. pp. 332 f.

[89] *Ibid.*, p. 250.　　[90] *Ibid.*, p. 334.

The human Soul therefore possesses three parts, *mens, ratio,* and *idolum,* to which is added, as a fourth element, the irrational Soul —in other words, the nature or complexion of the body. This doctrine is further enlarged by the addition of two intermediary entities, which reconcile the contrast between body and Soul and are therefore supposed to explain their union. First, in addition to the earthly body, the Soul possesses still another, more subtle cover consisting of the substance of heaven. This is called the ethereal body, or vehicle of the Soul, and is occasionally identified with the glorified body of the Souls that have passed away. This is an old Neoplatonic conception that survives in the most modern forms of superstition under the name of "astral body."

Let us return to the body closest to the Soul. The Magi call it the vehicle of the Soul, that is, the ethereal body received from the ether, the immortal cover of the Soul, which is round in its natural figure, because of the region of the ether, but transforms itself into a human figure when it enters the human body and returns into its former figure when it leaves.[91]

If one of the Platonists says that [the Soul] is always in the celestial vehicle, we answer that the Soul does not depend on the vehicle, but the vehicle on the Soul, and that the eternal Soul, according to the Platonists, always animates an eternal vehicle.[92]

According to the Platonists [the Souls] always have an ethereal body, but according to the Christians they will eventually have an eternal body.[93]

According to Ficino this vehicle has a very peculiar relation to the parts of the Soul. For the lower part of the Soul, the so-called *idolum,* is nothing but the image of the rational part communicated to the etheric body, and the *idolum,* therefore, is inherent in the etheric body and is related to it as the "nature" is to the earthly body.

[The Platonists] believe that the life impressed by the Soul upon the etheric vehicle as upon an eternal mirror always accompanies the impressing Soul, but that the life impressed upon the corporeal and de-

[91] *Ibid.,* p. 404. [92] *Ibid.,* p. 206.
[93] *Ibid.,* p. 375; cf. pp. 134, 162, *et passim.*

structible body does not always [follow the Soul]. For they think that the etheric body, being next to the Soul, is perpetually animated by the everliving substance of the Soul, while the elementary body receives life from the Soul through the etheric body only for a certain time.[94]

[The ancient theologians] do not say that the rational part of the Soul is directly inherent in the vehicle, but that the rational Soul . . . sends into the vehicle an animating act, which we have often called the *idolum* of the Soul . . . For as the light of the moon in a cloud produces paleness out of itself, so the Soul produces in the celestial body the *idolum,* as a comet produces its tail.[95]

Ficino attributes to the *idolum* a supernatural power of perception and phantasy [96] which is caused by the vehicle, a doctrine that cannot easily be reconciled with the basic conception that the *idolum* itself contains the natural forces of sense perception and phantasy.

Another intermediary entity between Soul and body, which, however, is much closer to the body and even occurs in medical discussions, is the so-called "spirit." The spirit is a thin, air-like body generated in the heart out of blood and spread from there throughout the whole body.

The Soul . . . is most pure, therefore it cannot be united to this thick earthly body, which is far away from it, except by a most subtle and light-bearing body, which we call "spirit" and which is generated by the warmth of the heart out of the finest part of the blood and spread from there throughout the whole body.[97]

[The bodies] move that warm and vital vapor which is in some way the knot of the body and of the Soul and is called by the physicists "spirit." [98]

The spirit plays a particular role in sense perception and is concentrated in the organs of the senses.[99] It is the first to receive im-

---

[94] *Ibid.,* pp. 149 f.   [95] *Ibid.,* pp. 404 f.   [96] *Ibid.,* p. 405.

[97] *Ibid.,* p. 177. Heitzman ("L'agostinismo avicennizzante," *Giorn. crit.,* 1935, p. 305) derives the theory of "spirits" from Alexander of Aphrodisias (*Op. om.,* p. 329). But the theory is very common in the whole medical tradition, as well as in the Neoplatonic tradition.

[98] *Op. om.,* p. 211.   [99] *Ibid.,* p. 178.

pressions from the objects of sense perception and so represents the passive factor in the process of perception. The Soul proper may therefore be considered a merely active factor.[100] The spirit also contributes more or less to all the other functions of the body. For this reason Ficino emphasizes its importance in the *De vita*.[101]

Since the spirit is also called the "vehicle of the Soul," it seems uncertain whether it is supposed to be distinct from the ethereal body. However, we must not be misled by verbal similarities. There is sufficient testimony to prove that Ficino clearly distinguishes the spirit from both the ethereal body and the earthly body, which is composed of four elements.

In like manner the Soul of man seems to behave with respect to its three vehicles: the ethereal, the air-like, and the composed body.[102] Many Platonists believe that the Soul uses three vehicles—the first, immaterial and simple, that is, celestial; the second, material and simple, that is, air-like; the third, material and composed, that is, made up of the four elements.[103]

The "idol" was considered the life inherent in the ethereal body, and the "nature," the life of the composed body. The logic of the scheme therefore leads to an inherent life being attributed to the air-like body, or spirit. The Platonists believe that the Soul

gives to the first [vehicle] an irrational but immortal life; to the second, an irrational but long-lasting life, which survives for a certain time in the simple body after the dissolution of the composed body; and to the third, a life irrational and to be dissolved with the dissolution of the body.

To these three degrees of life correspond different degrees of perception.[104] However, this elaboration of the scheme is wholly artificial. In other contexts Ficino recognizes idol and nature as separate forces, but he leaves no space between them for any other

---

[100] *Ibid.*, pp. 177 f., 211 f.; cf. chap. xii, above. See also Horbert, *op. cit.*, p. 20; Heitzman, "L'agostinismo avicennizzante," *Giorn. crit.*, XVI (1935), 305 ff.

[101] *Op. om.*, pp. 496 ff., 525 ff.   [102] *Ibid.*, p. 388.
[103] *Ibid.*, p. 405.   [104] *Ibid.*, p. 405.

function. Therefore he treats the spirit elsewhere merely as an appendix of the earthly body and concludes the series of Soul, idol, and ethereal vehicle of the idol with the "elementary body, either simple and airlike or composed, which is the vessel of the ethereal body." [105]

We have seen how consciousness exercises a number of empirical functions in addition to pure knowledge and how the observation that these different functions are independent of each other and even exclude each other in their actual workings led Ficino to the assumption of several distinct forces or parts of the Soul. But as mere faculties these forces of the Soul are not able of themselves to become operative. Hence consciousness, apart from the individual forces, must possess a particular capacity through which it can perform a certain function at a given moment and pass, in its actuality, successively from one activity to the other. This element, which we may call "actuosity," constitutes the essence and kernel of pure consciousness, after the particular powers of the Soul have been objectified and set apart. By a further step of objectification, this element of consciousness may itself be conceived as a special power of the Soul and be placed in a series with the other concrete forces of the Soul. This is the power of *ratio,* which we have mentioned briefly as the middle part of the Soul. In Ficino's thought *ratio* means the capacity of the Soul to act in a different way, intellectually or empirically, and to pass in perpetual unrest from one activity to another. In contrast to the other parts of the Soul, it is not bound to any established order, and hence it is the only one that is free. The peculiarity of the human Soul consists in its liberty and in the variety of its possibilities, therefore *ratio* is the essential and characteristic part of the Soul, which for that very reason is called rational, not intellectual.

All rational Souls have . . . an intellectual head, a rational center, and an animating lowest part. That middle force is the distinctive characteristic of the Soul.[106]

[105] *Ibid.,* p. 302.   [106] *Ibid.,* p. 298.

The middle [part of the Soul] . . . now . . . ascends to the mind
. . . and now descends to the animating power.[107]
Through those three parts [*mens, idolum, natura*] we are partly
bound and partly not bound to the order of things, but by the fourth
part we are primarily freed from it and belong entirely to ourselves.
This is the *ratio*, which we place in the middle between the mind,
head of the Soul, and the *idolum*, foot of the Soul. . . . *Ratio* is
placed in the middle, a force peculiar to the true Souls. . . . That rational faculty which is the peculiar nature of the true Soul is not limited
to one thing. For with a free movement it wanders upward and downward. . . . Consequently, though we are connected in some way with
the common order of things through mind, *idolum*, and nature—
through the mind with Providence, through the *idolum* with fate, and
through the particular nature with universal nature—we belong entirely to ourselves through reason, and, being free, we follow now this
and now that part. Sometimes reason is connected with the mind, and
then it is lifted up to Providence. Sometimes it obeys the *idolum* and
nature, and then, because of love, it is subjected to fate when it trusts
the senses and is distracted here and there by the occurrence of sensible things. Sometimes it leaves the other forces and retires into itself,
and at such times it either investigates other things by arguing or examines itself. To such a degree is this middle and peculiar force of the
Soul free and restless.[108]

The relation of the *ratio* to the other parts of the Soul must probably at first be conceived as follows: the other forces, being inactive
by themselves, attain actuality through the movement of the *ratio*.
But experience teaches that the empirical functions of life proceed
by themselves, as it were, objectively, consciousness not necessarily
participating. Accordingly, following certain Neoplatonic ideas,
Ficino attributes a perpetual, substantial thought also to the mind,
which, however, is only temporarily received into consciousness.

---

[107] *Ibid.,* p. 299; cf. Horbert, *op. cit.,* p. 21.
[108] *Ibid.,* p. 290; cf. Heitzman, "L'agostinismo avicennizzante," *Giorn.
crit.,* XVI (1935), 320 ff. Heitzman is mistaken when he explains *idolum* and
natura as "sensitive Soul" and "corporeal nature." A full analysis of Ficino's
doctrine concerning Providence, Fate, and Nature, and of its historical
sources is given by Heitzman, "La libertà e il fato," *Rivista di filosofia neo-
scolastica,* XXVIII (1936), 350–71; XXIX (1937), 59–82.

In both cases it is the *ratio* that elevates the objective functions of the other parts of the Soul into consciousness, and *ratio,* therefore, grants to the other parts of the Soul, if not absolute and objective actuality, at least the attribute of perceptibility and hence a kind of subjective and concrete actuality. *Ratio* therefore appears again as the principle of "actuosity" and as the carrier of consciousness.

When something reaches our extreme parts, for example, mind, *idolum,* or nature, it may be that the Soul immediately perceives it in some way; but the Soul does not become aware that it perceives the object until it passes into the middle force. For it is the middle force through which we are men, or rather through which we are ourselves, and anything pertaining to it evidently pertains to men. Colors or sounds often move the eyes or ears, and seeing and hearing at once fulfill their duties; the former sees, the latter hears, but the Soul does not yet become aware that it sees and hears if our middle force does not turn its attention to those things. This is obvious in people who fail to recognize a friend while they are thinking attentively of something else. So the higher minds always move our mind which is connected with them, but we do not notice this impulse, because the middle force, being distracted by lower things, turns away from the higher ones. Similarly, the *idola* of the higher Souls always move our *idolum,* but we do not recognize this influence when that middle force is speculating more strongly on something else. In like manner, the natures of the larger bodies continually irritate the nature of our body, and for the same reason we frequently do not notice this impulse.[109]

[The Platonists] believe that the divine act of the mind, which takes place through some intuition and through a kind of touch of divine things, is not interrupted in itself by the inferior activities, although with respect to the awareness of it, it is interrupted in the lower forces, and although the acts of rational intellect or of intellectual reason . . . are usually interrupted by the lower actions, and the converse. But why do we not notice such a wonderful spectacle of our divine mind? Perhaps because we ceased to admire and to notice it because of the continual habit of vision. Or because the middle forces of the Soul, *ratio* and phantasy, being in general more inclined toward the activities of life, do not clearly perceive the works of that mind, as when the eye sees something before it, but the phantasy, being occupied with something else, does not recognize what the eye sees. But when the middle

[109] *Op. om.,* pp. 290 f.

forces are at leisure, the sparks of that intellectual speculation flow down into them as into a mirror. . . . And it is no wonder that something happens in that mind that we do not perceive. For we become aware only of what passes into the middle forces.[110]

The fact that contrary to his usual procedure Ficino here combines the *phantasia* with the *ratio* and makes it participate in the functions of the *ratio* is not incidental, but is derived from Neoplatonic sources. In the passage in which Plotinus introduces the substantial thought he attributes the factor of consciousness or "actuosity" to phantasy, [111] while Ficino transfers the whole theory to the *ratio* and is almost forced to identify phantasy with *ratio* wherever he follows Neoplatonic doctrine closely.

As soon as we take *ratio* as the principle of "actuosity," the philosophical reasons for Ficino's theory of the parts of the Soul become clear. First, the distinction between *mens* and *ratio*—that is, between two different cognitive powers—is necessary because the *mens* constitutes a principle of pure thought, to which a substantial, unconscious activity is attributed, whereas the *ratio* represents the principle of consciousness proper and communicates the quality of consciousness not only to the acts of pure thought, but also to the empirical functions of life. On the other hand, being independent of tradition on this point, Ficino recognizes the powers of *phantasia,* sense perception, and nutrition as separate forces, but includes them all in one lower part of the Soul in order to create a kind of balance and symmetry between the upper and the lower functions of consciousness and also to put exactly in the center the *ratio,* the peculiar and characteristic power of the Soul, which as absolute consciousness produces, and explains, through its actuosity, the concrete change of the contemplative and empirical acts of consciousness.[112] For the sake of this symmetry Ficino, in contrast to Plotinus, cancels out the so-called nature from the series of the parts of the Soul and reduces it to a mere complexion of the body, while the nutritive power, which in Plotinus is peculiar to nature and

[110] *Ibid.*, p. 273; cf. Anichini, *op. cit.*, p. 61.
[111] *Enn.* i. 4; cf. Ficino, *Op. om.*, p. 1553.   [112] Cf. Dress, *op. cit.*, p. 58.

cannot be omitted from the functions of the Soul, is now separated from nature and connected with the lower part of the Soul, the so-called *idolum*. This characteristic modification of concepts accounts for a few smaller inconsistencies, perceptible especially in Ficino's account of Plotinus' psychology.[113]

The *ratio* not only contains the formal element of actuosity or consciousness but also possesses a peculiar and characteristic function, which Ficino calls "arguing thought" or "discursive thought." This thought consists in a process which ascends from individuals through the species to the most universal genera, and, conversely, descends from there to individuals, or proceeds from the last effects to the highest causes and returns from the causes to their effects. The method in this process is strictly logical and is accomplished by syllogistic demonstration. This arguing thought is inseparably connected with the concept of *ratio,* therefore the ascent and descent of the *ratio* to the other parts of the Soul, in which the element of actuosity was expressed, is consistently considered a kind of discursive reasoning.

Ratio is placed in the middle, a force peculiar to the true Souls, through which, in universal thought, they proceed in temporal succession from the principles of things to the conclusions, resolve the effects into causes, and deduce again causes into effects and proceed also in particular thought after the model of the universal reasoning. But in the case of the former, universal reasoning *ratio* is to be called intellectual, in the case of the particular reasoning, *ratio* is to be called thinking, and conjecturing.[114]

The middle part, that is, the faculty of reasoning . . . now . . . ascends to the mind, when it receives the principles of demonstration from the mind and seeks through reasoning the universal concepts of natural things. Now it descends to the animating power, when it believes in phantasy, listens to the senses, and flatters even the body.[115]

Is our reasoning not mobile, and does it not descend from one thing to the other when it seeks variety and ascend from one thing to the other when it examines something already found? [116]

[113] Cf. *Op. om.,* p. 384.   [114] *Ibid.,* p. 290.   [115] *Ibid.,* p. 299.
[116] *Ibid.,* p. 245; cf. pp. 201, 217 (where, however, the distinction between *mens* and *ratio* is not made).

Ficino gives examples to explain the arguing procedure of *ratio*. The *ratio,* he says in the sixteenth book of the *Theologia,* is first stimulated by phantasy to produce universal concepts in itself, and it thinks afterwards, in an act of reflection, individual things— that is, something indefinite, for example, "some" honey; then it thinks something definite, for example, "this" honey. Thereafter the *ratio* seeks the substance of the thing (What is this?), the cause of its quality (Why is it sweet?), and its relationship to other things (Is it sweeter than wine?); and it answers all these questions. After these particular discourses the *ratio* proceeds to more general questions (What is honey?), which it answers with general definitions received from the mind. It is therefore clear that union with the body is useful to the *ratio,* for without the body the *ratio* would be limited to universal knowledge. "But in this body, because of the senses, the *ratio* is accustomed to pass through individuals, to subject individual things to common concepts, and to develop the common into the individual." [117]

At this point it becomes definitely clear in what sense Ficino distinguishes *mens* and *ratio* as two kinds of cognitive power.[118] The *mens* is a power of pure contemplation, and its activity consists of an intuitive, stable knowledge of the intelligible entities. The *ratio,* which receives the universal principles from the *mens,*[119] is the power of logical consciousness, which proceeds by means of discursive knowledge from one concept to the other; therefore its object is not so much the pure essense of things as their mutual connection.

That mind which is the head and driver of the Soul, imitating by its nature the angels, attains, not by succession, but in a moment, whatever it desires—or rather by a habit and, as Plotinus says, by an act it contains all things together. And, rightly, after this stable mind of

[117] *Op. om.,* pp. 371 f.

[118] On the distinction between *mens* and *ratio* see also Heitzman, "L'agostinismo avicennizzante," *Giorn. crit.,* 1935, pp. 319 ff., 460 ff. But I do not agree with his statement that *mens* and *ratio* are to be identified, respectively, with *intellectus agens* and *intellectus capax.*

[119] Cf. *Op. om.,* pp. 245, 371 f.

the Soul, which imitates the angels, follows the mobile *ratio*, peculiar to the Soul.[120]

The highest [part of the Soul], that is, the mind, excels to such a degree that it never knows anything corporeal, being desirous of the divine things alone and stable by nature, instantaneous (*subita*) in its thought.

dialectic (Pico)

The *ratio*, on the contrary, now ascends and now descends.[121] The Platonists "are accustomed to call the intelligence "unity," because it takes place through simple intuition, but to call science "duality," because it proves the conclusion from the principle." [122]

This conception of the *ratio* manifests itself particularly in the interpretation of action and of the freedom of the will. As we have seen, human action, unlike that of the beasts, is not limited to definite effects, but can choose between different possibilities (see Chapter XIII). This choice, as Ficino explains in the ninth book of the *Theologia*, is made through a kind of practical reasoning in which thought proceeds from general principles to more and more special determinations, until final determination leads to concrete action. "From a general consideration no action can proceed, unless some particular estimate is added, because movements and actions are made about particular things." For example, "physical exercises are useful" is too general a statement to lead to execution. But when we examine specific exercises and their usefulness, we may choose one among them and act.

Because of its nature the intellect is occupied in considering universal concepts. Therefore, in order that some action may proceed out of its consideration, its universal conception must be developed into particular concepts. A universal notion contains many or rather infinite individuals. . . . Hence, that universal concept may be developed equally into different individual concepts. This development is followed by the judgment about how to act.[123]

Decision is therefore conditioned by a kind of practical reasoning, and in this lies freedom of will and action. Ficino considers this

[120] *Ibid.*, p. 290.   [121] *Ibid.*, p. 299.   [122] *Ibid.*, p. 389.
[123] *Ibid.*, pp. 206 f.; cf. Saitta, *op. cit.*, pp. 230 ff. See also *Op. om.*, p. 343; and Heitzman, "L'agostinismo avicennizzante," *Giorn. crit.*, XVI (1935), p. 313.

procedure as an analogy of the reasoning thought of *ratio* and compares the relation between pure will and the freedom of choice with the relation between *mens* and *ratio*. Every intellect conceives the first principles in the same manner, and every will desires the primal good in the same way.

Choice (*electio*) is an action connected with the human species, as is the discursive thought of *ratio*. For these two things are peculiar to man. Consequently, if men reasoned through a natural instinct, the opinion of all men about individual matters would be the same; and if they chose by nature, the choice of all would be the same. But in reality different persons choose different things in different ways, as they judge differently in reasoning.[124]

The parallelism of thought and will has been analyzed above (see Chapter XIII). Ficino here applies it in all details.

The power of *ratio* is, as we have seen, the characteristic part of the human Soul. Since *ratio* is inseparably connected with reasoning, the procedure of arguing appears to be peculiar to man and connected with the essence of the Soul.

These concepts are inseparably inherent in the Soul, which uses them always and directly according to its free will. The art of reasoning, which cannot be separated from the rational Soul, consists in these concepts.[125]
This is proved especially by the rational force, which is no less natural to man than flying is to birds or barking to dogs. Because of it Socrates is a man; because of it man is distinct from other species of animals. Rational force we now call that force of reasoning that looks at the consequences—in other words, gradually observes the results of everything and proceeds in orderly fashion from precedents to consequences. This is a kind of natural dialectic, in other words, an art of debating innate to men from the beginning. Through it boys and untutored people play their parts by conjecture as best they can. And all speech of man and all action and reflection of life is nothing else but a kind of arguing.[126]

The arguing method is therefore related to the inner peculiarity of *ratio* and of the rational Soul itself. Ficino obviously does not

[124] *Op. om.*, p. 209.   [125] *Ibid.*, p. 153.
[126] *Ibid.*, pp. 261 f.; cf. Saitta, *op. cit.*, pp. 211 f.

consider his own method of demonstration, which is essentially an accumulation of single syllogisms, merely an external and incidental form of exposition, but rather the consistent expression of the "natural dialectic" of human thought. The arbitrariness we feel in the repeated and varying connections of individual conceptual elements is only the freedom of the *ratio,* which presupposes the single concepts as objects existing in themselves, but which in mutually connecting these elements moves freely from one to the other according to its own choice.

The *ratio* is the principle of actuosity, and it unites itself now with the higher, now with the lower part of the Soul. On the other hand, it proceeds through discursive knowledge from one concept to the other, performing a continual movement, if we can call "movement" not only change in space but also any kind of change. If, however, we examine the hierarchy of existing things, we see that God and the angelic intellects are superior to any kind of movement,[127] and our own mind is likewise directed toward the divine entities in an unwavering perception.[128] The *ratio* and the rational Soul, of which the *ratio* is the characteristic part, thus constitute in the hierarchy of Being the highest and first entity in which the element of movement occurs, and the movement of *ratio* is therefore considered the primary and most excellent movement.

Following that stable mind of the Soul which imitates the angels is the mobile *ratio,* peculiar to the soul . . . Finally, that rational faculty which is the peculiar nature of the true Soul is not limited to one thing only; for it wanders up and down in a free movement. For the primary movement is that which is located in the peculiar nature of the Soul. . . . Yet the primary movement is not this or that movement, nor is it directed only here or there; but it is a common movement, and as the source of movement it flows freely and runs in any direction at any moment.[129]

Because the Soul possesses the primary movement in itself, it is also the cause of movement; and any lower form of movement, especially that of the body, must be derived from that of the Soul.

---

[127] Cf. *Op. om.,* pp. 85 ff., 115 ff.   [128] *Ibid.,* pp. 290, 299.
[129] *Ibid.,* p. 290; cf. Cassirer, *Individuum,* pp. 120 f.

All things that can be moved by another thing—for example, bodies and qualities—we have related to the Soul, which is movable by itself. I say "movable by itself," for if you descend from God through the Angel, both God and the Angel will appear stable to you, and the first thing which occurs to you as being mobile, will be the Soul.

Hence, the Soul is mobile by itself, and a sign of this is the fact that inanimate bodies are moved only by outward impulse, animate bodies by their own impulse and in any direction. The Soul makes the body capable of moving by itself; consequently, the Soul has this capacity to an even higher degree. Therefore the Soul is the source of movement.[130] The Soul is the cause which makes the body move; but the cause and possibility of that fact lie in the proper incorporeal movement of the Soul. The Soul, as Ficino says, "must first vigilantly prove its forces in itself before manifesting them in the body, and thus, as the corporeal substance is derived from spiritual substance, so the corporeal movement is produced by the spiritual movement." [131] Ficino illustrates this spiritual movement of the Soul by the metaphor of the painter who considers and paints the individual parts of a landscape in temporal succession and movement, while the real landscape is complete with all its parts together at one moment and remains without movement.

In a similar way, according to the Platonists, the rational Soul conceives or imagines God and the Angel through a perpetual light, desiring to paint itself after their image through speculation, habits, and action. While the Soul forms itself gradually, it is moved. This movement proceeds from the proper nature of the Soul itself which is the proper source of movement, that is, of action.[132]

In analyzing practical arguing and the choice of the will, we have seen how the spiritual movement of the *ratio* can produce a specific action and movement of the body. This relation of the corporeal movement to the spiritual change of the Soul is not limited to man; Ficino, accepting a Neoplatonic view, applies it to the whole universe as well. The spheres are moved by the activity of their

[130] *Op. om.*, p. 117.   [131] *Ibid.*, p. 118.   [132] *Ibid.*

Souls,[133] and since the Souls of animals are related to the world Soul, or to the Souls of the spheres, their movement, too, is ultimately derived from the spiritual movement of the cosmic Souls.[134]

The relation of the rational Soul, which contains the highest form of movement, to the stable substances, God and the angels, is frequently illustrated by Ficino with a metaphor which has particular significance because of its close connection with the famous metaphor of light. As we know, light is, according to tradition, the symbol of Being, particularly of intelligible existence. With reference to Plato's metaphor of the cave, God, the source of Being, is often compared to the sun, the source of light. Accordingly, Ficino compares the angelic intellects with the stars, and the rational Soul with the moon, which by its own nature subjects the homogeneous light of the sun to a temporal change.

The sun has light by itself and transmits it in a moment to Mercury. Mercury also receives its whole light in a moment and consequently remains fullest. In a moment the sun transmits the same light to the moon, but the moon does not receive it in a moment, but in time. For as it is directed to the sun differently at different times, it receives the light differently at different times, and through its own nature it is modified by the change of light. The sun represents God; Mercury, the Angel; the moon, the Soul. What I say about Mercury, you may understand as said equally about all other stars above the moon.[135]

Like the higher stars, the angels are converted to [God] like the sun; but the Soul [is converted] to Him like the moon, which is diversified by a change of the divine light and hence receives it as changeable, but perceives it as unextinguishable.[136]

Having clarified the theory of the parts of the Soul we can now determine the human Soul's place in the universe. To this end we shall begin with Ficino's gradation of existence by means of natural species, and we shall lay aside, for the moment, the theory of the five substances, which represents only a later stage of the development. The rational Soul is frequently compared to the angels, on the one hand, and to the Souls of beasts, on the other.

---

[133] Cf. *ibid.*, pp. 122 ff.   [134] Cf. *ibid.*, p. 401.   [135] *Ibid.*, p. 118.
[136] *Ibid.*, p. 219; cf. pp. 87, 222, 224, 402. See also Dress, *op. cit.*, p. 131.

The angels are pure intellects, not bound to any bodies.[137] Their activity consists in the pure contemplation of God, achieved instantaneously and changelessly.[138] Consequently, they possess no lower functions corresponding to the middle and lower part of the Soul. Beasts, on the other hand, possess, along with the body, the vital functions related to the body. They have also sensation and phantasy, but neither contemplative knowledge nor discursive thought.[139] They are therefore credited with having only a so-called "irrational Soul," which apparently corresponds not only to the *natura* but also to the lower part of the human Soul, the so-called *idolum,* since this part is also a carrier of sensation and imagination. This irrational Soul of beasts does not raise itself above the corporeal realm, and it is therefore not immortal, in contrast to the human Soul. It is occasionally qualified, like the irrational part of man, as the shadow of the rational Soul, and, as in the Neoplatonic theory, its essence is related to the world Soul or to the Soul of its own element.[140] As *anima rationalis* the human Soul resembles the angels in contemplation and in its higher part.[141] It resembles the beasts' Souls in its lower functions, that is, in the "nature of nutrition and sensation and corporeal complexion," while the middle part, the *ratio,* is characteristic of the rational Soul, as we have seen. Consequently, in the hierarchy of things the Soul stands midway between angels and beasts. This position gives rise to a series of attributes which we need not follow in detail.[142]

The general concept of *anima rationalis,* according to Neoplatonic views, contains not only human Souls but also a number of higher, cosmic Souls. In order to define the position of man in the universe, we must briefly consider his relation to these higher Souls. Various parts of Ficino's theory of the cosmic Souls seem inconsistent, partly because he does not always distinguish clearly his own opinion from that of the Neoplatonists. The following

---

[137] Cf. *ibid.,* pp. 87 ff., 227.   [138] *Ibid.,* pp. 368 ff.   [139] Cf. *ibid.,* pp. 207 f.
[140] *Ibid.,* p. 401; cf. the similar reflection on the Souls of plants (pp. 122 f.).
[141] Cf. *ibid.,* p. 290.
[142] *Ibid.,* pp. 218, 224, 227, 332, *et passim;* cf. Dress, *op. cit.,* p. 52.

scheme will give us some conception of it. The primary place is occupied by the world Soul, which is followed by twelve Souls of the spheres, corresponding to the eight celestial and the four elementary spheres, and then by the Souls of the individuals distributed among the different spheres and grouped respectively under certain leading Souls.[143] To the individual Souls belong first the Souls of the stars, then the Souls of men, and last the demons and heroes whose nature is not always clearly defined. Most of the latter live in the elementary spheres; but they also inhabit the celestial spheres.[144] All these Souls, like the human Soul, possess three parts, as well as a nature subject to the last part of the Soul,[145] and a body. There are, however, essential differences in the quality and attitude of these parts. The middle part of the celestial Souls, the *ratio,* is completely freed from the care of the body and turned toward the mind to share in its rest and stability. It is not subject to temporal movement as our *ratio* is, but attains knowledge of intelligible things in a 'kind of eternal movement.[146] Moreover, the lower part of the cosmic Souls, which, in this context, Ficino does not clearly distinguish from the *natura,* is sufficient in itself to guide the bodies. It produces corporeal movement when it passes through the whole series of forms in temporal succession, and through the forms generated in itself, which partake of the nature of germs, it brings forth successively the forms of corporeal things.[147] Finally, the cosmic Souls have either an etheric body, like the Souls of the celestial spheres and of the stars, or an elementary but simple body, like the Souls of the elementary spheres and of their demons, but not a composed body, like that of man, whose body is particularly difficult to guide be-

[143] *Op. om.,* pp. 122 ff., especially pp. 125 f.; cf. p. 250. See also Dress, *op. cit.,* pp. 51 f.; Horbert, *op. cit.,* pp. 17 f.

[144] *Op. om.,* pp. 223, 390.

[145] Cf. especially *ibid.,* p. 250. Ficino distinguishes between *natura terrae* and *natura universi,* that is, between the respective parts of the Soul of the earth and of the World Soul. Saitta apparently identifies both of them with God (*op. cit.,* p. 146). The same mistake is made by Hak (*op. cit.,* p. 95).

[146] *Op. om.,* p. 132.   [147] *Ibid.,* pp. 122 f., 132 f., 250.

cause it resists the influence of the Soul.[148] This imperfection of the human body is also expressed in its movement. The perfect form of movement, according to tradition, is the circular, and hence all cosmic Souls (except the demons, which in this point resemble the nature of man) give their bodies a circular movement. Only the human body, because of its gravity and composition, is incapable of circular movement and moves irregularly. The etheric body of man is capable of moving in a circular fashion, but it is prevented from exercising this power during life by the presence of the elementary body and can return to its appropriate form of movement only after death, provided it has not been aggravated and infected by earthly vices.[149]

Yet compared with the angels and the cosmic Souls the human Soul occupies the lowest place among all intellectual beings.

Which is that [last intellect]? It is the human intellect. . . . I believe our mind is the last one, as was the opinion of several ancient men, because it does not accomplish its acts simultaneously, but like Proteus changes its forms and thinks them successively, as the moon, being the last of the stars, changes its light successively, while the other stars do not change.[150]

The Soul of man, which in that part in which it is mind is the last among the minds and thinks only in a passive way, does not divide the universals into individuals.[151]

Such are the Souls of men, which because they are the lowest of all minds have not that force through which they can accomplish perfectly two different things at the same time—that is, contemplate divine things through human reason and govern the earthly bodies. But they must do both, for they are born for both. Therefore, they do successively what they cannot do simultaneously.[152]

Hence, the human Soul is the lowest of all intellectual beings (the beasts' souls having no intellect of their own and belonging completely to the corporeal world), but through its substance it belongs entirely to the incorporeal sphere of reality. On the other hand, it is connected with the body, and in the gradual ascent in

---

[148] *Ibid.*, pp. 379 f. [149] *Ibid.*, pp. 134, 380. [150] *Ibid.*, p. 222.
[151] *Ibid.*, p. 371; cf. Heitzman, *op. cit.*, p. 462. [152] *Op. om.*, p. 390.

the hierarchy of corporeal forms we can consider it the highest and last form of the bodies.[153] Thus, in spite of its purely intellectual substance the human Soul is placed in a special way on the border-line between the corporeal and the incorporeal and constitutes a kind of link between these two halves of reality. "By Divine Providence the Soul of man was graded so that it immediately follows the minds and comes just before the bodies." [154] As we shall see later, this concept receives its definite form through the doctrine of the double affection of the Soul and of the five substances of the world.

The theory of the two affections, or tendencies, of the Soul, which we shall now treat, has already been presented (see Chapters VII and X). But whereas before we were merely interested in understanding the attributes of the Soul as elements of an objective world system and did not examine the original meaning of these qualities as such, we must now try to interpret them on the basis of the facts of consciousness and to explain the cosmological conceptions derived from them in a new and definitive manner.

For this purpose we must start with the love of the Soul for its body. The empirical functions of consciousness, as we have seen, led to the assumption that there is a lower part of the Soul, clearly distinct from the power of knowledge, whose actual activity is in a certain contrast to the acts of the mind. However, the individual parts of the Soul are not substantially separated from one another, but constitute different aspects or forces within one Soul. Hence, Ficino tries to derive the empirical functions of consciousness directly from the unique nature of Soul itself, without respect to the parts of the Soul. In this sense he attributes to the human Soul a love for, or inclination directed toward, the body. Therefore the Soul has a natural inclination or a natural tendency toward the body. This accounts for all its empirical functions and acts, and the ontological concept of *appetitus naturalis* serves here, just as in

[153] *Ibid.*, pp. 226 f.
[154] *Ibid.*, p. 371. Cf. pp. 331 f.; Saitta, *op. cit.*, pp. 191 ff.

the case of the appetite toward God, to include a number of individual experiences of the consciousness under one objective principle.

Natural love united the Soul to the body; natural love detains the Soul in the body; the same love daily brings it to the care of the body.[155]
The rational Souls are by no means bodies, but through some natural affection they tend downward toward the bodies.[156]
Out of the Soul and the human body one natural compound results, and the Soul is endowed with a natural instinct toward the body.[157]
The individual Souls have a natural inclination to animate and to guide the individual bodies.[158]

Ficino compares this love of the Soul for the body to the love of a mother for her child,[159] or, characteristically, to the gravity of a stone. The Soul, which is inwardly divided "remains [in that state] only for a while, because the natural affection of its lower force draws it again to the care of the body, as a stone thrown upward is said to stay for a short while in the air between ascent and descent." [160] In this passage the doctrine of natural affection is strangely combined with the doctrine of the parts of the Soul. This combination, which obviously has to be considered secondary, occurs on other occasions as well. For example, Ficinio once speaks of the love of the entire Soul for the body, but shortly afterward he attributes to the higher part of the Soul a love for the middle part, to the middle part, a love for the lower part, to the lower part, a love for the vital complexion, and to this complexion alone, a love for the body.[161] Likewise, he says elsewhere that the *ratio,* through the three lower forces of the Soul, is inclined toward the body,[162] or that the Soul is full of love for its vital shadow in the body, in other words, for the *natura.*[163]

This natural affection for the body manifests itself not only in the empirical functions of consciousness during life but also as

[155] *Op. om.,* p. 381; cf. Saitta, *op. cit.,* pp. 254 f.
[156] *Op. om.,* p. 688.   [157] *Ibid.,* p. 416.   [158] *Ibid.*   [159] *Ibid.,* p. 206.
[160] *Ibid.,* p. 304; cf. p. 351. See also chap. x, above.
[161] *Ibid.,* p. 206.   [162] *Ibid.,* p. 382.   [163] *Ibid.,* p. 380.

the metaphysical cause leading the Soul, an incorporeal substance, to unification with the human body. "Natural love united the Soul to the body," so we read in a passage quoted above.

What binds [the Souls] to the bodies? Love, as Plato says, that is, the affection of an exuberant life, inclined to animate its neighboring things.[164]

Through the instinct of love different [Souls] adapt themselves to move different bodies.[165]

The same tendency of the Soul, as we have seen elsewhere, also furnishes a philosophical explanation for the Christian dogma of resurrection, since the natural affection remains unsatisfied for a certain period after death and finds its necessary fulfillment only in the ultimate union of the Soul with the resurrected body. The Soul has a natural appetite for the body, so we read in one passage; it cannot therefore remain separated from the body. The Souls

remain eternal after the destruction of the body. Anything that is against nature cannot be eternal. Consequently, the Souls will resume their bodies at some time.[166]

The natural inclination remains as long as nature remains. Hence, the Souls separated from the bodies will always naturally incline toward them. But a natural inclination and tendency cannot be forever in vain. . . . Hence, the Souls will at some time resume their bodies, toward which they are always directed by nature.[167]

The natural affection for the body, which has hitherto appeared as an objective and morally indifferent attribute of the Soul, becomes the actual origin of bad and imperfect conduct as soon as the Soul misuses it and gives it an illicit preponderance over its higher, spiritual possibilities. For example, the Soul often gives in to the body because of too great a love, just as a mother does to her badly raised child.[168] Among the most important causes of sin Ficino lists the too-great love of the Soul for the body.[169] In

[164] *Ibid.,* p. 299; cf. Saitta, *op. cit.,* p. 144.
[165] *Ibid.,* p. 299.   [166] *Ibid.,* p. 416.
[167] *Ibid.,* pp. 416 f.; cf. p. 351. See also chap. x, above.
[168] *Ibid.,* p. 206.   [169] *Ibid.,* p. 630.

the sixteenth book of the *Theologia* he derives vice from this affection of the Soul.

> [Through the lower forces] the *ratio* . . . descends through love to
> the body. Because of long inclination it acquires a habit of inclining
> more readily. This habit . . . we call vice.[170]

> The divine Soul is not vitiated or forced by the body, but because of
> love for the animated body, which is its work and instrument, the
> Soul itself stoops willingly toward it from its own state.[171]

> The Soul is never forced from outside, but by love it plunges into the
> body and by love it emerges from the body.[172]

> The Soul is not vitiated by the body, but it vitiates itself by loving the
> body too much.[173]

In a letter Ficino makes this affection responsible for the unhappy
life of the Soul that is dedicated to the outside world.

> The cause of all movement is natural, or animal, love; therefore you
> have all affection and fear for the body when you love it ardently, and
> you are troubled while having affection and suffer pain while having
> fear.[174]

The only salvation from the evils of the world is "to flee from the
love of the body and from the care of external things to the care
of the Soul." [175] The excessive love for the body which constitutes
the root of the external and imperfect life, also determines the
state of the impure Soul after death. For its state in the future life
is the continuation and fulfillment of the attitude chosen in the
present life, and the "preponderance" of love for the body manifests itself after death in the inherent force of gravity which leads
the guilty Soul to the lower place for purification and punishment.

> While [the Soul] descends to one extreme [of life], which it begins to
> do in the present [life] and finishes when it finally leaves [the body],
> it attains the middle [status] imperfectly and the opposite extreme not
> at all.[176]

Christians believe that guilty Souls precipitate themselves by affinity,

---

[170] *Ibid.*, p. 382.   [171] *Ibid.*
[172] *Ibid.* Cf. Saitta, *op. cit.*, pp. 255 f., and Cassirer, *Individuum*, p. 141.
[173] *Op. om.*, p. 383; cf. Anichini, *op. cit.*, p. 92.   [174] *Op. om.*, p. 738.
[175] *Ibid.*, p. 633.   [176] *Ibid.*, p. 375.

as by natural gravity, into the nine degrees of guilty demons to which they made themselves similar during life.[177]

With this theory of love for the body, Ficino attempts for the first time to derive from a unique principle two basic facts—the imperfect life and the empirical functions of consciousness. This natural affection, therefore, includes all negative, noncontemplative phenomena of consciousness, just as the desire for God unifies in itself all facts of the inner, contemplative experience (see Chapter XIII). The whole possible content of human consciousness is therefore expressed by the sum of these two affections, and the contradiction which seems to exist between them is essentially nothing but the contradiction, conceptually interpreted and transformed, between the inner experience and the elements of consciousness distinguished from it. Ficino does not eliminate or hide this contradiction, but in order to understand human existence as a whole he recognizes it as a real contrast and tries to overcome it. The attempt to comprehend the essence of the Soul in the contrast between the two natural affections was apparently effective in the interpretation and transformation of the individual facts of consciousness that led successively to the assumption of a desire for God and of an inclination or tendency toward the body.

If we look first at the contrast between the contemplative and the empirical functions of consciousness (the contrast which determines Ficino's point of view), we see that the assumption of two opposite tendencies of the Soul is evidently based on the same objective facts that had already been expressed in the principle of the incompatibility of different acts of consciousness and later in the separation between the higher and lower parts of the Soul, as well as in the upward and downward movement of the *ratio*. The two affections sometimes occur closely connected with the parts of the Soul.

There is in the Soul a force drawing downward toward sensible things, that is, imaginative and vegetative power, and there is a force higher than the former one, lifting it toward divine things.[178]

[177] *Ibid.*, p. 410; cf. p. 418. See also chap. x, above.   [178] *Ibid.*, p. 1369.

[The Platonists] believe that consequently the intellectual Soul is never inclined toward the body through the part by which it is intellectual, but is directed toward the bodies through that part by which it does not share natural intelligence.[179]

Since the clear scheme of two affections is lacking in the *De amore,* it may be that Ficino gradually passed from the theory of the parts of the Soul, through such indefinite formulations, to the clear doctrine as expressed in the *Theologia Platonica.* The human Soul, so we can formulate the important doctrine, possesses in its essence two opposite natural affections, or tendencies, one of which is directed toward the corporeal world, the other, toward the intelligible world. In this formula not only are desire for God and love for the body (conceptual expressions for the contemplative and the empirical, external attitude of consciousness, respectively) combined into one scheme comprehending the Soul as a whole but at the same time the Soul, through its two tendencies, is brought into an objective relationship to two different spheres of reality, the corporeal and the intelligible, and this relationship is given a definite ontological significance by the concept of *appetitus naturalis.*

[The Soul] ascends, because of a natural instinct, to the higher things and descends to the lower things. While it is ascending, it does not leave the lower things; and while it is descending, it does not abandon the higher ones.[180]

[We see] that our Souls have affection for the eternal things and affection for the temporal ones.[181]

We see that the Soul inclines both toward eternal and temporal things.[182]

Since our Soul is commonly and continually inclined toward both temporal and eternal things . . .[183]

Characteristically, Ficino compares the Soul to the two-faced Janus, looking simultaneously in opposite directions.

[179] *Ibid.,* p. 1570.   [180] *Ibid.,* p. 119.   [181] *Ibid.,* p. 219.
[182] *Ibid.,* p. 658.   [183] *Ibid.,* p. 473.

Although the Soul looks at both the corporeal and the incorporeal, through the nature of the third essence, just as the double-faced Janus . . .[184]
Hence, the Soul, like the double-faced Janus, seems to have a double face—that is, one of gold and one of silver. With the former it looks at the realm of Saturn; with the latter, at that of Jupiter [that is, the eternal and the temporal].[185]

Accordingly, Ficino speaks of the two eyes of the Soul, an expression which reminds us of the medieval mystics: "We . . . whose Soul seems to have two eyes, one looking upward and one downward." [186] Sometimes the principle of the double affection is related to the moral contrast between the perfect and the imperfect life; and this turn, as we have seen, is foreshadowed in the interpretation of the *amor corporis*. "Just as all tranquillity and virtue result from the love of divine things, so from the love of mortal things come all trouble and wickedness." [187]
From what has been said the philosophical foundation of the theory of the two affections of the Soul should be clear. But from this theory springs a series of further ontological conclusions which have already been considered and now must merely be illustrated in their relation to the facts of consciousness and to the attributes of the Soul. After the assumption of two natural affections, which mean an objectification of facts of consciousness, Ficino takes a step further and deduces from the two tendencies a double quality or nature of the Soul. For through its affections the Soul is related to the two objective spheres of the intelligible and the sensible world, and since each natural tendency presupposes an affinity between the desiring subject and its goal which exists in itself, the Soul must participate by its objective nature in the two different orders of Being. This doctrine of the two natures of the Soul, which cannot be entirely harmonized with the conception of parts of the Soul, in spite of their similar content, upon closer examination, is seen to contain a startling inconsistency. For the conclusion

[184] *Ibid.*, p. 375; cf. Dress, *op. cit.*, p. 54.   [185] *Op. om.*, p. 658.
[186] *Ibid.*, p. 430.   [187] *Ibid.*, p. 441; cf. p. 382.

which leads from the affections to the natures of the Soul would, in a strict sense, lead to the assumption of a corporeal nature in the Soul, which would entirely contradict all Ficino's other statements. He avoids this conclusion, however, by a clever device. Considering the two natures, he always begins with the contrast between eternal and temporal things, not with the contrast between intelligible and corporeal objects. This device, which conceals rather than overcomes the inner vagueness of the concept, is apparently used for the sake of the clear, speculative formula. Otherwise this inconsistency is clear proof of the fact that the two natures of the Soul are deduced from the two tendencies, a fact confirmed by Ficino's own testimony.

Since natural affections are based upon their own natures and different affections upon different natures, and since we see that our Souls have one affection for things eternal and one for things temporal, we rightly state that they [the Souls] are composed of two natures—one eternal and one temporal—as if we saw a body being moved by its nature almost evenly upward and downward, we should state that it is composed almost equally of gravity and lightness.[188]

In each natural thing we are accustomed to investigate the propriety of nature through its continual and natural inclination. . . . Our Soul is commonly and continually inclined toward both temporal things and eternal things, and therefore we conjecture that it has both natures, so to speak—an eternal one through the intellect and a temporal one through the sense.[189]

Different inclinations or tendencies are the result of different natures. From the very fact that we see the Soul inclined toward both eternal things and temporal things, we know that it is composed of both natures.[190]

From the double nature of the Soul, which is both eternal and temporal, it is deduced that its position is in the middle between eternal and temporal things. For if two objects or spheres have entirely opposite attributes and hence are contrasted as extremes, the general principle of mediation requires, as we have seen be-

[188] *Ibid.*, pp. 219 f.   [189] *Ibid.*, p. 473; cf. Dress, *op. cit.*, p. 54.
[190] *Op. om.*, p. 658.

fore, the existence of an intermediary entity, which shares in a
certain way in both opposite attributes and so reconciles the contrast between the extremes. This role is played by the Soul in respect to the eternal things and the temporal things, and the human
Souls, whose acts and attitudes were first interpreted as tendencies
and then as attributes, at last are given a definite and established
place in the objective hierarchy of things. "Between those things
which are only eternal and those which are only temporal there is
the Soul . . ." [191]

According to the Chaldeans [the rational Souls] exist on the borderline
between eternity and time. Through their substance they exist in eternity; through their actions, in time.[192]

The rational Soul . . . is placed on the borderline between eternity
and time, since it possesses an intermediary nature between eternal
things and temporal things; and because it is intermediary, it possesses
rational forces and actions ascending toward the eternal Beings and it
also possesses other forces and activities descending toward the temporal Beings.[193]

Our Soul, as is said by the Platonists, occupies an intermediary region
between eternal and temporal things. And since it participates in both,
it is moved at its will toward both.[194]

In the same passage Ficino mentions the double tendency of the
Soul, and in other arguments he relates the middle position of
the Soul, not to its opposite qualities, but to its two natural affections. In consequence we can now understand how the doctrine
of the central position of the Soul is founded upon its inner relation to the corporeal and intelligible objects—that is, upon the
fact that there are empirical acts and contemplative acts of consciousness.

It seems that nothing proves the intermediary nature of the human
mind better than its natural inclination toward both. For when it begins with the bodies through the intellect, it soon passes from there to

[191] *Ibid.,* p. 119.
[192] *Ibid.,* p. 227; cf. Thomas, *Summa contra Gentiles* II, 68, 81.
[193] *Op. om.,* pp. 657 f.
[194] *Ibid.,* p. 824; cf. p. 318, and Dress, *op. cit.,* p. 52.

the incorporeal things; and when it starts with the incorporeal things, it descends, conversely, to the corporeal images. Or when through the will it desires eternal things, it is meanwhile turned away from them by the affection for temporal things; and when it desires temporal things, conversely, it is often held back from them by reverence for the eternal things.[195]

The Soul was created on the borderline between minds and bodies and therefore not only desires divine things, but also is related to matter by a natural providence and love.[196]

Individual Souls naturally are inclined to animate and govern individual bodies. For that results from the nature and providence of a life that is placed between eternity and time and has a natural inclination partly toward eternal things, partly toward temporal things.[197]

The Soul, therefore, standing midway between eternal things and temporal things, has not only a definite place in the hierarchy of existing things but also possesses a peculiar significance with respect to other things and in the structure of reality as a whole. For the eternal and temporal things—that is, the intelligible and corporeal entities—are not arbitrarily chosen parts or sections of reality; they are the two halves of reality, which, put together, constitute the whole universe, the same two worlds that have dominated the history of metaphysics since Plato's day and whose dualism was modified, rather than overcome, by the principle of continual hierarchy. Hence, that which mediates eternal and temporal entities is not only a member in the series of objects but also the absolute center of all things. If any middle part, reconciling two extremes, contributes to the unity and continuity of the universe, then the center of things, which reconciles and connects the two halves of Being, may be qualified as the bond and knot of the universe, which makes the unity of the world possible and represents this unity in itself. The particular rank and the peculiar excellence of the Soul is based upon this connecting and mediating role, and Ficino clearly refers this mediating role of the Soul to the Soul's objective position between eternal and temporal things and to its double tendency toward both worlds.

[195] *Op. om.*, p. 346.   [196] *Ibid.*, p. 381.   [197] *Ibid.*, p. 416.

Since the Soul is the true center of all things made by God, it is obvious that it is created as much as possible in an intermediate and even manner.[198]

We have already often declared that the Soul of man is the center of things.[199]

If there are only these two things in the world—the intellect on the one hand and the body on the other—but the Soul be lacking, then neither will the intellect be drawn toward the body . . . nor the body toward the intellect. . . . But if the Soul, which is congruent with both, is placed between them, the attraction from both and toward both will take place easily. . . . Since . . . it [the Soul] is the center of things, it contains all things in its own way. . . . For in addition to being congruent with divine things on the one hand and on the other with transitory things, it also inclines toward both through its affection; meanwhile it exists completely and simultaneously everywhere.[200]

Ficino develops this doctrine most clearly in the third book of the *Theologia.* "Between those things that are only eternal and those that are only temporal there is the Soul, like a kind of bond between them." Each work becomes perfect through the unity of its parts, as the relation of the four elements shows. "Much more, there must be assumed a connection of the parts in the whole work of God in order that the work of one God may be one." God and Body are extremes, and the contrast is not even reconciled by Angel and Quality.

Hitherto all things have been extremes, and the higher and lower things, lacking a convenient bond, flee from each other. But that third essence [the Soul] placed between them is such as to keep the higher things without leaving the lower things, so the higher things are connected in it with the lower ones. For it is immobile and also mobile. By the former attribute it agrees with the higher things; by the latter, with the lower things. If it agrees with both, it desires both. Hence, through a natural instinct it ascends to the higher things and descends to the lower things. And while ascending it does not leave the lower things; while descending it does not abandon the higher ones. For if it abandons either of them, it will incline toward the other extreme and will no longer be the true bond of the world.

[198] *Ibid.,* p. 388.   [199] *Ibid.,* p. 403; cf. p. 404.   [200] *Ibid.,* p. 531.

The air mediates between fire and water; the light, between the sun and the elements.

Similarly, the third essence must adhere at the same time to divine things and fill mortal things. While adhering to divine things . . . it knows them. While filling the bodies . . . it animates them. Hence, it is the mirror of the divine, the life of the mortal, the connection of both.[201]

It possesses the images of the divine things on which it depends, the concepts and archetypes of the mortal things, which it produces in some way. And as it is the center of all things, it has the forces of all. . . . And because it is the true connection of all things, it does not leave any of them while passing to the others . . . so that it may rightly be called the center of nature, the middle of all things, the series of the world, the face of all, the knot and bond of the universe.[202]

We must also recall the fact that the Soul, as we have shown above, has entered the same ontological position which in an earlier work Ficino assigned to an abstract principle, namely, to love in a cosmic sense.[203] It is therefore very evident that the Soul must be considered the center and bond of the world chiefly through its double love, that is, its two natural tendencies. According to Ficino this mediating role of the Soul is not confined to the transitory earthly life. For since the Soul retains its tendency toward the body even after death, and since at the end of all days its desire for God is satisfied forever through eternal beatitude and its tendency toward the body through resurrection, the Soul will evidently be the bond and middle between the corporeal sphere and the intelligible sphere even in the final order of things after the movement of the world comes to rest.[204]

At this point we can understand the significance of the doctrine

[201] *Ibid.,* p. 119.

[202] *Ibid.,* p. 121. This central position of the Soul does not, however, exclude its "mystical" relation with God, as Dress (*op. cit.,* pp. 77 f.) believes, but contains that relation as one of its own aspects. Anichini's statement (*op. cit.,* pp. 41 f.) that Ficino concludes the immortality of the Soul from its central position is also incorrect.

[203] Cf. *Op. om.,* p. 1330. See also chap. vii, above.

[204] Cf. *Op. om.,* p. 689 f. See also chap. x, above.

of the five substances, which Ficino develops at length at the beginning of the *Theologia,* but which by no means constitutes the beginning of his philosophical considerations. It is, rather, the end —the final result and, so to speak, the outer layer of his speculation. For as a matter of fact there is a close connection between the scheme of the five substances and the central position of the Soul, as it appears from Ficino's own exposition. This does not mean that the central position of the Soul is merely derived as a conclusion or partial assertion from the scheme of the five substances, as previously established. On the contrary, the scheme of the five substances presupposes the central position of the Soul, and it was constructed by Ficino for the purpose of making the Soul appear the accurate center of a comprehensive ontological hierarchy. This fact, never wholly understood by Ficino's interpreters, needs no particular demonstration following the preceding discussions. For, as we have seen, the central position of the Soul is based upon its twofold natural inclination and hence upon the opposite attitudes of contemplative and empirical consciousness, through which the Soul inwardly participates in two different orders of Reality. It is by no means based upon the scheme of the five substances. This scheme was never presupposed in these considerations, and it even directly contradicts several of the respective arguments. This negative statement finds its positive confirmation in the genesis of the doctrine of the five substances, which we have analyzed in Chapter VII and therefore must mention but briefly here. In the early work, *De amore,* as we have shown in greater detail, Ficino did not yet know the scheme of five substances, but accepted completely the doctrine of Plotinus, who recognizes six hypostases altogether: God, Mind (Angel), rational Soul, Sensation, Nature, and Body. This older doctrine is still recognizable in several passages of the *Theologia Platonica* and constitutes a kind of lower layer of Ficino's speculation. Not until a later period, and then through a modification of the Plotinian scheme, did Ficino arrive at his own final hierarchical series, placing it visibly at the beginning of his principal work. The change lies in the fact that he eliminates the two lower parts of the Soul—that is, Sensation and Nature—and introduces instead Quality as a new element. So he obtains a symmetrical scheme of five substances, in which the two intelligible degrees are balanced by two corporeal degrees, while the Soul occupies the center and makes the connection between the contrasting halves of reality. In this transformation of the theory we see clearly Ficino's intention of elevating the human Soul to the center of a homogeneously constructed world system, and this intent is confirmed in the words with which he sums up the structure of his system in the third book of the *Theologia*.

And finally, to reach what we desire, let us again include all things in five degrees—that is, by placing God and the Angel at the peak of nature, Body and Quality at the bottom, but the Soul in the middle between those highest things and these lowest things, the Soul which we rightly call, in the Platonic sense, the third and middle essence, because it is the middle with respect to all things and the third from all sides. For if you descend from God, you find it on the third grade of the descent; and also on the third grade of the ascent, if you ascend above the body.[205]

The scheme of the five substances therefore rests on the central position of the Soul; the central position of the Soul, upon its double natural tendency; and this tendency, upon the difference between the contemplative, perfect consciousness and the empirical, imperfect consciousness. Here an insight of a more general character is manifest, and in it we may sum up the result of our entire interpretation: the speculative assertions of Ficino's metaphysics are determined essentially by his theory of the Soul. The theory of the Soul results from his continual effort to give a conceptual interpretation of a few basic facts of consciousness and so to transform those facts into objective principles. In other words, man and his attitudes constitute the point of departure of Ficino's philosophy. In this fact we must look for the secret of his historical, philosophical, and human influence and significance.

[205] *Op. om.*, p. 119.

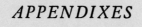

APPENDIXES

APPENDIX I

This appendix refers to Chapter VII

THE DOCTRINE of the place of the Soul in the universe provides Ficino with an opportunity to justify the Christian dogma of the incarnation in a new and special manner. In his opinion Christ is not only the mediator between God and men but also the mediator between the Creator and the creation as a whole. Because of this universal connection the Word of God was forced to choose man himself for His instrument as the universal link between all things. "Desiring to communicate itself to all things," we read in the *De religione christiana,* "infinite goodness did so most adequately at the time when it was united with man, in whom, as the middle species of the world, all things are contained." [1] This concept is more explicitly developed in the same context, where Ficino clearly emphasizes the middle position of the Soul and its universal character. The work of God is perfect in every way, therefore the created Being had to be at some time connected with the Creator.

The things above the rational Soul are only eternal; the things beneath it, only temporal. But the Soul is in part eternal and in part temporal; it imitates God through its unity, the Angels through the intellect, its own species through reason, the animals through sense, the plants through nourishment, the inanimate things through essence. Hence, the Soul of man is in a certain way all things, a matter we have discussed at length in our *Theologia.* . . . However it is meet that the universal creature be united in some way with God, the common leader of all things—I say not singly, because God is the highest unity, but in common. God, therefore, must be one with the human nature, in which all things exist. For if He were one with the things above man, as the extremes of things created, such a union would not reach to the middle of things or to the other extremes. It would be likewise

[1] *Op. om.,* p. 20.

if He were one with the things beneath us. In reality infinite Oneness united its works with each other and with itself to the highest degree when it first included all things in man and then united man with itself. That perhaps is what the prophet Habakuk refers to when he says: "O Lord, make Thy work to come to life in the midst of the years, make it known in the midst of the years." . . . For that work is fulfilled in the middle species of all things, which is composed of both orders: eternity and time.[2]

[2] *Op. om.*, pp. 20 f. See also Habacuc 3: 1 f.; Saitta, *op. cit.*, pp. 82 ff., 172; Cassirer, *Individuum*, p. 70; Dress, *op. cit.*, pp. 54 f.; Hak, *op. cit.*, p. 101; Anichini, *op. cit.*, p. 104.

APPENDIX II

This appendix refers to Chapter VII

A CONGRUENCE with Ficino's doctrine is clearly recognizable in Pico's famous *Oratio* on the dignity of man. The *Theologia Platonica* was printed some years before the writing of the *Oratio*, and Pico had certainly read it. There can be no doubt, therefore, as to Pico's dependence on Ficino. The *Oratio*, which was originally intended as the introductory lecture for the projected disputation in Rome, treats of the subject matter of its title only in the beginning.[1] Pico takes as a point of departure the dignity of man. Working from that point, he tries to understand the real goal of human life and to determine the part philosophy and its individual disciplines have in attaining that goal. So at the same time he prepares a systematic order of the nine hundred theses, justification of which takes up the entire second part of the *Oratio* and is repeated almost literally in the *Apologia*, which was written later. The *Oratio* begins with two quotations about man as the miracle of the world. One of these quotations, taken from Mercurius Trismegistus, occurs in Ficino as well;[2] while the other, which is similar, is taken from an Arabic writer.[3] In reference to the question as to what really constitutes the superiority of human nature, traditional answers are rejected as insufficient, among them that man is "the intermediary between stable eternity and fluid time and, as the Persians say, the bond of the world."[4] At this point we recognize

---

[1] Cf. now the partial translation by Mrs. E. L. Forbes (*Journal of the History of Ideas*, III [1942], 355–57), and Cassirer, "Giovanni Pico della Mirandola," *Journal of the History of Ideas*, III (1942), 123–44, 319–46.

[2] *Op. om.*, p. 310.

[3] *Ioannis Pici Opera Omnia*, Basileae 1572, pp. 313 ff.

[4] *Ibid.*, pp. 313 f.

Pico's divergence from Ficino's position. In order to explain satis-
factorily man's position and peculiar character Pico describes the
moment of creation. When the whole work of the universe was
complete, the Creator desired the existence of a Being capable of
meditating on the reason for that work, of loving its beauty and of
admiring its greatness. Thus He ultimately undertook the creation
of man. Ficino's concept that in thinking and loving man comprehends the whole world is rather vaguely indicated.[5] All gifts had
been distributed among the other creatures, Pico continues, allud-
ing to the myth in Plato's *Protagoras*.[6] Hence the Creator decided
that the Being for whom nothing remained to be assigned as its
peculiar property might at least have a share of all those gifts that
had first been assigned singly to the various beings. Man, therefore, has no clearly determined essence. He is neither celestial nor
earthly; neither mortal nor immortal. On the contrary, he may become all of these through his own will. For the Creator gave him
the germs of every sort of life.[7] According to the possibility he develops he becomes a plant, an animal, a celestial entity, an angel,
or is unified with God. In the mutability of man's essence lies the
true meaning of the old doctrine of the transmigration of Souls.
Man therefore possesses all possibilities within himself; it is his
task to despise the lower forms of life and to approach God in
infinite desire. Here the principal idea is the universal character
of man as expressed in the fourteenth book of the *Theologia Platonica*, while the place of man in the center of the world is mentioned only incidentally.[8]

A similar discussion on the position of man occurs in the
Heptaplus, written some years later, and again we recognize the
connection with Ficino. In the *Expositio quinta* Pico says that
man is the connection and juncture of the three worlds previously
mentioned, that is, the elementary, the celestial, and the invisible

[5] Cf. *Op. om.*, p. 310.
[6] 321 c ff.
[7] "Omnigenae vitae germina indidit," Pico, *ibid.*, p. 315.
[8] "In mundi positum meditullio; medium te mundi posui," *ibid.*, p. 314.

worlds.[9] This is a clear expression of the intermediary role of man in Ficino's sense, but the triple number of worlds detracts from the symmetry and therefore the concrete significance of Ficino's conception. Obviously referring to the *Oratio,* Pico continues that, just as a prince sets his monument in the center of the newly constructed city, where it may be seen by all people, so after the creation of the world God set man as His image in the center of that world.[10] The question as to what the dignity of man rests on and what is his affinity with God again occurs. The answer differs slightly from the *Oratio;* in reality man comprises the substances of all things and the fullness of the entire universe. Emphasis is given to the fact that man combines and unites the things not only through thought but also in reality (*re ipsa*), and this power he shares with God alone. The only difference is that God contains all things because He is the cause of all, and man because he is the center of all things.[11] Therefore, in God each thing exists in a better form than when it exists in itself; in man the inferior thing exists in a better form, the superior thing in a lesser form. The middle is conceived in terms of a hierarchical order as in Ficino. This accounts for the different effects on the extremes of the world, which Ficino also expresses in a similar form, though in a different context.[12] Pico then describes in detail how man contains all substances: the body corresponds to the elements; the spirit to the heaven; the vegetative Soul to the plants; sensation to the animals; and so forth. We must notice particularly that in this enumeration body and spirit appear as equal parts of the human essence, while Ficino always limits himself to the parts of the Soul in similar discussions. In this contrast lies the difference between the so-called Platonic and the Aristotelian definitions of man to which Ficino repeatedly refers. Pico ends the enumeration with the same quotation from Mercurius Trismegistus which we found in the

[9] "Complexus et colligatio," *ibid.,* p. 38.
[10] "In medio illius statuit," *ibid*.
[11] "Uti omnium medium," *ibid.,* p. 39.
[12] *Op. om.,* p. 310.

Oratio, and then he describes how all creatures serve man.[13] With obvious reference to Ficino, he calls man the bond and the knot of celestial and earthly things (*vinculum et nodus*). In addition he shows how all creation has a part in the moral attitude of man. Consistently, the discourse ends with the incarnation of God, a fact which is explained in Ficino's terms. "For it was meet that the invisible image of God and the first-born of all creatures in whom all things were founded should be joined in ineffable union with him who was created after God's image, who is the bond (*vinculum*) between all creatures and in whom all things are contained." [14] As we see, the question of world unity is no longer decisive for Pico. The hierarchical order of things is still recognizable in its outlines. Yet man apparently no longer stands as a fixed member in the series of things, but, detached from that series, he seems to float, as it were, in another dimension. Therefore, all of Pico's statements about man as the center, knot, and bond of the world have lost their precise original meaning. On the other hand, the doctrine of the universal character of man for Ficino is the final conclusion after a long series of considerations, while for Pico it is the starting point which he takes up and develops into independent significance. Hence, the congruence between Pico and Ficino is not merely a repetition; it is rather the expression of a living intellectual influence, the disciple leaving his own imprint upon the resulting philosophical conception.[15]

[13] Cf. *Op. om.,* p. 296.
[14] Pico, *ibid.,* p. 40.
[15] For the quoted passages of Pico and their connection with Ficino cf. Gentile, *op. cit.,* pp. 137 ff.; Cassirer, *Individuum,* pp. 88 ff.; Saitta, *op. cit.,* pp. 160, 176 f.; Dress, *op. cit.,* p. 54. For Pico's philosophy cf. Garin, *Giovanni Pico della Mirandola;* Cassirer, "Giovanni Pico della Mirandola," *Journal of the History of Ideas,* III (1942), 123–44, 319–46; Dulles, *Princeps concordiae.*

BIBLIOGRAPHY

BIBLIOGRAPHY

Primary Sources

Marsilius Ficinus, Opera omnia. 2 vols. Basel, 1561 (2d ed., 1576).
Supplementum Ficinianum, ed. P. O. Kristeller. 2 vols. Florence, 1937.

Secondary Sources

Anagnine, Eugenio, "Marsilio Ficino e la filosofia italiana del quattrocento," *La Nuova Italia,* VI (1935), 41 ff.
Anichini, Giuseppe, L'umanesimo e il problema della salvezza in Marsilio Ficino. Milan, 1937.
Baron, Hans, "Willensfreiheit und Astrologie bei Marsilio Ficino und Pico della Mirandola," in *Kultur- und Universalgeschichte, Festschrift, Walter Goetz zu seinem 60. Geburstag dargebracht von Fachgenossen, Freunden und Schülern.* Leipzig-Berlin, 1927, pp. 145 ff.
Carriere, Moriz, Die philosophische Weltanschauung der Reformationszeit in ihren Beziehungen zur Gegenwart. 2d ed. Leipzig, 1887.
Cassirer, Ernst, Das Erkenntnisproblem. Vol. I, 2d ed. Berlin, 1911.
—— Individuum und Kosmos in der Philosophie der Renaissance. Leipzig-Berlin, 1927. "Studien der Bibliothek Warburg," Vol. X.
Conti, Augusto, Review of Puccinotti, *Archivio storico italiano* (Series III), II (Part 2, 1865), 172 ff.
Corsano, Antonio, Il pensiero religioso italiano dall'umanesimo al giurisdizionalismo. Bari, 1937.
Corsini, Andrea, "Il 'de vita' di Marsilio Ficino," *Rivista di storia critica delle scienze mediche e naturali,* X (1919), 5 ff.
Corsius, Johannes, "Marsilii Ficini vita," in *Philippi Villani liber de civitatis Florentiae famosis civibus,* ed. by G. C. Galletti. Florence, 1847, pp. 183 ff.
Della Torre, Arnaldo, Storia dell'Accademia Platonica di Firenze. Florence, 1902.
Dress, Walter, Die Mystik des Marsilio Ficino. Berlin-Leipzig, 1929.
Ferri, Luigi, "Di Marsilio Ficino e delle cause della rinascenza del

platonismo nel quattrocento," *La filosofia delle scuole italiane,* XXVIII (1883), 180 ff.

—— "Il platonismo di Marsilio Ficino," *La filosofia delle scuole italiane,* XXIX (1884), 237 ff.

—— "Platonismo di Ficino, dottrina dell'amore," *La filosofia delle scuole italiane,* XXIX (1884), 269 ff.

—— "L'Accademia Platonica di Firenze e le sue vicende," *Nuova Antologia* (Series III), XXIV (July, 1891), 226 ff.

Festugière, Jean, "La Philosophie de l'amour de Marsile Ficin et son influence sur la littérature française au XVIe siècle," *Revista da Universidade de Coimbra,* VIII (1922), 396–564.

Gabotto, Ferdinando, "L'Epicureismo di Marsilio Ficino," *Rivista di filosofia scientifica,* X (1891), 428 ff.

Galeotti, Leopoldo, "Saggio intorno alla vita ed agli scritti di Marsilio Ficino," *Archivio storico italiano* (Series II), IX (Part 2, 1859), 25 ff.; X (Part I, 1859), 3 ff.

Galli, Ettore, La morale nelle lettere di Marsilio Ficino. Pavia, 1897.

—— Lo stato, la famiglia, l'educazione secondo le teorie di Marsilio Ficino. Pavia, 1899.

Garin, Eugenio, "Recenti interpretazioni di Marsilio Ficino," *Giornale critico della filosofia italiana,* XXI (1940), 299–318.

Gentile, Giovanni, Giordano Bruno e il pensiero del Rinascimento. Florence, 1920.

Giehlow, Karl, "Duerers Stich 'Melencolia I' und der maximilianische Humanistenkreis," *Mitteilungen der Gesellschaft für vervielfältigende Kunst,* 1903 (Supplement to *Die Graphischen Künste,* XXVI [1903], 29–41); 1904 (*ibid.,* XXVII [1904], 6–18; 57–78).

Giuliano, Balbino, L'idea religiosa di Marsilio Ficino e il concetto di una dottrina esoterica. Cerignola, 1904.

Hak, Henri Johan, Marsilio Ficino. Amsterdam, 1934.

Heitzman, Marian, "L'agostinismo avicennizzante e il punto di partenza della filosofia di Marsilio Ficino," *Giornale critico della filosofia italiana,* XVI (1935), 295–322; 460–80; XVII (1936), 1–11.

—— "Etudes sur l'Académie Platonicienne de Florence," *Bulletin international de l'Académie Polonaise de sciences et lettres, classe de philologie, classe d'histoire et de philosophie,* 1932, pp. 18 ff.; 1933, pp. 35 ff.

—— "La libertà e il fato nella filosofia di Marsilio Ficino," *Rivista di filosofia neo-scolastica,* XXVIII (1936), 350–71; XXIX (1937), 59–82.

Horbert, Werner, Metaphysik des Marsilius Ficinus. Koblenz, 1930. Dissertation Bonn.

Huit, Charles, "Le Platonisme pendant la renaissance," *Annales de philosophie chrétienne*, N.S., XXX (1895-96), 362 ff.

Huszti, Giuseppe, "La prima redazione del Convito di Marsilio Ficino," *Giornale critico della filosofia italiana*, VIII (1927), 68 ff.

Ivanoff, N., "La Beauté dans la philosophie de Marsile Ficin et de Léon Hébreux," *Humanisme et Renaissance*, III (1936), 12-21.

Kahl, Wilhelm, "Die älteste Hygiene der geistigen Arbeit: Die Schrift des Marsilius Ficinus De vita sana sive de cura valetudinis eorum, qui incumbunt studio litterarum (1482)," *Neue Jahrbücher für das klassische Altertum, Geschichte und deutsche Literatur, und für Pädagogik*, XVIII (1906), 482-91; 525-46; 599-619.

Kieszkowski, Bohdan, Studi sul Platonismo del rinascimento in Italia. Florence, 1936. Cf. my review, *Annali della R. Scuola Normale Superiore di Pisa* (Series II), VII (1938), 341 ff.

Klibansky, Raymond, The Continuity of the Platonic Tradition during the Middle Ages. London, 1939.

Kristeller, Paul Oskar, "Un uomo di stato e umanista fiorentino, Giovanni Corsi," *La Bibliofilia*, XXXVIII (1936), 242 ff.

——— "Per la biografia di Marsilio Ficino," *Civiltà moderna*, X (1938), 277 ff.

——— "Marsilio Ficino e Lodovico Lazzarelli, contributo alla diffusione delle idee ermetiche nel rinascimento," *Annali della R. Scuola Normale Superiore di Pisa; lettere, storia e filosofia* (Series II), VII (1938), 237 ff.

——— "Florentine Platonism and Its Relations with Humanism and Scholasticism," *Church History*, VIII (1939), 201 ff.

Lovejoy, Arthur Oncken, The Great Chain of Being. Cambridge, Mass., 1936.

Meier, Matthias, "Gott und Geist bei Marsiglio Ficino," in *Beiträge zur Geschichte der Renaissance und Reformation, Josef Schlecht zum 60. Geburtstag dargebracht*. München-Freising, 1917, pp. 236 ff.

Meylan, Edouard F., "L'Évolution de la notion d'amour platonique," *Humanisme et Renaissance*, V (1938), 418-42.

Moench, Walter, Die italianische Platonrenaissance und ihre Bedeutung für Frankreichs Literatur und Geistesgeschichte. Berlin, 1936. Cf. my review, *Giornale critico della filosofia italiana*, XVIII (1937), 205 ff.

Montano, Rocco, "Ficiniana," *La Rinascita*, III (No. 11, 1940), 71-104.

Nygren, Anders, Agape and Eros. 2 vols. London, 1939.

Olgiati, Francesco, L'anima dell'umanesimo e del rinascimento. Milan, 1924.

Panofsky, Erwin, Studies in Iconology. New York, 1939.

Panofsky, Erwin, and Fritz Saxl, Duerers 'Melencolia I,' Leipzig-Berlin, 1923. "Studien der Bibliothek Warburg," Vol. II.

Puccinotti, Francesco, Storia della medicina. Livorno, 1859.

—— "Della filosofia di Marsilio Ficino," *Nuova Antologia,* V (June, 1867), 211 ff.

Pusino, Ivan, "Ficinos und Picos religiös-philosophische Anschauungen," *Zeitschrift für Kirchengeschichte,* XLIV (1925), 504 ff.

Robb, Nesca Adeline, Neoplatonism of the Italian Renaissance. London, 1935.

Rocholl, R., "Der Platonismus der Renaissancezeit," *Zeitschrift für Kirchengeschichte,* XIII (1892), 47–104.

Saitta, Giuseppe, La filosofia di Marsilio Ficino. Messina, 1923.

Saxl, Fritz, "A Marsilio Ficino Manuscript Written in Bruges in 1475," *Journal of the Warburg Institute,* I (1937), 61 ff.

Schelhorn, Johannes Georgius, "De vita, moribus et scriptis Marsilii Ficini commentatio," in his *Amoenitates literariae* (Francofurti), I (1730), 18–118.

Semprini, Giovanni, I platonici italiani. Milan, 1926.

Shorey, Paul, Platonism Ancient and Modern. Berkeley, 1938.

Sieveking, Karl, Die Geschichte der platonischen Akademie zu Florenz. Goettingen, 1812.

Stein, Heinrich von, Sieben Bücher zur Geschichte des Platonismus. Göttingen, 1875.

Symonds, John Addington, Renaissance in Italy. 7 vols. London, 1875–86.

Taylor, Henry Osborn, Thought and Expression in the Sixteenth Century. 2 vols. New York, 1920.

Thorndike, Lynn, A History of Magic and Experimental Science. 6 vols. New York, 1923–41.

Toffanin, Giuseppe, Storia dell'umanesimo. Naples, 1933.

Trinkaus, Charles Edward, Adversity's Noblemen; the Italian Humanists on Happiness. New York, 1940.

Weitenweber, Wilhelm Rudolph, Ueber des Marsilius Ficinus Werk 'De vita studiosorum.' Prague, 1855.

Miscellaneous

Anagnine, Eugenio, G. Pico della Mirandola. Bari, 1937.

Baron, Hans, "Renaissance in Italien," *Archiv für Kulturgeschichte,* XVII (1927), 226–56; XXI (1931), 95 ff.

Borghi, Lamberto, "Alamannus Donati de intellectus voluntatisque excellentia," *La Bibliofilia,* XLII (1940), 108–15.

Buck, August, Der Platonismus in den Dichtungen Lorenzo de' Medicis. Berlin, 1936, Cf. my review in *Giornale critico della filosofia italiana*, XIX (1938), 149 ff.

Burckhardt, Jacob, Die Kultur der Renaissance in Italien. Basel, 1860.

Burdach, Konrad, Reformation, Renaissance, Humanismus. 2d ed. Berlin-Leipzig, 1926.

Cassirer, Ernst, "Giovanni Pico della Mirandola," *Journal of the History of Ideas*, III (1942), 123–44; 319–46.

Dulles, Avery, Princeps Concordiae. Cambridge, Mass., 1941.

Ferguson, Wallace Klippert, "Humanist Views of the Renaissance," *American Historical Review*, XLV (1939), 1 ff.

Garin, Eugenio, Giovanni Pico della Mirandola. Florence, 1937.

Hönigswald, Richard, Denker der italienischen Renaissance, Basel, 1938.

Huizinga, Johan, "Das Problem der Renaissance," in *Wege der Kulturgeschichte*, Munich, 1930, 89–139.

Kibre, Pearl, The Library of Pico della Mirandola. New York, 1936.

Kristeller, Paul Oskar, "Augustine and the Renaissance," *International Science*, I (1941), 7 ff.

Kristeller, Paul Oskar, and John Herman Randall, Jr., "The Study of the Philosophies of the Renaissance," *Journal of the History of Ideas*, II (1941), 449–96.

Landinus, Christophorus, Carmina omnia, ed. by Alessandro Perosa. Florence, 1939.

Olschki, Leonardo, Geschichte der neusprachlichen wissenschaftlichen Literatur. 3 vols. 1919–27.

Picus, Joannes, Opera omnia. Basel, 1572.

Politianus, Angelus, Opera omnia. Basel, 1553.

Winckelmann, Johann Joachim, Kleine Schriften und Briefe. 2 vols. Leipzig, 1925.

INDEX

INDEX